Baseball in Europe

Baseball in Europe

A Country by Country History

JOSH CHETWYND

McFarland & Company, Inc., Publishers
Jefferson, North Carolina, and London

LIBRARY OF CONGRESS CATALOGUING-IN-PUBLICATION DATA

Chetwynd, Josh, 1971–
    Baseball in Europe : a country by country history /
Josh Chetwynd.
      p.   cm.
    Includes bibliographical references and index.

    ISBN 978-0-7864-3724-5
    softcover : 50# alkaline paper ∞

    1. Baseball — Europe — History.   I. Title.
GV863.42.C44   2008
796.357094 — dc22   2008023344

British Library cataloguing data are available

On the cover: (left to right) Holland player Han Urbanus (courtesy
of Hans Urbanus); Curaçao pitcher Shairon Martis (Renato Fer-
rini/FIBS)

Manufactured in the United States of America

McFarland & Company, Inc., Publishers
  Box 611, Jefferson, North Carolina 28640
   www.mcfarlandpub.com

To my parents, Lionel and Gloria:
thank you for your love and friendship

Acknowledgments

A book of this breadth requires a tremendous amount of patience, support and kindness from so many people. Charity started at home on this project and I must thank my wife Jennifer and my son Miller. Jennifer's proofreading and translation skills in Spanish and Italian were essential. Miller's smile always kept me moving forward. My parents and my brother Michael were also a tremendous help, each reading chapters (along with Jennifer) and offering excellent suggestions.

Outside the family, words cannot express my gratitude to Bill Arce, who has done more to raise the standard of baseball throughout Europe than probably any other person. He showed an enthusiasm for this book, and his willingness to supply photos and answer questions about his journeys to nearly every nook of Europe's baseball community was priceless.

A number of great friends also came through for me. Clive Russell proved that his kindness to me knows no bounds; translation help came from Peter Janssen (Dutch and Flemish) and Erik Janssen (French); and Jason Holowaty shared his deep knowledge of and thoughtful perspective on European baseball.

For many of the countries I covered, there was somebody there to offer support, great insight and/or feedback. They included: Jan Bagin (Czech Republic), Alper Bozkurt (Turkey), Mats Fransson (Sweden), Joan Garcia Pagan (Spain), Roland Hoffmann (Germany), John Fitzgerald (Ireland), Jim Jones (Czech Republic and Spain), Chris Kabout (Netherlands), Martin Miller (Germany and Europe generally), Gaston Panaye (Belgium and Europe generally), Andrew Sallee (France), Riccardo Schiroli (Italy), Peter Schöön (Sweden), Jimmy Summers (Croatia and Netherlands) and Han Urbanus (Netherlands).

Finally, the scholarship of others played a key role in this book. Although I have only met a handful of these writers personally, I must offer thanks to all of them for their past works: Jeff Archer (Great Britain, Netherlands and Germany), Gary Bedingfield (Great Britain and Europe during World War II), Brian Belton (Great Britain), Arvydas Birbalas (Lithuania), David Block (baseball's pre-history), Daniel Bloyce (Great Britain), Peter Carino (Italy), Peter Cava (Olympic baseball), John J. Chernoski (Lithuania), James Elfers (professional tours), Jeff Elijiah and all the writers at the now-defunct *International Baseball Rundown*, Kim Steven Juhase (Russia), Alan Klein (Italy and Germany), Mark Lamaster (professional tours), Peter Levine (professional tours), Tom Mazarakis (Greece), Roger Panaye (Europe), Richard Puff (Russia), Blair A. Ruble (Russia), Harvey Shapiro (Netherlands), Ian Smyth (Great Britain), Marco Stoovelaar (Netherlands and Europe generally), M. E. Travaglini (Germany) and Tim Wolter (World War II European POW baseball).

Table of Contents

Preface

Although I didn't realize it at the time, research for this book began in 1996. In April of that year, I casually wrote an e-mail to the British Baseball Federation (BBF) asking about the sport in that country. I was born in England but grew up in the United States and was curious about baseball opportunities abroad. I had played NCAA Division I college baseball for four years at Northwestern University and had a brief stint in the Frontier League, an independent professional circuit, but, at 24, I still had a thirst to play competitive baseball.

When Kevin Macadam, then BBF vice president, responded that Great Britain had a national team and asked if I'd be available to play for the squad at the European (B-pool) Baseball Championships that summer, I jumped at the chance. It was the beginning of a long relationship with European baseball. I played for Great Britain for ten years, participating in four top-level European Championships as well as that 1996 "B-pool" event (now known as a qualifying tournament) in which we took the gold medal.

In addition, I've played in two European domestic leagues. In 2003, I was a professional import player in Sweden, helping my team (Oskarshamn) to a share of the regular season crown and a spot in the Swedish Cup finals. I then won a national championship in Great Britain in 2007 as player/coach for the London Mets. In total, I've competed against national or club teams from 21 different European countries (from Italy to Ireland) and I've played the game in ten different nations from the continent (from the Netherlands to Norway).

Off the field, I've also held other roles in the European baseball community. I currently cohost television broadcasts of major league baseball games on network TV in the United Kingdom (although, with satellite, the show is seen by viewers in numerous other European countries); I spent a year and a half as the communications executive in Major League Baseball's London office, which is responsible for game development, licensing and merchandising for Europe, the Middle East and Africa; and I served briefly on the board of the British Baseball Federation.

My background certainly informs this book, and, when appropriate, I've made reference to personal experiences. But for the most part my travels serve as merely a backdrop for the sweat-of-the-brow research that represents the vast majority of this work. Surprisingly, current baseball leaders in some European nations possess only a vague knowledge of the game's history in their country. In other instances, official sources were difficult or impossible to contact. Moreover, the amount of scholarship on this topic has been limited. There have been only two small booklets—produced by European baseball's governing organization in 1978 and 1993—that even skim the whole continent's baseball history.

As a result, this book required piecing together from many sources. A key component of this history was contemporaneous news reports. I searched through newspapers and magazines dating back to the nineteenth century to find what was written when events actually happened. I also spent time at the Confederation of European Baseball archives in Switzerland, sifting through official documents as well as programs and statistics from sanctioned events.

In some countries, such as the Netherlands, Italy, Great Britain and Russia, there have been historical accounts or personal recollections produced. I'm grateful for authors whose work (duly noted in my text) added a tremendous amount to my chapters on those and other countries. To buttress what I could find that was written, I also interviewed founding fathers, current organizers, and former or current players and coaches of the game whenever possible. In all, I spoke or corresponded with more than two dozen European baseball pioneers and participants who, in some cases, mined memories dating back more than six decades.

This book is meant to be a starting point for a historical understanding of the game's roots in Europe. Ideally, my work is a beginning upon which future authors will build, uncovering more stories and other elements of the vibrant and colorful history of European baseball.

Introduction

The dream of baseball in Europe is more than one hundred years old. It's a vision that has been shared by baseball Hall-of-Famers, Italian royalty, Dutch school teachers and British captains of industry. It is also one that has yet to be fully realized.

In March 2007, I traveled to Lausanne, Switzerland, to spend some time at the Confederation of European Baseball (CEB) archives. All the time, the governing body shared nondescript offices with the International Baseball Federation (IBAF). While busily looking through the material, an IBAF executive happened into the room where I was working. He asked me what I was doing, and I explained I was working on a book on European baseball. He snickered, shook his head and walked out.

On a continent with an estimated 728 million people, approximately 100,000 people play baseball. If numbers were the sole criteria to judge the weight of a sport — or any activity — European baseball would be worth a chuckle. But the game's influence and importance in Europe cannot be judged solely by numbers. European baseball must be examined in light of a host of other factors that underscore its relevance and importance. There is the considerable effort Americans have made to proselytize Europeans to the ways of baseball. There are the telling political and cultural reasons why the establishment in some European nations has shunned the sport. And, finally, there is the baseball band of brothers — both indigenous and foreign — that has persevered through decades of sweat and toil to assure that baseball is played in some form in almost 40 European nations. Their stories in many cases are intrinsically compelling.

American Influence

Beginning with an 1874 tour of Great Britain and Ireland by professional ballplayers, Americans have longed to inculcate their European cousins with a passion for baseball. The reasons for this goal have been varied. One, of course, has been cultural pride. Harry Wright, the son of a cricketer and organizer of the 1874 excursion, was born in Sheffield, England. One of his motivations was a conviction that his former countrymen would find the American sport worthy as pastime.

Baseball and sporting-goods mogul Albert Goodwill Spalding, a man of seemingly limitless ambition, had, in part, similar goals when he organized his 1889 tour, which spanned the globe and included France and Italy along with stops in the United Kingdom and Ireland. Spalding was a fervent patriot who believed that baseball was an embodiment of American spirit. The Hall-of-Famer was also an ardent capitalist, and his tour and motivations in Europe were financially directed as well. He knew that if he could firmly plant baseball on the European sporting scene, he would be in the prime position to serve as the main supplier of equipment for the continent. To the extent that he helped prop up small leagues in France and Great Britain, his baseball equipment business benefited — but that income was far less than the money he pumped into those fleeting circuits.[1]

In the twentieth century other motivating factors would drive Americans to push for baseball in Europe. In the case of Leslie Mann, ego was a factor. The diminutive Mann, who enjoyed a somewhat successful professional baseball career, was hell-bent on making amateur and international baseball his legacy. "He was a hot dog," recalled U.S. Olympic Committee member Bob Paul in 1985, "with the mustard."[2] Regardless, he worked hard to put European baseball on firm footing. He served as a key recruiter for professional baseball in England in the mid–to late–1930s and he was a tireless proponent of Olympic baseball. His efforts were essential in earning baseball a spot as a demonstration sport at the 1936 Olympiad in Berlin.

But for many Americans who played the game in Europe, baseball was simply a diversion during two world wars. Before football and basketball became behemoths in their own right in the U.S. sporting world, baseball was the country's game of choice. So when GIs had precious free time while fighting on European soil during both World War I and World War II, it made sense for them to play baseball. For many of these men, there were no ulterior motives to sell baseball to the locals. If the French, Dutch or Italians liked the game, then that was a bonus, but the main goal was simply recreation. "Baseball was a lifesaver for our troops," commented one World War II soldier. "It was a real morale booster, and a strong reminder of baseball home traditions."[3] Still, there were some exceptions to this recreational rule. Most notably, baseball was seen by U.S. military officials as a tool in post–World War II Germany to help in the transition from the fascist Nazi regime. Baseball was important in "help[ing] mould German minds along democratic lines," explained Lt. Col. Robert C. Hall, one of the architects of youth activities in post–World War II Germany.[4]

Today, Major League Baseball (MLB) continues to carry the torch. The organization has offices in London, responsible for merchandising, licensing and game development in Europe, the Middle East and Africa. While the development programs have been somewhat streamlined in recent years, MLB is still active in youth programs like Play Ball!, which is a baseball starter program for kids, and more elite development, like individual country academies as well as a pan–European academy, which has led to a number of the continent's best teenagers inking contracts with big league teams. In addition, Major League Baseball has sponsored an "envoy" program, which sends qualified coaches to countries throughout Europe to teach the game.

European Attitudes

Whatever American motives may be, Europe's mainstream has often looked at baseball with suspicion. Reactions by the vast majority have either been disinterest or, in some instances, disdain. When Americans made their first foray into selling baseball to the English in 1874, the British media "just ignored baseball," according to sports historian and sociologist Daniel Bloyce.[5] During Spalding's 1889 world tour, the British media did take more notice but were dismissive. "Although American enthusiasts consider it [baseball] decidedly superior to the English game [cricket], it is not very likely that people in this country will share the opinion ... to compare it with cricket is a piece of audacity of which only an American can be guilty," wrote the *Lancashire Evening Post*. "In cricket there is vastly more, a great deal more science, ever so much more of the picturesque; in short, language fails to describe its superiority."[6]

Of course, this English aversion to the American game could easily be interpreted as knee-jerk cultural protection of its own domestic bat-and-ball sport, cricket. The idea of America — Britain's younger cousin — replacing England's beloved cricket with upstart baseball is totally anathema to some, even today. "If baseball is to hold sway in this country a new British nation will have to be born and that will never be," wrote Lord Tennyson, seemingly speaking for the mainstream, in a July 1933 edition of the *Daily Mirror*. "Give me cricket all the time."[7]

But most other European countries have not had a popular home-grown bat-and-ball sport in need of protection. Nevertheless, baseball faced obstacles. In some places, tangentially related politics served as a barrier for the sport. In the late nineteenth century, Spain banned baseball in Cuba — and presumably looked down on the sport at home — because the game was played by those calling for Cuban independence. During the world wars, being an enemy of the

United States also generally meant forsaking anything American. With few exceptions, countries opposing the United States or those occupied by America's opponents saw a halt to any momentum baseball was gaining. In the second part of the twentieth century, the Soviet Union became a staunch baseball opponent. In 1952, the *New York Times* reported that a Soviet youth magazine described "beizbol" as a "bloody fight with mayhem and murder."[8] As for those countries under the Soviet sphere of influence, they also shunned baseball. In places like Czechoslovakia, Yugoslavia and Poland, where baseball had made some inroads, the fear of communist leaders, who saw baseball as a wholly American endeavor, slowed or stopped any growth.

And yet these issues have not served as an impediment in every European country. In some, baseball just hasn't been able to compete against the king of sports— soccer. Part of this is because the early proponents of soccer were more aggressive in pushing their game. Sure, Spalding and Wright, among others, tried world tours, but, in the formative years of organized sports, there was a greater critical mass of British soccer missionaries throughout Europe expounding their sport's greater virtues than there were American counterparts. "[S]occer spread at the end of the nineteenth century, initially through the medium of British expatriates and then via local elites as they adopted the game," wrote authors Stefan Szymanski and Andrew Zimbalist. "This process contrasts sharply with the more inward-looking and commercial development of baseball during the same period."[9] Soccer also benefits from a simplicity that baseball does not have. To play soccer at its most basic level all you need is a ball, makeshift goals and an understanding that the objective of the game is to kick the ball into the net. In contrast, baseball requires more equipment and even the simplest explanation of the sport's rules takes some time to master. In other words, while the two sports are equally complex at their most advanced degree, baseball requires more commitment from beginners.

Baseball in Europe

In spite of these barriers, baseball does exist throughout Europe and enjoys a vibrant following in some pockets. The sport's European practitioners are often stubborn in nature. They have to be in order to continually push for a sport that many of their compatriots tell them doesn't — or shouldn't — exist in their country. Sometimes this hardheadedness has been a hindrance for the sport. In some countries, like Great Britain and Spain, baseball organizers have fought for control of their sport like lords battling for fiefdoms. Not surprisingly, this type of friction over such little turf has had undermining consequences.

But there are many examples of inspiring perseverance. For example, in the Czech Republic, Jan Bagin had a dream of a proper baseball complex in Prague. He fought with the communist regime for it and even cut through

Baseball can draw healthy crowds in Europe. At both the 2005 European Championships in the Czech Republic and the 2007 Euros in Spain, thousands of fans showed up for marquee match-ups. (Courtesy CEB, Renato Ferrini/FIBS.)

enough bureaucratic red tape to reach the cusp of his goal. But when liberalization led to changes in property laws, he was told he'd essentially have to start all over again. Bagin didn't give up and today his Prague facility is one of the best in Europe. In Croatia, during its bloody conflict with Serbia in the 1990s, players in the Serbian border town of Karlovac continued baseball activities despite bombings and daily military duty requirements for many of the players. In Sweden, a team in the town of Skellefteå, which is located just 200 kilometers from the Artic Circle, would travel some sixteen hours to take on teams from the southern part of the country in league games.

These local efforts have been bolstered by the acts of some Americans who have made a commitment to the European game for no other reason than their love of the sport. During the Battle of the Bulge, Bill Arce was a member of Gen. George Patton's Third Army. Injured in the fighting, Arce prayed to God. He promised that if he were to survive, he'd spend his life in a meaningful way. Arce would go on to become a university professor, administrator and baseball coach — and would give to European baseball like no other. Often paying out of his own pocket, he was the first professional American coach to hold baseball clinics in Sweden (1962), Czechoslovakia (1969) and Yugoslavia (1979). All told, he's worked in fifteen different European countries and is the only person to coach two different countries — the Netherlands (in 1971) and Italy (in 1975) — to a European Baseball Championship. Other coaches have also made major personal commitments. For example, Ted Thoren, who was the longtime skipper at Cornell University, spent a tremendous amount of time teaching the game in such nations as Croatia and Austria. Jim Jones, another coach, worked extensively in both the Czech Republic and Spain.

For nondomestic players, Europe has also been a great place to play the game. For years, teams in both Holland and Italy have hired former college and professional players from the United States and Canada as well as Latin America, Australia and South Africa. Now, in a sign of the growing sophistication of baseball in a number of countries, other domestic leagues have followed suit. Foreign import pros can be found in circuits in Germany, Czech Republic, Sweden, Belgium, Spain and Austria, among other places. What is most telling about these players is that so many of them come back year after year to compete in Europe. Ian Young, a former NCAA Division I baseball player at University of Hawaii–Hilo and Centenary (Louisiana) College, may be the extreme example. He has played for teams in Great Britain, Sweden, the Netherlands, Germany, Portugal and France. "It's a great personal experience, but I also find myself wanting to help baseball each place I go," Young said. "In so many places, the people I play with are so committed, which is inspiring."[10]

Ultimately, the combination of local stalwarts like Bagin and Americans with a true loyalty to the European game like Arce will assure that baseball has a permanent home on the continent. But can the sport grow in Europe?

The Future

Baseball organizers in Europe have numerous hurdles to navigate if there is hope for mass interest in the sport. From a financial standpoint, the International Olympic Committee's decision in 2005 to remove baseball and softball from the Olympic program was a huge hit. No matter what the groundswell of interest is in a sport, money is necessary to assure that those interested have facilities and equipment to enjoy the game. Olympic status guaranteed a working budget for baseball in so many countries. With the loss of that money, baseball is sure to struggle in numerous European locales. While some observers suggest that Major League Baseball's World Baseball Classic will replace the void created by no Olympic tournament, MLB is more limited in its value to helping grow baseball in less developed playing nations like many of those in Europe.

Beyond the money issue, perception may be baseball's biggest problem. In 2000, Mark McGwire was still at the height of his popularity. The specter of performance-enhancing drugs hadn't clouded his reputation yet and he was still looked at as a representative figure of America's pastime. Upon hearing that baseball was going to open that season in Japan, McGwire objected. "Our game is too international as it is," he said dismissively.[11] If McGwire was willing to make that sort of comment about big-league forays into the baseball powerhouse of Japan, it did not portend good things for the sport in Europe. Many disagreed with McGwire at the time and international efforts have grown since then. Nevertheless, McGwire's statement represents a sentiment that still exists. In 2003, a number of players, including Derek Jeter, Jason Giambi and Shawn Green, endorsed the idea of major leaguers playing in Europe, but the view was not unanimous. Houston Astros outfielder Lance Berkman said about the idea: "It's a long way to go, and it would disrupt the rhythm of the players who did it ... I'm not sure that what baseball would get out of it from a public-relations standpoint is worth the harm you'd do to the players who had to make the trip." [12] For baseball to succeed in a place like Europe, undivided support from the American baseball community would serve as a massive boost.

Attitudes by some within Europe's mainstream sporting community don't help the situation either. While drug-testing policies and the fact that the United States will not send its top baseball players to the Olympics (because they occur during the MLB season) were the most cited reasons for the sports' dismissal from the Games, anti–American sentiment also seemed to be percolating in the decision to drop baseball (and its sister sport softball). International Softball Federation president Don Porter was careful but clear when he said after the decision: "Softball and baseball hold deep American roots, and their removal reflects the IOC's heavy European influence."[13] It may be that some in the European sporting elite suffer from the same cultural protectionism illustrated by the British views on cricket. While baseball may no longer unanimously be

Ian Young (above) grew up in Australia and played NCAA Division I college baseball in the United States. Yet, like many players who were trained elsewhere but have come to play baseball in Europe, Young has developed a keen affinity for the continent's brand of the sport. He has competed for club teams in Great Britain, Sweden, Holland, Germany, Portugal and France. (Photograph by David Young.)

America's favorite sport (football now draws the biggest TV-viewing audiences), it is still seen by many as wholly American. The loss of baseball may reflect an attitude that baseball is not fully welcomed among some Europeans.

The main tragedy with this perception is that European baseball already has its own ethos and culture that is distinct from America's. One recurring statement from American players and coaches who have spent time in the European baseball world is that there were often moments when they said to themselves: "Baseball is played so differently in Europe." To some degree these statements reflect the lower level of play in many European countries. But there is also a sense that the everyday world that impacts the lives of European baseball players carries over to the diamond.

In those European nations where baseball has a firm toehold, some key characteristics do recur. Influential locals have taken a serious and lasting interest in the game. In the Netherlands, baseball's first founders were teachers, lawyers and businessmen. Throughout the successful history of Dutch baseball there have been practitioners of the game who have gone on to successful careers outside of the sporting world. For example, Leo van Wijk, the former president and director general of the airline KLM, grew up playing baseball. Similarly, in Italy, baseball's first president was Prince Steno Borghese. A member of the ruling elite, Borghese's connections were helpful in securing recognition for baseball by the country's sporting powers. Facilities are also essential. In Germany, where baseball participation has boomed in the 2000s, dozens of high-quality diamonds are available. The Czech Republic has also had excellent field development, which has helped the game gain broader recognition. But in Great Britain, where the domestic game has been stagnant despite a rich history, there is a paucity of decent places to play the sport.

European baseball has provided enough international achievement to support the argument that some nations on the continent are getting it right. At the 2007 baseball World Cup, Cuba and the USA each lost just one game en route to the finals. In both cases, the traditional powerhouses lost to European teams: Cuba fell 2–1 to the Netherlands and Italy beat the Americans 6–2. The Dutch ultimately placed fourth in the 16 team field, finishing above better-known baseball countries like Chinese Taipei, Korea, Mexico, Australia, Canada, Venezuela and Panama.

My goal in this book has been to chronicle the story of baseball in Europe and to show that in most countries on the continent baseball does, in fact, have a vivid history. My desire is that after spending time with these histories, the reader will appreciate the struggle that many have taken to develop European baseball and the important role the game has played throughout the continent. At the least, the myth that baseball is not played in Europe can be dispelled.

1

*The Netherlands**

What's in a name? The Dutch word for baseball is a sign that Holland is a small yet sturdy outpost of serious baseball on a continent of sporadic interest in the sport. Unlike countries where America's pastime goes by a phonetic version of the word "baseball" — like *béisbol* in Spain or *baseboll* in Sweden — the Dutch call the sport *honkbal*. This unique expression is merely one indication of how the sport is not just an American offshoot, but a vital part of Dutch culture.

Baseball has reached a respectable level in Holland for a handful of reasons. There was serious early and sustained acceptance of the game by Holland's sporting establishment. In addition, the Dutch Antilles and Aruba, both parts of the Kingdom of the Netherlands and not far from the baseball-rich country of Venezuela, have offered an essential resource for staffing Dutch baseball teams — both at the national and domestic levels. These players not only have a zest for the game but are also great athletes who have chosen baseball first — even over king soccer. Moreover, organizers were aggressive in seeking out high-quality American coaches and foreign competition in order to develop. And, most important for any minor sport looking for respect, Dutch baseball teams have won and they've won often.

A look at the Netherlands record against their European competition shows just how much the Dutch have dominated on the continent. Consider this: Through 2007, the Dutch national team played their European counterparts 188 times at the European Baseball Championships. Their overall record in those

---

The arrangement of this book's chapters are based on historical performance in the European Baseball Championships. (See Appendix 3 for details on this performance.)

contests is 157–31 and if you exclude their closest competitor — Italy — they have an amazing 115–1 record against the rest of Europe. All told, the Dutch have won 20 European Championships (second best: Italy with eight).

While Italian baseball tends to get more attention from American media, it is the Dutch who have quietly risen to the level where they can consistently compete with the world's greatest baseball powers. At the 2000 Sydney Games, the Netherlands became the first country to beat the vaunted Cubans at the Olympics. At the 2005 World Cup, the Dutch finished 7–1 in pool play (defeating the likes of Canada, South Korea and Panama). They then knocked off Puerto Rico 10–0 en route to a fourth place finish out of 18 teams. Then, in the prestigious Intercontinental Cup in 2006, Holland finished second in a field that included Cuba, Japan, Taiwan, Australia and South Korea. The Dutch actually led Cuba 2–1 through six innings in the finals only to fall 6–3 in 11 innings.

Proving those performances were no fluke, the Netherlands placed fourth at the 2007 World Cup — a result that included its second international victory against Cuba. That Dutch triumph broke a streak of 32 straight Cuban wins at that event.

Unlike most other countries in Europe where the sport was launched and pushed by Americans, Holland's first substantial introduction to the game came from a true Dutchman. Although baseball had been played sporadically in the Netherlands beginning sometime around 1905, it was J. C. G. Grasé, an Amsterdam native, who planted the sport firmly in Holland in the 1910s. During this period, the Amsterdam Association for Physical Education was founded. Soccer was already established as the great winter and fall sport, but the board concluded that there was no direct complement for the summer months. Enter Grasé, who taught English in Amsterdam and had fallen in love with baseball on a vacation to the United States. Upon his return home, he pitched it as the ideal summer activity. It probably helped that Grasé pointed out that baseball bore a resemblance to an ancient Dutch game, called "tripbal," which had been played by American colonists. Holland, like England, Poland, Russia, Germany and others, can lay some claims to the roots of baseball. This historical basis likely pleased the Association board, which lauded baseball immediately. One of the educational inspectors spoke glowingly of baseball, likening the sport to "knighthood, courage, confidence and mental accuracy combined with underestimated physical strength," according to Marco Stoovelaar, Dutch baseball's preeminent historian. The inspector would go on to endorse baseball saying, "Baseball deserves to be a summer game for those who played other sports in the winter season."[1]

Grasé had the ideal skills to help get baseball on its proper footing. As an English teacher he took the rules of the game and translated them, and coined the name *honkbal*. Despite Grasé's efforts, there was a little lost in translation. "He and a group of Dutch enthusiasts sat down to study baseball from [famed

When it comes to European baseball, the Dutch have more than double the number of continental championships of their next closest rival. Above: celebration after winning the 2005 European Baseball Championships. (Courtesy CEB.)

baseball organizer A. G.] Spalding's rules," the *Washington Post* recalled in 1928. "They got most of it right, except that the pitcher threw the ball underhanded."[2] Regardless, the sport got an auspicious debut in 1910 with a pick-up game on a small field near one of Amsterdam's most famous landmarks, the Rijksmuseum. A year later, rules were printed and official games began. From the start, baseball was aided by the support of members of the country's established class. The first club created was the Amsterdamsche Honkbal Club (Amsterdam Baseball Club), made up of businessmen, doctors, engineers, lawyers and teachers, and it was soon joined by a second club comprised of students.

While those teams couldn't be sustained, Grasé pushed forward, founding the Dutch Baseball Union on 12 March 1912. The following year, two key clubs were formed: Quick Amsterdam and Hercules. Quick, which started on 1 March 1913, is Europe's longest continuously running baseball club. Its founder, Emile Bleesing, would ultimately become Holland's most important baseball pioneer. Chosen as the Dutch Baseball Association's president in 1914, Bleesing served as an essential organizer and baseball missionary. He traveled the country giving lectures on the game, setting up exhibitions and conducting clinics for future umpires. He also worked his players at Quick hard. Indicative of Bleesing's efforts, a little more than a decade into the club's founding he added indoor training sessions in 1925. Bleesing used these workouts to improve player stamina through running. Bleesing and other team leaders decided the players would gain "iron muscles, strong kidneys and reach the speed of a young goat" thanks to the strenuous activity, according to historian Stoovelaar.[3]

But before Bleesing's running strategy was put into place, World War I gave Dutch baseball enthusiasts their first serious interaction with North American players. American and Canadian soldiers set up the Belgium-Holland baseball league.[4] The seven-team circuit included teams from the Dutch cities of Rotterdam and The Hague. Although a team based in Brussels won the pennant, the Americans celebrated both the Dutch and the Belgians for their ability to follow the game.

After the war, baseball became firmly established on the sporting scene. The key reason baseball was so accepted: two of the most famous soccer clubs in the country, Amsterdam's Ajax and Blauw-Wit, decided to take the game on as a summer sport. Ajax's choice to play baseball was a particular coup for the sport's organizers. Founded in 1900, AFC Ajax is historically one of the three teams that have dominated the Netherlands national soccer league (Eredivisie), having won the Eredivisie championship 29 times. The club has also hoisted every major European Championship trophy at least once. Baseball knowledge was present from the very founding of Ajax, thanks to the club's inaugural coach, John Henry (Jack) Kirwan. A former national team member for Ireland, Kirwan skippered Ajax from 1911 until the outbreak of World War I. He had played club soccer in England for, among other teams, North London's Tottenham Hotspur. Along with being a soccer power, Tottenham also triumphed on the baseball diamond. Kirwan shared in both successes. He was a member of Tottenham's 1901 soccer squad that captured the country's most important trophy—the FA Cup.[5] He also played baseball for the Hotspur's 1906 British national champion baseball team.

Although Ajax formally began playing baseball after the Great War and Kirwan was replaced as head coach at the club by 1915, it's quite possible he gave Ajax its first taste of the bat-and-ball sport. While not nearly as prominent as Ajax, Blauw-Wit's entrance into the baseball world offered further legitimacy for the game. Organized in 1902, the squad would spend a sustained period as a professional club, playing its games beginning in 1928 in Amsterdam's prestigious Olympic Stadium.[6]

Along with adding respect for baseball, the two soccer teams' baseball involvement also provided assurances that great athletes would take up the game in Amsterdam. As soccer was the country's most popular sport, it attracted the most athletic aspiring sportsmen. Over the years, these athletes would play America's pastime because of their affiliation with Ajax or other soccer clubs.

Among the notable crossovers were Johan Cruijff, Johan Neeskens and Cor Wilders. Cruijff is one of Holland's—and Europe's—greatest all-time soccer players. He was a three-time winner of the trophy for European Footballer of the Year (1971, 1973 and 1974) and, in 1999, he was named European Footballer of the Century by the International Federation of Football History and Statistics. He was also a committed baseball player until he was 16 years old. "As [a] catcher for the Ajax youth squad at the end of the 1950s he learned all about team spirit," according to an International Baseball Federation newsletter.[7] Showing his interest in baseball continued later into his life, the 60-year-old Cruijff even attended the 2007 European Baseball Championships in Barcelona.

As a soccer midfielder, Neeskens also had an impressive career. He was a key member of the Dutch national team that finished as runners-up in both the 1974 and 1978 FIFA World Cups. In all, he represented Holland 49 times and scored 17 goals for his country in international competition. While his soccer career may not have been as star-studded as Cruijff's, Neeskens was probably a better baseball player. "Johan Neeskens was a member of the Dutch youth baseball team and was voted best batsman at the European Youth Baseball Championships in Rome in the sixties," according to the 10 August 2005 edition of the *Guardian* (UK).

Wilders, who played soccer and baseball for Blauw-Wit, is one of only three athletes to ever represent Holland in both baseball and soccer. He proved his skill as a pitcher in 1948, twirling one of the country's first recorded no-hitters.

While Cruijff, Neeskens and Wilders would come along later, Ajax and Blauw-Wit turned out successful squads nearly immediately. The first league formally commenced in 1922 with four teams: Ajax, Blauw-Wit, Quick and Hercules. Quick, which was organized by Bleesing and, as a result, had relatively more experience on its side, would capture the first title, but Blauw-Wit would win the league in 1923 and Ajax would take the first of its four national crowns in 1924. (Blauw-Wit would finish first in the country an impressive nine times.) With only four teams—all of which were relative baseball novices—it's not surprising that the early games were high-scoring affairs. In other words, a modern-day observer watching a nascent match-up might not have characterized the baseball as very good. "In these early years," quipped Chris Kabout, a keen follower of Dutch baseball history, "people could talk for days about a scoreless inning." In addition, these early players may have been too polite to fully succeed at baseball. "In those days, you were considered a bad sport if you bunted or took advantage of the lack of control by a pitcher," Kabout wrote.[8] "It was considered a humiliation to get a walk. It was far better to hit a fly out than reach base on four balls. Baseball was [also] played in shorts."

Bleesing was aware that in order to take his beloved sport to a higher level Dutch players needed more interaction with experienced ballplayers. He searched diligently for solutions. Along with pushing the publicity side of the game by writing about baseball in different newspapers, he also sought out tougher opponents for Dutch players. To that end, Bleesing would contact U.S. Navy ship captains whenever a U.S. Navy ship docked in Amsterdam's harbor. The request was simple: let's play a game of baseball. The first official contest of this nature occurred in 1923 between a Dutch representative side and the crew of the USS *Pittsburgh*. The score in that first match-up is not included in Dutch baseball history books, but it is noted that Holland lost. The score was likely one-sided as a formative Dutch national team would take on the USS *Pittsburgh*— as well as other ships like the USS *Preston/Bruce*, the USS *Detroit* and the USS *New Orleans*— over the next few years and lose handily. For example, the USS *Pittsburgh* prevailed in two contests in 1926. The result in the second game: the Dutch lost 27–1. But the score didn't really matter as the Dutch were getting needed experience and were clearly getting better, as evidenced by their 8–2 triumph over US Destroyer 217 on 11 September 1927 in Amsterdam.

Along with the players, Dutch spectators were also learning the game. An Associated Press article explained: "A Dutch audience reacts differently to baseball from what an American does. While in the United States, the spectators in the bleachers seem happy when a ball is hit there, and men vie with one another to catch it, everybody in Holland within apparent reach of the ball ducks as it approaches and there is great commotion."[9]

In all, Dutch teams would play eight games against American competition between 1923 and 1928 and would go 1–7 in those contests. While the on-field improvements were somewhat slow, Bleesing was making marked strides. Besides, he was a salesman and infused drama into how his Dutch Baseball Federation sold the game to potential fans and players. A two-page leaflet, complete with diagrams, described the game as "[t]he constant struggle between the fielders and base runners ... the competition in speed and dexterity — all this makes the game especially lively and attractive." By 1928, the pitch had succeeded enough to earn expansion outside of Amsterdam. In 1923, a team had been established in Haarlem, a town little more than ten miles from Amsterdam. As was the case with soccer-baseball connection in Amsterdam, Haarlem benefited from crossover athletes. For example, Joop Odenthal was a solid shortstop and third basemen for the Haarlem-based club EDO in the late forties and early fifties. He also made a name for himself on the soccer field. His move from the soccer branch of EDO to HFC Haarlem in 1949 was a big story, as both teams were from Haarlem, according to Dutch baseball historian Stoovelaar. Like Amsterdam's Wilders, Odenthal would represent Holland on both the soccer pitch and the baseball diamond.

By the 1930s, baseball was a Dutch sporting fixture. The national team was now not only playing American competition but also setting up competitions against other European countries. On 26 August 1934, the Dutch national team played its first game against another country — Belgium — in the town of Heemstede located near both Amsterdam and Haarlem. Although Holland's second basemen Jan Baas collected five hits in six at bats, the Belgians prevailed 21–12. Later that summer, the Netherlands would get revenge, beating Belgium 19–17 in the Belgian city of Antwerp for its first international triumph. Through the end of the 1930s, a Dutch national team would play regular games against both Belgium and France and would begin to emerge as the strongest baseball country of the three. Between 1937 and 1939, Holland boasted a 7–2 record against the two European opponents.

Domestically, foreigners were also giving the Dutch stiff competition. In 1939, a team of Mormon missionaries called the Seagulls were invited by Bleesing into Holland's preeminent league and promptly won the national championship losing only two games all season. The country's top circuit also had its controversies during this period. In 1937, the national championship pitted Haarlem's EDO against Amsterdam's Blauw-Wit in a close-fought match that ended in dispute. The reason: at the time, Dutch baseball held an unfortunate vestige to its soccer ties—the game featured a clock that required the contest to be completed in two hours. With EDO winning at the end of a completed inning and the full time seemingly elapsed, EDO's players thought they'd won. But the umpires pointed out that there were actually three more minutes left on the clock, so a new inning commenced. Blauw-Wit engineered a comeback and took the championship. The controversy did have a positive effect: starting in 1938, all games in Holland's top league would last nine innings.

All this seemed very inconsequential when the Germans invaded the Netherlands in May 1940. World War II effectively shut down baseball throughout most of Europe. But in Holland the sport was able to continue in some fashion. Materials were scarce but a form of baseball remained. Han Urbanus, who is one of Holland's all-time greatest players, began his career during the heart of the war in 1942. The following year he was a regular fixture in Dutch baseball, which appeared to continue unabated. Nevertheless, there were some changes. Recounts Urbanus: "There was a competition during World War II, but it was what we called a 'emergency competition.' We did not have normal leather baseballs but we played with baseballs made from highly compressed cork. They looked liked [field] hockey balls. Baseball bats were made in Holland and also gloves, but they were not the finest. When it was raining a little bit it was very dangerous to be confronted with a fastball pitcher because the balls became very slippery. But we survived."[10]

Quipped Dutch baseball organizer Jan Herzog in a 1961 interview about the war years: "We used a cork ball, which usually broke into pieces when it was hit. But the guy who caught the biggest piece had the ball according to our rules."[11]

This modified version of baseball may not have been optimal, but the fact that the sport persevered during the fighting not only showed a unique level of European enthusiasm for the game but also gave Dutch baseball development a huge boost. As a result, the immediate postwar era saw a quick return of

From the early days of baseball in Holland, the country has produced talented ballplayers. Among the best was Han Urbanus (above) who not only dominated Dutch domestic baseball in the 1950s, but also went to spring training with the New York Giants twice. (Courtesy Han Urbanus.)

proper baseball. American military personnel introduced softball in the decade after the war, but baseball's growth during this period was particularly bolstered by a concerted effort on the part of Americans at home to support the Dutch baseball movement. This was not uncommon throughout Europe. Successful American immigrants from other countries—most notably Italy—were sending equipment to buoy baseball interests in their lands of origin. In the case of the Netherlands, large Dutch-American populations in the Great Lakes region worked hard to elevate baseball in their ancestral home. For example, Honkbal Headquarters, Inc., a committee of Western Michigan businessmen, ran a baseball-gear drive in 1948. The committee shipped more than 1,000 top-grade baseballs, 361 bats, more than 100 uniforms and a large supply of gloves, shoes and catcher's equipment, according to an Associated Press dispatch.[12] With this assistance, baseball boomed again with 165 senior teams (squads with players over 16 years old) playing in Holland by 1952.

The national team also resumed play following the cessation of hostilities. In 1946, the squad returned to its best source of competition: playing against U.S. Navy teams. That year, the Dutch split two games against the USS *Little Rock* (a loss) and the USS *Houston* (a win). In addition, contests against Belgium became a yearly fixture again in 1948. Some of these games drew impressive local interest. For example, a Netherlands-Belgium match-up in 1953 attracted 6,000 spectators to Ajax's stadium on 28 June.[13] The Dutch dogged determination to continue playing — however piecemeal — during the war clearly played a key role in their impressive return to international competition. To date, Belgium has beaten the Netherlands just twice since the war in some fifty match-ups.

All this headway did make the Dutch discerning about baseball organization on the continent. In 1953 when five countries decided to form a pan–European federation, the Dutch didn't join.[14] "The Dutch Federation was not very confident in the new organization," longtime European and Belgian baseball organizer Gaston Panaye recalled in 2007. "[T]hey joined after two years when they saw that F.E.B. [Federation of European Baseball] was doing a good job." When the Netherlands did join, they were at the point where they could dominate. Beginning in 1956, the first year the Netherlands participated in a European Baseball Championship, the Dutch won every continental championship they entered until 1973 — a total of ten straight titles.

In 1956, when the Netherlands finished 4–0 to win their first European Championship, the national team was described as "[a] dark horse team" by one news account but that should not have been the case.[15] The Dutch were a legitimate baseball country thanks in large part to their ability to leverage U.S. connections to help their strongest athletes improve. This era's biggest star, pitcher Han Urbanus, is a prime example. With the help of Albert Balink, editor of the Dutch-American magazine *The Knickerbocker*, Urbanus would attend spring training with the New York Giants in 1952 and 1953. The right-hander, who made his debut at the adult level as a 15-year-old in 1942, was already the Netherlands ace when he headed to Phoenix, Arizona to work out with the Giants in 1952. His American immersion gave him a tremendous education.

Although Urbanus was so overpowering that he had not been relieved during a start in some 150 games over eight years in Holland, according to *Time* magazine, he had never been taught how to throw a change-up.[16] He threw a fastball, which Urbanus said he hoped some day would be as good as Cleveland Indians ace Bob Feller's, and a curveball, which he said he "invented" himself. In addition, Urbanus had never pitched from a mound, as that wasn't a regular feature on Dutch diamonds by this point. (This problem would be fixed not long after Urbanus's return.)

Nevertheless, the lessons learned in 1952 did not bear fruit immediately when he returned home. Apparently, at first, Urbanus lost his control while trying to master his newfound repertoire that now featured off-speed pitches including a curveball taught to him by Giants star pitcher Sal Maglie.[17] But by the end of the 1952 season, it all clicked for Urbanus. He had pitched a no-hitter, two one-hitters and averaged 12 strikeouts a game. Moreover, he'd led his club, another baseball-soccer combination, Amsterdam's Op Volharding Volgt Overwinning or O.V.V.O ("Perseverance Leads to Victory"), to its fourth straight Dutch championship.

Despite his considerable talent, Urbanus was truly modest about his skills. He never went to the United States with major-league stars in his eyes. "I don't know if I would accept an offer," Urbanus told *Time* in 1952, "because I wouldn't get one ... [I'm going] just to learn." Nevertheless, when Urbanus returned to the United States in 1953, his development earned him a contract offer from the Giants. But Urbanus had other plans. "I was offered a baseball contract, which I denied because I was finishing my studies as [certified public accountant] that year and was planning to marry in November," recalled Urbanus in 2007. "Both were realized. So in the end I chose against a professional baseball career for a career as a professional auditor, which I did for 35 years. I played baseball just for fun."[18]

The fact that he wasn't professional didn't mean Urbanus took a cavalier approach to baseball. Armed with an instructional film given to him by the Giants, Urbanus offered clinics on the correct way to play the game. *Time* reported that after his 1952 experience, Urbanus returned home and "taught rival pitchers how they, too, could throw American style." As much as other players benefited from Urbanus's sojourn to the United States, it was the talented Urbanus who reaped the biggest rewards. By the end of his career he would throw a record seven no-hitters (five after he visited the States) in Holland's top league, the *hoofdklasse*. He was also named the country's best pitcher five of the first six years the award was given (1953–1958).[19]

An opportunity to go to America and play with North American professionals must have been priceless. Urbanus was the first, but he was not the only Dutch player to get that chance. In the two decades following World War II, players like Jan Smidt, Herman Beidschat, Wim Crouwel and Martin Jole also had stints in camp with major league organizations. Each of these players returned to dominate in Holland. Smidt was pitcher of the year in 1955; Beidschat won the same award an amazing 10 times; Crouwel captured three batting crowns; and Jole, who worked with the Cincinnati Reds, also earned a pair of hitting titles. After playing with and against top U.S. competition on American soil, it should come as no surprise that when these players faced European competition, they had great self-confidence. For instance, Urbanus and Smidt dominated at the 1956 European championships. Urbanus won two games and Smidt also won a pair, including the Netherlands victory in the final. He struck out 13 in that game against Germany and 16 in his other win against Belgium.

The value of these excursions was best summed up by Ferdinand Rocky Van Beringen in 1965. A third baseman for the top Dutch club Haarlem Schoten,

Van Beringen trained with the Detroit Tigers for two weeks during spring training that year in Lakeland, Florida. "I hope to learn a lot," an excited Van Beringen told the Associated Press before his American experience began.[20] "I will note everything. I will keep a diary of what I see and learn so I can give the information to the [Dutch] league and benefit the players." The purpose of these excursions was not just to get better but to ultimately raise the level of baseball play throughout their home country. While Italy also sent players abroad, no European country sent more athletes to major league camps than the Netherlands.

Getting individual players to work out at big league spring training was one of a multi-pronged effort to achieve dominance in European baseball. The Dutch were also early pioneers in taking whole teams to the United States. Using connections with Dutch-Americans in western Michigan and drawing support from the National Baseball Congress, a prominent baseball organization based in Wichita, Kansas, the Netherlands played early on in the United States on a number of occasions. After their victory at the European Baseball Championships in 1956, the national team was invited to the Global World Series. Set up by a Milwaukee, Wisconsin, businessman, the event drew a handful of amateur representative teams from around the world to Milwaukee. The Dutch played two games, losing 14–2 to Puerto Rico and 7–1 to Colombia. Another tour occurred in 1961. The Dutch traveled to Michigan to play a club team called Sullivans in Grand Rapids and an All-Star squad from Kalamazoo. The Dutch dropped eight straight, but the games started a long relationship with the Sullivans club.

Dubbed "the Furnituremen" by Grand Rapids locals, the Sullivans were established in 1953 by Bob Sullivan, owner of Sullivan's Carpets and Furniture. For years, the club was one of the elite amateur baseball organizations in the United States. Future Big League stars Al Kaline, Kirk Gibson, Willie Horton and Jim Kaat were just a few of the more than 50 Sullivans alums who would go on to play at baseball's highest level. Beginning in 1963, the Michigan club would travel to Holland more than a dozen times to play in its marquee event, Haarlem Baseball Week, winning it five times. In lieu of competition against U.S. sailors, the Sullivans always assured the Dutch a top-notch American opponent. They also gave Dutch players and fans something to aspire to. Wrote Shirley Szelkowski in a 1982 *Grand Rapids Press* story: "The Sullivans were mobbed by fans at every game [at Haarlem Baseball Week]. From the moment they entered the gate until they returned to the bus after the game, fans clamored after them with scraps of paper and pens. During the games, Dutch boys would stretch out on the roof of the dugout and dangle pens, baseballs and programs hoping for autographs."[21]

To complement the strong competition, the Dutch also needed a higher standard of teacher to take their baseball prowess to the next level. While Americans had coached Dutch teams in the past, these men were not professionals.

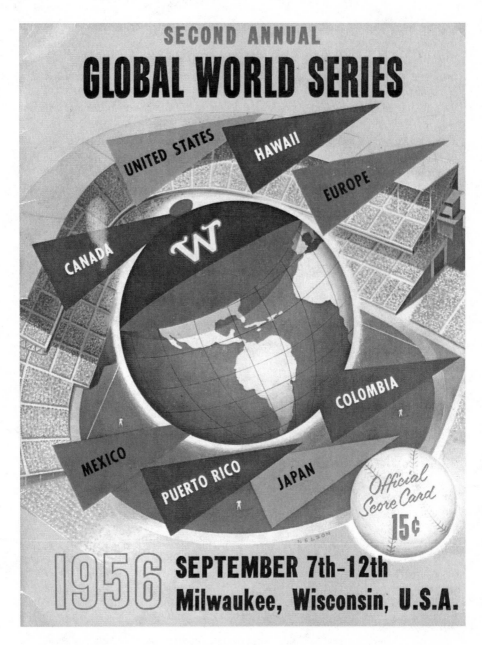

Following its victory at the 1956 European Championships, the Netherlands stepped onto the world stage, competing in the second annual World Global Series (above: program from the event). The Dutch struggled, losing both its games by a combined score of 21–3. Still, they earned valuable experience.

In 1958, they found their first top-notch coach. Ron Fraser had been a relief pitcher at Florida State University before a hitch in the Army took him to Germany. During his stint in Germany, he took the reigns of the German national baseball team and guided them to a bronze-medal performance at the 1958 European Baseball Championships in Amsterdam. Although the Dutch had won the gold, they must have been impressed with Fraser because they hired him away from the Germans. Fraser brought a level of intensity to his workouts, focusing heavily on the fundamentals. For example, during one training session in the area of Bloemendaal he told his players to remove their spikes during sliding practice because he feared that the hard surface might lead to injury. Yet, after a while, he grew frustrated with his charges' performance so he decided to show them how it should be done. The only problem: he didn't take off his cleats. The result: Fraser broke his shinbone.[22]

Broken leg aside, his efforts paid off as the Netherlands swept through the 1960 European Baseball Championships in Barcelona. The team won the gold, finishing 3–0 and outscoring opponents 24–1. What happened next is illustrative of how baseball was more than just a minor sport in Holland by 1960. As Fraser told the story, he met with the Dutch prime minister after the Barcelona triumph. "I'm at the summer home of the prime minister of the Netherlands, and he asks me what it would take to keep me there as baseball coach," recounted Fraser to *Sports Illustrated* in 1992.[23] "Well, I came up with what I thought was a fantasy: $19,000 a year, which was a lot of money in those days, and a few months in the States. And the prime minister [said] O.K. Believe me, I never made that mistake again in negotiations."

At the 1962 Euros, Holland would again win, going 5–0. Interestingly, it was Fraser's connection to Dutch baseball that would land him the job that would make him a legend in college baseball circles. Following the 1962 championships, Fraser was asked to be a contestant on *What's My Line?*, a game show in which panelists would try to guess the profession of the guest. Fraser stumped the panel who, not surprisingly, didn't expect Fraser's job to be Dutch baseball coach. Unbeknownst to Fraser, Henry King Stanford, the president of the University of Miami, saw the show and he was impressed by the coach. As a result, he asked Fraser to run the school's baseball program. Fraser would turn the University of Miami into a power. The Hurricanes would qualify for the College World Series twelve times under his stewardship and win two national championships.

The Dutch had lost a star coach with Fraser's return to the United States, but the country's baseball powers now understood the value of experienced American coaches. Including Fraser, the Dutch federation would employ seven different American college coaches to run their national team during the 1960s. From that group, Holland was particularly lucky to nab another talented teacher immediately after Fraser. Bill Arce's entry into European baseball was mere happenstance. "I was on a plane trip with a professor from Stanford going to a convention in New York," recalled Arce about his 1960 introduction to the European game. "At the bottom of a sports page I noticed an item saying Holland had won the European baseball tournament. I commented that would be a great way to spend a leave from college, working with baseball players in a country like Holland."[24] Sometime after that he received a letter from a friend who was serving as the American consul in Amsterdam saying that they were looking for a coach, and he replaced Fraser in 1962. Arce, who served as athletic director and head baseball coach at Claremont–Harvey Mudd Colleges in California, jumped at the opportunity.

Arce would become not only a tireless teacher for the Dutch but also a master organizer. As Urbanus put it years later: "Bill Arce became one of the most famous and trustful coaches in our baseball history." On Arce's initial trip, he took a leave of absence from his U.S. academic commitments and spent more than a year working with Dutch players. For years after that, he brought college-aged teams over to Holland to play and coach. Along with the Sullivans, Arce's players were central figures in improving play in Holland. So much so that "the impact it had on Dutch baseball is still felt there today," wrote longtime Atlanta Braves scouting director Bill Clark in 1995.[25] A top-flight coach, he would also lead the Netherlands to a European Baseball Championship gold medal in 1971 and finished his college coaching career with a 606–472–7 record. He was inducted into both the National Association of Intercollegiate Athletics Coaches Hall of Fame and the American Baseball Coaches Association Hall of Fame.

Arce's arrival in the Netherlands coincided with great baseball expansion in the country. In 1963, the first real baseball stadium, named after one of Holland's greatest athletes, Pim Mulier, was erected in Haarlem. In addition, *honkbal* was spreading outside of its strongholds in Amsterdam and Haarlem. Rotterdam, which had always prided itself on being a city of sports and had some baseball presence since the 1940s, came to the fore. In 1963, Rotterdam's Sparta club won its first Dutch national championship. Between 1963 and 1974, the club would earn nine titles. Overall, by 1970, the number of Dutch baseball teams had more than tripled to 588 in less than twenty years.

Beyond the efforts of the likes of Fraser and Arce, another movement in Dutch baseball increasing talent levels was the integration of players from the Netherlands Antilles and Aruba. These Caribbean islands (the Netherlands Antilles most notably includes the island of Curaçao) are autonomous members of the Kingdom of the Netherlands. Located close to the developed baseball nation of Venezuela, both Aruba and the Netherlands Antilles have strong baseball histories. Aruba joined the International Baseball Association in 1950 and the Netherlands Antilles competed in baseball's World Cup as a separate participant eleven times beginning in 1952. Although Urbanus remembers Antillians playing in Holland beginning just after the war, these Caribbean players, who were great athletes and knowledgeable players, really changed the face of the *hoofdklasse* in the 1960s.

Throughout Dutch baseball history, concerted efforts have been made to offer clinics for developing players. Above: instructors at a 1963 baseball camp held in Eindhoven. Top row (L–R): Charles Urbanus, Rudy Doma, Boudewijn Maat, Wim Crouwell and Bill Arce; Front row (L–R): Jan Schaefer, unidentified, and Wim Sorge. (Courtesy Bill Arce.)

Rotterdam's Sparta featured three of the greatest: Hamilton Richardson, Hudson John and Simon Arrindell. Richardson, who played briefly in the Chicago White Sox organization, was the best of them all. He would win seven hitting titles in Holland's top league — five of them with a batting average over .400. A six-time league most valuable player, Hamilton would ultimately be named a Knight in the Order of Oranje-Nassau, a prestigious distinction given by the Dutch government. Complementing Richardson were John and Arrindell, who were two of Holland's most feared power hitters. John led the league in home runs four times and Arrindell twice. John's 17 home runs in 28 games in 1971 particularly stand out.

Besides raising the standard of the top league in the Netherlands, the Caribbean players were also key additions to the national team. At the 1965 and 1973 European Baseball Championships, Richardson was named MVP. The impact of Richardson and his fellow islanders reverberated throughout European baseball community, particularly rankling Holland's biggest European nemesis, Italy. In 1969, the Italians protested to the European Baseball Feder-

The quality of both domestic and national team play has been raised substantially by the involvement of athletes from the Netherlands Antilles. For example, Curaçao native Shairon Martis (above) pitched the first no-hitter in World Baseball Classic history for the Netherlands in 2006. (Photograph by Renato Ferrini/FIBS.)

ation, complaining that the use of players from the Netherlands Antilles should be banned because they were born outside of Europe. The Dutch Baseball Association responded with vigor, calling the Italian grumbling "discrimination," especially considering the players for the islands "possess[ed] the nationality of [the Netherlands] for 100%."[26] The Italians ultimately relented and to this day the players from Aruba and the Netherlands Antilles play essential roles on the national team.[27]

Beyond changing the make-up of the national squad, the Caribbean players have also influenced baseball culture in Holland. Many observers have pointed out that the players from the Netherlands and those from the islands have a completely different way of playing the game.

Bill Arce explains it this way:

> I consider it a matter of the climate differences which lead to different lifestyles. I come from a warm Southern California climate so I was used to ball players [like the Dutch Antillians] being loosey goosey in their movements. The cold climate in Holland caused Dutch players to be slower in their movements, somewhat stiff looking and awkward as they made plays. A non-baseball example would be dancing. The first time I saw Dutch jitterbugging it was a far cry from the jitterbugging we did or the Antillians did. Antillian hitters had an all-out loose, fast and explosive swing at a pitch. Dutch players had a deliberate, place-the-bat-on-the-ball type of swing. Defensively, the Dutch were slow and deliberate, with almost no rhythm in their movements, with a few exceptions like Han Urbanus.[28]

For Jimmy Summers, who both played and coached in the Netherlands *hoofdklasse* from 2000 to 2006, the differences were even more stark. "Antillians are basically crazy," said Summers in a 2007 interview.[29] "In 2000, we were shagging balls before batting practice and there was a can of Coke in the dugout. It was a Sunday morning and there was whiskey in the can before the game. Without a doubt they are great athletes, but I have seen lots of guns in bags. [One teammate] had a 9mm [gun] and I asked, 'Do you take it everywhere?' and he says, 'You never know.'"

Summers, who played college baseball at Malone College in Canton, Ohio, and professionally for five seasons in war-torn Croatia before competing in the *hoofdklasse*, said that the Dutch-born players were more team-oriented, but did play "soft" at times. "They are very influenced by soccer," Summers said. "You can get yellow cards in [baseball] games in Holland. They want to look good. The Croatians get dirty [and] hard-nosed. The Dutch style is [that] a player will be upset if [his uniform isn't] perfect."

The unique Dutch baseball culture is also seen off the field. Most notably, many Americans who have come to coach in Holland have been taken aback by the aggressive nature of the media. Today Ron Fraser is lauded by the Dutch as the first professional American coach to skipper the national team, but in 1960 the media lambasted him. "Before we won the European championship in 1960," he said, "the Dutch press was on my ass, accusing me of being a taskmaster and tyrant." Harvey Shapiro, who managed both in the *hoofdklasse* and the Netherlands national team, faced similar difficulties from the Dutch press. "[T]he Dutch media could be annoyingly negative," Shapiro said. "In the United States I was used to reporters being generally positive in their analysis, reporting the outcome and key happenings in the game.... However, the

Dutch media dealt with their players and teams like we do in the tough media cities of New York and Boston."[30]

In his book, *Strike Four*, Jeff Archer, who coached a season in Holland's top league, believed that the press had a particular anti–American bias. He supported this claim by pointing out that when the media covered news of a Dutch pitcher throwing a no-hitter, the focus was on the fact an error was made by American shortstop Eddie Rose. The headline read: "Rose's Error Foils Perfect Game."[31]

One place where the culture has seen a remarkable transformation is in the stands. *Hoofdklasse* games can attract attendances in the thousands. Today, those supporters can be as raucous as any in the baseball world, but that development has been gradual. In 1952 *Time* magazine described the crowds as sedate. "Though the Dutch are careful to follow all the American rules, the game is strictly amateur and considerably more gentlemanly than the sometimes rowdy U.S. variety," the article said. "The Dutch have no equivalent for the Bronx cheer; no one ever boos; no one would dream of suggesting that the umpire be killed." A generation later the energy level had been ratcheted up a notch. "It used to be that they would watch baseball like people watch tennis," Arce told a *Los Angeles Times* reporter in 1970. "Now they're developing a little bit of partisan rooting." By 2003, the fans in Haarlem were downright loud when the home team was playing. At the European Championships that year singing and dancing was not uncommon among the Dutch fans.

Whatever cultural quirks the Dutch bring to the sport, their on-field play continues to improve. While the 1970s saw some turmoil in the domestic league — for example, in 1972, the great soccer club Ajax ended its baseball program and, in 1977, O.V.V.O's soccer team faced a scandal that lead Han Urbanus to leave the club — the decade also saw the first born-and-bred Dutchman make the Major Leagues.[32] In 1979, pitcher Wim Remmerswaal, a native of The Hague who had been named the best pitcher at the European Championships in 1973, broke into the big leagues with the Boston Red Sox. Although he lasted only two seasons at baseball's summit, he offered inspiration for young Dutch players.

On 29 August 1993, Dutch native Rik Faneyte got the start in centerfield for the San Francisco Giants in the second game of a doubleheader against the Florida Marlins. "To my left was [former two-time National League batting champ] Willie McGee. To my right was [future home-run king] Barry Bonds. And I was stuck in the middle," Faneyte said recounting the experience. "I tried to concentrate on the game."[33] Faneyte went one-for-five and the Giants won. The son of a baseball player from the Dutch Antilles and an Amsterdam softball player, Faneyte was first chosen for the Dutch National Team at age 16. In 1987, at 18, he was named the MVP during the European Championships. Faneyte's major league career would last only 80 games over four seasons, but he would return to Holland to both hit and pitch for the Amsterdam Pirates/

Expos for many years. A season after Faneyte's debut, Robert Eenhoorn broke into the big leagues with the New York Yankees. Although Eenhoorn's career was even shorter than Faneyte's—he played just 37 big league games in four seasons—he did have the distinction of being the starting second baseman on the day that Dwight Gooden threw a no-hitter in 1996. Eenhoorn's commitment to Dutch baseball runs deep. Not only did the Rotterdam native return to the Dutch league following his release from U.S. professional ball, but he went on to become the head coach of the national team and run an academy for young players. Like Urbanus nearly a half-century before, Faneyte and Eenhoorn take their responsibility to develop Dutch baseball. It's this attitude that keeps the Dutch improving, according to Claudio Liverziani, a member of the Italian National team who spent time playing professionally in the United States. "The best [Dutch] prospects go to the U.S. and when they come back, they come back with that background and share it with other players," Liverziani said.

Today, the stream of Dutch players going to play in the United States continues. Of course, a number of Antillians have made it to the Major Leagues—most notably All-Star centerfielder Andruw Jones. In addition, Rick Vanden Hurk became the second born-and-trained Dutch product to pitch in the majors in 2007 (although he did begin his U.S. playing career at 16 years old). All told, about two dozen Dutch and Dutch Antillian players were members of North American professional clubs in 2006. Some of these players have not come cheap. Left-handed pitcher Alexander Smit, a native of Geldrop, Netherlands, received a reported $800,000 signing bonus from the normally frugal Minnesota Twins in 2002.[34]

At the same time the *hoofdklasse* continues to develop. Although not a completely professional league, salaries are doled out to both foreigners and star Dutch players. Unlike in Italy, where many former Major Leaguers have gone to end their careers, there have been only a couple of ex–big leaguers to play in Holland's top circuit who didn't already have Dutch ties. (One of these was Stan Bahnsen, a 16-year major league veteran, who played in Haarlem as a 46-year-old in 1992.) One reason for this is that the Dutch don't seem to pay for the Major League title the way the Italians might. A top player in Holland can receive a couple of thousand dollars a month but in Italy a former major leaguer can easily get twice that amount. Contributing to that might be that some Dutch clubs are gun-shy about overspending for talent. The Haarlem Nichols, a team that won twelve Dutch championships and played thirty consecutive years in the country's highest division, went bankrupt in 1994—in part because it extended itself too far with players' salaries. That said, there remain a number of very healthy clubs with strong sponsorship ties in the *hoofdklasse*. Rotterdam's Neptunus has become the country's preeminent club. Between 1981 and 2005, Neptunus won eleven national titles. The club boasts a great youth program, a beautiful stadium and a professional approach.

OFFICIEEL PROGRAMMABOEK

16E
HAARLEMSE HONKBALWEEK

1992

10 - 19
JULI
1992

DIT IS EEN UITGAVE VAN HET ORGANISATIECOMITÉ
VAN DE 16E HAARLEMSE HONKBALWEEK.

This page and the following three: Netherlands baseball facilities are among the best in Europe. This has allowed the country to host top international events, including the European Baseball Championships and Haarlem Baseball Week, which draws national teams from such countries as the United States and Cuba.(Above: programs from *Haarlem Baseball Week* and the 1973 Euros.)

Despite a successful domestic league and increasingly impressive performances internationally, the international baseball community continues to question whether the Dutch can continue to develop and compete with more traditional baseball powers. Some are skeptical. Harry Wedemeijer, a veteran Dutch scorer, points to the 2005 World Cup as an example of the limitations of baseball in the Netherlands. "The financial report on the World Cup tournament in 2005 was finally published, and it showed a deficit of 350,000 euros," Wedemeijer said in 2006. "Because of this, it will be harder in the future to interest businesses to sponsor baseball teams or baseball tournaments. Baseball will see a dip in the future, and not the increase in members that was hoped for by the [federation] when it organized the World Cup."

Former Dutch national team head coach Harvey Shapiro also has his doubts about Dutch hopes of competing with the likes of Cuba and the United States. "Since it is a small country, with a limited pool of baseball players from which to choose, along with inclement weather and the dominance of soccer, Dutch baseball will be hard pressed to reach higher levels," wrote Shapiro in 2006. "The availability of the Antilles players with professional baseball backgrounds can significantly improve the team's tournament stature. However, it would not be realistic to think that baseball in the Netherlands could reach the echelon of a world baseball power."[35]

And yet their victories against Cuba at the 2000 Olympics and the 2007 World Cup as well as a second-place showing at the 2006 Intercontinental Cup suggest an even more promising future for the Dutch. In addition, the country's squad at the World Baseball Classic in 2006 was comprised of many players who compete in the *hoofdklasse*. That squad acquitted itself well, beating Panama 10–0 and hanging tough with the Dominican Republic for five innings before falling 8–3. (The team also lost to Cuba.)

Even if there is stasis in the world of *honkbal*, the sport has proved itself to be a durable part of life in the Netherlands. When the soccer great Johan Cruijff played baseball, his teammates included Leo van Wijk, the former president and director general of the airline KLM. For many in Holland like van Wijk, baseball isn't about becoming an elite athlete but about having fun while growing up. In that way *honkbal*, for all its differences in name, is a true cousin of Cuba's *béisbol*, Japan's *yakyu*— and America's baseball.

2

$$\diamond$$

Italy

Anyone who has ever played in Italy has a story about the country's unique baseball experience. First, it is an ideal setting to play the game — the fields are often perfectly manicured and the stadiums are located near some of the most picturesque terrain.

But it's the Italian culture, which has crept into the practice of Italian baseball that often leaves Americans a little mystified. Ken Hickson, a former college player at the University of California, Berkeley, spent time playing and coaching in Italy. He once recounted how a pitcher he was managing declined to issue intentional walks because they reflected badly on his masculinity.[1] Daniel Newman, a native of Cleveland, Ohio, who has played so long in Italy that he has dual nationality and has represented Italy in numerous international events, also admitted that the Italians approach the game a bit differently than Americans. "The Italian players do some interesting things," he told the *Akron* [Ohio] *Beacon Journal* in 2000. "They celebrate whether they win or lose. They drink coffee and smoke during innings. And I don't know why they do this, but when they warm up before a game, they wear a plastic cup on the outside of their uniform."[2]

Whether Newman was pulling a journalist's leg with the last statement (I've played in Italy against the national team in Parma and never saw a single Italian jockstrap), it's clear that the sport has grown up in its own special way in Italy. That said, there are a lot of similarities between the Italian and American versions of baseball. The reason: after more than a half-century of playing the game seriously, Italian ballplayers who may do things differently on the margins, know at their core how to play the game.

Baseball's first major foray into Italy came from a man who truly knew how to spark passion. In 1889, baseball Hall of Famer A. G. Spalding led a group of players on a world baseball tour. Among the tourists' stops was Italy, where the teams, whose players included nineteenth-century great Adrian "Cap" Anson, soaked up the country's beauty and played some competitive baseball. America's pastime had made a brief appearance in 1884 in the Italian port town of Livorno, but Spalding — a showman of the highest order — offered it on a grander platform.[3] Spalding was using his world tour to open new markets for his sporting goods company by offering up baseball in fertile, untapped locales throughout the world. The barnstormers were made up of two teams: Spalding's Chicago White Stockings and a team of other professionals dubbed "All-America."

Their inaugural Italian stop was Naples, where All-America pitcher John Montgomery Ward, a future Hall of Famer, wrote in his first Italian dispatch in honor of the area's awe-inspiring beauty: "*Vedi Napoli e poi muori.*" (See Naples and then you can die.) Not surprisingly, the Naples contest was staged in a breathtaking setting. It was late February, so the Apennines were snow-capped in the distance behind the game's venue, the Campo di Marte, with the famed Mount Vesuvius smoking beyond deep center.

The event drew approximately three to four thousand spectators. Unfortunately, what was likely the first baseball game ever played in Naples ended in near bedlam. The field lacked a barrier to keep fans apart from the players and as the game developed the spectators inched closer and closer to the diamond. In the top of the fifth, chaos ensued as the All-Americans were mounting a massive six-run rally that broke a deadlocked 2–2 contest. One of the All-Americans hit a foul ball into the ever-closing crowd, striking a middle-age man over the eye. He was knocked out cold, leading frenzied spectators to rush the field. The game had to be stopped, and the experience did not endear the sport to the bewildered and slightly frightened onlookers. Wrote Mark Lamaster in his book *Spalding's World Tour*: "Certainly these events would do nothing to quell suspicions about the 'vulgar' nature of his sport or its traveling exponents — to say nothing of the nation from which they came."[4]

It was an inauspicious beginning, but Spalding was not deterred when he and his party moved on to Rome. Spalding tried — unsuccessfully — to stage a game at the Coliseum but was understandably rebuffed. (He ultimately settled for a photo opportunity at the site with his players in full uniform.) As for actually playing baseball, the game was held in another more suitable site: the gardens at the Villa Borghese. Featuring some of the most lavish gardens on the continent, the Villa Borghese and its grounds were an ideal setting for baseball. The game was contested at the Piazza di Siena, which was described by one of the tourists as "a picturesque glade, its surface as smooth as any ball park at home."[5] Although the Italian King Umberto did not attend due to illness, the Italian queen and a number of other members of the royal family showed up to enjoy the closely contested game, which was won by the Chicago side.

The Italian leg of the trip was completed in Florence at a large park called the Cascine. The event apparently put Florence's high society "in a flurry" and two thousand spectators flocked to the match-up.[6] They were treated to a tight contest won by the All-Americans 7–4. Despite the lavish locations and generally supportive attention, baseball did not earn a big bump from the tour. Part of the reason for little development at the time is that there was scant follow-up from Spalding and his agents. In contrast, Spalding had lined up coaches to develop baseball in England. The result there was a short-lived professional league in England's north. For the most part, the baseball was an interesting spectacle that was probably seen like a circus—a fun diversion when in town but just a faded memory when it moved on.

That said, in at least one instance, the game stuck in a most unexpected way following the tour. Spalding's 1891 guide reprinted a letter from a "Mr. Stacey," weaving the following tale:

> During my sojourn in Rome while taking a stroll through one of the great parks on the outskirts of the town, I witnessed a surprising sight. It was a game of base ball between two teams composed of monks, and what was more surprising they played the game well.... The monks were attired in their official robes, long flowing black gown, a broad, red ribbon tied around the waist and hanging down on one side, and black, broad-rimmed felt hats. Such an outfit is not very well adapted for [a] base ball uniform, still the monks played a fairly strong game. The catching was especially good ... [t]he infielding was necessarily loose, because the long robes made a clean handling of grounders almost impossible. Long flies were almost sure to be gathered in by the outfielders, but grounders invariably went through the fielders who would then gather up their long robes and scamper after the ball.[7]

Despite this fascinating holy attention, the overall lack of interest generated by the Spalding tour was underscored by the reception received by another group of major leaguers in 1913. Like Spalding's excursion, the Chicago White Sox, led by its powerful owner Charles Comiskey, and the New York Giants, headed by Hall of Fame skipper John McGraw, conducted their own round-the-world tour in 1912–13. The teams landed in Naples in mid–February 1913 to a warm, but small reception. According to author James Elfers in his book *The Tour to End All Tours*: "While there were some Italian Americans playing baseball ... the game itself was essentially unknown in the Land of Caesars."[8] The team was unable to play a game in Naples because a suitable field couldn't be found. In Rome, Spalding's over-the-top approach might have been the only thing remembered about the last baseball escapade in the Italian capital. Spalding's ambitious efforts to secure the Coliseum as a game site possibly didn't sit well with the Romans, posits Elfers. "Perhaps reports of Spalding's irresponsibility and long memories on the part of the Roman politicos gave the city's leaders a false impression as to what baseball was all about." As a result, the capital's establishment was wary about another baseball exhibition. According to Chicago journalist G. W. Axelson who was on the trip, officials "demanded that a net be placed in front of the spectators and that a few innings be played behind closed gates that they might be sure that no danger could fall."[9] Although Comiskey, McGraw and their crews agreed to the requests, the weather was not conducive to baseball. The big leaguers spent about a week in Italy but didn't play a single game.

As a result, the sport was generally forgotten. It did reappear — albeit in pockets—following World War I. In France and Great Britain, American GIs gave the sport a big push following the hostilities. That effort led to modest staying power among the Brits and the French. But Italy seemed to only get an incidental taste of baseball. One of the few dispatches about baseball in Italy after the Great War came from the *Washington Post*. The paper reported in 1918: "The credit for staging the first real game in the Italian peninsula lies with a group of air service mechanics who were going through a school term at the Fiat automobile factory in Turin. The boys took advantage of the Italian national holiday to pull off a game at Valentino Park, in Turin, and after first puzzling the natives, have now aroused in them a desire to do a little pitching."[10]

Turin was a serendipitous locale for this makeshift game as a year later one of the town's native sons would begin bringing longer lasting baseball interest to Italy. The sport's early sustained development in Italy is credited to Max Ott (born Mario Ottino), who brought a keen enthusiasm for the sport to his birthplace upon returning to Turin from the United States in 1919. Ott, along with Guido Graziani, a professor in Rome who organized games beginning in the early 1920s, are deservedly credited as the fathers of Italian baseball. Both men had spent time in the United States and brought a devotion to baseball back to their home land. Their work was duly noted in one of the most popular baseball books of the day: the *Spalding Base Ball Guide*. In the annual's 1922 edition, Spalding's editorial team wrote: "Italian residents who have been to the United States and have picked up some playing points of the game, as well as a thorough interest in the sport, will organize teams of their own which will excite Italian curiosity." Those efforts were buoyed by the work of H. Chase Ballou, the sports director for Rome's YMCA. He also offered exhibitions of the game in Rome in 1920 at the Stadio Nazionale and the Piazza di Siena.

Baseball got an unexpected push from the academic world during this period as well. The Accademia di Educazione Fisica della Farnesina (UISM) sent a group of students to the United States to study the rules of the sport in the early 1930s. Upon their return, the students performed several exhibitions in Rome and in San Remo and even displayed the sport at an international physical education congress in 1931.[11] The sport must have been somewhat popular at the school because a photo depicts the UISM's 25-man baseball team, all with matching uniforms and gloves, and even two players in catchers' equipment. In 1932, efforts were continuing at the university, as professor Attilio Poncini published a sports guide that included details on baseball.

But by 1935, baseball was falling out of favor in Italy. That year, Benito Mussolini's fascist government instituted "sabato fascista" (Fascist Saturday), in which sports or military exercises were mandatory on Saturdays. According to Italian baseball's official history, baseball's American roots prevented it from being included in that program.[12]

Thankfully for the world, Mussolini's rule would come to an unceremonious end in 1943 and less than a year later baseball's Italian future was being cemented by American GIs hitting the beaches of Anzio. These soldiers' efforts would not only help liberate the country but would also firmly place baseball on the Italian sporting landscape. Ever since, the sport has enjoyed a robust — although sometimes overlooked — history in Italy.

As American soldiers fanned out across Italy following the Anzio landings in January 1944, they brought baseball with them. The most notable hotbed was the small seaside town of Nettuno. Not far from the beaches of Anzio and within about 40 miles of Rome, Nettuno was chosen as the site

Max Ott (above) was born in Turin but spent a large portion of his formative years in the United States. He developed an affinity for America's pastime and would return to his native land to become one of the founders of Italian baseball. (Courtesy FIBS.)

to bury American soldiers who perished in bloody fighting with the Nazis near the end of the war. In 1947, Lt. Charles Butte was assigned as the officer in charge of the cemetery. Butte commanded a small detachment of American GIs and hired approximately 40 to 50 locals to dig graves and maintain the cemetery grounds.

According to Butte, who was interviewed by the *Palm Beach Post* in 2007 about his Italian baseball experience, the Italian workers at the cemetery were fascinated by the American pastime. "One day, when we were working at the cemetery, a couple of the workers came up to me and asked me if I ever played baseball," Butte told the *Post*. "In those days, the major leagues were dominated by the Italian players, the DiMaggios."[13]

Butte secured some equipment and play began. As Italians are known for their elaborate and colorful storytelling, a few of the accounts of baseball in the country are a bit contradictory. Some reports say that softball — rather than baseball — started first. This is possible, as softball would have been a good introductory sport for baseball novices. The second story is likely apocryphal:

the tale goes that in early games at the cemetery, headstones were used as bases. It's doubtful that the Americans—or the Italians—would have gone for such an indiscretion.

Regardless, baseball soon spread from the graveyard. Butte contacted his superiors in Rome and got permission to use the cemetery's grave-digging equipment to build a stadium. "We had earth movers, bulldozers, road graders," he said. "We never did it on working time. We always did it in the evenings and on Saturdays and Sundays."

The stadium was built on the land of Prince Steno Borghese, a local nobleman of the royal Borghese family. Butte understated that Borghese "liked sports" and so was willing to donate land for the baseball project. In reality, Borghese fell in love with baseball and his involvement as an organizer, fundraiser and establishment face on the minor sport would be essential for baseball's Italian growth over the years.

Even with Borghese's support, ingenuity was as valuable as funds during this postwar period when resources where limited. To that end, Butte utilized materials that were readily available. Using sheets of pierced-steel planking that still sat on the beaches of Anzio following the American invasion, he fashioned the stadium's grandstand. Canvas bags were stuffed to make bases and a tree trunk was cut and fashioned to serve as home plate. He also made uniforms out of surplus khaki uniforms he requisitioned from the Army.

The Italians who had been gravediggers were now baseball players. Butte told the *Post* that the locals were quick to look for games against the Americans. The Italian players were athletic, but their passion for baseball didn't include the finer points of the game. "They never watched the coach for signals," Butte remembered. "You might want them to bunt, but they didn't want to bunt, they wanted to knock the ball out to show how they could hit."

Butte left the cemetery in 1949 and his legacy could have been short-lived if not for his replacement Horace McGarity. It was McGarity who took Nettuno baseball to an almost mythical level in Italian baseball. A fiery man, McGarity, who would be inducted into the Italian Baseball Hall of Fame for his coaching efforts in Nettuno, turned the fishermen of the tiny hamlet into champions. Under McGarity's tutelage, Nettuno would win five of the first ten Italian national championships. He brought a certain American enthusiasm to the game. A *Los Angeles Times* article in 1953 described him in this way:

> The manager, the Wild Man of Italian Baseball, is an American, the man who has the soothing philosophical job of supervising and tending of the graves of our war dead on the peaceful Italian shore. But on the diamond, Horace J. McGarity is excitable and more operatic than most Italians. He is the only man of any nationality to be twice singled out by the Federazione for special distinction. First, following a riot he led against the team which beat his outfit at the end of the season, he was last year banned from Italian baseball for life, banished forever. Next, at the beginning of this season, he was reinstated with full managerial powers.[14]

While the larger-than-life McGarity was probably the most visible of the first wave of Americans to offer baseball to the Italians, he certainly was not the only one. For example Pvt. August M. Bermen and Pvt. Kurt Weismuller began teaching Romans baseball just months after the Americans reached the Italian capital. "We just picked up a ball and glove and went at it," Bermen told the *Los Angeles Times* on 1 October 1944. "[I]n no time at all there was a crowd around, as if it were the first game of the World Series." Following Bermen's and Weismuller's play, the Italians burst into applause.

A more prominent American player in Roman baseball was Joe Lubas. He served as a soldier based in Italy at the end of the war and then returned to Rome after the armistice to marry an Italian woman. In 1947, he noticed kids experimenting with baseball near the Tiber River. Lubas quickly became their instructor. With a knowledge of both Italian and baseball, be began holding baseball clinics and was hired by the YMCA to hold a five-week course on how to play, manage and umpire. Fifty people showed up for his course including city police and Italian Army officers. He would later play and manage Libertas Roma, which would go on to win the country's first unified national champions in 1950.

It's impossible to discount the importance of American GIs in baseball's flowering in Italy, but to give them sole credit would undermine the importance that native Italians had in the sport. Generally speaking, minor sports do not gain any prominence without locals who show a sincere zest for the game and Italian baseball was no exception.

For Italy, those natives were led by Max Ott, who had worked to develop the game before the war and served as a journalist during the hostilities. Following the fighting, Ott went to work for the American pastime again. In Milan, he linked up with a law student named Franco Milesi to spur the game locally. Milesi and his friends played softball with American GIs in the mid–1940s, but Ott helped them refine their play into actual baseball. Ott also used his connections at Istituto Leone XIII to get baseball going in a meaningful way at the school. Ott's son had attended the institute and Ott approached its president, suggesting that baseball should be played. At Ott's urging, the school requested and received the necessary equipment from its American sister school, Fordham University, to set up the sport properly. On 27 June 1948, the first official baseball game between Il Milano and the Yankees was contested in Ott's nascent Lega Italiana Baseball. The first game was a success—if for no other reason than the fact that Coca-Cola sponsored it, providing two refrigerators full of drinks. The people who attended thought it was a curious novelty, according to writer Igino Scafella.

This was only the beginning for Ott's league. On 3 October 1948 in Bologna, the circuit held a championship between Libertas of Bologna and Milan's Yankees. The score indicates a bit of a sloppy affair as Libertas prevailed 25–19, but the event did attract all-important media attention. Thanks to Ott's journalistic connections, *Gazzetta dello Sport* writer Franco Imbastaro began covering the game.

From there, two leagues emerged — one was the Guido Graziani–led l'Associazione Italiana Baseball and the other was Ott's Lega Italiana Baseball. Between the two circuits, many cities were now playing baseball. Among them: Rome, Milan, Bologna, Turin, Florence and Modena. Consolidation occurred in 1950 with a top league, the Italian Baseball League being organized. Federazione Italiana Palla Base, which is still in existence today as Federazione Italiana Baseball Softball (FIBS), formally took over as the sport's governing body.

During this period, Italian baseball was developing its own style. In the 1953 season, an American journalist Blake Ehrlich chronicled the early days of organized baseball in Italy.[15] He recognized that the overall level of play was still in the nascent stage and described the Italian game as follows: "The beauty and grace on local diamonds may seem severely limited to anyone used to big-league, or even semi-pro play, but there is a nervous elegance and operatic melodrama peculiarly Italian about it all. When an outfielder drops a fly ball, you feel sure that he will kill himself by eating his mitt, if his teammates don't kill him first."

As in the United States, fans in Italy took the game seriously — even in the embryonic years. Still, the intensity of fans seems to have been akin to the most rabid in America. For example, reported Ehrlich, the batter "stepping into the box is frequently advised that if he makes a solid hit, his ears will be cut off and mailed to his grandmother." A base runner was warned, according to Ehrlich, that "[y]ou steal home and my gang'll catch you outside the stadium and break both your legs."

Following up on the GIs' informal efforts at the end of the war, the United States Information Service was looking to continue the baseball boom in the 1950s. In 1952 they printed — and distributed for free — thousands of copies of a baseball rule book, entitled *Regolamento Tecnico del Gioco del Baseball*. Films featuring the great Italian-American slugger Joe DiMaggio and other big-league stars were also imported.

What could not be imported were umpires, according to the American Joe Lubas. "We don't study the batters — we study the umpires," Lubas told Ehrlich. "Some of them call all low balls strikes and that sort of thing. The strongest point in Italian ball playing is the pitching. These boys have wonderful arms. So you teach the kids to throw curves and you've got a pitcher with a beautiful sinker. What happens? The umpire can't see the corners. There are no corners on an Italian plate with an Italian umpire."

While the umpires may have been lackluster, Italian baseball did develop some decent baseball prospects immediately. The best of them all was Giulio Cesare Glorioso. A right-handed pitcher, Glorioso, who began playing in 1948, put up jaw-dropping numbers in Italy's top domestic league. From 1953 to 1967, Glorioso led the league in strikeouts eleven times, averaging more than

150 a season. This is particularly awe-inspiring when you realize that those seasons usually ran 18 games long. At the height of his career —from 1961 to 1967 — he won 108 games and lost just 8. His earned run average was an incredible 1.29. His greatest season was 1961 when he won every one of Milano's 18 games, striking out a total of 218 batters.

At six feet, 180 pounds, Glorioso was not a dominating figure on the mound, but he combined a live fastball with a slow curve that even got him a shot at the major leagues. In 1953, Glorioso traveled to the United States for a tryout with the Cleveland Indians. Glorioso went to spring training in Daytona Beach, Florida, and performed well enough to earn a contract offer, according to his coach in Italy at the time, Kenneth Opstein, a former journalist from Ohio. But, according to a 1953 *Los Angeles Times* article, Glorioso had to decline because of military commitments in Italy. Whatever the reason, Glorioso returned to Italy as a combination of Cy Young and a bit of Babe Ruth. (He won two batting titles, with a .432 average in 1960 and a .444 average in 1961.)

Glorioso, who studied law at university, knew how to make the most of his commodity status, bouncing around a number of clubs. The Rome native began his career for his hometown team Lazio before spending time with perennial powers Nettuno and Parma. He also led Milano to three championships (known as *scudetti* or "pennants") between 1960 and 1962. According to one account he was wooed by Nettuno with the promise that the club would get lights. A true ambassador of the game, he used his prominence in 1968 to bring top-level baseball back to the Eternal City. When Glorioso decided he wanted to play in Rome, members of the Italian baseball establishment jumped. "A bit of wheeler-dealer antics with the assistance of the Lazio Sports Club and the Incom kitchen cabinet company landed a bankrupt Bologna franchise and Rome was back in the 'A' League," reported a 7 July 1968 *Washington Post* article. As in Nettuno, Glorioso fought hard to get floodlights as he believed that night games were essential for growing baseball. Beyond his savvy off-field efforts, his baseball acumen also earned him international respect, as he served as a scout for the Cincinnati Reds. A learned man, Glorioso has also been a baseball philosopher. In David Bidini's nonfiction account of baseball in Nettuno, *Baseballissimo*, Glorioso is quoted: "There is something that occurs in man ... when you give him a stone or a ball. There is something appealing [about this], for some reason, which is outside, immaterial. All popular games involve balls. Baseball is like language. It just happened."

While Glorioso was certainly Italy's biggest and brightest star, he was not the only Italian to get a major league look in the formative years of Italian baseball. Two years after he displayed his skills for the Indians, two other players crossed the Atlantic to prove their worth. Shortstop-centerfielder Franco Tavoni and catcher Angelo Rizzo were brought over by the Washington Senators on a two-month visit arranged by the State Department and the United States Information Service. Tavoni and Rizzo were very good players, but nowhere in the league of Glorioso. Not surprisingly, the pair was overwhelmed at their first sight of Major League pitching. "My friend," said Tavoni to Rizzo while watching future All-Star Camilo Pascual throw batting practice, "We have never seen anything thrown that fast in our country."[16] Unfortunately for other aspiring Italians, this trip did not end well. Rizzo overstayed his visa and, as a result, the State Department offered no further invitations to Italian ballplayers.[17]

Despite that disappointment, the era did produce Italy's most mythical major-league moment: the day Joe DiMaggio played baseball in Nettuno. Every chronicler of Italian baseball has been drawn to this story. Most recently, the 2007 documentary *City of Baseball* and Bidini's 2005 book *Baseballissimo* reveled in the tale. Most agree with how it started. In the summer of 1957, DiMaggio, who had retired six years earlier from the New York Yankees, traveled to Rome on vacation. When he heard a baseball game was being played in the nearby hamlet of Nettuno, he took a side trip to the coastal town.

From there, the Italian love of storytelling leaves the details a little hazy. *City of Baseball* has a whole segment with different Nettuno oldtimers telling variations on what happened next. As the legend generally goes, the 42-year-old DiMaggio agreed to take a few swings against a local pitcher. After the Italian hurler threw one pitch by Joltin' Joe, the slugger took off his jacket and began hitting home run after home run. Some accounts had him hitting dozens of majestic shots into the sea. In 1998, 72-year-old Nettuno native Rolando Belleudi recounted the story this way to *USA Today*: "In the early '50s, Nettuno had a great fastballer, Carlo Tagliaboschi, so we dared DiMaggio to hit him. DiMaggio watched pitch after pitch until we started jeering. Then, suddenly, he slipped off his jacket and strode to the plate in his shirtsleeves. He hit three homers on three pitches and walked away." According to the article, "Joltin' Joe's third shot, legend has it, carried out of the since-demolished stadium and plopped into the Mediterranean Sea."[18]

Contemporaneous news stories do confirm the event, but leave out much of the drama supplied by locals. DiMaggio apparently did hit three home runs in the 10-minute hitting display, according to a 17 June 1957 *Washington Post* account.[19] "I guess I was a bit over-ambitious," said DiMaggio, who injured his back slightly at the event. "It's nothing serious, just a little sore.... All I'll have to do is take it easy for a few days and have a few steam baths." If in fact he did blast even one ball into the sea, it would have been particularly impressive, as DiMaggio said he'd swung a bat only one other time "in years."

DiMaggio's exploits must have fueled baseball dreams throughout Italy. After all, the Italian-American DiMaggio was well-known throughout the country. But the growth of baseball in Italy would require more than dreams. For that, Italian baseball was lucky to have Prince Steno Borghese. Just the tacit involvement of a man of Borghese's noble background — the King of Italy came from the Borghese family — would have been enough to help legitimize the cause of baseball. But Borghese, along with donating land for Nettuno's field, was a tireless worker for the sport. Along with other Italian baseball promoters, Borghese was a key figure in convincing the president of Italy's Olympic sports committee (a friend) to recognize baseball in 1957. This gave baseball cachet in the Italian sporting world. A year later, he traveled to the United States to court Italian-Americans keen on helping baseball burgeon in their homeland. His efforts were fruitful. A number of organizations were established to procure equipment and funds for baseball. They included Baseball for Italy, Inc., a nonprofit organization headed by Lou Perini, the president of the Milwaukee Braves, and television personality Ed Sullivan. Another group, the Baseball International Foundation, even held a special dinner in New York City to raise money for Nettuno baseball that was attended by Yankee greats Yogi Berra and Bill Skowron. This was not his only trip to the United States, and the Prince often attended major-league games on his American sojourns, according to longtime European baseball official Gaston Panaye.

All told, Borghese headed Italian baseball's governing body from 1949 to 1960. In addition, his devotion to the sport reached outside Italian borders. In 1953, when organizers decided to form a European baseball federation, Borghese was picked to be its first president. Panaye, who was vacationing in Italy at the time, was dispatched to convince the nobleman to take on this bigger cause. "Prince Borghese was a very sympathetic gentleman," Panaye recalled in 2007. "We spoke in French (he also spoke English and Spanish) and [it turns out] he had the same idea about a European federation. He was very enthusiastic." Borghese took his role seriously, attending all the meetings of the organization's executive committee and congresses as well as being on hand for each European Championship. Even after he was replaced as the head of European baseball's governing body, he continued as a presence, showing up at European Championships throughout his life.

Borghese's participation in the pan–European baseball movement was not only a boon for a sport trying to organize over a continent but also helped Italian baseball specifically. Borghese's contacts made it easier to begin setting up international games between Italy and other countries.

The Netherlands and Belgium had played some international contests before World War II and Italy aggressively followed suit in the early 1950s. Its first contest was 31 August 1952 against Spain. Held in Rome's Stadio Nazionale, the result was not what fans of *la nazionale azzurra* (aka "The Blues") would have expected. A packed audience, which included Prince Steno Borghese and actor Gregory Peck (who threw out the first pitch) watched with surprise as the Italians fell behind in the fourth and eventually lost 7–3. Even at this early juncture, the Italian baseball community had a lot of pride and the loss was a heavy blow. According to a 1 September 1952 *New York Times* article, many of the more than 15,000 in attendance left the game after the seventh inning complaining that the contest was too long. Presumably, a stronger performance by the home team, which committed 13 errors and were losing handily by the sev-

PRIMO INCONTRO DELLA NAZIONALE AZZURRA
DI BASEBALL

SPAGNA - ITALIA

STADIO NAZIONALE - ROMA - 31 AGOSTO 1952

Following World War II, Italy plunged headfirst into baseball. In 1952, the country's national team hosted its first international contest against Spain in Rome (above: postcard from event). It was a high-profile game, with American actor Gregory Peck throwing the honorary first pitch.

enth, would have kept them in their seats. Organizers regrouped and decided that they were not properly choosing players. Local sportswriters complained that the absence of four players from Italy's top team Nettuno was a key reason for the loss, according to the 1952 *Times* article. Those players had been barred from the game because of a dispute with an umpire two weeks previous. The venerable Max Ott was named technical director of the national team and was charged with setting definable standards for members of the squad.

Following the changes, Italy didn't waste time in trying to regain their honor on the field. A second match against Spain was set up in Madrid in August 1953, followed by a contest against Belgium in September. Spain proved too powerful again for the Italian team, as the Blues fell at the Estadio Metropolitano de Madrid 8–4. But Italy's first international victory came against Belgium the following month. Interestingly, although the great Glorioso had started on the mound for *la nazionale azzurra* in the two tilts against Spain, he did not pitch when Italy beat Belgium 7–3. It was Tagliaboschi, the pitcher who faced Joe DiMaggio, who picked up the win.

Despite the mixed performance in their inaugural international games, it didn't take long for Italy to taste success on the European circuit. At the first European championships in 1954, Italy prevailed, settling an old score with Spain by beating them 7–4 and overcoming the Belgians again 6–1. But it took a little longer for Italy to take its place alongside the Netherlands as an elite team on the continent. Through the end of the 1950s, Italy did not hoist another European Championship crown, placing second once, third twice and fourth once. It wasn't until the 1960s that Italy began to dominate. In fact from 1960 through 1999, Italy finished either first or second at every European Championship it entered.

How did the Italians rise to the top? It was a combination of factors. First, facilities were getting better and better. In Milan, for example, a pristine baseball field was erected in 1964. The field dedicated to U.S. president John F. Kennedy had finely cut grass and boasted a large manual scoreboard in centerfield sponsored by Coca-Cola. Along with improved facilities, the national team also stepped up its competition against international foes. Each year the Italians made a point of playing American clubs. The team also lined up top competition against other countries. By the late 1960s, Italy was playing the Netherlands in a one-on-one series (1967), competing in Europe's most prestigious non–European Championship event, Haarlem Baseball Week (1968) and even playing a series of games against Cuba (also 1968). While the results were not always pretty — Italy lost to Cuba seven straight times by a combined score of 96–5 — it did leave them battle-tested and far superior to European clubs that weren't seeing such competition.

In addition, Americans were being used far more strategically. U.S. coaches with high-level experience were playing an increasingly important role. Individuals like Chet Morgan and Bill Arce added a level of professionalism to

In 1954, Italy won the first-ever European Baseball Championship. A photo of the team featured many of the fathers of Italian baseball, including: (Standing) Horace McGarity, coach (1st from left); Giovanni Ugo, manager (6th from the left); Calro Tagliaboschi, pitcher (2nd from the right); and (Seated) Giulio Glorioso, pitcher (1st from the left). Other players are unidentified. (Courtesy CEB.)

Italian baseball. Morgan had enjoyed a substantial minor-league career that included a stint as Hank Aaron's teammate before arriving in Parma in 1967.[20] He would also work with the national team. Arce, a college coach and baseball administrator from California, achieved tremendous success leading the Dutch national team before skippering *la nazionale azzura* to the European Championship in 1975.

Along with pursuing American coaches, Italian clubs also began aggressively pursuing Americans—particularly Italian-Americans—to supplement their rosters. This practice began in 1971, according to a 1977 *Washington Post* article.[21] Over the years the quality of the imports (known as *stranieri*) has improved, with numerous major leaguers seeing time in Italy. But in the early years most of the Americans were college-level players. What role Americans would play has been a big issue in Italy—as in other European countries. In 1977, for example, the *Post* described the rules as allowing three Italian-Americans and one American on the field during one game (with rosters carrying as many as seven Americans). In contrast, by the start of the new millennium, teams were limited to two foreign players on the field.[22]

All these efforts created critical mass, so that by the 1970s Italy's place—

alongside the Netherlands—as a powerhouse on the European baseball landscape was secured. Beyond national team success, Italian clubs were also dominating their counterparts on the continent. In 1963, Europe's baseball federation established the European Cup. The trophy would be contested by the league champions from each country and, starting in 1969, Italian teams dominated the event. From 1969 to 1999, Italian teams won twenty-five European Cup championships. The club from Parma was Italy's brightest light, winning thirteen titles. Parma's success should not be surprising as its facilities were simply breathtaking. The Stadio Europeo, located in the heart of Parma, would be the envy of many minor league organizations below the AA level. Immaculate, with a fine scoreboard, closed-in bullpens, numerous hitting tunnels and a smooth playing surface, it was an idyllic place to play baseball.

Chet Morgan (above) was one of a handful of professional coaches who helped improve player performance in Italy beginning in the 1960s.

But Parma was not alone. The fishing town of Nettuno continued to be a power, winning four European Cups. Rimini, a resort town located near the Adriatic Sea in the Emilia-Romagna region, also developed into a baseball hotbed. A great location combined with a beautiful stadium has made Rimini a popular place for top talent to play, as evidenced by the town's ten national championships and three European Cup triumphs. In addition, Bologna, a town known for its sports, has been an energetic baseball locale for decades. For a period, Milan was also a major player. Presumably, the brief tenure of Glorioso and the new stadium led to the club's fleeting success. From 1960 to 1970, Milano won seven national championships and two European Cups. Alas, today they do not even play in Italy's top league.

On paper, baseball appeared to be booming in the 1970s. After all, Italy won three straight European Championships in 1975, 1977 and 1979 and captured all but one European Cup club title during the decade. In 1975, former major leaguer and longtime broadcaster Joe Garagiola traveled to Italy to do reports for his NBC TV show "The Baseball World of Joe Garagiola" on Italian baseball. In an article he wrote in *The New York Times*, Garagiola explained that Italian baseball was looking a lot like its American baseball cousins.[23] "I guess I figured on finding a game that would be much different from the baseball we know in this country," he said. "In fact, I found a lot of similarities I didn't expect." Most notably, he recognized that there was true baseball talent in Italy.

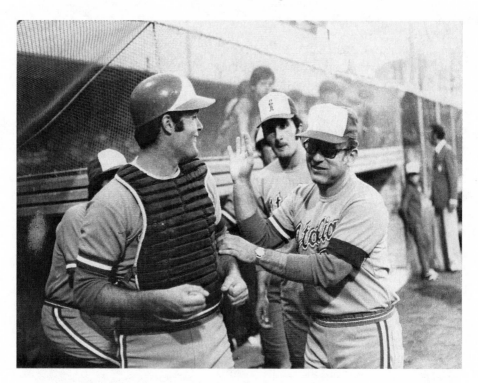

Italy had a great run of international success in the 1970s, winning the European Base-ball Championships three times in the decade. Behind the coaching of Bill Arce, the national team also performed well against traditional baseball powers, beating both the Untied States and Taiwan at the 1973 Intercontinental Cup. Pictured here at the 1973 event: (L–R) Bruno Laurenzi, Giorgio Costantini and Arce. (Courtesy Bill Arce.)

"The caliber of play would have to be measured by the eight teams in [the top league, Serie A1]," he wrote. "I'd guess that an all-star team from that league would be the equivalent of a top college team over here."

A generation before, it was Giulio Glorioso who stood out as the big tal-ent. Now Italy's baseball superstar was catcher Giorgio Castelli. Like many ele-ments of Italian baseball, Castelli's foray into American baseball is glossed with a level of dramatic Italian tale weaving. Author Peter Carino recounts it this way: "Castelli was scouted by American teams and after his rookie season in 1968 was offered a contract to be groomed as a backup for Johnny Bench, but the deal fell through when the Reds signed talented prospect Bill Plummer."[24] Of course, there are other versions to the story. The 1977 *Washington Post* story on Italian baseball explains the situation this way: "Everyone loves to tell the story of how the Cincinnati Reds were ready to bump a guy named Bench out to first base to make room for Castelli, who showed up at a Florida baseball camp in 1968 as a 17-year-old unknown and had scouts crawling all over him after two days. The Reds, in fact, were ready to sign him when the long arm of the Italian family scotched the deal. His mother didn't want him so far away from home."

Whatever happened, there is no dispute that Castelli was a first-rate catcher and hitter. Even Garagiola, who spent nine years as a catcher in the majors, said in 1975 that the 23-year-old Castelli "definitely is a major league prospect." Added former Italian National team skipper Bill Arce: "He was the real thing: good size, strong, good running ability, smart, could hit and had some power and coachable ... he was definitely a prospect."[25] Of course, Castelli never got there and, instead, became one of Italy's greatest all-time hitters. He spent his entire career in Parma and from 1968 to 1978 he won eight batting crowns. Five of those titles came with a batting average well over .400 and, in two of those seasons, he hit over .500. By far, 1974 was his best season. That year, he won the Italian triple crown, batting .515 with 26 home runs (known as *fuori-campi* in Italian) and 79 RBI in 44 games. His final career stats would be impressive in any league: a lifetime .423 average, 163 home runs and 696 RBI in 605 games.

Even with a superstar like Castelli and consistent success throughout Europe, Italian baseball remained consigned to the second tier of Italian sports in the 1970s. "'Where have you gone, Joe DiMaggio?' is the anthem and lament of Italian baseball, which struggles along in relative obscurity behind king soccer and royal-pretender basketball in the country's line of sports succession," the *Washington Post* dourly said in 1977. The article pointed out that there was a disparity between the powerhouses with their beautiful stadiums and robust budgets and the weaker clubs. "Many boxes read like rugby scores," wrote the *Post*. "Parma recently mowed down Bollate in a three-game series by scores of 23–10, 10–0 and 16–3." The article quoted one player explaining why baseball couldn't compete with the country's most popular games. Baseball's deliberate pace was "very much contrary to the Italian mentality," he said.[26]

The lack of extensive popular backing has not deterred those involved with Italian baseball. In fact, major sponsors for the sport, which have varied from Danesi (a coffee company) to the bank Cariparma, grew increasingly ambitious in the 1980s and into the 1990s. While big leaguers may have trickled in as early as the 1970s, the first prominent player to ply his trade in Italy was Lenny Randle. A 12-year major-league veteran, Randle had put up some decent numbers in a journeyman's career that featured stops with the Washington Senators/Texas Rangers, the New York Mets, the New York Yankees, the Chicago Cubs and the Seattle Mariners. His best season was 1974 when he finished seventh in the American League in hitting with .302 and swiped 26 bases for the Rangers. But in 1983, at age 34, he was out of the major leagues and looking for a job. "Playing baseball in Italy was like finding the fountain of youth," Randle told the *Tampa Tribune* in 1995. "Guys over there learn how to relax and enjoy the game. It's easy, because there's no stress." It was probably easy for Randle to relax because he performed very well for Nettuno. Playing from 1983 to 1986, he won a batting title in his first season, hitting .475. Three years later, he led the league in stolen bases with 32. At the time, aluminum bats were still being used in Italy's top league and Randle made the most of the power advantage metal offered over the traditional wood bats he would have used in his U.S. professional career. In 1,138 games in the Major Leagues, he hit only 27 round trippers, but in approximately 200 games in Italy he slammed 47 *fuori campi*.

Among the other big leaguers who played in Italy in the 1980s were Harry Chappas, Rick Waits and Joe Ferguson. Five-foot-three shortstop Harry Chappas was one of the shortest men ever to play in the majors. His stature didn't prevent him from being a home-run hitter in Italy. He hit eight homers in 56 games during one mid–1980s season for the Tuscan club Grosseto after mustering a single four-bagger for the Chicago White Sox in a three-year 72-game career. Waits, who was known for his top-shelf curve ball, brought his whole family with him to Italy in the late 1980s. He played in Rimini and Parma after a 12-year major-league career primarily with the Cleveland Indians. Joe Ferguson, who spent 14 seasons as a back-up catcher, also had a stint in the country.

Enhancing the level of foreigners did make a difference in the quality of play in Italy, according to Jim Mansilla, who coached Italy at the 1984 Olympics. "Ten years ago, we were like a college program," Mansilla said. "Now, with the influx of American players, we have gotten much better. I would say that our league is comparable to [the highly competitive minor-league level of] Double A."[27] Italian baseball historian and FIBS communication manager Riccardo Schiroli sees the standard a little differently: "Italy is more like the independent Atlantic League. Double A is full of young prospects, the best players here are veterans."[28]

The incursion of major leaguers was not the only way in which Americans were being used to ratchet-up Italian play. The country's national team was increasingly being populated by Italian-Americans who were able to obtain dual nationality. At the 1984 Olympics, Italy was Europe's sole representative, finishing fifth out of six teams but impressing with a 10–7 victory over the Dominican Republic. Yet that team featured nine players (on a squad of 20) who were born in the United States. Understandably, Italy has had to grapple with the demands of being on the big stage. As one of the top two teams in Europe, the Italians have earned spots at elite events like the Olympics, the World Cup, the Intercontinental Cup — and, more recently — the World Baseball Classic. Any competitive advantage has been essential to ensure that the club merely stays on the field with perennial powers like the United States, Cuba and Japan.

Moreover, the Italians generally require that these players compete in the Italian league. Therefore, just being eligible to wear the blue for Italy has not been enough. In fact, in 1996, the Italian baseball federation planned to bring in three Italian-American pitchers—including future major leaguers Jason

Former major league baseball players have been a staple in Italy's top league (Serie A1) for more than a generation. Ten-year big league veteran Giovanni Cararra (above: pictured pitching for longtime Italian powerhouse Nettuno), is one of the more than 100 ex-major leaguers who have competed in Italy. (Photograph by Renato Ferrini/ FIBS.)

Grilli—for the Atlanta Olympics. The team balked at their inclusion and the players were sent home. In the end, Italy performed admirably in Atlanta, beating South Korea and Australia en route to a sixth-place finish out of eight countries. Ironically, one notable exception to the outsider rule was the World Baseball Classic, wherein the class of professionals required Italy to bend their rules. On the team, along with the likes of Mike Piazza, was pitcher Jason Grilli who had been spurned in 1996.

Even with the increase in foreign involvement in the 1980s, Italy was still able to develop its own talent. The greatest player of this generation was Roberto Bianchi. The outfielder from Milan began his career in 1981 in Bologna with a bang, leading the league in his rookie season in RBI with 43 in a 40-game season. That year he hit a home run out of Baltimore's Memorial Stadium when the Orioles apparently showed interest in the young slugger. But, according to one report, the Italian baseball federation "turned thumbs down" on Bianchi playing in the United States.[29] He was still being noticed by talent evaluators in 1984 when longtime San Diego State University head coach Jim Dietz tabbed Bianchi as a pro prospect in the *Los Angeles Times*. As was the case with Glorioso and Castelli before him, Bianchi instead made a name for himself at home. By the time he retired, he held the coveted all-time Italian home-run record, hitting 288 homers. His greatest year was likely 1987 when he hit .474 with 27 home runs and 72 RBI, although there may be an argument for 1985, when, in a 66-game season, he set the single-season record for RBI with 102. Equally as important as his performance on the field was his affection for the game, which was palpable. "I love baseball more than I love myself," he told the Fort Lauderdale *Sun-Sentinel* in 1996.

Despite all his success, Bianchi serves as a reminder that baseball — even for its greatest players— is merely a blip on the Italian radar. By 1996, Bianchi had already proved himself the Babe Ruth of Italy, but he could walk down the street unnoticed. Or even worse, a puzzling figure. "People see me in this uniform," he said pointing to his Italia jersey, "and they say, 'What is that, a soccer team? When I tell them baseball, they say, 'Baseball in Italy? You're kidding.'"

Still, Italy's top league, known as Serie A1, continues to draw former major leaguers. In 2002, Chuck Carr, who led the National League in steals for the Milwaukee Brewers in 1993, was rumored to have been paid a massive sum of money for playing a season for Rimini. Americans and top Italians without pedigrees the likes of Carr or Jaime Navarro, a former 17-game-winner in the majors, can make in the vicinity of $2,500 to $5,000 per month — or more — plus accommodation and a car.

More interesting than the big league players who played their twilight years in Italy are those who used their experience in Italy to enhance or resurrect their careers. Jason Simontacchi, for example, played in Italy before making it to the big leagues with the St. Louis Cardinals in 2002. He dominated for Rimini in 2000, posting a 15–1 record with a 1.56 ERA and 136 strikeouts in

133 innings. He even credited developing his change-up to his time in Italy. Ed Vosberg pitched briefly for the San Diego Padres in 1986 and the San Francisco Giants in 1990, but found his career was stalling. After spending some time in the minor leagues, he got his career back on track in Italy, playing for Novara in 1992. Two years later, he returned to the major leagues for eight additional seasons, highlighted by a World Series championship with the Marlins in 1997.

The strength of its league has also helped the national team remain one of Europe's two most consistent performers on the international stage. Along with the Netherlands, Italy became the first European country to participate in the World Cup in 1970. Since that time, Italy has hosted the 1978, 1988 and 1998 World Cups. The 1998 competition was successfully organized throughout Italy and included venues in such cities as Milan, Reggio Emilia and Livorno. It was also the first Baseball World Championship event open to professionals, and included such notable guests as former International Olympic Committee President Juan Antonio Samaranch and current IOC President Jacques Rogge.

For years, Italian baseball has been a reliable representative of Europe. The country has played in every Olympics since the sport became an official event at the Barcelona Games in 1992 (although they did not qualify for the 2008 Beijing Games). Overall, they have won eight European Baseball Championships, with the most recent triumph coming in 1997. And, at the 2007 World Cup, Italy was the only team to beat the USA, who won the event. In addition, Italy has played a unique role in the sport's worldwide growth. The country's native Aldo Notari, a player in Italy's early years and later an adept front-office man, served as president of the International Baseball Federation (IBAF) from 1993 until his death in 2006. Indicating some toehold in Italian popular culture, the sport has even drawn the support of Italian pop band Elio E Le Storie Tese. In conjunction with Major League Baseball, the band, which has members who play the sport, has worked hard in the past to publicize baseball.

Major League Baseball, which is televised in the country, has also aided in grassroots development. MLB has sponsored youth development for beginners and, in conjunction with the *Federazione Italiana Baseball Softball*, has hosted camps in Italy for elite young players from throughout Europe and Africa. In 2002, 12-time All-Star Mike Piazza, whose father's family comes from the Sicilian town of Sciacca, conducted a clinic and hitting exhibition in Rome as part of MLB's international game-development program.

Italy also remains a resource for on-field talent for potential major league prospects. The country regularly sends players to the U.S. minor leagues but has yet to produce a truly born-and-bred big-league Italian player. Author Peter Carino suggests that the failure of stars in Italy like Claudio Liverziani and Andrea Castri to last longer in the minors is a bad reflection on Italian baseball. But the increasing number of Italians getting a chance should mean more experience at home and should bode well for the next generation of Italian

players. Moreover, the pipeline doesn't seem to be slow-
ing. In 2007, for example,
17-year-old Italian pitcher
Andrea Lucati was signed
by the Houston Astros out
of Major League Baseball's
European Academy. He was
the fourth Italian to receive a
contract from a big-league
club since the camp was
formed in 2005.

As for the direct impact
of the country's natives on the
major leagues, six Italian-
born players have made it to
the majors. The most recent
was Reno Bertoia. Born in St.
Vito Udine, Bertoia played
ten seasons for five different
teams. The infielder broke in
with the Detroit Tigers in
1953 and made his final
appearance in the majors in
1962. While Italian-born athletes are not abundant in
big-league lore, players with
Italian heritage account for

**Including some former major leaguers, Italian
baseball has also produced some prospects of its
own, including Alex Liddi (above), who has played
in the Seattle Mariners organization. (Photograph
by Ezio Ratti/FIBS.)**

many of the game's all-time greats. From New York Yankees Hall of Famers Joe
DiMaggio and Phil Rizzuto to recant greats like Piazza, the influence of Italy
undoubtedly looms large in baseball history.

Beyond that, it's the unique approach to the culture of baseball that Italians offer that should never be understated. Baseball is truly a family affair in
Italy. While Italian crowds of more than 1,000 are not wholly common nowa-
days, those who do attend are true fans. Instead of beer, ballpark fare skews
toward espressos or cappuccinos. And, instead of hot dogs, there are usually
sandwiches or pastries for sale. Sometimes elaborate lunches are held, including both teams—between games at doubleheaders!

There has been talk for some time of a joint venture between Major League
Baseball and the Italian federation to set up an MLB-affiliated (or at least tac-
itly supported) professional league throughout Italy. Observations from the
likes of sports sociologist and author Alan M. Klein suggest such an ambitious
venture might be too difficult to pull off. "Because [Italian] clubs are bought

On a nice Italian night, baseball is still a draw for many locals. Pictured here is Grosseto's jam-packed stadium at the country's 2007 national baseball finals. (Photograph by Renato Ferrini/FIBS.)

[by wealthy locals] for reasons of vanity and ego satisfaction, an understanding prevails among owners to close ranks against anyone who would reform or rationalize the sport," Klein wrote in 2006. "[Italian baseball club] owners like to socialize as a group, consider themselves members of a tight little cartel."[30]

Yet, the idea of seeing future major leaguers playing with the Tuscan hills rolling behind the stadium in Florence or chatting with fans at a small café next to the field in Grosseto seems perfect. The combination of awe-inspiring environs and deep rosters of top-notch talent could be great for the game of baseball in Italy, Europe and beyond.

3

Spain

A number of European countries have encountered turbulent times with baseball. For much of the late twentieth century, the Soviet Union and its satellites shunned baseball because it was seen as too American. Then there's Great Britain. For more than 100 years, large chunks of the British populace have turned their backs on the sport because it wasn't British enough. But Spain may be the only European nation that actually *banned* baseball.

In the late nineteenth century, Spain was trying to maintain control of Cuba, a small but valuable colonial outpost, and baseball was serving as an unwanted agent for change by the local population. From nearly the date of its invention, baseball was a popular sport in Cuba. The game was first played in the United States in the 1840s and by 1864 students returning to the island from the U.S. brought the sport with them. The hitch was that these students— and those who took most to the game in Cuba—were not part of the Spanish ruling elite. To the government leaders, respecting Spanish sports like bull-fighting was a key way to pay homage to mother Spain. Baseball simply didn't fit.

Moreover, baseball was becoming an ethnic yardstick. It was a way of distinguishing between true Spaniards on the island and *criollos*, the children of Spaniards born in Cuba, according to Cuban baseball historian Gilberto Dihigo.[1] Cuban baseball observers have readily used the sport to underscore cultural differences between what they've described as the battle between the freedom-seeking Cubans who were increasingly influenced by the United States and their outdated and dictatorial Spanish leaders. "Baseball was a sport played in defiance of the Spanish authorities, who viewed this American invention as vaguely secessionist and dangerously violent because of the use of sticks," wrote author

Roberto González Echevarría in 1999.[2] "Cubans celebrated the modernity and progress implied in baseball, associated with the United States, and denounced the inhumanity and backwardness suggested by bullfighting, associated with Spain," added writer Louis A. Perez, Jr.[3]

This cultural tension probably wouldn't have been enough to earn baseball an island-wide ban from the powers in Madrid if it weren't for the fact that baseball was quickly becoming the game utilized by dissidents and revolutionaries in their quest for independence. "Baseball was not played by the Spanish. They called it 'a rebel game.' To a certain point they were correct, because baseball players used the opportunity to collect money for the fight for independence from Spain," Dihigo explained. "Baseball was a meeting place for rebels. Emilio Sabourin, who is one of the founders of Cuban baseball, was a prisoner of Spain in Ceuta [a Spanish prison in North Africa] for his role in the independence struggle. And there is a long list of baseball players who died fighting for the independence of Cuba. Baseball clearly distinguished Spaniards from Cubans, and this is where the Cuban love of baseball begins." As a result baseball was outlawed by the Spanish government in 1869 — just after the beginning of the Ten Year War, which was the start of Cuba's long struggle for independence. Of course, the ban had little impact on the growth of the sport in Cuba, where the game remains a central part of its culture.

Despite the strong animus toward baseball by authorities, the sport made its way back from Cuba to Spain by 1889. When A. G. Spalding put together his 1888–1889 baseball world tour, Spain was a serious candidate for an exhibition because of its ties to the game. "There isn't a 'good base-ball town' on the Continent, unless Barcelona and Madrid be excepted, whither the game has been imported from Cuba," explained a 6 April 1889 article in *Harper's Weekly*. (Ultimately, the tourists did not venture to the country because "[c]ircumstances rendered a Spanish journey out of the question." Presumably, those "circumstances" related to logistical issues.)

Even with the Spalding snub, Americans were at least sporadically playing in Spain the beginning of the twentieth century as U.S. sailors were organizing games during shore leave in Barcelona, according to Spanish baseball pioneer Fernando Garrido.[4] This led to more formalized baseball activities. In 1914, a *Washington Post* dispatch from Paris reported that "[c]oincident development of the game in Spain is noted in a challenge from a nine in Barcelona, which the racing club here has accepted."[5] Four years later, the *Christian Science Monitor* reported a contest between a Spanish squad and an American team led by William Ormesby, a U.S. Navy paymaster and Brown University alumnus. Spain won the 22–12 slugfest. The newspaper reported that the "Spaniards are said to like the game, but consider it 'very complicated.'"[6]

Even with these promising reports, U.S. observers were mixed during this era in their assessment of the American pastime's prospects in España. On the one hand, there was the opinion of veteran baseball journalist William A.

Phelon: "Baseball is full of thrills and fast, sensational happenings; this caught the fancy of the Cubans, and it didn't take long for the game to win its way into their hearts," he wrote in the January 1914 edition of *The Baseball Magazine*. "Their Spanish kinsmen, however, will never take up the diamond game, for the European Spaniard is far slower, more pompous, less eager for speed and sparkle, than the Cuban." On the other hand, the *New York Times* had a more sanguine judgment in its 31 August 1913 edition: "Spaniards are quick to embrace any branch of sport that carries the element of keen excitement," the *Times* wrote. "With the falling off in the interest in bullfighting and the establishment of branch houses of the leading American commercial firms the opportunity for the introduction of baseball on a firm basis appears encouraging."

The *Times* appeared right on this matter as within the next decade and a half, a Barcelona league was running, with four clubs — Catalonia, Munseratti, Catala and Olympic — taking part in 1929. The sport secured enough of a following that at Barcelona's International Exposition in 1929 a pair of international games were conducted. A French "national team" defeated the Spanish 10–6 and then a group of Paris-based Americans also beat the Spanish 11–4.[7] In Madrid the game was also being played. *Madrileños* were putting down baseball roots, as evidenced by the founding of the Piratas Béisbol Club in 1927.

Overall, those inroads were likely slowed by the Spanish Civil War which plunged the country into a severe depression in the late 1930s. This might have put an end to the Barcelona circuit which lasted for only a brief time. Still, the baseball interest developed in the 1920s did have some staying power. Madrid's Piratas would continue to play baseball into the modern era, winning three national championships (1966, 1967, 1981). In Barcelona, baseball also endured and was even played at the Industrial School of Barcelona, as evidenced by the story of Joseph Gusi. After learning baseball at the Industrial School in the early 1940s, Gusi would settle down in the Catalonian town of Viladecans, paving the way for a 4,000-seat stadium in the small town.

By 1944, there was enough critical mass for a national championship tournament. Baseball got an early boost from interest in the sport by some of Spain's most heralded soccer clubs. Spanish sports clubs are renowned for fielding a diversity of teams and when baseball became organized it was a logical step for four of the country's most successful soccer organizations — Real Madrid, FC Barcelona, Atlético de Madrid and R.C.D. Espanyol — to start baseball sections.

FC Barcelona formed a baseball team in 1941, thanks to the efforts of Fernando Garrido. That year, he approached the club about starting up an affiliated baseball squad. His pitch was simple: all the team would need from FC Barcelona were simple uniforms and a place to play. The powerful soccer team's knowledge of baseball was clearly limited — they called the sport "Pelota-Base" (literally "Ball-Base"), according to Garrido — but FC Barcelona's general manager nevertheless agreed to welcome the baseball side. Garrido would assemble a team of 15 players from across Catalonia and they would practice every

The participation of high-profile soccer clubs, like Real Madrid (pictured above), helped baseball's early development in Spain. Real Madrid would win a total of eight national baseball titles. (Courtesy RFEBS.)

Sunday at El Campo de la Bordeta, sharing the space with rugby and field hockey. Within a few years, they were a top baseball team. Although they lost in the finals in 1945, they won the national title in 1946 and 1947 behind the pitching of Panamanian hurler Joaquin Borrel, who Garrido dubbed "la bomba de hidrógeno" ("the hydrogen bomb").[8]

Real Madrid's prominence in baseball coincided with the reign of one of the club's most famed and revered figures, Santiago Bernabéu Yeste. He became club president in 1943 and rejuvenated Real Madrid, turning it into one of Europe's elite football organizations. At the same time, baseball would become another area of success for the club. Bernabéu's team would win eight national baseball championships between 1945 and 1963. In fact, the four soccer clubs that played America's pastime would dominate early Spanish domestic play, winning 12 of the first 13 crowns. While the fan enthusiasm likely came nowhere close to the excitement when these clubs met on the soccer pitch, it would have been fun to see two of the greatest rivalries in European sports played out on the diamond. Historically, Real Madrid and Atlético de Madrid have battled it out for the hearts and minds of the Spanish capital's sporting faithful. Equally as contentious is the Real Madrid–FC Barcelona rivalry. The two teams are seen as more than just competing sports organizations — they are the spiritual representatives of two differing regions of Spain: Castile and Catalonia. Unfortunately, today only FC Barcelona continues to field a baseball team. Although Real Madrid still has a basketball team (a squad that was established in 1932), it dropped baseball sometime after its final national championship in 1963.

The loss of the likes of Real Madrid to the Spanish baseball community must have been a blow because it's clear that the professionalism those organizations brought to the sport in the decade following the war gave baseball España a huge organizational and talent boost. In the years in which the Spanish soccer teams dominated on the diamond, the country also emerged as one of Europe's best and most forward-thinking baseball-playing countries.

Spanish baseball's governing organization was officially formed in 1944 under the name La Federación Española de Béisbol and domestic play immediately commenced.[9] As Europe began to calm somewhat after World War II, the thirst for international competition became great. In 1951, federation president Luis Barrio and the organization's secretary Jose R. Alvarez toured Europe with one goal: convincing organizations in the continent's other baseball countries to unite to form a European federation. The pair visited Italy, France, Germany, Belgium, Holland and England, "studying the possibilities and the strength of the existing organizations," wrote longtime European Federation official Roger C. Panaye.[10] Describing Barrio and Alvarez as "determined," Panaye said that they continued their efforts in 1952, proposing a meeting in July. While Belgium, Italy and Holland were receptive, representatives from France, Germany and England could not attend, so the confab never took place.

Ultimately, it would take the bureaucratic might of the Belgians — who had actually started the process for a European federation before the Spanish — to seal the deal on the formation of the Federation of European Baseball in 1953. Still, Barrio's and Alvarez's outreach allowed Spain to be on the forefront of national team competitions. There had been informal international matchups in the past between European countries — most notably between the Netherlands and Belgium before the war — but in 1952, Spain and Italy planned something on a grander scale. On 31 August 1952, Italy would play its first international contest at the Stadio Nazionale and Spain would be its opponent. Italy, which had taken to baseball enthusiastically following the war, would enter the game confidently. Their top pitcher Giulio Glorioso, who was one of Europe's greatest players of the era, was in his prime and would take to the mound. The game was more than just baseball — it was a coming-out party for Italian baseball. There were nearly a hundred articles written about the contest. A key reason for the interest was that one of the world's biggest movie stars, Gregory Peck, was on hand to throw out the game's first pitch. (Many articles focused on the Peck angle). Whatever the reason for the attention, the stadium was packed with spectators. The Stadio Nazionale was not configured for baseball. The field was all grass and the dimensions did not seem conducive to baseball (the left field fence appeared to be particularly short). That said, practically every seat was taken for the baseball battle.

The Spanish, who were dubbed the *Furie Rosse* or "Red Furies" by the Italian media (presumably a nod to the Spanish national soccer team's nickname "The Red Fury"), started slow in the contest. The Italians scored in the opening inning and kept the Spanish off the board for the first three frames. But the mound work of pitcher Juan Manuel Becerra, a Puerto Rican native living in Spain, kept the Spanish in the game and in the top of the fourth, the Red Furies exploded for four runs. Although the Italians answered in the bottom of the frame with two of their own, the Spanish closed the door on the home team with three in the seventh. The final score: Spain 7, Italy 3. Becerra was the star, allowing just two hits and striking out ten batters, including six in the final two innings.

Following the game, some Italian politicking began. Italian baseball observers blamed the loss on the organizers who chose an under-achieving squad to represent the *Azzurra*. Negotiations quickly commenced for a rematch in Madrid in 1953. On August 16, the two countries squared off again, this time at the Stadio Metropolitano di Madrid. In one sense, the game provided insight into why Italy would develop into one of Europe's top two baseball powers, while Spain would ultimately fall into a category just below them. When the two teams met in Italy, the stadium was filled to capacity. But in Madrid, the attendance was spotty. Seats behind the outfield at Metropolitano di Madrid were completely empty. Surely, baseball had support in Spain, but Italy appeared to be winning on that front. On the field at this point it remained a different story. Italy had claimed to have solved its roster issues and early indications suggested the problem had been cracked. The Italians jumped out to a 1–0 lead — just as they had in Rome. But, again, the Spanish answered. With two runs apiece in the second and third innings, Spain held a 4–1 advantage. The Italians would claw back with three in the fourth, but the Red Furies would break the Blues' hearts with three in the fifth and an additional run in the sixth to run away with an 8–4 victory. Unfortunately, the triumph was marred by a new controversy. Italy claimed that the Spanish national team had used Puerto Rican players in the Madrid game — a no-no, as the international tilt was supposed to feature only Spanish and Italian natives. The Spanish countered that the Puerto Ricans were considered as Spanish in Spain, but the European federation wasn't buying it. Pointing out that Puerto Rico was a part of the United States, the federation banned the Puerto Ricans from representing Spain in future sanctioned competitions.

Beyond the triumphs against Italy, Spain's national team did have at least one more glorious international moment in the early years of pan–European baseball. At the first European Baseball Championships in 1954, Italy exacted revenge from the Spanish, beating them in the finals 7–4. It was a sloppy game, with the Spanish making eight errors. But the following year, the Spanish hosted the championships in Barcelona and gave the locals something to cheer about.

Spain and Italy tied 0–0 in their game, but the Red Furies won their three other games to capture their one and only European title. The final, a 2–0 pitchers' duel against Belgium, even attracted a solid crowd of 3,000. Still, the Spanish couldn't shake the specter of unfair play. During the tournament, Federation of European Baseball president Prince Steno Borghese received an anonymous telegram claiming that the Spanish player Bernardo José Luis Menéndez was carrying a false Spanish passport. Menendez was a central player on the Spanish squad, having pitched Spain to its 0–0 tie with Italy and then earning the finals victory versus Belgium. Although the Italian publication *Gazetta dello Sport* claimed that Menendez was a Venezuelan, the tournament's technical committee found no proof of falsification and the pitcher was allowed to play. (It is worth noting that the technical committee at the time was chaired by Spain's Barrio and the committee's secretary was Barrio's compatriot Alvarez.)

The 1955 tournament also illustrated that the Spanish laid back "siesta" reputation could possibly be applied to their baseball endeavors. A new baseball stadium was constructed at Montjuich-Barcelona for the Barcelona event. But the day before the championships were set to begin, European federation dignitaries were dismayed when they visited the new ballpark. The reason: several mounds of sand were on the playing field. The officials asked how the Spanish would manage to get the field ready in time for the start of the festivities the next morning. After all, the field didn't have lights and the evening was quickly approaching. The Spanish were nonplussed and simply replied "a la luna" ("by moonlight"). Sure enough, the field was ready by the time the opening ceremonies commenced.[11]

In spite of all the tension and recriminations, the 1955 Euros victory gave Spain a unique opportunity on the world baseball stage. The championship earned Spain an invitation to the inaugural Global World Series in Milwaukee, Wisconsin, in 1955. The event was the brainchild of a Milwaukee industrialist

Spain - Champion 1955

Despite a nineteenth century baseball ban in Cuba, Spain excelled when the sport was organized across Europe. In 1955, the national team (pictured above) won the European Baseball Championships. (Courtesy CEB.)

named Dick Falk and the games were played at County Stadium, which at the time was the home of the Milwaukee Braves and would later house the Milwaukee Brewers. Along with Spain, other countries represented were the United States, Japan, Mexico, Colombia, Hawaii (which was yet to become a state) and the Commonwealth of Puerto Rico. Although the Spanish did not make the finals, they did become the first European national team to face squads representing countries outside Europe.[12] Ironically, the finals, which were aired on ABC and featured the United States beating Hawaii 7–4, drew only 1,500 — about half the number of fans that saw Spain beat Belgium in Barcelona the year before.

Despite the Red Furies' early success, the national team would have to settle with a somewhat diminished status following its European Championship crown. The country has yet to win another gold or silver medal, although it has captured 11 bronze medals. With the exception of the Spanish win in 1955 and a Belgian crown in 1967, the Netherlands and Italy have won every European championship. In fact, in 1967, neither the Dutch nor the Italians played at the event for political reasons.

So why did the Spanish drop a notch below the Italians, a team they beat handily in 1952 and 1953? One thing is for certain, the fall was not immediate. The Spanish national team might not have been cracking the top two at the European Championships, but Spanish club teams continued to be among the elite into the 1960s. In 1963, the European baseball federation began running a tournament to decide the best club team on the continent. Unlike the European Baseball Championships where the Spanish would have to worry about whether a roster member was Spanish or Puerto Rican or Venezuelan, the European Cup would be more lax in this area. Thus, the best non-nationals who played domestically in Europe could compete in the European Cup. Even though the Spanish soccer clubs — with the exception of FC Barcelona — were stepping away from baseball, the domestic league in Spain must have still been robust in this era because clubs from that circuit won four of the first seven European Cup competitions. In the inaugural Cup, Picadero Jockey Club, a team from Barcelona, topped teams from the Netherlands, Italy, Germany and Belgium to win the crown. In 1964 and 1967, the longtime club from Madrid, the Piratas di Madrid, hoisted the Cup. As part of the 1964 victory, the Piratas bested two of Europe's most illustrious clubs, Italy's Nettuno organization and Sparta Rotterdam from the Netherlands.

In 1968, Picadero would capture its second European club title which would be Spain's last. After that, the fall from elite status in European competition can be attributed to a couple of factors. First, both the Netherlands and Italy were aggressively courting and using professional American coaches during this period. The influence of men like Bill Arce and Ron Fraser was instrumental in the development of baseball in those countries. Although the Spanish would embrace this type of coaching later, it's unclear whether they had the same level of management at the time. Second, Spanish baseball suffered through regional squabbling that undoubtedly hindered the game at some level. Baseball had grown independently — and quite successfully — in both the Castillian city of Madrid and the Catalonian town of Barcelona. The success of Madrid's Piratas and Barcelona's Picaderos attests to this. But the two regions have always been fierce rivals and in 1970, this disdain manifested itself in the baseball world. According to European Baseball Federation documents, tensions between clubs in Barcelona and Madrid were causing problems. At the time, British baseball was suffering a schism in which teams from the south of England were trying to break away from teams in the north. In a 31 January 1970 document, Spain reported that "similar difficulties have arisen in Spain. There is a dispute between the clubs from Barcelona and Madrid." The north-south disagreement in Great Britain did lead to difficulties assembling the best national team for that country and also limited domestic play. Whether similar problems occurred in Spain is unclear. That said, as a minority sport everything must run well for optimal success, so any controversy must have been a hindrance.

By the 1980s, the center of Spanish baseball had moved away from the city centers of Madrid and Barcelona to Viladecans, a town of about 60,000 just outside of Barcelona. The sport came to Viladecans in the 1940s and, as journalist John Kernaghan wrote in the *Hamilton* (Ontario, Canada) *Spectator* in 1992: "[I]t's difficult to find anyone in this town ... who isn't touched by the game, either as a player, official or fan, making it the largest pocket of béisbol aficionados in Spain."[13] The Viladecans Baseball Club's president at the time, Andreu Comellas, explained that "[t]his sport, which to some people appears very complicated and even a little stupid, has been a principal reference of Viladecans." There is a good reason why: from 1981 to 2002, Viladecans won *every* Spanish national championship. The string places it among the most successful domestic clubs in European history. There isn't a tremendous secret to the Viladecans performance, according to Jim Jones, a longtime coach in Europe who worked with the Spanish National Team at the 2003 and 2005 European Championships. The club did it by finding local athletes and turning them into baseball players.

The Olympics must have helped in the recruiting process. The 1992 Barcelona Games marked the first time that baseball was an official Olympic sport and Viladecans was one of the sites for the tournament. Facilities were built up and the event served as a showcase for Spanish baseball. Conventional wisdom dictated that the Spanish would not only lose but lose big throughout the tournament. After all, at the 1988 World Championships, Spain finished 0–11 and was outscored 160–9. But the squad was a bit more talented than anyone expected.

In Spain's opening game, they drew the United States. The American team boasted such future major-league All-Stars as Nomar Garciaparra, Jason

Giambi, Jason Varitek, Charles Johnson and Phil Nevin. Some 4,800 partisan fans came out to the game chanting "España! España!" throughout. While the Spaniards could not pull off the epic victory, they did hang tough. The pitching of Felix Cano and Juan Damborenea held the Americans to just five hits. Garciaparra, Giambi and Nevin went a combined 0–10. Damborenea's pitching even received praise from the Team USA skipper Ron Fraser, who told the *Baltimore Sun*: "Give [left-handed reliever Damborenea] credit, he pitched well, and we didn't adjust."[14] In the end, a two-run home run from another future major leaguer, Michael Tucker, was the difference, as the Spanish lost 4–1. After that game, the Spanish did struggle in their next five games, getting roughed up mightily by the likes of Cuba, Taiwan and Japan, the teams which would win the gold, silver and bronze medals, respectively. But the Red Furies showed tenacity in their final game against a far more experienced Puerto Rico team.

During the Games, a Barcelona newspaper cartoonist described Juan Carlos, King of Spain, as "The Ubiquitous One" because he seemed to show up everywhere during the 1992 Olympics. His omnipresence included a stop at the Olympic baseball venue for the Spain–Puerto Rico game. The Puerto Ricans had beaten both the Dominican Republic and Italy, and appeared on their way to another win against Spain through 8 innings. Going into the bottom of the ninth, Puerto Rico led 6–4, but the Spanish rallied for three runs in their final at bat to earn their first — and only — Olympic victory. In a *USA Today* article, Felix Cano, the team's top star, who blasted a grand slam in the Puerto Rico game, attributed the win to Juan Carlos. "Before the game," Cano said. "I said that the king would bring us luck, just like he's done at other venues."[15]

Cano, who *USA Today* dubbed "the Babe Ruth of Spanish Baseball," was one of a number of talented players on that Spanish team. At 40 years old, the evergreen Cano was still representing his country — and representing it well — at the 2005 European Championships. The slugger drove in six runs in seven games played and was named the tournament's outstanding designated hitter. Xavier Civit, a 19-year-old pitcher at the Barcelona games, found some professional success in the United States. The right-handed pitcher posted very respectable numbers during a three-year professional stint with the Montreal Expos and the Cleveland Indians organizations. From 1996–98, he registered a 3.63 ERA and struck out 146 batters in 156.2 innings pitched. Unfortunately, he never made it above the Class-A minor-league level. More recently, left-handed pitcher Carlos Ros and shortstop Javier Zabalza played professionally for independent minor league teams.

Yet, with all these developments, Spanish baseball remains where it's been, following its heady days in the 1950s and 1960s: near the top of European baseball but still unable to compete successfully with Italy or the Netherlands. For some Spanish baseball observers, there was a lot of disappointment that the 1992 Olympic Games did not lead to a bigger spur in baseball interest. It didn't help that the best field for the Olympics was converted to a soccer stadium after the games. In fact, a local baseball club plays on a dirt field in the shadow of that facility, former national team coach Jones said.

Beyond the Olympic disappointment, the biggest concern about Spanish baseball in some circles today is that it is increasingly dominated by foreign talent. Cuba has always had strong ties to Spain, and other Latin American countries—most notably Venezuela—have seen many baseball players immigrate to Spain. "The Latin and South American influence is strong," Jones said. "Any club that competes for the championship has key 'import players' and many immigrant players eventually get their citizenship and become 'Spanish players.' To that end, the national team now features many players who were born in either Venezuela or Cuba."[16]

As a result, the center of Spanish baseball has shifted. Interest in Madrid has waned tremendously. In fact, Rivas Ciudad Del Deporte, which was the only club in 2007 from Madrid in Spain's top league, La Liga Nacional de Béisbol—División de Honor, was relegated leaving the capital unrepresented in 2008. The Catalonia region (centered in and around Barcelona) and the Navarra region (most notably in Pamplona) both have clubs in the top circuit, but the

Spain's national team boasts a long string of solid international performances, having won the third-most medals in the European Baseball Championships. At times, Spain has relied heavily on Venezuelan-born players. Caracas native and former Major Leaguer Alejandro Freire (above) is one of many of these players. (Photograph by Ezio Ratti/FIBS.)

Top: Barcelona has an enduring baseball history that continues today. The beautiful stadium at Montjuic (above) illustrates the city's enduring interest in the sport. (Photograph by Ezio Ratti/FIBS.) *Bottom*: Baseball in Pamplona has seen growth. The city's local field (above) was the host of the 2005 European Junior Baseball Championships. (Courtesy CEB.)

Manuel Olivera (above), who pitched at the Double-A professional level in the United States in 2007, was a key member of the Spanish national team at the 2007 European Championships. (Photograph by Renato Ferrini/FIBS.)

Canary Islands, a Spanish archipelago located southeast of Spain off the African coast, is now home to the country's best clubs. Teams from Tenerife, which is the largest of the seven Canary Islands and has extensive ties to Latin America, captured the 2004, 2005, 2006, and 2007 Spanish national championships and facilities on the island are becoming top-notch. "The Canary Island facility has just recently been covered with artificial surface and is as good as any facility that I've seen in Europe," says Jones, who has coached throughout the continent.

For some, this use of foreign talent causes concern. Martin Miller, who is president of the Confederation of European Baseball, is a strong proponent of developing born-and-bred talent. He points to Spain as a country that may be focusing a bit too much on seeking international players. Still, it's hard to argue that the influx of import players has not increased the standard of play in Spain. According to Jones, when an import pitcher gets on the mound in a domestic game, it's "probably [NCAA] Division II [level] or a low[er] pro level ... [but] Division III when the Spanish pitchers are on the mound." Whether Miller is right and the use of foreign developed players is a detriment or whether the additions force domestic players to raise their level of play, one club that has been hit by the influx of Latin players is the former perennial champions Viladecans. They continue to focus on home-grown talent in their area but have fallen short of a championship since 2002. "For many years Viladecans dominated the Spanish top league with local development," Jones said. "However, lately they cannot compete because they do not bring in enough import players."

On the plus side, the current baseball administration is focused on increasing Spain's baseball profile, as evidenced by the fact that the Barcelona area — including Viladecans— hosted the 2007 European Championships, garnering television coverage and respectable crowds when the home team played. In a 2006 *Sporting News* interview, Pau Gasol, the National Basketball Association All-Star and former rookie of the year, was asked about baseball in Spain. Gasol comes from Sant Boi de Llobregat, which is the home of one of Spain's most high-profile facilities (it was one of the venues for the 2007 Euros). In addition, Gasol played basketball for FC Barcelona, which to this day also fields a baseball team. Yet Gasol's response to the question was that "baseball is so-so" in Spain.[17] Spanish baseball officials must hope that high-profile events and more international wins will change that perception of the game.

4

Belgium

There's little denying that Belgium likes being at the center of organizations. The country is the bureaucratic hub of the European Union and the headquarters of the North Atlantic Treaty Organization (NATO). It's no different in the world of baseball. When it came time to form a pan–European baseball confederation, the Belgians paved the way.

In 1949, the secretary of the Belgian Federation, Tony Dudermans, contacted various Olympic committees, asking a simple question: where was baseball actually played in Europe? His goal was to unite these small baseball programs in order, among other things, to push for the Olympic recognition for baseball. Dudermans' successor Vincent Caers continued these efforts and, along with Spanish officials, the Belgian identified a clutch of countries enjoying America's pastime. In 1951 and 1952, the Spanish attempted to move things forward but had little success.

So, in January 1953, the Belgians took charge again. Roger C. Panaye, president of the Belgian Federation, proposed a meeting in Paris and convinced delegates from Italy, France, Spain and Germany to attend. With Panaye as the event's chairman, the Belgian delegation proposed a series of statutes that were accepted by the five countries on 28 April 1953. The result was the formation of the European Baseball Federation. If for no other reason, Belgium's legacy in the European baseball community was assured on that day.

Along with their administrative acumen, the Belgians should have possessed a prestigious baseball history, at least judging from their early days on the field. Known as the Southern Netherlands until the Belgian Revolution in 1830, Belgium and their Dutch neighbors appeared to be baseball equals before

World War II. Between 1934 and 1936, the two countries squared off six times, and the Belgians prevailed in four of those contests.

Alas, since then, the neighbors have diverged on the path of baseball development. While Belgium has some sturdy baseball facilities and has been competitive in the context of Europe throughout much of the past half-century, Holland has become Europe's brightest star on the international scene. Emblematic of the two nation's differing directions: after Belgium's 4–2 head-to-head start, the Netherlands has won all but three matchups in the more than 50 games between the two countries.

The first notice of Belgian baseball in the American press dates back to 1897. A small blurb in the *Washington Post* on 5 April that year makes mention of a T. Devrovre of Brussels, who was the president of the Baseball Association of France and Belgium. Baseball had first come to Belgium's southwestern neighbors in 1889 and had made some impact there. The French, who have had a large cultural influence on much of Belgium, probably extended its limited interest in baseball across the two nations' shared border. This initial foray in both France and Belgium was limited and, while baseball continued in France, it did not appear to endure in Belgium during the twentieth century's first decade.

Baseball reemerged in the lowlands during World War I as American soldiers stationed there played ball in a combined Dutch-Belgian league. Interest from locals was so great that the *New York Times* claimed in September 1919, "Although baseball has failed to supplant cricket as the national pastime of the English sporting public, much progress was made toward popularizing the game in Belgium, Holland and France."[1] In 1919, a team from the Belgian capital of Brussels captured the championship in the Belgium-Holland baseball league — much to the thrill of the 200 American GIs stationed in the city.

The military league comprised of army and navy soldiers from Antwerp and Brussels in Belgium, Rotterdam and The Hague in Holland and Hamburg and Danzig in postwar Germany. One of the key purposes of the circuit was to introduce the game to locals. "All the soldiers were happy ... for they felt they had done important missionary work in baseball," the *Times* reported. "The Belgians and the Hollanders have progressed to such a point that they can easily follow the game."

In Holland, where the efforts of locals dating back to 1911 had created a true domestic beachhead for baseball, the soldiers' play buttressed interest in the game. But in Belgium, the military games offered only the sort of artificial spike that comes from the influx of foreign enthusiasts; it lacked true grassroots support. Belgium — like most European countries— required the steadfast interest of local baseball zealots for any sustained growth.

For Belgium, those trailblazers would begin to emerge in 1923, with a little help from some Japanese sailors. The game's true introduction to Belgians came that year from members of the Japanese Maru merchant shipping line. Ships would regularly call at the Belgian port city of Antwerp, with the crews passing their leisure hours playing baseball on shore at a field known as the Wilrijkseplein. Young boys living in the neighborhood would come to watch. They became instant fans and began joining in, and the excitement from the pickup contests led to the formation of the Antwerp Baseball Club. Known as the Antwerp Cats, it was the first true Belgian squad and still exists today. "Japanese ex-players living in Antwerp organized the Antwerp Cats and coached the team," according to longtime Belgian and European baseball official Gaston Panaye.[2]

An informal league soon ensued, with the Cats, Beltelco B.C. and General Motors playing. Baseball was featuring locals, but the influence of Americans remained, as GM and Bell Telephone (the Beltelco club) were both integral. Still, unlike GIs who had a level of impermanence, these companies would play a large role in the Antwerp baseball scene for decades. In addition, the Japanese influence continued during this period, and from 1934 to 1936, almost weekly games were played with teams from the Nippon Yusen Kaisha Navigation Company.[3]

Local baseball players took on Japanese sailors in the early days of the sport in Belgium. In 1930, Antwerp baseball played Terukun Maru (above). Identified players: (Back row) Jules Van Looy, umpire (2nd from left); Frans Van Haute, catcher (4th from right); (Seated) Roger Gillet (boy, 1st from left), Alfons Dom (boy, 2nd from left). Other Antwerp players in photo: Caluwe, Hendrickx, Max Verstraeten, Jim Paine; Other Japanese players: Hatori, Myata, Tahatshi. (Courtesy CEB.)

Enthused by the local competition, Jaak Palmans, who would later become Belgian baseball's first president, contacted the Dutch Federation about a cross-border contest. The first game between the two countries was staged on 26 August 1934, and the result illustrated the rudimentary level of baseball at the time: The Dutch won 21 to 12. With international games taking place, the organizational element to Belgian baseball kicked in further. The *Belgische Baseball Federatie* was officially established in 1936.

With a governing body in place, the Belgians set up more international tilts. According to Dutch baseball historian Marco Stoovelaar's book *Honkbalgids 2000*, the two countries squared off twelve times between 1934 and 1939. Antwerp hosted six of these international affairs. Holland won seven games and Belgium earned five victories.[4] Scores in the later years suggest that the level of play was becoming more respectable. In 1939, when the two countries split a home-and-away series, Belgium won the first game on July 23 in Antwerp by a score of 4–3 and the Netherlands team was victorious 9–3 in the final prewar encounter on August 20 in Amsterdam.

It goes without saying that World War II placed tremendous hardships on the region. In 1940, Belgium was invaded by the Nazis during its blitzkrieg offensive. The country was then occupied by the Germans until the winter of 1944–5, when it was liberated by Allied troops. One relatively small by-product of the occupation was the end of baseball activities—with the exception of a bit of indoor play. This halting would be the first step in creating a disparity in playing levels between the Netherlands and Belgium. In contrast to the Belgians, the Dutch continued domestic competitions throughout the war — albeit in limited ways.[5]

Even if the Belgians had begun to fall behind, baseball did pick up steam again after the war. As was the case in World War I, the U.S. military influence was ever-present. Following the liberation, GIs stationed in the country meant that baseball gear was available. Equally important, U.S. forces stationed at the "Top Hat" camp on the left bank of Antwerp's Schedlt River joined in with revived prewar teams, according to Gaston Panaye. Brothers Gaston and Roger Panaye would play a large role in reenergizing Belgian baseball. In 1951, Gaston got into the game through Roger, who was an employee at the Antwerp town hall.

"A colleague of my brother working at town hall and playing for the Antwerp Cats tried to start his own club named Stadhuis [town hall]," recalled Gaston in 2007. "My brother and other colleagues joined the new club together with some outsiders (me and others). My brother played first base and I played shortstop." Gaston, whose day job was as a Chevron Oil sales manager, would go on to be an influential baseball writer in Belgium, penning a baseball column for the *Gazet van Antwerpen* from 1965 to 1987. He would also hold key positions in Europe's governing body for the sport. As for Roger, along with serving as president of the Belgian Federation and playing a central role in the founding of the European Federation, he was a historian of European baseball. Roger Panaye's 1978 booklet, *European Amateur Baseball: 25 Years*, provided the first pan–European history of the game. (Gaston would pen a 1993 update entitled *European Amateur Baseball: 1979–1993*.)

While the Panayes and other Belgians were keenly involved in the game, the American corporate influence remained prevalent. General Motors continued to have a key role in Belgian baseball, winning the first three officially recognized Belgian national titles in 1947 through 1949. (A GM Giants team also captured the crown in 1952.) The squad offered the Belgians a high level of baseball competition. "General Motors would have been a better-than-average small-college team," said Bill Arce, who, in 1962, was the first American baseball coach to conduct professionally run baseball clinics in Belgium.[6]

General Motors was also helpful in offering an early baseball diamond. The automobile company's field was located in Luchtbal, in the middle of the

Belgium's Roger C. Panaye (above, seated 1st from the left) played a central role in the formation of the European Baseball Federation. Here are the federation's founding fathers ratifying the organization's constitution on 27 April 1953 in Paris. Back row (L–R): Jean Warot (France), G. Charrier (France), Giovanni Ugo (Italy), Rene Goulka (France), Jose Ramon Alvarez (Spain), Henri J. Martin (Belgium); Seated (L–R): Panaye (Belgium) Norbert Schoffers (Germany), Prince Steno Borghese (Italy), Th. A. Blanchard (France); Luis Barrio (Spain). (Courtesy CEB.)

company's manufacturing facility, according to Gaston Panaye. What made this diamond unique by European standards is that it had regular dimensions. Unlike the military push for baseball, which stemmed from both a yearning by GIs for a recreational activity that would remind them of home and an effort to export American culture through its national pastime, the GM impetus for baseball may have been far more simple. General Motors had teams in other sports, according to Panaye, and opted for a wide-ranging baseball program to provide a Little League option for the son of an executive at the company. In the early 1960s, the GM facility was one of the best in Europe. "The General Motors field was a good small-college field," says Arce. "There was a pitcher's mound on the field, which was rare, and there were fairly good mounds in the bullpens." Ultimately, the GM facility would move to another factory site located about twenty kilometers from the original plant, but the company would remain involved with baseball until 1985.

Along with General Motors, Bell Telephone also maintained its participation in the sport under the moniker the "Pioneers," a team that still exists today.[7] In addition, a team called the Brussels Senators, which was composed of personnel from a number of different American companies located in the Belgian capital, played in the 1950s, winning championships in 1953, 1958 and 1959. The U.S. influence must have helped raise the level of play because Belgium was among the top four or five baseball-playing countries in the postwar years. The Belgians hosted the first-ever European Championships in 1954, earning a bronze medal behind the Italians and the Spanish. At the next two Euros in 1955 and 1956, the Belgians earned back-to-back silver medals. Then, in 1967, Belgium became one of only four countries (along with Holland, Italy and Spain) to win a gold medal at the continent's championships.

Yet, the scope of those triumphs is somewhat limited. The Dutch didn't compete at the 1954 and 1955 Euros (they hadn't yet joined the federation) and they were also absent in 1967 due to political squabbles that kept Italy out of the event as well. If the Dutch had been at those tournaments, it would have surely diminished Belgium's standing. The reason: the two countries were no longer comparable on the field. Bill Arce, who had already coached in Holland by the time he went to Belgium in 1962 to work with the Belgians' senior and junior national team programs, saw a definite talent disparity. "Belgium had five to seven good ballplayers, whereas the Dutch had about 16 or 18," Arce says.

In explaining the differences, one of Holland's all-time greatest players Han Urbanus ironically suggested that it was the superior organization of Dutch baseball that made the difference. While the Belgians excelled in the "big picture" administration and development of baseball, they were a step behind in structuring growth on the field. "In Holland the sport spread around the country more [than in Belgium]," Urbanus said in a 2007 interview. "American coaches were invited and more games were played with a better scheme ... [In contrast] Belgium has been standing still — there has been no development at all."[8]

Some in Belgian baseball circles recognized this growing problem in 1954. In the country's official baseball newsletter, a front-page article in the summer of that year asked "What is holding our sport back?" The number one answer: nurturing young players. "There are still too many clubs that disregard the potential of a junior league," the article strongly asserted. "Too cumbersome, time consuming and laborious, they say. And the clubs that have junior sections don't allot the talent and time of their coaches to a small bunch of 'wild horses'.... As far as the rules of the game are concerned, no attention is given to that 'page of the book.'"[9]

Along with a superior ability in creating an efficient player-development structure, the Netherlands emphasis on professional coaching was also a main factor in Holland's supremacy. Americans with some experience were available in both countries, but serious improvement only comes from top-notch instruction. By 1960, Dutch baseball already had retained the services of Ron Fraser, who would later go on to have one of the most successful coaching careers in NCAA Division I college baseball history. Fraser, who would win two national championships at the helm of the University of Miami's baseball program, spent approximately two years coaching full-time in Holland. A number of other American coaches would follow. Again, some Belgians recognized this problem, although it appears it wasn't immediately rectified. "As an old Flemish saying goes 'Training results in performance,'" said the 1954 front page article in the country's official baseball newsletter. "However, we lack in this respect. More training coaches should be available to inspire our players, who then will become more motivated and show off better results."[10]

Still, Belgium wasn't altogether without talent. Vital Verbert showed both talent and guts as one of Belgium's early baseball heroes. In 1953, Belgium traveled to Milan to face Italy in a major international match. Verbert took the mound for the Belgians and although the Italians won 7–3, Verbert's performance became legendary as he logged a complete game — most of it after sustaining a broken jaw. In the third inning, Verbert fouled a ball off his jaw while hitting. The pain became more intense as the game continued, but the pitcher persevered. After the contest he went to the hospital where doctors diagnosed a fractured jaw bone.

Pitcher Jos Robijn, who played on the Belgian national team from 1954 to 1969, was another of the country's early home-grown stars. Robijn, a teacher by trade, could dominate. In 1955, the teenager beat a heavily favored Italian squad 7–4 at the European Championships in Barcelona. Showing his longevity, the five-foot-seven hurler was named top pitcher more than a decade later at the 1966 European Cup.[11] In 1971, as a 34-year-old, he was one of two Belgians selected to play on a pan–European team called the "Continental Cavaliers," which toured South Africa.

Not surprisingly, Robijn played his club baseball in Luchtbal. The Antwerp suburb was not only the home to the General Motors team but also another highly successful club — the Luchtbal Greys. Robijn's Greys[12] captured a commanding 19 national titles between 1956 and 1990. In fact, the Antwerp area has been the heart of Belgian baseball throughout its history. Such early national-team stars as catcher Francois Tanghe, shortstop Gilbert Naessens and pitcher Frank Mathijs were all from Antwerp and its suburbs. In a theme that is constant throughout Europe, baseball's relative minority status on the sports landscape requires regional success. In addition to General Motors, the Luchtbal Greys and the Antwerp Cats, the Flanders port also hosted the Antwerp Eagles (seven-time national champions) and the Brasschaat Braves (eleven-time champs).

Today, Antwerp's suburb of Brasschaat owns one of Belgium's best baseball facilities. The park boasts cement stands, a scorer's box, lights for night games and a great clubhouse that has beer on tap. Since 1996, it's served as the site for the Flanders International Tournament that attracts national teams from other European countries, as well as American touring teams. That said, Brasschaat's facility has its limits. It seems clear that baseball organizers had to take what they could get in terms of the field dimensions. The rectangular plot of land results in a very short fence in right field. In other words, it's a left-handed hitter's paradise.

Despite the physical shortcomings, Brasschaat was a successful enough organization to lure two former major leaguers to the club in the 1990s. Left-handed pitcher Joel McKeon, a former first-round draft pick who registered 43 appearances with the Chicago White Sox, was ready to follow in the footsteps of other cup-of-coffee big leaguers, and play in Italy in 1992, when his contract fell through. A friend made a call to see what other opportunities were available on the continent. The result: Brasschaat, sponsored by Levi Strauss & Company at the time, stepped up — and McKeon accepted the deal. Tom Magrann, who played in nine games for the Cleveland Indians, also spent a year in the Antwerp suburb. Their performances give a sense of the Belgian standard at the time. In three years, McKeon didn't lose a game on the mound. "For the first year, I couldn't catch him," Brasschaat catcher Karl Onzia told the *International Herald Tribune* in 1994. "He throws a forkball and I had bruises all over me. Sometimes it went left, sometimes it went down, sometimes it went right. Mostly it hit me on the wrist. Sometimes I just missed the ball."[13] As for Magrann, who was hitless in his ten major league at bats, he won the Belgian batting triple crown in 1992, hitting .605 with 18 home runs in just 15 games. (As a right-handed hitter, he didn't even get any help from Brasschaat's short right-field porch.)

While it has never reached the lofty heights of its Dutch neighbors, Belgium has earned a level of achievement outside its borders. All told, Belgium has captured one gold medal, two silver medals and six bronze medals at the

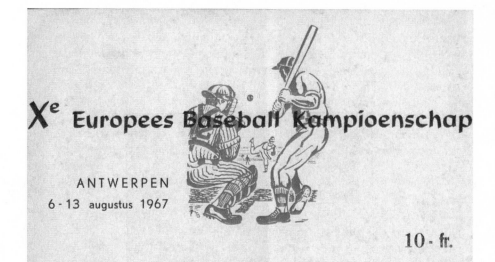

Xᵉ **Europees Baseball Kampioenschap**

ANTWERPEN
6 - 13 augustus 1967

10 - fr.

TERREIN GENERAL MOTORS CONTINENTAL — NOORDERLAAN

P R O G R A M M A

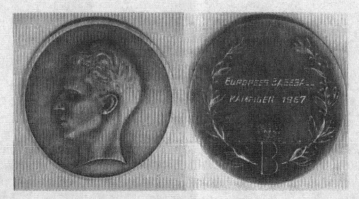

Begiftigd met de medaille van Z.M. Koning Boudewijn

Belgium's biggest international triumph came when they country hosted 1967 European Baseball Championships (above: program from the event). With both Italy and Holland not participating, the locals won the gold medal.

With a nice clubhouse, cement stands and a decent playing surface, the baseball facility in the Antwerp suburb of Brasschaat is one of the best in Belgium.

European Championships. The Belgian national team has even stepped onto a bigger international stage than Europe twice — albeit somewhat unsuccessfully. In 1978, Belgium competed in the 25th Baseball World Cup, which was held in Parma, Bologna and Rimini, Italy. The Belgians finished last, going 0–10. Among the losses was a 16–0 defeat to the eventual champions, Cuba. In 1986, the Belgians fared slightly better going 1–10 at the 29th World Cup in Haarlem, Holland. Belgium did beat the Netherlands Antilles 4–1 and nearly upset Colombia, losing 6–5. In the category of very slender silver linings, the Belgians did get the opportunity to face such future major leaguers as Steve Finley, Mike Remlinger and Scott Servais when they played Team USA. Unfortunately, the final score in that contest was 19–0 in favor of the Americans.

Even though Belgium has scored a mixed performance on the international field (good at times in Europe, but not against greater baseball powers), the Belgians' zest for organizing led to one of international baseball's most audacious plans in 1983. That year, Belgium figured they should — and could — host one of world baseball's most prestigious events— the Intercontinental Cup.[14] This was an ambitious idea for a few reasons. First, the event had been previously hosted by far more developed baseball countries like Cuba, Canada and Nicaragua. (The only other European country to have hosted the tournament at that point was Italy, which had far more infrastructure.) Second, Belgium wasn't even going to play in the tournament. In fact, Belgium is the only country in the history of the Intercontinental Cup to host and not even play in it.

To this day, Gaston Panaye describes the event as Belgian baseball's biggest success. "We had about 300 new kids starting to play and in one week we had a daily attendance of 8,000 to 9,000 [spectators]," remembered Panaye, who said that, in all, 60,000 fans came to the Cup from 13–25 July. "With no financial help from the government or the Olympic Committee, we took an impossible risk. But we broke even in 1983 thanks to sponsors."

The Belgian spectators were treated to some great baseball. Belgium played an exhibition game at the start of the event against a selection of players from the seven teams competing, but the big fireworks came from Cuba. Behind the hitting of Cuban national team star Victor Mesa, who batted a robust .567 at the competition, Cuba won the Cup. Team USA was Cuba's biggest nemesis at the event. Among its players, Team USA boasted a tall, skinny slugger from the University of Southern California named Mark McGwire. In Belgium the future major leaguer's prodigious bat could not overcome Cuba, which beat Team USA three times at the event, including an 8–4 victory in the finals. Interestingly, McGwire was not even the America's top home-run hitter at the tournament. That honor went to Eric Fox, who would go on to hit five major league home runs in 116 big-league games (a number that matched Fox's homer total in Belgium).

In the past quarter century, Belgian baseball organizers have tried to build upon the Intercontinental Cup accomplishment. Media coverage is not huge, but scores from the top league are reported in the major Belgian newspapers, and local TV and print publications also cover baseball happenings. As might be expected in a country known for its affinity for bureaucracy, the Belgian government has played a central role in legislating how Belgium baseball can organize. Sports are a part of the Ministry of Culture and, in 1987, the ministry insisted that there be two organizations—one Flemish and the other French-speaking—for all sports in the country. "If you didn't create two leagues, you lost governmental financial support," Gaston Panaye says.

Although there are a number of general cultural difference between the Flemish and French parts of Belgium, Panaye insists that there is no major rivalry between the two leagues. "The Flemish players approach the game the same way as the Francophone players," he says. Baseball is improving in the Francophone areas, which doesn't have the same baseball tradition as the Flemish. This is evidenced by the Namur Angels which is currently the region's only competitive top-tier team.[15] Namur, a decidedly French-influenced city, was under French control from 1794–1815.

Even with this growth into Francophone Belgium, the country's place among the top European baseball nations has come into question during the past decade. Belgium's recent player development pales in comparison to a number of its rivals. Most notably, Belgium has yet to send a player to the minor leagues in the United States—an achievement reached by at least six other European countries. In the late 1980s, Oswald Boermans, a pitcher from the town of Borgerhout, had a tryout with the Cincinnati Reds but did not get a contract. At least one of the country's top players, catcher Kevin Knollenburg, did spend a year playing college baseball in America. Knollenburg played at the NAIA school Ottawa University in Kansas. In addition, Knollenburg and a number of other talented Belgian players have crossed the border to Holland where the quality of the top league is far greater than that in Belgium. "The level of play [in Belgium's top league] was comparable to a Division III college program at best," recalled Chris Lavoie, who played college baseball at the NCAA Division I level before spending a season in Belgium's highest circuit with the Pioneers in 1999. "The only decent pitching that I saw was from the imported American pitchers ... I was used to seeing mid– to upper–80s [miles per hour] at the University of Vermont and I am guessing the average fastball was upper–70s from the Belgian pitchers."

In 2003, this lack of marked progress in Belgium's domestic league caught up with the national team at 24th European Championships. By that point, only Spain, Italy and Holland had played in more Euros and, if history was a guide, Belgium should have been confident of at least a respectable result. After all, they'd only finished below sixth place (in the 12-team tournament) once. But maybe it was a harbinger that the one subpar performance—a ninth-place result—came in 2001 at the previous European Championships. Times were changing among the top tier of European baseball. The Eastern European countries such as Russia, Czech Republic and Croatia had steadily gained ground on Belgium. In addition, other Western European nations, such as Great Britain, were relying more and more on passport holders who had learned their baseball in the United States, Canada or Australia. As a result, the Belgians finished in 11th out of 12 teams and were relegated to the continent's second tier of baseball.

It was a bitter pill to swallow and it was exacerbated by the fact that Belgium hosted qualifying tournaments to return to European baseball's top pool in both 2004 and 2006 but were unable to make it back. It may be difficult for Belgium to return to its halcyon days, but Panaye remains optimistic: "After 50 years at the top of European baseball and two participations at the World Championships, the Belgium team has been relegated ... [but] with the young players of good quality there is hope for the future."

The ultimate hope would be a return to the time when Belgium and Holland could stand toe-to-toe on the baseball diamond. But that dream may be a bit too much. "With a history of about 80 years' activity in Holland and more help from the Dutch government and local authorities, there is still a difference of 30 years with Belgium," Panaye said. "Historically Holland is Belgium's greatest natural rival, but not in baseball. We know by experience that Holland is a lot stronger."

5

Great Britain

You don't have to look any further than a blustery day more than a century ago to get a taste of British baseball's intriguing history. On 12 March 1889, the Prince of Wales settled into his seat at the Kennington Oval, one of England's most famous cricket grounds, to watch baseball. The game between teams of American professionals was part of a tour set up by the great baseball entrepreneur, manager and player A. G. Spalding, and featured, among others, future Hall-of-Famer Adrian "Cap" Anson. By all accounts, the man who would become King Edward VII watched every move intently, asking questions about the spectacle and staying until the last out as the Chicago White Stockings beat the "All Americans" 7–4 in a muddy, rain-soaked game.[1]

Following the contest, the future king of England had begun to stroll away when a newspaper reporter caught up to him and asked for his impressions of the game. The Prince of Wales looked the journalist in the eye, thought for a moment and then agreed to answer the reporter's query in writing. He jotted down a note and walked away. The next day, the Prince's statement was printed as part of the game account: "The Prince of Wales has witnessed the game of Base Ball with great interest and though he considers it an excellent game he considers cricket as superior."

For more than a century since, the British royal has, for the most part, seemed to speak for an entire nation. While the sport has enjoyed periods of legitimate attention in Great Britain, it has faced some daunting obstacles, notably, a sports culture that can be inhospitable to games that aren't seen to be entirely British, world events that stunted baseball's biggest growth periods, regional disputes, and sporadic lapses in funding and vision. Nevertheless, inherent characteristics that have helped Britons through the ages—namely resilience and an abiding optimism — have also assured that in down times, British baseball has persevered.

Baseball in the British Isles started in 1874, when the Boston Red Stockings, winners of America's professional championship the summer before, traveled to England with the Philadelphia Athletics to introduce baseball to Britons. Harry Wright, one of baseball's great pioneers, organized the event, in part because he was "so 'impressed by the ease with which the new game replaced cricket in America' that he was 'led ... to think that British sportsmen would, if they saw baseball played at its best, undergo the same conversion.'"[2]

Indeed, curious crowds attended these events (31 July to 25 August) in such cities as London, Dublin, Liverpool and Manchester. Regrettably, the format was unusual. In most of the exhibitions, the Americans would play some baseball and then compete in cricket against a local team. The odd format appears to have come at the behest of the powerful Marylebone Cricket Club. "It was indicative of the power of the MCC that [the Americans] felt constrained to agree to their demand that cricket matches be included in the tour," wrote British baseball historian Daniel Bloyce.[3] The odds were in favor of the Americans, who would field eighteen players to the customary eleven playing for the

Spurred by Harry Wright, a future Hall-of-Famer who was born in England, the first European tour of professional players went from the United States to the British Isles in 1874. The Boston Red Stockings and the Philadelphia Athletics competed in a series of games.

British teams. This undermined the exhibitions. Newton Crane, a British baseball organizer and former U.S. Consul in Manchester, England, wrote in 1891
that the tour failed to spark interest because "the game of baseball was not
understood, and in the short hour or two devoted to the exhibition matches
but little idea of it could be acquired by the bewildered spectators."[4]

It took fifteen years and one of baseball's great early visionaries, Albert
Goodwill Spalding, to bring longer-lasting attention to the sport in the British
Isles. Spalding, who played every role in the world of baseball—player, manager, owner, sports equipment manufacturer—arranged a world baseball tour
in 1888. A key player and organizer in Wright's 1874 tour, Spalding took two
teams of baseball players—the Chicago White Stockings, the club he managed
back in the United States, and a mixed squad of players dubbed "All America"—
around the globe. Stops included the Sandwich Islands (Hawaii), Australia,
New Zealand, Ceylon, Egypt, Italy, France and finally to Great Britain. Baseball writer Patrick Carroll, who has done considerable research on Spalding,
refers to him as "a Gilded Age archetype," and describes the venture as "a typical mixture" of Spalding's "passionate missionary zeal for the game, go-get-
ting business 'push,' and his often Machiavellian politicking."[5]

The Americans arrived in England in March 1889 and played eleven games
throughout the country, drawing considerable crowds. Some 8,000 spectators
attended the game in London that was attended by the Prince of Wales and 4,000
watched a match in Bristol later in the tour despite the weather being "exceed-
ingly unpropitious," according to British baseball organizer Crane. "Most of
the games [were] played in fog, rain, and snow, and on grounds which were
wet and slippery." There was another serious problem from the fan's perspective: rather than put on the best show possible, the American teams took each
game very seriously, playing to win. This apparently decreased the crowd's
enjoyment, as the Duke of Beaufort, who helped host the baseball party, noted:

> Of course, the jealousy between All America and Chicago, while it kept all the
> players up to mark and made them do their best to prevent their opponents from
> scoring, made the game dull to on-lookers, who did not understand it. If they
> could have played a few games not to be counted in their wins and losses against
> each other, in which the pitchers would give easy balls and enable the hitters really
> to make fine hits and give a chance to the field to make the splendid catches they
> are able to make, the game would have taken the fancy of the British public much
> more, as it would have thoroughly astonished them.[6]

The British reaction to the tour was, in the words of author Peter Levine,
"lukewarm,"[7] while Bloyce described the media attention as "minimal," suggesting that what little coverage did occur was generally negative, laced with
sentiments of "[n]ational pride and anti–American feeling."[8]

The tour might have failed like the one in 1874 if it hadn't been for a group
of young American collegians who followed up the Spalding extravaganza by

spending their 1889 summer vacation in England. Instead of just playing, they actually taught the game. They also set up matches throughout the country, establishing teams that mixed American and British players—a marked difference from the professionals' approach before them. As there is no substitute for playing, the Britons who got a taste of baseball were hooked.

In October 1889, a group of enthusiasts formed the National Baseball League of Great Britain and, with the help of Spalding and his associates, planned a professional league to commence play the following season. The organizers found that "the football [soccer] clubs ... whose efforts were confined to the winter months, were disposed to encourage the movement," according to the 1890 edition of *Spalding's Official Base Ball Guide*. Three of England's top soccer clubs—Aston Villa of Birmingham, Preston North End and Stoke (along with a fourth team from Derby County)—decided to start franchises in the new professional baseball circuit. There was one big hitch: very few British athletes had played more than a game or two of baseball before. With that in mind, the organizers advertised for six to eight young Americans to serve as instructors. They received nearly 1,000 applicants. The teachers were given a round-trip ticket from New York to London and 3 to 4 guineas a week (the equivalent today of between £200 and £270 per week).

When play began in May, the performance of the players was "gratifying." "The novices being experienced football players, [were] finely trained in hand, limb and eye," noted *Spalding's Official Base Ball Guide* of 1890. While the Spalding guide couldn't be considered an unbiased publication considering Spalding's involvement, it's worth pointing out that Jack Devey, a British native who also played for Aston Villa's soccer team, beat all the foreign imports to win the batting title with a .428 average. As for attendance, the Spalding guide claimed it was "satisfactory, and toward the close of the season, especially at Preston, were quite as large as the average Minor League cities in the United States."

But there were problems. As with the 1874 tour, many in the media were not keen to accept baseball, fearful that the sport might encroach on cricket's dominance in the summer months. Some reporters did not believe that there was genuine interest in the game. "The baseball business is being 'boomed' with a vigour of which is a little too obviously artificial for the average Englishman," said a 16 June 1890 article in the *Birmingham Daily Post*. "The phlegmatic Briton does not care to have a pastime which has considerable amount of the advertising element about it foisted upon him."

There was also on-field controversy. The Derby team, which was run by a leading industrialist Sir Francis Ley, had more foreign players (three) than any other club. As a result, within the first month of the season, Derby won enough games to clinch the championship. The other teams protested and Ley agreed to only use his ace American pitcher against Aston Villa, the league's second-best team. When Derby reneged on that promise, however, the other team leaders were furious and Derby pulled out of the league. Aston Villa was then named the league's champion, while Preston North End won the separate Baseball Association of Great Britain and Ireland Cup competition. Preston is regarded by today's British baseball organizers as the first English champion.

Off the field, the league had financial problems, losing an estimated $25,000, according to William J. Barr, a former American diplomat who managed the Aston Villa team. The tremendous costs included advertising, recruiting players and maintaining an office in London. While Spalding appears to have bankrolled much of the endeavor, one of his representatives did not completely live up to the promised financial aid, which upset the British teams. A Spalding agent who was in England to promote baseball left the county with more than £300 which had been designated for the players, according to one newspaper account. Perhaps because of the high cost and no immediate attendance boom, Spalding never fully invested in British baseball again and the circuit folded after just one season.

Still, the league was not a complete failure. In at least one place — Derby — baseball proved that it could make money. That team took in about £150 from the gate and had expenses that didn't exceed £100. Moreover, as a result of the initial attention generated by the league, the sport made substantial progress as an amateur game during the next twenty years. A number of the country's top soccer clubs followed the lead of the teams from the 1890 season and developed baseball teams for the short summer off-season. Derby, which continued to be a force in baseball, eventually opened its home to the local soccer club and until 1997 the Derby County soccer team played at the old baseball field. As a result, that stadium was known as "The Baseball Ground." In addition, such soccer powerhouses as Arsenal, Tottenham Hotspur and Nottingham Forest also took up the game. Many top soccer and rugby stars played baseball, including Steve Bloomer, who represented England in soccer 23 times and played for Derby, and John Kirwan, who played soccer for Tottenham Hotspur when it won the prestigious Football Association Cup in 1901.

By the start of the twentieth century, baseball had a place in British society. In 1906, the British Baseball Cup attracted around 2,500 fans to White Hart Lane soccer ground in the north end of London to watch the home team, the Tottenham Hotspur Baseball Club, win the national championship. The following year, a baseball season ticket for Tottenham baseball games cost five shillings (about twenty dollars today).

Part of the reason for this early success in London was a combination of support from wealthy American expats and good, old-fashioned grassroots efforts. In the early 1890s, a handful of baseball enthusiasts went to Battersea Park in southwest London to play some baseball, only to be greeted by almost immediate disgust from the local establishment. "[T]hey were warned off the ground by a policeman who scented danger of life and limb," reported Richard Morton in a contemporaneous article in the *Badminton Magazine*. "Argument availed to nothing, and six Americans who desired to play their national sport had to seek another location where rules and regulations were capable of being stretched by more tolerant officers of the law."

The players went deeper into south London, to the expansive Clapham Common, which featured a series of flat open fields. This time the locals took to the game and it quickly became a spectacle in the vicinity. At first, the reaction of native Londoners was skeptical. "[C]heering, when there was any, [was] sarcastic and derisive; for the Clapham folk felt they

A number of British soccer greats also played baseball, including Steve Bloomer (above) who represented England twenty-three times in international soccer.

had progressed beyond rounders, and somewhat resented a fantastic display of the schoolboy recreation by able-bodied men," wrote Morton. But by 1892, true Brits were playing on the common and it was not uncommon for a thousand people to come to watch games. "The number of English converts [is] increasing every day, and [they] are now assisting to promote the game in every way in their power," Morton continued. "When they compare [baseball] to cricket, it is not at all to the advantage of the latter."

In 1894, the London Baseball Association was formed to oversee the sport's development in the capital. This organization was supported by hefty American resources. One team was sponsored by Dewars, the great whisky producers, while Remington Typewriter Company and Fuller's Cakes sponsored other clubs. London's famous West End theater community, which included numerous Americans, also got involved. A team called the Thespians were one of the era's most successful and, according to an article at the time in the *Strand* magazine, it was suggested that a music-hall regular spent close to £2,000 in support of baseball, which was an awesome amount of money for the era. Great facilities were also been used during this period. Crystal Palace, where every final of the prestigious Football Association Cup was contested from 1895 to 1914, agreed to take on baseball. The managing company of the facility offered "splendid inducements ... to make baseball one of the main attractions of that popular pleasure resort," according to Morton.

Although the average Londoner was clearly taking to America's pastime, it was equally apparent that the London ruling-class shuddered at this alien baseball boom. According to an 11 May 1911 article in the *Boston Globe*, the London County Council banned baseball on its public commons, ending games at locations like Clapham Common where the game had built momentum. The *Globe* said that the council was concerned that "[t]he American game is dangerous to spectators." Still, the article pointed out that cricket, football, lacrosse and hockey were all allowed on the public commons. This effectively stopped the growth of the sport in the country's biggest city.

Others also suggested the big corporate support shown by some American concerns were not wholly sincere. On 23 May 1906, prominent British baseball observer William C. J. Kelly told the *Los Angeles Times* that baseball failed to fully blossom during this period because the U.S. businesses only looked at the sport as a way to get attention and did not focus on grassroots development. "[S]everal of the big companies ... played baseball as a mere advertisement, and the general public did not take any interest in the game," Kelly said.

In the official history of British baseball, there are no national champions listed between 1912 and 1933. Even Spalding's own guide was somewhat downcast about the game's status in 1912. "Base ball is played in England, but more by American players who reside in England and by English players who have played the game in the United States and returned home, than by the population in general," said the 1912 *Spalding's Official Base Ball Guide*.

Nevertheless, during this period, in 1913 and 1914, Major League Baseball did try to spur international interest in the game with its first world tour since Spalding's 1889 effort. If the Americans had hoped to woo the British public on their London stop, their actions did just the opposite. The London leg of the four-month tour between the New York Giants and the Chicago White Sox was booked for mid–February. The great sportswriter Grantland Rice presciently wrote in the 27 October 1913 issue of the *Chicago Record-Herald*: "Now we are far from being endowed with a gambling disposition, but any citizen who wishes to wager that the Giants will be able to edge in one-third of their February London schedule will be accommodated up to our ultimate kopeck."[9] As Rice suggested, the weather held the tourists to a single game in London on 26 February 1914. This limited what the group could exhibit, a group which included some of baseball's greatest players of the day, including future Hall of Famers Tris Speaker, Sam Crawford and Urban "Red" Faber, and Olympic hero Jim Thorpe.

Even worse, American hubris overshadowed any on-field action in the tour's London visit. Before the single contest occurred, one of baseball's greatest all-time managers, the Giants' John McGraw did little to ingratiate baseball to the British public. In an interview with the Pall Mall Gazette, McGraw said that "American soldiers are superior to the British because of the athletic discipline in the United States and because every American soldier has learned to play baseball and through that game has benefited his mind as well as his body."[10] The game itself, which was held at Chelsea Football Club's hallowed Stamford Bridge Grounds, was a success, as the White Sox won 5–4 in an exciting 11-inning affair.

After the game, King George V, who was in attendance, asked the U.S. ambassador to "tell Mr. McGraw and ... [White Sox owner Charles] Comiskey that I have enjoyed the game enormously." Still, the words of McGraw probably resonated more than any goodwill the game produced. The *London Sketch* wrote, following McGraw's outburst, "The impudence of the Yankee knows no limits; and their baseball visit has afforded another opportunity for the display of it."[11] In fact, some newspapers had called for a boycott of the game, based on McGraw's statements. Between this and McGraw's ill-chosen words, it's not surprising that baseball was already losing momentum. "At such a time when our political relations are so friendly with America it seems almost an unfriendly act to allege that their great national pastime leaves us cold," London's *Daily News and Leader* said. "It is, I think a game for a warm climate and a people temperamentally more excitable than ours."[12]

Of course, there was another key factor that halted all domestic baseball efforts: World War I. As would later be the case during World War II, baseball did not have deep enough roots to sustain interest during wartime. The influx of Americans into the country during the war did lead to extensive play, but it was almost exclusively among American and Canadian soldiers. In 1918, the Anglo-American League was set up in the London area for the entertainment and recreation of the American and Canadian Forces. The biggest baseball event took place on 4 July 1918 at Stamford Bridge, the home of the famed Chelsea Football Club.

The clash between the U.S. Navy and the U.S. Army attracted a crowd of 38,000, including King George V, British Prime Minister David Lloyd George and the future Prime Minister Winston Churchill. With the media in the mood to support strong bonds between Britain and the United States, some suggested that baseball was a way to create cultural bridges. "If Waterloo was won on the playing fields of Eaton, it may be that it will be said hereafter, in the same symbolic sense, that the Great War was won on the baseball ground at Chelsea," wrote the *Illustrated London News* following the game.

But following the war, the game had difficulty getting going again. In the fall of 1924, baseball supporters did set up a series of exhibition games between the Chicago White Sox and the New York Giants in London, Liverpool, Birmingham, Dublin and Paris. Unfortunately, the games did not get a full welcome. The trip cost a pricey $20,000 and, according to a 30 November 1924 *New York Times* article, "[m]ore money was taken in for the two games played in Montreal and Quebec [Canada] before the teams sailed than for the entire six games played in England and France."

Overall, the media was dismissive of the tour — although the games did receive one positive review. The British playwright George Bernard Shaw, though not a sports fan of any sort, remarked after a Giants–White Sox game in London: "To go back to cricket after baseball is like going back to Shakespeare played in five acts with fifteen-minute intervals after seeing it played through in the correct Shakespearean way."[13] Ultimately, though, the game had been diminished by the war.

It took a man who had made his fortune in the world of gambling to facilitate baseball's golden age in Great Britain. Sir John Moores, who founded the Littlewoods Football Pools Company in 1923, took his biggest gamble on baseball. His pools remain today a legalized form of gambling and — although the Moores family no longer runs it — by 2002 the Liverpool-based company had grown into a powerful organization with a mail-order business and 189 stores. Moores first became involved with baseball in 1933, when he formed the National Baseball Association in response to a challenge by the president of Major League Baseball's National League, John A. Heydler, to spur British baseball growth. Within a few months of the challenge, eighteen amateur baseball teams in two leagues had been formed in Moores' Liverpool, according to William Morgan, a publisher of British baseball periodicals. Heydler was so impressed that he donated the league trophy — a silver cup. With Moores' business acumen and financial backing, baseball began to flourish. In 1934, there was domestic baseball being played throughout the country, including Liverpool, Oxfordshire, Birmingham and the London area.

The sport even attracted one of the country's greatest sporting legends: Dixie Dean. In the 1927–1928 season, Dean scored an English record 60 goals for the club Everton — a mark that was akin to Babe Ruth clouting 60 home runs in 1927. Like Ruth, with whom Dean once had a chance encounter, the prolific goal scorer also had an affinity for baseball.[14] Dean would play for the Liverpool Caledonians and prove to be a competent baseball player — as well as a great draw. In a game down in the London borough of Harringay in 1936, 17,000 came out to watch Dean play ball for his Liverpool team. This was a much larger crowed than the usual 4,000 Harringay drew. Showing his penchant for showmanship, Dean reveled in his two-sport status. "Dixie signed for the Caledonians and I was a pitcher for Littlewoods," recounted Albert Finnis years later, "As I was almost ready to pitch to him, someone in the crowd shouted, 'Why don't you head it, [Dixie]?' [Dixie] just smiled and to everybody's amusement went through the motions of heading the ball."[15]

Not satisfied with top draws like Dean for amateur play, Moores became more ambitious with his baseball interests and in 1935 he decided to form a professional league called the North of England Baseball League, based around Manchester.[16] The reaction of some in the baseball community was trepidation. "This is a daring move," wrote the *Liverpool Echo* on the eve of the pro circuit's debut. "I know that sound judges would have liked such a development to have been deferred until [British baseball was at] a more mature moment. The time was not quite ripe."[17]

Undeterred, Moores barreled ahead with the new venture. The players were mostly Americans and Canadians with solid baseball credentials and respected athletes from other sports like soccer and rugby, such as Jim Sullivan, who is regarded as one of the greatest Rugby League players of all time. (Dean played only at the amateur level.) Typical of the foreigners was Stanley Trickett, a player for the Belle Vue Tigers who was billed in one media report as the former captain of the University of Kentucky's baseball team. So could these guys play? Players with little baseball experience certainly attacked the sport with gusto. Benny Nieuwenhuys, for example, a South African soccer player for the famed Liverpool Football Club, was lauded after his baseball team the Hurst Hawks won because "his headlong dives for the bags were very effective if not spectacular."[18]

But it was clear that mastering the rules of baseball would not happen overnight. Controversy in the 1935 season stemmed from officials complaining that excessive base stealing was leading to bloated scoring (a team scoring 20 runs in a game was not uncommon). The promoters considered banning stealing all together, but the Americans and Canadians protested vigorously. The reason for the high number of steals was not a flaw in the rules, said one experienced player, but the result of English pitchers not being able to effectively hold the runners on. For some unknown reason, the English pitchers were throwing out of the wind-up — a no-no with runners on base — instead of the stretch. Players also often faced inhospitable playing conditions as some teams competed in soccer stadiums, which featured baseball-diamond dimensions that were too small and playing surfaces so torn up by football boots that ground balls would often bounce head high.[19]

Despite these problems, most teams in the league drew between 1,000 and 3,000 spectators with games between front-runners getting 5,000 or more. "Clubs produced remarkably large profits and gates were surprisingly big," crowed one paper after the season.[20] Founder Moores was elated by the performance of the first season and in an interview with the *Ashton-Under-Lyne Reporter* boasted that the National Baseball Association had "already gone ahead of the five-year plan originally set out."[21]

The next year, Moores formed two new professional leagues — the Yorkshire League and the London Major Baseball League — to go along with the North of England Baseball League.[22] With three pro circuits spread throughout the country, Moores was now covering a tremendous amount of territory. He was also attracting the interest of the British sports establishment as evidenced by the BBC radio broadcasting its first live baseball game — a contest between the Oldham Greyhounds and the Rochdale Greys — in 1936.

In its second season, owners in the North of England League became more aggressive in their recruiting. The expansion Liverpool Giants had six members with American playing experience and — between the North of England League and the nascent Yorkshire League — every decent ballplayer in the northern part of the country seemed to be a pro. The *Liverpool Echo* lamented that this meant that amateur leagues, the lifeblood for sustained growth of the sport, were suffering. The professional leagues were "claiming (top players), but at much too rapid a pace to allow their places to be filled adequately ... that has been a big defect of the early introduction of professionalism in baseball ranks." Despite the local British talent, top foreigners dominated early in the 1936 season. The Ashton Hawks, for example, were battling to stay out of last place in the North of England league when the team brought over a Canadian pitcher named Ross E. Scott. The results were immediate. In his first four league games, Scott struck out 58 batters (an average of 14 per start) and the Hawks finished the season well clear of the cellar.

While the Yorkshire and North of England Leagues were competing for players in the Midlands (central England) and the North, the London Major Baseball League had its pick of top talent in the South of England. In 1936, there was little doubt that the London league was the best in the country. London's star player was West Ham's Roland Gladu, a French-Canadian who had previously played minor league baseball for the Montreal Royals. Gladu, dubbed "the Babe Ruth of Canada," would eventually go back to North America and play in the Major Leagues with the Boston Braves in 1944. Unlike many of the contests up north, London Major Baseball League games tended to be low-scoring affairs. Also, when teams in the league did compete against their rivals from up north, the London clubs dominated. The London league was so strong that following the Olympics in Berlin, the U.S. Olympic baseball team traveled to the British capital to play two teams, White City and West Ham. (Baseball had been an exhibition sport at the 1936 Games.) Although the Americans prevailed against White City, West Ham beat the Olympic squad 5–3.

Both the London and Yorkshire leagues matched — and in some cases surpassed — the North of England Baseball League in interest. In London, West Ham could draw crowds in excess of 4,000 and the Romford Wasps attracted 3,000 for some games. In the Yorkshire League, Hull brought out 9,000 for marquee matchups, and Sheffield's first home game attracted 6,000. Financially, the Yorkshire League topped the other two leagues. Hull, which had an average gate of £70 a game, and Sheffield, with an average of £50 to £60 a game, were particularly successful. These matches did have a mood that was quite different from American contests. "The big difference over [in the United States] is in the shouting," the *Scarborough Evening Post* wrote on May 16, 1936. "The Yanks make such a hubbub, both on and off the field, that it's like listening to a wagonload of escaped baboons." Ellis Harvey, who attended Romford games in 1936 and 1937, found that British baseball fans were also more reserved than those who attended soccer matches at the time.

One reason for this difference could have been the British fans' relatively limited knowledge of the game. Harvey says that he went to games because "British folk tended to dismiss it" and he wanted to see what attracted so many thousands of Americans.[23] He was a cricket fan and, while his knowledge of the game grew with each game he attended, it took a while before he and other fans got to the point where they felt comfortable badgering the umpires for bad calls. (Today, although the number of spectators at most games is minuscule, fans are far better educated about the sport. Major League Baseball games are telecast on British network television twice a week during the summer and with the Internet it's relatively easy to follow the game.)

In 1937, the Yorkshire League became the top circuit, replacing the London Major Baseball League as the place to play. The Yorkshire teams heavily imported American and Canadian players to enhance their squads, and they poached some of the London league's best foreign players, leaving very few British athletes on the field. Yorkshire's Leeds franchise, for instance, had only one English player. The money was reasonably good for these professionals with an average salary, according to British baseball historian Ian Smyth, of £2 per week, a solid wage for the era.[24] A star player could make even more and would receive accommodation and additional employment. But Smyth points out that the influx of excellent foreign talent — particularly on the mound — led to some complications up north with low-scoring games becoming the norm. For the uninitiated baseball spectators, pitchers' duels — like the ones played in the exhibition games in 1889 — were relatively boring. Nonetheless, many fans still came out, as evidenced by the 11,000 who watched Hull win the National Baseball Association Cup against the Romford Wasps 5–1.

But down south, baseball was beginning to fail as a professional sport. Stadium operators in London grew restless when the game didn't quickly produce sizeable dividends. In 1937, only the Romford Wasps and the West Ham Hammers had top-caliber players and the losses did seem considerable. "[B]aseball in England cost promoters £2,684 last season, making the total loss on five seasons £8,087," wrote London's *Daily Mirror* in May 1937.[25] After that season, the league folded and teams like the Wasps became amateur clubs. Moores' rapid expansion left too few good players to go around. With some top players defecting, the London league suddenly had a marginal product.

Even in the north where interest was much stronger, the sport was also beginning to stumble, as organizers began purging foreign players, with dire consequences. In 1938, the Yorkshire Baseball League and the North of England League merged to become the Yorkshire–Lancashire League. The major difference with the new circuit: each club was limited to only two professionals. This was done to allow British players to develop, and it effectively dropped the top level of baseball from professional to semi-professional. (An ill-fated renegade league called the International League started that year but went out of business after only a few weeks.) By 1939, attendance appeared to be waning. The loss of professional teams, which certainly lessened the quality of play, probably led to a dropoff in interest.

The professional leagues aside, perhaps Britain's greatest success in the

Baseball AT
WEST HAM STADIUM

WEST HAM BASEBALL CLUB

UNLESS OTHERWISE STATED ALL SATURDAY AND SUNDAY GAMES PITCH - OFF 3.30 P.M.

Professional baseball flourished for a brief period in 1930s Great Britain. Teams in both the north of England and in London (pictured above: 1936 program from London's professional West Ham team) played competitive baseball, thanks in large part to the patronage of Liverpool business magnate John Moores.

global baseball community took place in 1938 when the country won the first-ever World Amateur Baseball Championship. The story began in August 1938, when the U.S. Olympic baseball team arrived in Plymouth for a five-game "test series" against England. At the time, there was no talk of a world championship. The U.S. squad was prepping for the Olympic Games that were planned for Tokyo in 1940. The team was comprised of high school and college players who had been picked the month before at the U.S. National Amateur Baseball Trials in Lincoln, Nebraska. Former major leaguer Leslie Mann coached the team.

The English squad was made up almost entirely of players born in Canada. England's top player, Ross Kendrick, was described in a game program as a "pitcher with a very clean style of hooks, speed and endurance." Kendrick would become a legendary fixture in British baseball, playing well into middle age — one eyewitness claimed seeing 60-year-old-plus Kendrick pitching a game many years after the world championship triumph.

The series was set for August 13–19 in Liverpool, Hull, Rochdale, Halifax and Leeds, and attendance was impressive. In front of 10,000 fans in Liverpool, Kendrick defeated curveball pitcher Virgil Thompson to lead England to a 3–0 first-game victory. Kendrick threw a two-hitter, striking out 16. Two days later, England won 8–6 in front of 5,000 spectators in Hull. The Americans took the next game, 5–0, in Rochdale, but England won the next two games. In Halifax Kendrick returned to the mound, shutting out the United States for the second time, 4–0, and then England won again 5–3 in Leeds. Following the series, the International Baseball Federation designated the series as the first World Championships and named Great Britain the inaugural World Amateur Champions. To this day, that bureaucratic decision may be GB's greatest baseball victory.

The quality of professional baseball in 1930s Great Britain was made evident by the performance of its top players against an American national team that came to England in 1938. The British squad (pictured above) won four out of five games to capture what is today considered the inaugural World Championship.

We'll never know whether British baseball players would have ever reached the levels of their North American counterparts because World War II ended the Yorkshire–Lancashire League as players of all nationalities went off to war. During the hostilities, Allied soldiers did set up recreational baseball on the British Isles. The London International Baseball League was a highly competitive eight-team circuit that played in front of large crowds of mainly Allied soldiers. Unlike the previous war, British players were at least marginally more involved with baseball, as a British team called the Hornsey Red Sox played against North Americans throughout the war years. In addition to league games, many exhibition games were played during the war. On 7 August 1943, for example, the U.S. Air Force played the U.S. ground forces at Empire Stadium, Wembley, before 21,500 spectators. Still, the game lost its hold on the British consciousness and a British championship would not be contested again until 1948.

After the war, baseball tried to reclaim its place in the British sports landscape. With a huge number of North American soldiers still in Britain, the sport had enough experienced players to return to minor prominence. In London, baseball received solid coverage in local newspapers, and teams up north — most notably in Hull and in Stretford near Manchester — were also developing very capable baseball teams. But the quality of the leagues depended on foreigners. Andy Parkes, who played for the Stretford Saints in the postwar era, recounts that the team leaders would run over to local factories and firms whenever they heard an American or Canadian had started work. One of the Saints' (and Northern England's) top players in this period, Wally O'Neil, was recruited through this very approach. O'Neil, a Canadian, had come to England to work as an electric control engineer but soon was enlisted to play baseball and went on to lead the Saints to numerous championships.

If North Americans weren't joining the British, they were running their own teams. The Burtonwood Bees, for example, a squad from a U.S. Air Force base, dominated in the 1950s. But financial support and general interest from Britons was limited. George Livsley, an organizer of the Stretford Saints, recalled that by the end of the war there was very little equipment available for British teams and that in some cases the equipment could not be afforded.[26] Chuck Cole, a player from that era, recounted how baseball was included at the Festival of Britain exhibition in London in 1951. While baseball was demonstrated in an exhibition for some four to five weeks during the summer, he only remembers "one or two inquiries" from potential players interested in taking up baseball.

During this period, U.S. and Canadian military games could still draw big crowds of mainly other soldiers, but audiences for British contests were much smaller. For example, a game in 1954 between the U.S.A.F. Cowboys and R.C.A.F. Langar attracted more than 4,000, while in contrast a team in the northern city of Leeds, which could easily draw 1,000 spectators to a game

OLDHAM GREYHOUND STADIUM.

WATERSHEDDINGS.

Saturday, May 7th 1949.

oooooooooooooooooooooooooooooooooooooooooooooooooooooooo

AMERICAN AIR FORCE

V

Manchester and District League.

oooooooooooooooooooooooooooooooooooooooooooooooooooooooo

IF YOU HAVE NOTHING TO DO TO-NIGHT

DANCE

WITH THESE BOYS

AT CHADDERTON TOWN HALL.

GRAND BAND   LICENSED BAR.   ADMISSION 3/-

Programme   -   -   Threepence.

Programmes are being sold by Chadderton Grammar School Rover Crew. in aid of Bob-a-Job Fund.

TORRENS (Printer), 566, Middleton Rd., Chadderton.

Following World War II, baseball reemerged in a number of regions. British teams would often take on American military personnel who were still stationed in England. These match-ups, like one between the U.S. Air Force and a British All-Star squad in Oldham in 1949 (above: program), could draw sizeable crowds.

before the war, had only 300 watch them lose to the Kingston Diamonds. The bottom line was that baseball's modest success in the 1950s was largely due to foreign players. This fact was not lost on British baseball pundits. The 16 July 1953 issue of *Baseball News*, a British baseball publication, ran an editorial revealing the concerns about non–British involvement:

> The scarcity of "home-produced" players has led to an increasing demand for the services of visitors to this country who are "ready-made" ballplayers. Whilst U.S. Servicemen are in England it is natural that there will be a large number of them competing in British baseball [but] there will naturally be a difference should there be a future decline in the numbers of "guest stars" available. It is for this fact alone that all teams should concentrate on building up "local talent" side by side with the experienced men.[27]

A decade later, little had changed. The Stretford Saints' Parkes said to a newspaper reporter in the mid–60s that the "Americanism" of baseball was inevitably hindering the game's growth, "I think it's bound to put some people off," he explained. "But the game is American. All the terms are American. There aren't English words for them."

Still, organizers were unwilling to let British baseball go quietly. Although some businesses, most notably Ford Motor Company, bankrolled individual teams, gone were the days of substantial financial support from the likes of A. G. Spalding or John Moores. Nevertheless, in 1963, a National Baseball League was formed with teams from all areas of the country — Stretford, Hull, Nottingham, Coventry, Manchester, Birmingham and London. The league, designed to start competition at the end of the soccer season and play until the soccer started again, survived until 1972. But the game was strictly amateur and any hopes of reclaiming a professional place in the British sports world seemed remote.

Overall, the quality of baseball also appeared to be diminishing during this era. Jeff Archer, in his book *Strike Four*, wrote about his efforts to develop baseball in Great Britain in the mid–1970s and early 1980s. He described the sport as being in a sad state of affairs. Archer recounted an incident in 1975 in which his team, leading by a large margin, lost a shutout in the eighth inning. After the run was scored, the opposing manager, who was apparently drunk, staggered onto the field and apologized to the starting pitcher on Archer's team for breaking up the shutout.[28] Archer later tried to set up a league in London that would draw paying customers, but his efforts ultimately failed and he moved to Holland, where baseball was more developed.

One factor that probably contributed to baseball's stagnation was that the sport had become regionally fragmented. Signs of this appear as early as 1952. In June that year, an England squad traveled to the Netherlands to play and was criticized by London's *Evening News* for having a bias against southern players. According to the paper, the Sutton Beavers, which was a particularly strong team in the London area, sent the names of its three top players, but they were rejected. In the end, only one player from the South was named to the team. Later in the summer, southern organizers retaliated by forming their own squad — dubbed an England team — to play an international game against a Canadian all-star team.

By the late 1960s, organizers in the north (centered in Hull) and the south (with teams mainly in London and the surrounding "home counties") clearly appeared to be focusing on their own areas. Despite winning the silver medal at the 1967 European Championships in Belgium, the country had difficulty putting together a consistent, cohesive national squad. International play in 1969 was emblematic of the factional nature of the game in that period. Representative teams from both South Africa and Zambia traveled to Great Britain to play separate series. Instead of British baseball's governing body forming a single squad, various regions put up all-star teams against the foreign competition. In domestic leagues, four areas emerged as baseball centers between the late-60s and mid–90s: Hull, Nottingham, Liverpool and greater London. During this period, teams from in and around those cities won practically every national championship.

Organizers worked hard for the game, but regional disputes between the game's power centers did create problems. This tension reached its greatest climax when two competing bodies vied for recognition from the European baseball's governing body. In 1971, two federations emerged: the established organization that included the National Baseball League (NBL) and the Baseball-Softball Association of Great Britain, which was based in the south of England. The conflict grew so great that the NBL banned its members from playing in the South-of-England leagues.

This schism was not fully resolved for years. In 1975, Myron Ferentz, who had formed a baseball-equipment company, "took the initiative in calling a meeting aimed at getting the warring factions in British baseball to sit around a table and attempt to sink their differences," according to the leading British baseball publication of the time, *Baseball Mercury*. Not since 1969 had representatives from the main baseball-playing areas — the Southeast, Midlands, Merseyside and Humberside — met face-to-face. The meeting must have been some kind of a success as a number of issues, including matters relating to England's national team, were resolved.

Tensions like these stunted any hopes of an overall strategic development of the British game, said Mike Carlson, who was Major League Baseball's representative in Great Britain between 1990 and 1994. "To a certain extent, the problem [in Great Britain] is the club structure," he said. "You can't get to a wider area; you can't disseminate the sport beyond small areas. There were a lot of little fiefdoms. People liked running their small program. They'd rather be a big fish in a small pond."[29]

In fairness, another obstacle was the cost of travel. A lack of funding often

AMERICAN BI-CENTENARY
BASEBALL
INTERNATIONAL

★

GREAT BRITAIN
v
U.S.A.F. BASES
(United States Air Force)   (U.K.)

SUN., 19TH SEPTEMBER, 1976
HARVEY HADDEN STADIUM
WIGMAN ROAD, BILBOROUGH

**PITCH-OFF
3 P.M.**   **ADMISSION BY PROGRAMME
AVAILABLE AT GROUND - 40p
UNDER 16's - 30p**

By the mid–1970s, British baseball was grappling with issues of regionalism. Still, there was still room for some high-profile events like a contest between U.S. Air Force personnel and a Great Britain squad (program pictured above).

made team travel up and down the country every week too costly, and to this day, teams from the North and the South rarely meet — except in major events. Nevertheless, a willingness to work together could have overcome any logistical difficulties. After all, the NBL had originally included teams from London in the south to Hull in the north.

The cyclical moments of optimism and bouts of despair about the future of British baseball have continued up to the present day. In 1987, Scottish Amicable Life Assurance Society, a British-based insurance company, agreed to sponsor British baseball. The three-year sponsorship was said to be worth £300,000. With the funding, the British Baseball Federation formed the Scottish Amicable National League. Its purpose, according to the organization's official newsletter, was to provide British Baseball with a "'Shop-window' that gives [the] sport credibility by staging games for the sporting public to the best possible standards."

Many involved with baseball at the time said that the game was gaining ground on other sports. It also helped that Major League Baseball was being televised by the national network Channel 4 and by Sky Sports. British baseball leaders staged several high-profile events to draw attention to baseball. In 1988 when cricket great Graham Gooch battled Hall-of-Famer Ernie Banks in a home-run derby at the famed Oval cricket grounds in London as part of the festivities surrounding that year's British baseball national championship. Banks, 57 at the time, was well past his prime but he beat Gooch three home runs to zero. (One report actually had the score at 5–0.) Gooch, who was 33 at the time, said after the contest: "I hit a number of balls right ... [on] the screws but the wind was against me and they just fell short." Banks blamed Gooch's failure on technique. "It came down to swings," Banks told the *Boston Globe* following the competition. "I tried to teach him to swing up and get the ball in the air. He was used to a low, straight swing of cricket, and every time he tried to swing up, he'd pop the ball up." Another highlight: in 1989, the British National Team took on a traveling all-star team of former major leaguers including Hall-of-Famers Bob Feller, Willie Stargell and Billy Williams, called "The Legends of Baseball," at Old Trafford Cricket Ground in the Manchester area. (The old-timers won 16–3.)

But then in 1990, the 100th anniversary of organized baseball in Great Britain, Scottish Amicable pulled out, for reasons still unclear. Some suggested that British baseball's leadership had misused funds, while others insisted that the sponsorship had just ran its course. Whatever the case, future sponsors of Great Britain's National League — including Coors and Rawlings — were not as generous as Scottish Amicable. British baseball continued to have problems during this period. In 1991, entrepreneur Malcolm Needs organized a new league — the National League — to play in large stadiums and attract British fans back to the game. But a disagreement between Needs and British Baseball Federation president Mike Harrold led the National League to break away from the BBF. Its players, who were among the country's best, were banned from BBF-related organizations—including the national team. In 1994, baseball's governing body in Europe got involved and Needs left British baseball, while the National League players were welcomed back into the BBF fold.

Some suggested that British baseball was also hurt by a foreign-player limit put into place in 1988. The restriction, which followed a long history of fear that non–British players would dominate the domestic game, seriously curtailed participation, according to Alan Smith, a longtime British player and organizer. More specifically, the limit on foreigners caused the demise of the Surrey Baseball Association and the dismantling of three major adult teams: the Oxshott Orioles, the Woking White Sox and, most importantly, the Cobham Yankees, which was founded six years earlier and had won the All-England club championship four times. Still, those who governed the game at that time argue that the rules we put in place to encourage further growth. "We did not want to create a situation where a foreign player could not play," said Paul Raybould, who was a member of the British Baseball Federation board at the time. "The main purpose of this rule was to encourage foreign players to spread their talents to different teams in the region or possibly consider setting up a club where none existed."[30]

Whatever the effect of the rule changes, by the mid–90s the number of people playing baseball diminished to minuscule levels. But at the start of the new millennium, hope sprung up again. In 2000, the BBF joined with the Baseball Softball Federation under the umbrella BaseballSoftballUK banner in an effort to bundle resources. Starting with just Mike Carlson and a single assis-

A big problem today in Great Britain is the quality of playing facilities. Most fields require the use of snow fences for outfield walls (as seen above in a 2007 game in London between the London Mets and the Windsor Bears) and other makeshift elements. (Photograph by Alex Phipps.)

tant in 1990, MLB's operation in London, which is now run by Clive Russell, a former aide to British Prime Minister Tony Blair, has offered some support. Although the office is responsible for both game development and TV and merchandise licensing for MLB in Europe, the Middle East and Africa, it has offered office space and other help to British baseball and softball.

In 2002, Frubes, a children's yogurt dessert brand of Yoplait, became the first-ever title sponsor of MLB and BaseballSoftballUK's Play Ball! program, which gives kids a chance to play baseball and softball both in and outside of school. Along with MLB's efforts, BaseballSoftballUK (BSUK) now has a paid professional staff. In the past, unpaid part-timers did the work of developing the game. The hope is that a handful of full-time employees will increase baseball and softball's profile in Britain. To that end, in 2005, baseball and softball received a £300,000 grant from Sport England, a public entity that supports athletics in the country. This is the largest amount of public funding these sports have ever received in the United Kingdom. Still, by 2007, BSUK had changed its focus to macro-development, while the British Baseball Federation had taken over the day-to-day administration of the game. This will require a lot of time and effort from BBF volunteers.

The use of foreign players is no longer as controversial in Britain's domestic leagues as it was in decades past. The problem today is a dearth of experienced players. In 2003, British baseball organizers created a program to lure American collegians to play in the country's top league. Although that program ended abruptly because of financial difficulties, organizers continue to look for ways to lure solid foreign baseball players to Britain to supplement local talent. While some still worry that too many non–British players may stunt domestic player development, they now understand that a core group of good foreign players are needed as role models, especially since with the end of the Cold War most American and Canadian soldiers have returned home. Only one military base — the U.S. Air Force facility at Menwith Hill in the north — still actively plays baseball.

It's hard to tell if baseball is finally ready for sustained growth in Britain. Major League Baseball games are now shown twice a week on Five (TV), one of the five national television networks in the country. In addition, a pay cable network, NASN, which is owned by ESPN, has been successful broadcasting baseball along with other North American sports. A televised game on Five or NASN can attract a healthy viewing audience, but there has been little connection between a loyal viewing public and people willing to take up the game. Britain is not a "sporting nation" in the same way as the United States, where not only children but also adults flock to play organized sports. More Britons watch than play.

Yet, while the number of those who actually play baseball in Great Britain is small, their passion is huge. Some of the best players have begun going to America to play at U.S. universities. One British pitcher, Gavin Marshall, played two seasons in the Frontier League, an independent professional league in the Midwest. A handful of other British players have competed at the college level and one former player, Liam Carroll, worked as a student-coach at the University of Las Vegas, Nevada. The national team also showed signs of life in 2007 when it won the silver medal at the European Baseball Championships. It was the country's first medal in forty years and while the team was almost exclusively composed of expats who qualified for British passports, there is hope that the success could spur greater domestic interest. Alas, despite earning entry into a special final Olympic qualification event with its Euros' performance, GB did not send a team for financial reasons. Organizers said they couldn't raise the £40,000 they estimated was needed to properly compete.

To prosper, baseball in Britain will need new benefactors—like John Moores and A. G. Spalding of the past. For, more than ever, English culture appears determined to protect traditional English sports. A popular anti-baseball chant among detractors is that baseball is "glorified rounders," a child's game that bears a resemblance to baseball. Alas, this comparison hasn't changed in more than a century.

6

Germany

Long before baseball existed as we know it, Germans were pitching balls, swinging bats and looking to score runs. The centuries-old German-Austrian game of *schlagbal* featured a pitcher throwing a ball to a batter who tried to swat the pitch as far as he could. There were three lines—a bat line, a run line and a field line—that served as de facto bases and a run was scored when a batter made it back to the bat line. In 1796, German writer Johann Christoph Friedrich Gutsmuths even devoted seven pages in a book on sports to a game he called baseball.[1] Although Gutsmuths' game appears different than descriptions of *schlagbal*, he also discussed a sport quite similar to *schlagbal* elsewhere in his work, according to David Block, an expert on the roots of baseball.[2] The bottom line: Germans were playing ball well before there was even an America to have a pastime. In fact, some suggest that *schlagbal* was one of the early games that came to an infant America and was thrown into the stew of European bat-and-ball sports that ultimately became baseball.[3]

While this early play suggests that Germans should have a penchant for baseball, the traditional game of *schlagbal* never hit it big in Germany. In fact, there was little sign of an enduring affinity for bat-and-ball sports in Germany by the time baseball was emerging as America's game in the late nineteenth century. For baseball to make German inroads, it required Americans who steadfastly exported the sport in the twentieth century. Two seminal events satisfied this need: the 1936 Olympics in Berlin and the German rebuilding effort after World War II. As a result it appears that maybe that long-ago history with bat-and-ball games has finally begun resonating deep inside some Germans. Today, some 30,000 Germans play baseball, making the country home of one of Europe's biggest domestic baseball communities.

Although the first real push for baseball in Germany began just before the 1936 Berlin Games, the sport's inaugural game, according to the American press, occurred in 1909 at the Botanical Garden Parks in Berlin, wrote the *New York Times* on 19 September 1909. The full staffs of the American Embassy and Consulate General were in attendance. Moreover, the sport was played in the country by American GIs during the waning days of World War I and afterward, but Germany never received the same baseball interest from major leaguers that other significant European nations encountered in the late nineteenth and early twentieth centuries. When A. G. Spalding conducted his world tour from 1888 to 1889, he made a point to stop in Italy, France and the United Kingdom. Germany was on the itinerary but was removed when the tourists learned upon their arrival in Europe in February 1889 that a foot of snow covered Berlin. In 1912–13, the Chicago White Sox's Charlie Comiskey and the New York Giants' John McGraw led another Major League Baseball world tour, but Germany was overlooked. As with the Spalding trip, the ballplayers stopped in Italy, France and the United Kingdom, but Germany missed out on a big-league exhibition. A 1924 follow-up tour by Comiskey and McGraw was limited to just France, Great Britain and Ireland.

Maybe it was that Germany didn't work on the McGraw-Comiskey trip schedules or that the players were more interested in the attractions of Paris and London than the lush, bucolic beauty of Germany. According to an 11 August 1913 *New York Times* article, the first tour didn't include games in Germany because the country would be experiencing inclement weather at the time of the tour making "outdoor baseball an impossibility." Regardless, the result likely left baseball more remote in the minds of Germans in the early 1900s than it was in the consciousness of most other Western Europeans.

Leslie Mann looked to change that situation. The outspoken Mann had a colorful baseball history. On the field, he was best known for driving in the Boston Braves' winning run in game two of the 1914 World Series en route to a Braves series sweep of the Philadelphia Athletics. Off the field, he was a magnet for attention. Mann was among the players who controversially jumped to the outlaw Federal League following the 1914 season. Although he returned to the majors the following year, he was again in the eye of the storm as a member of the National League–winning Chicago Cubs in 1918. He led a group of players fighting for a bigger share of the purse at the 1918 World Series. Mann and Harry Hooper, a representative of the Boston Red Sox, tried to broker a raise for the players. They sat down eye-to-eye with three of baseball's ruling elite — American League president Ban Johnson, National League president John Heydler and Cincinnati Reds president August Hermann — but negotiations failed. Despite delaying game five of the Series in a last-ditch effort to convince the potentates who was in charge, Mann and the other players finally capitulated and played without the raise.

If nothing else, Mann's experience with professional baseball proved he was tenacious and willing to take chances. After his playing days, he concluded that his great legacy to the game should be masterminding the development of international baseball. His efforts were already underway before he set eyes on Germany as the location from which to springboard the game internationally.

Germany in 1936 was probably not the best place and time to shine the spotlight on baseball. Adolph Hitler and his malignant Nazi regime had other plans for the Berlin Games. In early February 1936, the Nazis had already used the Olympic movement as a propaganda tool. The Winter Games, which occurred in the Bavarian towns of Garmisch and Partenkirchen, were seen as a dry run for the Summer Games. While anti–Semitism and racism already existed in Germany at the time, Hitler wanted to give the impression otherwise. He ordered that all anti–Jewish signs be removed from the southern Bavarian region. Hotels in the area were ordered to show tolerance to visiting foreigners of all races and religions. Moreover, the German press was instructed to avoid printing any stories that might suggest a racist or anti–Semitism undercurrent in Germany. Despite these efforts, many countries did show some protest. The official Olympic salute involved extending the right arm in a manner very similar to the Nazi salute. The American Olympians refused to perform the salute as did the teams from Estonia and Finland. For the summer games, the Nazis redoubled their efforts to provide a benign image. Hitler himself directed the equivalent of a $25 million building project to not only create top-notch facilities but also make sure that the streets were immaculately clean and that all outward signs of state anti–Semitism were withdrawn.[4]

Baseball was a complementary vehicle for these propagandist efforts. In 1936, America was still undecided about the Nazi regime. Some leading U.S. figures were sympathetic and Hitler was eager to increase his support in the sleeping giant. Allowing an exhibition of baseball was a perfect way to ingratiate himself with the United States.

It's doubtful that Leslie Mann cared too much about the political subtext while making his pitch. After all, he'd been scheming to get baseball in the Olympics since at least 1928 and had already started making his mark on the European baseball scene by helping develop the sport in England. Professional baseball flourished briefly in the British Isles from 1935–39 and Mann had served as a key recruiter of players for the new pro leagues. In Germany, his initial plan was for the United States to square off against other nations in a demonstration tournament. To that end, Mann constructed a solid squad composed of many of the leading collegiate players of the day. After preliminary tryouts in Maryland, California and Michigan, finalists for spots on the Olympic squad worked out at a camp in Baltimore, Maryland. The team ultimately included players from such top collegiate programs as Stanford University, University of Georgia, Temple University, University of Maine and University of Nebraska. Included on the final roster was one Jewish player, a Brooklyn College product named Herman Goldberg.

While many of the baseball players were likely oblivious to the political issues involved with playing in Germany in 1936, Goldberg had contemplated the matter carefully. A number of organizations and publications, including the NAACP, the American Federation of Labor, the *New York Times* and the *Nation*, had called for a boycott. Goldberg, who was one of about five or six Jewish athletes in an American Olympic contingent of more than 300, discussed the possibility with the other Jewish members of the team. "We came to the conclusion that if the entire team would boycott, we would also do so," said Goldberg years later. "But we were really American athletes of Jewish religion. It didn't make sense to us to be the only ones to boycott. We were not Jewish ballplayers ... we weren't Jewish sprinters; we weren't Jewish basketball players; we weren't Jewish pistol shooters; we weren't Jewish weight lifters. We were American athletes, selected by the team to represent our country."[5]

Hindsight makes it easy to identify the tensions and impending conflict, but at the time things weren't as clear and most of the baseball team sailed to Germany on the USS *Manhattan* in relative bliss. One player, Dow Wilson, a middle infielder and the squad's youngest member at 19, played cards with Olympic hero Jesse Owens throughout the voyage. Other players were tangentially involved in the Games' first big scandal. Swimmer Eleanor Holm, who had won an Olympic gold medal at the 1932 Olympics, was kicked off the 1936 team for drinking champagne and shooting craps on the ship. Dick Hanna, a U.S. baseball player who played his college baseball at Stanford University, recalled that the baseball team was seated next to the women's swimming team in the ship's dining room, and some of the ballplayers were actually with Holm when she drank the illicit alcohol.

The enjoyable voyage was a marked contrast to the news the team received upon their arrival, according to Paul Amen, one of the team's top hitters. "There were supposed to be a number of nations represented in baseball, even though it was just a demonstration sport," Amen recalled. "But when we got to Berlin we learned that they had all dropped out, most of them because they couldn't afford to send teams. There was a worldwide depression going on at the time."[6]

Still, the Americans were resolute about one thing: they would demonstrate baseball to the German public. A split-squad exhibition game was planned for the final day of the Olympics. Until then, the team practiced, attended other sporting events and organized clinics focusing on introducing baseball to the German audience. Their baseball efforts did capture some local media interest. "There was a series in a local newspaper ... and the headline read '*Baseball*' *Was es Das?*" Goldberg recounted. "[T]he story went on to explain how difficult it would be to understand baseball, so they were publishing a week-long series on how to watch a baseball game. I remember [they gave] the names of the positions, in German, of course. Left field, for instance, translated as *linkausen*, meaning 'way out in the left side.' ... A pitcher was *der werfen* (the

Germany was the home to one of baseball's largest single events: a baseball exhibition at the 1936 Berlin Olympics (above: ticket). Although estimates vary, as many as 125,000 spectators attended the U.S. Olympic team split-squad game.

'thrower-in') and a catcher was a *fangen*. They couldn't come up with a word for our shortstop position, though, so it remained *shortstop*."[7]

Years later, many of the players reflected on the Nazi presence during the downtime. For example, American second baseman Les McNeece, who was 20 at the time, remembered that "when the Olympic team marched into the stadium there were thousands of Nazi S.S. troops lining the road.... We thought they were honoring us."[8] Even though baseball was not on the official Olympic program, Hitler and his mistress, Eva Braun, took a particular interest in the sport. Wilson, the 19-year-old who played cards with Jesse Owens on the trip to Germany, said "they both had this fixation with American ballplayers.... I never figured out why." Wilson, who wasn't aware of the political climate, spoke with Hitler every day for a number of days. Oblivious to the Nazi leader's abhorrent beliefs, Wilson made small talk with the dictator. Looking back, Wilson tried to explain why he was so nonchalant about the conversations at the time. "I was 19, what do 19-year-olds talk about?" he said. "[Hitler] was polite and seemed like a nice man who obviously became a very bad man."[9]

Braun was also very interested in the baseball. During the games, Braun came to a baseball practice and asked to talk with the U.S. baseball captain. Pitcher Carson Thompson was chosen to talk with her because he spoke some German. "She told me that Hitler had given her exclusive rights to do [a documentary on] the event and since baseball was an important event, she wanted background on the game," said Thompson in an interview in 1984. Thompson remembered Braun as being a particularly striking woman. "She was the most fascinating woman I ever met," he recalled. "She was beautiful with reddish brown hair. I couldn't figure out what she saw in that Hitler."

As he was already aware of the evils of the Nazis, Goldberg's time in Berlin reinforced many of his fears. Although the Germans he met were polite and civil, there were a number of hints of the institutional prejudice. "When they listed the house of worship in some of the publications, there was no mention of Jewish synagogues," Goldberg said. "They had all the others, but never these. I was especially concerned when I read in an American newspaper that Hitler had forbidden the use of the word hallelujah at all religious services in all churches because it was a Hebrew word." In each player's room was a book entitled *Germany*. The propaganda in this publication also served as a warning. "Taking the time to read this book carefully, I could sense the beginnings of their war machine," Goldberg said. "They were telling us, throughout this book, that they were getting ready for war, although they didn't call it that. They just called it the 'preparation of Germany for expanding its borders.' It went on and on, and we were somewhat disturbed by it."

Politics aside, there was baseball in Berlin at the games. On August 12 at 8 P.M., the sport finally took the field at the Olympic Stadium. Although estimates have varied, a crowd of as many as 125,000 were on hand. That number would make the attendance the largest-ever for a baseball game. Because the United States had the only team in Germany, the squad was divided into two sides, the World Amateurs and the U.S. Olympics. It was August, but the weather was chilly, according to Goldberg. "We didn't have jackets to go over our uniforms, so we were given blankets to keep us warm on the sidelines," he said.[10] As baseball was new to the German people, it's not surprising that the field conditions were not optimal. "The lights only went about 50 feet into the air," said Hanna, who played outfield in the game. "I remember one ball went into the air and I had no idea where it was. It came down right into my glove." Other shortcomings included no outfield fence, no pitcher's mound and a cage that was snugly placed around home plate. The fencing around home was erected to minimize the chances of any neophyte spectators getting hit by a foul ball. The field dimensions were also irregular. Because the field had to be shoehorned inside a track, the right-field line was an extremely short 200 feet while left field ran the full length of the 400 meter track straightaway. Beyond those idiosyncrasies, there was a far more disturbing element: Hitler's box was located ten feet inside fair territory in right field.

U.S. pitcher Bill Sayles marveled at the spectacle. "Before the game started, a whole gaggle of German generals came down — I later recognized [Hermann] Goering as one of them," Sayles said years later. "We were told that under no circumstances were we to hit a ball into right or right-center field. Well, being Americans, you never saw so many line drives hit to right in warm-ups."

To assure that the predominantly German crowd would remain interested — even if they got befuddled by what must have been a very foreign game — the Americans employed Tiny Parker, a Miami native, to serve as umpire. Parker was particularly animated in calling balls and strikes. For those who could comprehend the attraction, there was a lot to enjoy. The game was played for just seven innings rather than the usual nine, and it was deadlocked 5–5 going into the final inning. Les "Rabbit" McNeece came to the plate and smacked a ball past the outfielders. With no fence to contain the hit, the fleet-footed infielder (hence the moniker "Rabbit") flew around the bases for an inside-the-park home run. The four-bagger gave the World Amateurs a 6–5 win. "The German crowd was not quite sure what had happened," McNeece told Fort Lauderdale, Florida's *Sunshine Magazine* in 1994. "But they knew it was something good, so they applauded."

After the contest, Dr. Carl Diem, the secretary of the German Organizing Committee, descended to the field to congratulate the players. "I have come officially to advise you that this has been the finest demonstration of any sport that any nation has ever put on at any Olympic Games," Diem said. "We congratulate you and speaking for my people, you have made over 100,000 friends here tonight and as you go home America's baseball players' praises will be sung by all." Considering such lofty praise, one might expect that baseball made huge progress among the German people following the 1936 Olympics. In fact, the game in Germany did enjoy a bit of a spike following the games. Teams emerged around Berlin after the Olympics and even some play in the southern Germany, according to former German baseball federation president Martin Miller. In Miller's hometown of Ingolstadt, which is located in central Bavaria along the banks of Danube, the mayor told Miller in the 1980s that he'd played baseball as a child before the war.

When World War II began, sports were no longer seriously pursued. In particular, baseball was shelved in Germany. Like communist regimes during the Cold War, the Nazis perceived baseball as an American sport. With the United States entry into the war on the side of the Allies in 1941, America's national pastime was not welcomed under the Nazi regime.

That didn't mean that baseball was not played on German soil. Most movie fans will recall the iconographic scene in *The Great Escape* with Steve McQueen playing with a ball and glove while in solitary confinement. In fact, a lot of baseball was played under Nazi captivity by American GIs. In reality about 90 percent of the "baseball" in POW camps was what we'd call softball. Still, while a softball might have been used, it was baseball in spirit, according to Tim Wolter, author of *POW Baseball in World War II*. "[T]he majority of play [is] not what we recognize as hardball," Wolter wrote in his book. "But I think that is an unfairly narrow viewpoint. Players made do with what they had and modified the rules to fit the circumstances. The limited amount of open space within the camps often dictated use of a softer ball, as there were some understandable difficulties retrieving balls hit 'out of the park.'"[11]

Americans were first captured and sent to the infamous stalags in the early days of 1943. By the end of the war an estimated 90,000 Americans served as POWs. The conditions were difficult, but sporting equipment — even baseball equipment — was available to these GIs. The YMCA was vigilant in collecting gear to send to U.S. soldiers behind barbed wire. In a letter sent to returning POWs in 1945, the YMCA, according to Wolter, said it distributed more than 1.7 million "sports articles."

Nearly every camp housing Americans within Germany's borders had some sort of baseball or softball on its grounds. At Stalag Luft I, which was located near Barth, Germany on the Baltic Sea, a number of leagues were running by 1944. An indication of just how far from home these players were: betting was prevalent on the games — a baseball no-no back in the States. At Stalag Luft III,[12] which was the model for the movie *The Great Escape*, upward of 200 teams were playing at its baseball peak in the summer of 1944. The baseball was so serious that there was tremendous competition between teams for new prisoners with extensive baseball experience. "The competition for good players was intense, and inducements did change hands," Wolter wrote. As one prisoner paper said: "Block 56 is in the market for a couple of .400 hitters. There's chocolate in it, boys!" Talented baseball players could definitely be found throughout these camps. For example, Mickey Grasso played ball at Stalag IIIB near Furstenberg, Germany, which was about 60 miles southeast of Berlin. Grasso served as a sergeant in North Africa before being captured. He had been a minor-league catcher before the war and was a star in Stalag IIIB. Despite dropping 60 pounds during his time in the Stalag, he returned to baseball once the hostilities ended. Following the war, Grasso would play parts of seven seasons in the major leagues, mostly for the Washington Senators. In all, he logged 322 games as a big-league catcher.

As the war came to an end in 1945, baseball players in Allied-occupied Germany were now playing outside POW camps. Some of the sport's top players — still serving as part of U.S. ground forces — excelled in German-based U.S. military competitions. Among the notables was the great pitcher Warren Spahn. The Hall-of-Fame lefthander, who had made a brief appearance in the big leagues before joining the army in December 1942, rose to the rank of second lieutenant as a member of the 276th Engineer Combat Battalion and 1159th Engineer Combat Group. Although he was wounded in the Battle of the Bulge, it did not affect his playing career, which would last 20 seasons after the war and include thirteen 20-win campaigns. But before he returned home, he had a brief period of baseball domination in Germany. Following the Nazi surrender in May 1945, Spahn represented the 115th Engineers Group in a series of games at the University of Heidelberg, which is located in southeast Germany between Stuttgart and Frankfurt. In a four-game stretch, Spahn allowed just one run and nine hits while striking out a jaw-dropping 73 batters.[13]

Right-handed pitcher Ewell Blackwell was another major leaguer who competed with much distinction in Germany. After the war, Blackwell was a six-time All-Star and the 1947 runner-up for the National League Most Valuable Player award while playing for the Cincinnati Reds. At the 1945 Third Army Championship Series in Augsburg, Germany, he almost single-handedly led his team, the Seventy-First Division Red Circlers, to a three-games-to-two-games triumph.[14] In game two of the series, Blackwell fired a no-hitter in a 7–0 win. Then, in the deciding fifth game, the California native twirled a two-hitter as his team was victorious 5–0. A week later, Blackwell was back toeing the rubber at the U.S. Ground Forces Army Championships played in Mannheim and Nuremberg. The Seventy-First Division Red Circlers swept, so Blackwell only threw once, winning the opener. But Blackwell's remarkable run would come to an end at the European Theater Operations (ETO) Championships, which were played in Nuremburg and Rheins, France, from 30 August to 8 September. Blackwell lost two 2–1 contests to the OISE All-Stars.[15] Not surprisingly, OISE had a big-time player of its own: Leon Day. A pitcher who was a star in the Negro Leagues both before and after the war, Day could also play the infield and the outfield and was inducted to the Baseball Hall of Fame in 1995. A half-century before his enshrinement he pitched and hit his team to the win in game two of the series, collecting the victory and delivering four hits.

Within a brief time after those championships, all these major leaguers returned home. It's doubtful that their experiences had much of an impact on the local Germans. The military games at that point were, for the most part, played for other military personnel. Said Erik Petersen, a first lieutenant from Fontana, Wisconsin, in *Stars and Stripes*, the military newspaper: "Baseball was a lifesaver for our troops. It was a real morale booster, and a strong reminder of baseball home traditions."

Still, baseball, through the American military personnel who remained in Germany in the years of occupation following the war, would have a more lasting impact. In a surprisingly eloquent passage for a military document, U.S. officials described just how important sports like baseball were going to be in reconstructing Germany:

In the spring of 1945 the American troops taking up occupation duty in the defeated Third Reich found ruins and rubble where once splendid cities had stood. As the long columns of troops threaded their way through the ruins, they were watched with sullen or frightened curiosity by the crowds of weary and hungry civilians in the shattered cities. To the average soldier these shabby crowds were one with the mounds of rubble. At first he was indifferent to both, having seen too much of the destruction of war and too many frightened people crowding the roads over which he had fought. Then, the small children who frequently clustered about the soldiers during halts in towns and villages caught the soldier's attention and often his sympathy.... Broken and hesitatingly shy efforts at conversation and games soon followed the handouts of candy and food. From such spontaneous beginnings developed the first concerted actions by which American military personnel befriended German youth. Probably without realizing it, let alone without being trained or prepared for it, these men were dealing with one of the many formidable social problems emerging from the chaos of war.[16]

From those beginnings, the Supreme Headquarters Allied Expeditionary Forces (SHAEF) started devising programs that could help transition both Germany's war-torn youth back into a peaceful environment and also inculcate them with democratic ideals. The main program was generally known as the German Youth Activities (GYA) program. Through local committees, the U.S. military built recreational buildings and secured equipment for German children. Activities were organized by religious and trade groups, and sporting organizations. Strangely, the first structured effort by occupying U.S. forces to teach sports did not include the instruction of baseball. In the summer of 1946 at the Theater Athletic School in Stuttgart, 350 young Germans, along with military personnel, were given instruction in "coaching methods, game demonstrations, and opportunities to participate actively in athletic contests." Baseball was not included at the event, but softball, along with tennis, received the greatest interest from Germans at the camp.

Nevertheless, baseball quickly became an important element to the German Youth Activities program. In April 1949, Lt. Col. Robert C. Hall, who was the chief of the GYA, recalled that in the first three years of the program, baseball was one of the sports that the military especially stressed, in part, because the sport "help[ed] mould German minds along democratic lines."[17] Beyond

Baseball was a key part of Germany's rebuilding process following World War II. With the help of the German Youth Activities program, many kids played the game. (Above: Berlin's Babe Ruth Club, which won the 1947 GYA championship)

the formal efforts, the military also encouraged spontaneous baseball education by U.S. GIs. "Of all the high policy and low policy directives that have
been handed out lately, the suggestion that American soldiers—in their own
free time—begin to teach German boys the fundamentals of the American
national game has met with the greatest response," Edwin Hartrich of the *New
York Herald Tribune* wrote in 1946.[18]

Indeed, baseball did flourish in a number of German areas thanks to the
efforts of regular soldiers. One of the most successful baseball endeavors in the
immediate postwar period was the Babe Ruth Club based in Berlin. Run by Sgt.
Charles F. Buss, the team was organized in 1946. The following year they won
the USAFE's all–U.S. Zone championship and by 1948 they went 14–3 against
squads of U.S. military personnel, which was startling since the Babe Ruth Club
was composed of German kids ages 14 to 16. The club is an interesting study
in the effort to meld American ideals with ingrained German characteristics.
Some elements of "being German" were complementary to success on the baseball field, according to journalist Caroline Camp Leiser, who wrote a feature
article on the club in May 1949.[19] Despite many of them having jobs, the
teenagers diligently practiced ten to fifteen hours a week and took a "scientific
approach" to the game, learning all the details of a rule book provided by the
coach. But other local cultural elements created problems. "For instance, the
old German custom of handshaking was seriously delaying the beginning of
each practice," wrote Leiser. This, apparently, represented what the coach
thought was unacceptable German tradition. "He objected because it was symp-
tomatic of the boys' attitude toward him. He was on a pedestal of authority.
His decisions couldn't be questioned and he couldn't be joked with because he
was a superior.... The sergeant finally had to explain that all this formality just
wasn't necessary."

Coach Buss did make efforts to respect some German traditions. When
the team had a dance, he instructed the small band to play Viennese waltzes
and low fox-trots rather than popular American tunes. But the underlying effort
to sell American ideals was always present. "Because their coach feels that an
ingrained familiarity with democratic procedures is even more important than
baseball, the boys vote on every club issue that comes up, no matter how triv-
ial," wrote Leiser, who recounted how the boys voted on minute elements for
setting up the team dance.

The Berlin team was not alone in its development. Germany was parti-
tioned after the war with sectors under Soviet, British, French and American
control. The United States had a portion of Berlin, a small enclave in the north
around Bremen, and a large swath of territory to the south in Bavaria. The
children of Bremen showed some interest in baseball, as a 1948 roll of youth
organizations in the city showed 57 youngsters playing the sport. But the
greatest groundswell for the game came in the South around such cities as
Mannheim, Ramstein, Stuttgart, Nuremberg and Munich.

Mannheim, with its robust industrial area and particularly large American contingent, became a key home for the development of German baseball talent after the war. From this area came three players who would play a large role in German baseball history both on and off the field: Claus Helmig, Norbert Jaeger and Roland Hoffmann. All three were longtime members of the German national team and would be involved in leadership roles in German baseball development. In the late 1940s, Hoffmann and other kids would go to Mannheim's stadium to watch an American team called the Heidelberg Tornados play. "This is where we got the broken bats and baseballs to play," Hoffmann recalled in 2007.[20] He added that formal American youth activities were also very generous in providing equipment.

While baseball was growing, it was limited by geography and opportunity. Clearly, in the non–U.S. zones of the country, there was no baseball and, where U.S. soldiers were not playing the game, the sport did not put down roots. Nevertheless, the sport had developed enough of an administrative apparatus that in 1953 West Germany, which due to the Cold War split became a separate entity in 1949, was one of the five founding countries of the European Baseball Federation. The generation of young Germans who began playing the game just after the war was now running the show, according to Hoffmann. Claus Helmig was the national team's first coach. He was also one of Germany's and Europe's top players. Helmig and his brother Jürgen would sign professional contracts with the Baltimore Orioles and play briefly at the Class D minor league level — Claus for the Paris (Texas) Orioles in the Sooner State League and Jürgen for the Thomson (Georgia) Orioles in Georgia State League.[21]

Underscoring their place in European history, at the opening game of the inaugural European Championships in 1954, Claus Helmig was Germany's starting pitcher and Jürgen was at first base against Spain. In 1978, longtime European baseball official and historian Roger Panaye wrote about the brothers: "These players are still active in the German national team today and we think this is a ... record that has not been equaled in Europe."

In these early days, led by the Helmig brothers, Jaeger and Hoffmann, West Germany showed promise on the field against its European counterparts. At the 1955 European Baseball Championships in Barcelona, West Germany earned the bronze medal and even beat powerhouse Italy 5–4 at the event. This ability should have come as no surprise, as the German players spent more time during this period playing seasoned American GI teams than competing against other Germans. "There was no league," said Hoffmann about German baseball in the 1950s. "When we played a German championship, we'd play a few teams because the traveling was so far away. There would be a couple of games against Munich and Frankfurt. But we played almost every week against [U.S.] Army and Air Force teams."

Two years after the national team's strong showing in Barcelona, West Germany hosted the European Championships in Mannheim. Hardcore interest by those who played the game in Germany did exist, but others didn't appear as interested at the 1957 championships. "The European baseball championships currently under way here have failed to arouse interest in the game among sports-loving Germans," the *Washington Post* reported on 13 July 1957. "Championship matches between national teams from the Netherlands, Belgium, Italy, Spain and West Germany are played before empty stands with practically only the non-playing teams watching."

Attendance was only one of a handful of problems the Germans endured at the '57 championships. "The players were lodged in military barracks and the weather was so hot that it was impossible to sleep under these conditions," Panaye wrote. "The first game, Holland [versus] Italy, had to be stopped and replayed because the organizers had not appointed an official scorer and spotty transportation to and from the field had games starting hours late."[22]

Even worse, the German players became embroiled in an embarrassing on-field situation. On the second day of the event, German players "attacked" a Belgian umpire in their game against Holland, according Panaye. Helmig would defend the outburst years later: "The umpire was from Belgium, and he was drinking beer. He made some of the calls for his umpire brother, terrible

Fans flocked to the 2001 Euros in Bonn (pictured above), Cologne and Solingen. Crowds like this would have been hard to come by in the early days of German baseball. At the 1957 European Baseball Championships in Mannheim, spectator attendance was sparse.

calls. Then it was about the sixth inning, and we couldn't stand it anymore, you know. We charged him, and had some kind of melee, you know. A few of our guys got thrown out, and we lost the game."[23]

Nevertheless, the action was enough for the European federation. They decided to take the organization from the German Federation and a special commission was appointed to handle the tournament. "The German trouble-makers were suspended and two American umpires were added to the European staff," Panaye wrote.

If leadership appeared to be an issue, it seems that Americans were there to help fill the void. Unfortunately, according to some observers, this American influence actually hurt the growth of German baseball by the 1960s. "The problem with the Americans is that one of two things would happen," former German federation president Miller said. "Either teams would be all Americans or some Americans would set up a team and then depart leaving no Americans." In the 1960s, the German–American League was formed and numerous professional baseball players—many of whom were on duty during the height of the Cold War—were playing in West Germany. For example, in Garmisch and Partenkirchen, West Germany, in 1961, four major leaguers—including the Detroit Tigers' Jim Bunning, who would go on to the Hall of Fame—served as instructors at the U.S. Air Force European baseball school.

It would have been hard to avoid the American military influence at this time if for no other reason than that they were a key resource for facilities. In 1969, West Germany hosted the European Baseball Championships again — this time in Wiesbaden — and the competition was played at the U.S. Lindsey Air Station. The Americans even played an exhibition game as part of the event. At the very least, the American influence must have had some positive influence on the development of elite players in Germany because along with its medal-winning performance in 1955, West Germany made the podium at the Euros again in 1957 (silver), 1958 (bronze), 1965 (bronze), 1967 (bronze) and 1972 (bronze). The success was somewhat limited since against stronger competition Germany didn't perform as well. In 1971, the national team traveled to Managua, Nicaragua to compete in the World Cup and went a disappointing 0–15.

Basically, the best players were still getting good competition thanks to the Americans, but efforts to increase domestic grassroots growth wasn't taking place. A German championship title was first bestowed in 1951 but between 1969 and 1981 there wasn't a single national champion crowned. There was baseball — but it was conducted through the U.S. military bases. In fact, by 1979, there was only one German club — the Mannheim Tornados— playing the sport. Miller blames the decay of baseball during this period on an old guard that in many instances didn't lay the groundwork for the next generation of domestic baseball players. "Many of the players who learned the game right after the war didn't really teach their sons how to play," he says. In 1980, an effort to rectify a decade of decay began. Throughout the postwar years, the German baseball community never registered their sport as an official organization with German authorities. While it had minimal substantive impact, the official registration of the Deutscher Baseball und Softball Verband (DBV) as the governing body for the sport did symbolize the beginning of a dedicated effort to truly develop baseball in the country.

In the mid–1980s baseball began showing signs of life, in large part because of a subtle cultural shift in West Germany. Student exchanges had always been a popular vehicle for young Germans to see the world. In the past, the United Kingdom had been the preferable stop for those looking to spend time in an English-speaking country. But flight prices became less expensive in the mid–1980s and more and more Germany students were choosing to go on exchanges in the United States. As a result, more German teens were returning home after time in America with interest in and knowledge of baseball. While these new players had developed a love for the game, they also wanted to have more control.

The tension from the American influence peaked in 1989. Former national team members and Mannheim teammates Norbert Jaeger and Claus Helmig were on opposite sides of the American debate. In the early 1980s, Helmig developed a 10-team league from the U.S. Army bases with each team being required to play only two Germans in every game. "Claus thought this was the best way to promote baseball in Germany ... he argued that the quality of baseball would be too low [otherwise]" wrote Jeff Archer in his book about European baseball, *Strike Four*. On the other hand, Jaeger was looking to offer more opportunity for German players. This tension boiled over in 1989 when Jaeger's Mannheim Tornados and Helmig's Mannheim Amigos had an on-field fight that was so intense that the police became involved. It's unclear who won the fight on the diamond, but the contingent arguing for limiting American baseball involvement won off the field. Helmig and his German-American baseball league were banned from German baseball. Helmig, who had served as vice president of the European Baseball Federation, appealed to the continental body, but that organization said it was a German issue. Nevertheless, Europe's governing body stepped into the fray in 1990. In August 1990, the confederation wrote a reminder that Helmig was suspended from European baseball and that a $1,000 fine would be levied against any clubs that competed against his team.

The conflict was eventually mediated and Helmig was elected to the DBV's Hall of Fame in 2006. But the course of German baseball had been altered. "They didn't understand how negative the involvement of the Americans [was]," said Miller, who became president of the DBV after the Mannheim altercation. For the next decade, German baseball would make a slow but steady ascent in the baseball world. Miller's strategy was to build membership before anything else. From less than 2,000 players in 1989, German baseball now has nearly 30,000 people playing the game. In addition, the country boasts numerous top facilities. The stadium in Regensburg is breathtaking, with a sunken diamond, pristine grass and perfectly manicured clay infield. Just off the first-base line is a series of batting tunnels that holds its own with any baseball facility in Europe — including those in the Netherlands and Italy. Elsewhere, the college town of Paderborn boasts a nice facility as does Bonn, Solingen and Cologne, among other locales. The country's top circuit, the Bundesliga, sits at a level of competitiveness and management just below Holland and Italy. In direct contrast to the German–American League which made accommodation for only two Germans on the field at any time, the Bundesliga allows teams to carry a very limited number of non–Europeans on their rosters — and most of

German baseball has had a lot of celebration in recent years (seen here: the 2005 European Championships). The country has the highest participation of any on the continent, its facilities are respectable and its national team qualified for baseball's 2007 and 2009 World Cup. (Courtesy CEB.)

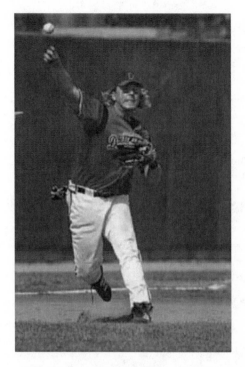

those players have either U.S. professional experience or an extensive college baseball background.

The commitment to German players continues at the national team level. In the increasingly competitive world of European baseball, a number of countries have worked hard to recruit players with dual nationality who learned their baseball outside of Europe. Germany has taken a different route. In 1999, the German brain trust decided that half the members on their junior national team that year would be members of the senior squad by 2001 when Germany was set to host the European Championships. True to their word, the squad not only included those juniors but is also one of the few throughout Europe that is essentially made up of exclusively born-and-bred native players.

Claus and Jürgen Helmig were the first Germans to play professional baseball in the United States, signing with the Baltimore Orioles in the 1950s. In recent years, many of their countrymen have also received minor league opportunities. Mitch Franke (above) started the contemporary trend, earning a contract with the Milwaukee Brewers in 2000. (Photograph by Ezio Ratti/FIBS.)

There have been hiccups to this approach. Most notably, Germany was relegated from the top level of European baseball in 2003. But they won a second-tier qualifying tournament in 2004 and returned in 2005 to their greatest international glory in decades. The team placed fourth in the tournament and qualified for the World Cup. Indicating its staying power, Germany placed fourth again in 2007, qualifying them for a second straight appearance at the Worlds.

Equally important, the country is developing major-league prospects. In 2000, Mitch Franke became the first player from the baseball Bundesliga to sign an American professional contract. The Milwaukee Brewers inked him as a bit of a project and although Franke did not progress far in the organization, he opened the doors for other Germans. He was followed by right-handed pitcher Tim Henkenjohann, who played parts of three seasons in the Minnesota Twins organization (2002–2003, 2005), and catcher Simon Gühring, who spent two campaigns (2002 and 2003) in the minors with the Brewers. Since then, the big leagues have continued to mine Germany for talent. In 2007, for example, seven members of Major League Baseball's European Baseball Academy were signed to minor-league contracts and three of those players were German — the largest contingent from any single country on the continent.

Despite the progress, some believe that German baseball culture still has room to grow. Andy Johnson, an American who played college baseball at Hamline University in Minnesota and has competed in both the Swedish and German domestic leagues, believes that the German players need to be less literal in their approach to the game.

"I would say there is a German approach but in many ways German baseball is struggling to find its identity," he says. "Compared to Japanese baseball, which seems to have its own unique culture, German baseball battles itself in search of a culture distinct from American baseball. They tend to be technical, seemingly believing that by raising their elbow or widening their feet it will result in a hit (point being, if I do it right, success will follow) versus the American approach which has a strong focus on mechanics but emphasizes what works as being more important regardless of the technique."[24]

This search for identity is something organizers recognize on a macro level. "The idea is not to have Germans identify baseball as American," said George Pascal, a sports-marketing executive who has worked on selling baseball in German. "It's Baseball Germany! [Like] Baseball Japan, [Germans must] have their own brand of the game."[25]

Adjustments on the field will come with time, but identifying the need for a unique style of baseball by those charting the sport's future in Germany is a positive sign. It suggests that promoters are committed to making the game a sturdy fixture on the country's sporting landscape and may lead to a day in the not too distant future when Germans are teaching Americans a thing or two about baseball.

7

Russia (and the Soviet Union)

For some baseball fans, the first thought that comes to mind when the words "Russian baseball" are uttered is a 1992 television movie called *The Comrades of Summer,* which starred Joe Mantegna as a fading ballplayer trying to teach the Soviets baseball in the waning days of the communist empire.[1] In the vein of *The Bad News Bears,* hapless-baseball-players-improving-enough-to-compete-with-the-big-boys genre, the Soviet team ultimately proved its worth against major-league teams. While today's democratized Russia may not be a world baseball power, *The Comrades of Summer* didn't fully give the real Russians their due. In more than a quarter-century of dedicated baseball playing, the country (and the Soviet Union before it) has sent a number of players to the minor leagues and has posted some solid performances against countries with far greater histories in the game.

Yet, even before the communists embraced baseball in the 1980s, there was a time when Russia actually controlled baseball. Well, to be wholly accurate, they controlled baseballs. In the years preceding the 1917 Russian Revolution, the country, led by Czar Nicholas II, was heavily invested in exporting horsehides. To be exact, the Tartar horse, a breed indigenous to Russia and reared for its hide, was essential in the manufacture of baseballs—including those used by American professional leagues. In fact, all top-end balls selling then for more than 23 cents used the Tartar hide.

"The Russian product is much stronger than the skins grown on any other kind of horse," the *Washington Post* reported on 11 June 1911. "It can furthermore be shaved very thin and still have the strength, durability and toughness required for the abuse a ball cover receives in a good lively batting game ... no hides have proved so satisfactory for this particular purpose as that of the Tartar pony grown in Russia."

Four years later, the importance of the Russian hides was used more as a political hot potato than a baseball when discussing the future relations between America and the czarist power. At a speech in New York in 1915, Curtis Guild, the former U.S. ambassador to Russia, argued to the American Manufacturers' Export Association that trade relations between Russia and the United States had to be further fostered with such instrumentalities as a Russian-American bank. One of his key reasons, according to a 14 March 1915 issue of the *Washington Post*: "If trade with Russia is not continued there will be no more baseball." Whether Guild's warnings led to a warming between the two nations is unknown, but it's likely that Americans began going elsewhere after the unrest created by the Russian Revolution and the subsequent communist approach to business with the West.

Baseballs aside, this era did produce at least one effort to export the sport itself back to Russia. Glenn Adams, a Chicago native, traveled to the Siberian city of Irkutsk in 1917 as a YMCA secretary for the area. One of his big goals was to establish baseball. The game was so foreign to the locals that Adams had to come up with alternative phrases for common baseball lingo. The catcher was renamed "one who receives"; the batter was "one who strikes"; and fielders, oddly, were "the reserves," with the shortstop being "the chief reserve," according to a 6 April 1947 *Chicago Tribune* article. The only problem for Adams was coming up with a word for an error. He'd already used the term "mistake" for a foul ball, leaving him with little room to maneuver. In the end, the quality of play, which was very low, made the point moot. "We had nothing else but [errors]," Adams told the *Tribune*. As a result, the term was omitted from the lexicon.

Adams might have been remembered as the Johnny Appleseed of Russian baseball if not for the fact that a bloody revolution was unfolding before him. He ultimately spent much of his time in Russia helping refugee children flooding into Irkutsk before the Red Army's advances. At one point he lived on a train for four days while the Red and White armies battled over control of a train depot. Adams left Russia after that harrowing experience and eventually completed a 40-year career with the YMCA back in his native Illinois.

While Adams saw firsthand the horrors of the revolution, some American publications were suggesting baseball as a tongue-in-cheek cure to Bolshevism during the first years of the communist reign. Under the heading of "Baseball and Politics," the 8 May 1919 edition of *Life* magazine argued that "[a]bsolutism and baseball do not go together.... Baseball seems a natural product of successful democracy." The article continued to say that "[t]he basic idea of Bolshevism is that every man shall be his own umpire, or at least that each side shall umpire for itself. Baseball could no more exist on Bolshevist principles than representative government can. The author's conclusion: "When Russia develops baseball it will mean that Bolshevism is done for."

Life wasn't correct in its prediction because for a brief time in the 1930s, it appears that baseball was going to take off in Soviet Russia. In the spring of 1933, American workers living in Moscow, Leningrad (now St. Petersburg) and Petrozavodsk organized games. A team dubbed the Moscow Anglo-Americans drew 25,000 spectators to an exhibition game at the city's famed Dynamo Stadium, according to the *Moscow News*.[2] The next year, baseball classes were opened at Moscow's Physiculture Institute.[3] The game was being taught by Americans and a Russian who learned to play in Japan. The Soviet's Supreme Council of Physical Culture even reported extensive baseball growth with teams springing up in Petrozavodsk, Kondopoga, Leningrad, Gorki and Erevan. Inter-city competition began on 6 June 1934 with the Moscow Foreign Worker's Club beating the Gorki Auto Plant 16–5 in an all–American tilt at Dynamo Stadium. Along with the company teams, the U.S. ambassador to the Soviet Union, William Bullitt, assembled squads from the U.S. diplomatic corps.[4] Maybe Bullitt, who was a close friend of Sigmund Freud and would also become an outspoken anticommunist, was trying to subtly push baseball on the Soviets. Whatever the case, the ambassador ordered equipment for four teams — there would be two made up of embassy staff and two others comprised of Americans in Russia. Bullitt, who was 43 in 1934, agreed to play for one of the teams. His greatest piece of diplomacy on the issue: he secured the use of a field from the Soviet government. The 1935 season was shaping up to be a big one. Uniforms were being made by the Central Sports Equipment Laboratory at the Institute of Physical Culture, and the Dynamo Sports Goods Factories in Moscow and Leningrad were producing other equipment. One Moscow team had a budget of 8,000 rubles and scheduled two out-of-town baseball trips. Even the Stalin Auto Plant in Moscow, which was one of the country's biggest factories, had plans to start a team.

Alas, the efforts of Bullitt and other Americans failed, as baseball seemed to be wiped off the Soviet sporting landscape faster than it took for it to become popular. What happened? In their article "Soviet Baseball: History and Prospects," Kim Steven Juhase and Blair A. Ruble suggested that the rise and fall of baseball in this era mirrored the prevailing politics of this turbulent time.[5] In November 1933, the United States recognized the Soviet Union. That fact plus the large number of Americans in the country at the time made baseball palatable to the communists' sporting culture. But Juhase and Ruble point out that "[a]fter 1935, Russia was engulfed in the turmoil of communist purges and show trials. Nazi Germany was preparing for war. The central authorities apparently saw no need to continue to support a foreign sport that did not directly contribute toward building a strong armed force as would parachute jumping, a frequently referred-to popular sport."

Whatever the reason, the result meant that baseball was done — at least

During most of the twentieth century, due to communist rule, the Soviet Union shunned baseball. Still, other bat-and-ball sports were allowed. In Estonia, for example, *pesapallo*, a Finnish offshoot of baseball, was a game accepted by Soviet leaders. Above: the cover of a 1965 *pesapallo* rulebook published in Tallinn, Estonia.

Russian-born Victor Starffin (above) was one of the greatest players in Japanese baseball history. He was elected to the country's baseball Hall of Fame in 1960.

officially — on Soviet soil. Still, it didn't mean that every Russian wasn't playing baseball. The unlikely story of Russian Victor Starffin illustrates that great baseball players can come from the most unlikely corners of the globe.

The son of an officer in Czar Nicholas II's army, Starffin was born in 1916 in Nizhnii Tagil, a small village in the Russian Urals. The year after Starffin's birth, the revolution forced his family to flee from its home. Their harrowing 3,000-mile journey to relative safety in Manchuria included being forced to travel in a train full of typhoid patients and hiding in a truck transporting corpses.[6] The family lived the Manchurian city of Harbin, which included a large Russian population, as they attempted to secure entry into Japan. Eventually, the family had to sell what little family keepsakes remained to raise the 1,500 yen necessary to immigrate. In 1925, they resettled in the northern Japanese city of Asahikawa, which boasted a large Russian expat community. Baseball was a growing Japanese sport at the time and Starffin, who was six feet tall by the age of 12 and showed tremendous natural athletic ability, was drafted to pitch for his school. He dominated and, according to writer Richard Puff, Starffin "became an idol throughout the island of Hokkaido."

Starffin's ability did more than just wow spectators — it also saved his father's life. In 1935, Constantin Starffin was accused of murdering a young Russian girl who worked at a local tea shop. Although his guilt never seemed to be fully confirmed, the older Starffin was jailed for eight years and his family seemed poised to be deported. They were saved by Starffin's pitching. Now six-foot-four, the robust righty reluctantly agreed to join the Japanese All-Star team (he was loyal to his local team). As a result, Constantin's sentence was reduced to two years, his mother was whisked away to Tokyo and the family was not deported.

In 1936, Japan established its first professional league and Starffin was one of its original and most enduring stars. As a member of the storied Tokyo

Kyojin (Giants), Starffin threw a no-hitter in his second season. His statistics from his 19-year professional career are downright gaudy: He was the first player in Japan to amass 300 victories; his lifetime ERA was 2.09; he still holds the record for most wins in a season 42 (in 1939); and he was a two-time league Most Valuable Player selection.

Despite so much success on the field, the Russian's personal life was a tragedy. Throughout World War II, Starffin was constantly suspected as a spy for the Soviet Union, which was now a mortal enemy of the Japanese. It became so bad that he changed his name to Hiroshi Suda. Despite his fame, he spent time in a detention camp and was bedridden with pleurisy. Even baseball was briefly taken away from him when the Giants stopped playing Starffin for fear, according to Puff, that a foreigner on the squad could give the government reason to ban baseball as "a sport of the enemy." The war years took their toll. Starffin could not keep his marriage together and the pitcher began drinking heavily. He eventually died in a car wreck less than two years after he retired from baseball. Starffin had been driving under the influence of alcohol. He was just 40 years old. Still, the Russian is remembered today in both his native Russia and his adopted country. A youth tournament in Moscow has been played between Russian and Japanese teams in his honor and the 25,000-seat municipal ballpark in his adopted Japanese home city of Asahkawa is called the Victor Starffin Stadium. Starffin is also enshrined in the Japanese Baseball Hall of Fame.

Starffin's success undoubtedly did little to soften the U.S.S.R.'s view of baseball, though fighting a war on the same side as the United States might have changed the baseball perspective of even the hardest man. By 1945, rumblings of Soviet baseball were beginning. An Associated Press story carried by the *New York Times* on 15 Oct. 1945 said: "Russia may take up soon many other games, such as baseball, which were not played here before the war." In September, Congressman Karl Mundt, a Republican from South Dakota, suggested that a yearly baseball matchup between the Soviet Union and the United States be scheduled. Following a victory by Russian chess players against a group of Americans, Rep. Mundt quipped, "If you learn to play baseball as well as chess, the American players better beware."[7] The following year a concrete plan to develop baseball in the Soviet Union was considered by the Army and Navy Union. The organization pondered a resolution to send enough equipment and uniforms to Russia to outfit 1,000 baseball teams. The declaration, which was presented at the organization's 58th national encampment in Milwaukee, stated: "The rulers of Russia are not to be confused with the people of Russia. We must treat the rulers with fairness and firmness, but we must treat the people as fellow human beings and friends."[8]

The Army and Navy Union likely never got too far with its plan as the Cold War's increasing chilliness in the 1950s made any such interaction with the Red Menace nearly a treasonable offense. With tensions growing, baseball's intentions and lineage became the battleground in the two countries' propaganda war. In 1952, a Soviet youth magazine described "beizbol" as a "bloody fight with mayhem and murder," the *New York Times* reported.[9] This must have caused some rancor because a Penn State University professor took it upon himself later that year to explain to the *New York Times* that such an opinion might have been isolated. William Edgerton, an assistant professor of Russian, wrote in the 22 September 1952 edition of the *Times* that baseball was officially described in the *Large Soviet Encyclopedia* as a sport that "demands great agility, speed and coordinated action among all members of the team. With highly developed technique the game becomes a genuinely athletic physical exercise. In the U.S.S.R. baseball is not very widespread."

The debate over baseball's image in Russia was exacerbated by questions of the sport's roots. Starting the 1950s — all the way to the waning days of the Soviet Empire — many communist publications insisted that baseball was a direct offshoot of the Russian game *lapta*, which is a bat-and-ball sport dating back to the fourteenth century.[10] In 1959, a Russian weekly magazine claimed that *lapta* was brought to the United States and Canada by Russian immigrants and that baseball came from it. In the official Soviet newspaper *Izvestia*, writer Sergei Shachin claimed in 1987 that *lapta* "was taken to America by the first Russian settlers, and has now returned to us in a different form and with a strange, foreign name."[11] The writer added: "It is just a shame that we allowed *lapta* to be undeservedly forgotten while baseball fans were aggressively promoting it."

Even the great Joe DiMaggio got involved in the *lapta*-baseball debate. In 1962, the retired New York Yankees slugger flew into Moscow during a European business trip. He insisted he wasn't in the U.S.S.R. to teach baseball, but did offer this wry comment about *lapta*: "According to what I read in the newspaper, they have claimed they invented it [baseball]. But I've never been able to find their names in our record books."[12]

These conflicts surely didn't help encourage a burgeoning of baseball in Russia. Until the late 1980s, very little effort was made to use baseball as a form of détente. On the unusual occasions that the sport did make an appearance it was not presented as America's pastime. In 1970, a Russian sports newspaper, *Soviet-Sky Sport*, made a rare reference to baseball — but it was described as a Cuban game, according to the 23 February edition of the *Chicago Tribune*. The article detailed how three Cuban student teams were going to play in the Ukrainian port city of Odessa. Cuba, fellow communist outpost and world amateur champion, had numerous students in the Soviet Union. These teams from Odessa would then play Cuban students in other cities. According to another source, Nicaraguans, Cubans and other Latin American students played pickup games in Moscow parks in the early 1980s.[13]

Despite all this, the Soviet attitude toward baseball took an abrupt 180-degree turn thanks to the Olympic movement. On 13 October 1986, the International Olympic Committee announced that baseball would join its official program. Likely in anticipation of that decision, the Soviet State Committee for Physical Culture announced eleven days earlier that it would make baseball an official Soviet sport. On 7 October, the first official Russian baseball game pitted athletes from Moscow State University against players from Patrice Lumumba Friendship University, a college that included numerous Latin American students. The game, which was played in the center of a horse-racing track at the edge of Moscow, featured mainly Nicaraguans and Panamanians against Cubans, according to a *Chicago Tribune* report the following August, and the play was apparently sloppy.[14] Nevertheless, it was a beginning, and baseball teams began popping up throughout the communist empire, from Moscow to Tashkent.

In August 1987, a Soviet baseball federation was founded, with Ramaz Goglidze, a member of the Georgian parliament, elected chairman. Goglidze, who set up the federation's offices in the Georgian capital of Tbilisi, certainly viewed baseball philosophically in the context of the U.S.S.R.'s changing relationship with the West. "Lenin said that we should take that which is best in other countries, and baseball is one of the best things you have," he told an American journalist. "Baseball should be one of the fruits of perestroika [restructuring], one more thing that our two countries can share."[15]

That year, a national team was culled from the best that domestic squads had to offer. As expected, athletes with skills seemingly fit for baseball were recruited. For example, javelin throwers and team handball players were scouted as potential pitchers. Without blinking an eye, the new Soviet national team took on a Nicaraguan touring squad. The results of the initial game were uglier than the first official game played a year before: the Soviets lost 22–0. Still, the country's propaganda machine was undeterred. "At least the Soviet team managed to prevent the guests from scoring runs in two innings," wrote the official news agency Tass.[16]

The vastness of the Soviet empire was illustrated by the first domestic tournament held in Moscow in the summer of 1987. Eight teams from across the country took part and as many as six languages were on display. "The Riga team argued in Latvian, the Tashkent in Uzbek, the Tallinn in Estonian and the Moscow team in Russian," recounted the *Washington Post* in its 6 July edition. The patchwork led not only to linguistic confusion but also a breakdown in basic rules. "One team plays by Japanese rules, another by Cuban, and a third by rules from God knows where," explained Slava Smogin, a Soviet student who was one of the event's organizers, to the *Post*.

Progress was slow but steady in the early years. At the second national tournament in 1988, Steve Wulf covered the event for *Sport Illustrated*. He wrote in his 25 July article: "What is surprising is that the Soviets play [baseball] so well so soon. The best Soviet teams are about as good as most American high school junior varsity teams." At this tournament, the influence of the world baseball

Beginning with javelin throwers and other athletes playing sports that required arm strength, the Soviet system developed a number of technically adept pitchers. This trend continued after the fall of the communist government. Nikolay Lobanov (above) shows good form while pitching for Russia in 2007. (Photograph by Ezio Ratti/FIBS.)

community was apparent. On the one hand, the top Moscow team — D.I. Mendeleyev Institute of Chemical Technology — was coached by American Richard Spooner, who would show his team videotapes of recent National League games. In contrast, a team from Kiev in the Ukraine was learning baseball, in part, from Cuban and Nicaraguan advisors. Regardless of the coaching, the players were still attempting to master some basic points of the game. Most notably, second baseman would hold runners on the base leaving a huge hole on the right side of the infield and cutoff men were not used from the outfield. Unwritten rules were also still to be learned. For example, according to Wulf, batters would writhe in pain when hit by a pitch, something more experience players would just shake off.

But Russian baseball has always taken the philosophy that the best way to improve is to face better competition. Domestic teams went abroad early on to seek higher levels of competition. Mendeleyev, for example, played in an international tournament in Prague in 1988 and also went to the United States to take on Johns Hopkins University. (They were swept in a series against Hopkins, losing by such lopsided scores as 16–0.) Another team, Tiraspol APF, traveled to the United States in 1991 to play games and receive instruction from teams in Florida, Indiana and Illinois. The national team did the same. In 1989, an 18-player Soviet National Team traveled to the United States and went 0–11 against such college opponents as George Washington University, the U.S. Naval Academy and the University of Maryland. The following year, they returned to America to play even higher competition at the Goodwill Games. The Games, which were created by Ted Turner during the tumult surrounding the U.S. boycott of the 1980 Olympic Moscow Games and the 1984 Soviet boycott of the Olympic Los Angeles Games, attracted teams from the elite echelons of baseball-playing countries. The Soviets finished the tournament 0–5, losing to Team USA 17–0, Japan 14–0, Puerto Rico 13–0 and Mexico twice, 9–1 and 14–4. Still, if a journalist's assessment of their play was any indication, the team was making progress. Wrote Debbie Becker in the 27 July 1990 edition of *USA Today*: "The Soviets ... compete at about the NCAA Division III level." This would be a huge improvement for the high school junior varsity description *Sports Illustrated*'s Steve Wulf gave just two years earlier.

Beyond their travels abroad, the Soviets were also able to convince a group of American pros to tour their country.[17] In late fall 1989, a select team of players from the Class AA Eastern League took a 17-day tour of the Soviet Union — dubbed the "Diamond Diplomacy" tour — in an effort to "help the Soviet grasp the rudiments of baseball," according to a 4 December article in the *Sporting News*. What was so remarkable to the touring American pros was the resilience of the Soviet players. "We beat the Soviet national team by 20 runs and they still wanted to play more. Whenever you show them anything, they get their notebooks out, write it down, and store it [in their heads]," said Troy Neel, who would go on to play three seasons in the major leagues for the Oakland A's. The trip was indicative of the increasing thaw in the Cold War at the time. The tour, which went to such Soviet Republics as Estonia and Ukraine, culminated in Moscow with a "unity dinner." The Soviets were given a trophy dubbed the A. Bartlett Giamatti Bowl, named after the Major League Baseball commissioner who had died earlier that year. It was intended to be the cup for the annual Soviet club champion.

In the context of European baseball, all this play against far better teams paid off for the U.S.S.R. In late summer 1989, the Soviets headed to Parma, Italy, to compete in a qualifying tournament for the European Baseball Championships. After playing against such future major leaguers as Aaron Sele, Scott Hatteberg, Paul Byrd and Darren Bragg at the Goodwill Games, taking on the likes of Germany, Switzerland, Poland, Czechoslovakia and Yugoslavia must have seemed elementary. The U.S.S.R. won the event, earning elevation to the top flight of European baseball. (The following year, the team, which would be the only one to represent the Soviet Union at Europe's highest level, would place sixth out of eight teams at the Euros in Italy.)

Unlike other European baseball countries, which may have some government support but must rely mainly on private benefactors, the Soviets received

In 1987, the Soviet Union squared off against Czechoslovakia at a soccer stadium in Tbilisi, Georgia. The contest's scoreboard (above), which was likely one of the first baseball scoreboards ever to use the Cyrillic alphabet, shows the CCCP (Soviet Union) losing to the CSSR (Czechoslovakia) 2–0. The word at the bottom of the digital display is "baseball" in Cyrillic. (Courtesy Jan Bagin.)

considerable state aid. For example the Red Army agreed to release any serviceman from military duty who volunteered to play for the national baseball team. National team players also received a weekly salary of 238 rubles ($368 in 1988), which, according to writers Juhase and Ruble, was more than the average Soviet worker might earn.

The sport also got private help. The biggest boost: Dr. Shigeyoshi Matsumae, the president of Tokai University in Japan, who along with other Tokai benefactors donated $3.2 million to build a 1,500-seat stadium that opened in Moscow in 1989. The park offered everything a team would want, including locker room and showers—although many purists would bristle at the fact that the playing surface is artificial turf. Amenities aside, Dr. Matsumae hoped that the field would serve a higher purpose. "He hoped international peace would come through the globalization of baseball," explained former Los Angeles Dodgers president Peter O'Malley, a friend of Dr. Matsumae who died in 1991.[18] The facility remains today the country's one and only true ballpark.[19]

Beyond the Moscow field, elements of baseball's growth also illustrated the country's increasing embrace of capitalism during the era of *glasnost.* When the U.S.S.R. National Baseball Team toured the United States in 1989, they were sponsored by Taco Bell. The fast-food company purchased uniforms for the squad (complete with "Taco Bell" patches) and the players made a number of publicity stops for the fast-food company during their tour.

Capitalism wasn't the only movement stirring baseball during the waning days of the Soviet empire — nationalism was also affecting the sport. According to Juhase and Ruble, two top pitchers from the Soviet Republic of Georgia left the team after a regional dispute. A Lithuanian player also quit the squad because "he refused to wear the national team uniform stating they would kill him in Lithuania if he wore it," wrote Juhase and Ruble.

On 8 December 1991, leaders of Russia, Ukraine and Belarus signed a declaration officially dissolving the Soviet Union. The end of the U.S.S.R. marked a diaspora of its fledgling national baseball team. A number of former republics established their own national team. Ukraine, which played in its seventh top-tier European Baseball Championships in 2007, has been the most successful.

Despite the break-up, Russian baseball continued. In 1992, the Russian League featured the emergence of the country's early super team: the Moscow Red Devils.[20] The squad, which was an outgrowth of the Mendeleyev College of Chemical Engineering team,[21] would win the first four Russian League crowns (1992–1995). In the first championship, the Red Devils defeated one of the country's oldest clubs, AFP Tiraspol.[22] Although the Muscovites won the best-of-five Russian Series 3–0, the three games were highly contested. In game one, the Red Devils broke a 4–4 tie in the top of the ninth with a two-out RBI single by the team's star infielder Yevgeny Puchkov to win 5–4. In game two, they won by scoring five runs in the top of the ninth to erase a 5–3 deficit and, in the final game, the Moscow team fell behind 5–1 through six innings, but scored eight in the seventh to earn the title.

The most telling sign of Russian baseball's development in the early 1990s — and the dominance of the Red Devils — are the adventures of Russian Series hero Puchkov, Rudolf Razhigaev and Ilya Bogatyrev. In 1992, the three players (two of whom, Puchkov and Bogatyrev, were Red Devils) signed with the California Angels. The signing bonus: $1,500 apiece. "I believe in ten years Russia will be producing major league players," a sanguine Bob Fontaine, director of Angels scouting, told the *Phoenix* (Arizona) *New Times* on 9 September 1992. The three Russians were typical in many ways of the elite Russian baseball players: they had come to the game late in life and they had shown success in other sports. Bogatyrev, for instance, had been a kayaking champion at Moscow State University before sustaining an injury which led him to take up baseball. Puchkov was formerly a promising tennis player at Moscow State and Razhigaev was a distance runner from Siberia who impressed coaches with his wiry six-foot, two-inch frame. All of the Russians — each of them in their early 20s — had played baseball for just a few years when they got the opportunity to play minor league ball for the Angels.

The trio was sent to the lowest rung of organized professional baseball — rookie ball in the Arizona League. In fact, the Angels had to get special permission to have three players in their twenties playing on the same time. (The rule at the time was only one player older than twenty per squad.) The move to the United States must have been the height of culture shock. To get themselves prepared for the experience, they studied a Russian-dubbed version of *Bull Durham*. Once in the United States, their teammates taught them a bit about golf (not a big Russia sport) and the value of the 7–11 convenience store's 44-ounce Big Gulp. That said, the players came with confidence.

"They got here with the attitude that they were going to be Big League players," Meza Angels manager Bill Lachemann, who coached the three Russians, told the *Los Angeles Times* in the paper's 23 August 1993 edition. Despite their promise — and success in Russia — the troika struggled in the Arizona sun. They lasted two seasons, with Puchkov and Razhigaev both getting looks at the Class-A level. The biggest stumbling block, according to Lachemann, was that they were taught baseball by the numbers. "All three of them were [very mechanical]," said Lachemann. "They learned a lot from watching videos, so they were trying to do things step by step. We've tried to get them to be more fluid." Following the 1993 campaign, the three players returned to Russia, causing some disgust by supporters of the Russian baseball movement.

Upon the players' return, some were highly disappointed with the chance the Russians had been given. John Lehr, an American who was heavily involved with Russian baseball in the 1990s, wrote a blistering critique of the Angels' actions. He claimed that two of the players and the Russian Baseball Federation were not properly notified of the releases and that the offer by the Angels to help develop baseball in Russia in a long-term, meaningful way was disingenuous. "Other nations should heed the warning of the Angels' conduct: beware of professional baseball scouts bearing bats and balls. They might be more modern-day colonialists than baseball ambassadors," Lehr wrote.[23]

Lehr's complaints were probably too harsh, as the experience did aid Russian baseball on a couple of fronts. The American adventure certainly helped those players develop. At the 1995 European Baseball Championships, Puchkov hit .500 and was named the tournament's outstanding third baseman. As late as 1997, Puchkov and Bogatyrev were both still playing in the Russian League. In limited play, Bogatyrev hit .483 and Puchkov batted .478.

The three players also opened the door for other Russians to compete in America's minor leagues. In 1995, catcher Andrei Selivanov played rookie ball for the Atlanta Braves' West Palm Beach team in Florida. Second baseman Alexander Nizov spent two years with Angels rookie affiliate the Butte (Montana) Copper Kings in 1997 and 1998. He hit .278 in limited action in his first campaign and .208 in his second year. On the positive side, the speedster Nizov stole five bases without being caught in 1998 and proved that the Angels had not abandoned Russia altogether.

More recently, Oleg Korneev represented the biggest prospect to sign with a major-league club when he inked a deal with the Seattle Mariners in 2001. Anyone who saw the six-foot-seven Korneev pitch that summer at the European Championships in Germany would recognize a true baseball talent. The son of a former star on the national team, Korneev threw a 90-mile-per-hour-plus fastball and had a nasty, biting curveball. In 2002, Korneev posted a pedestrian 4.50 ERA but struck out 12 batters in 12 innings for the Mariners' rookie team in the Arizona League. Unfortunately, injury derailed Korneev's career and, while he still played for the Russian national team in 2005, his hopes for big-league glory were behind him. No Russian-bred player has made it to the Major Leagues, although Victor Cole — who was born in Leningrad in 1968 but grew up in the United States— pitched 24 innings for the Pittsburgh Pirates in 1992. (He also threw for the Russian national team in a 2003 tour of the independent Northeast League.) In total, 11 players have signed professional minor league contracts to play in the United States between 1992 and 2007.

Beyond big-league aspirations, Russian baseball has been an impressive presence in the European baseball world during the past two decades. At the youth level, the Russians are near the top of the continent. Between 2001 and 2006, a Russian team comprised of 11- and 12-year-olds has qualified for the Little League World Series five times. In 2007, Russia's junior national team (under age 19) put forth an impressive performance at the European Junior Championships in the Netherlands. The team won the silver medal, losing to Italy in the finals by a narrow 4–2. At the club level, Tornados Balashika —featuring former pro Korneev — has battled it out in both the 2005 and 2006 European Baseball Cup, Europe's most prestigious club event.

As for the adult national team, which has always been a driving focus of the federation since its inception, the team has yet to reach its goals of winning a European title or qualifying for the Olympics. The squad's overall record in the European Championships is a subpar 23–45 through the 2007 championship. Still, the team did have one remarkable performance at the 2001 European Championships in Germany. The Russians won the silver medal, upsetting perennial powers Italy in the semi-finals 2–0 and Holland in the preliminary phase 4–3. Although they lost 4–0 in the finals to the Netherlands, the Russians became the first European team other than the Dutch or the Italians to finish first or second at the championships since 1967.

Why were the Russians able to break the Dutch-Italian stranglehold on the top spots of European baseball? The squad was talented, but they were not necessarily more adept as a number of other European countries. In fact, at the fateful 2001 Euros, the Russians lost to Spain, which placed sixth, and Great Britain, which finished tenth at the tournament. What is unique about the Russians is their level of confidence. You might even call it arrogance or cockiness.

Case in point: at the 1999 European Baseball Championships, I was catching for Great Britain in a tight game against the Russian team. It was the top of the ninth inning and the Russians were clinging to a 6–5 lead. As their first batter came to the plate, I figured I'd engage in a little small talk. I look up from my crouch and said, "Great game; it's really a close one." The Russian dug in his back foot and then looked back at me and replied: "It is close, but we will win." His team then proceeded to put five more runs on the board en route to an 11–5 triumph. Against Italy in the 2001 semifinals, they showed no nerves against a team that at the time had won more European Championships (eight) than the Russians had even participated in (six). Maybe all the trips abroad to compete against top international talent had paid off. After all, more fans likely showed up at each of the eight games against teams from the independent Northern League earlier that summer in the United States, than were at the Italy-Russia contest at the Euros.

The flipside of this approach is that the Russians can come out flat against teams they assume they'll beat. Focus appeared to be a problem in 2005 when the former hub of the Soviet empire placed dead last at the European Championships. While they fell in a highly contested one-run game to the Italians,

After a series of very credible performances in international play — highlighted by a silver medal result at the 2001 European Championships — Russia has endured a drop in performance. At the 2005 European Championships, the Russians placed last, and in 2007 the squad finished 10th out of 12. This included a loss to their rivals Ukraine (above) in 11 innings. (Photograph by Jason Holowaty.)

they also lost to the Ukraine and Greece — two countries that they should have beaten.

Despite this seeming attitude quirk, a hallmark of Russian baseball continues to be that Spartan work ethic that was emblematic of the Soviet sports machine. In 2005, Adam Souilliard, a Pittsburgh Pirates scout, traveled to Russia for a two-week tour and was wowed with the Russian approach to the game. "They're raw, talented kids who work their butts off for their coaches, and do exactly what their coaches say," Souilliard told the *Los Angeles Times* on 9 February.

Another plus is that a generation of Russians who grew up with the game are now adults. The likes of Oleg Korneev, who learned the sport from his dad Leonid, are now old enough to pass his knowledge down to a new generation. Dmitry Kiselyev can remember seeing his first baseball game as a child in the 1980s. In 2005, the 33-year-old was the president of the Russian baseball federation.

How badly baseball's loss of Olympic recognition will impact Russian baseball will be something to watch closely. At the 2005 European Championships, Russian officials seemed particularly sullen about the damage the International Olympic Committee had done. This makes sense, as state involvement with the sport was initially spurred by the thirst for Olympic glory. Following the IOC announcement, the country has struggled along, finishing last in the 2005 European Championship, and tenth (out of twelve) at the 2007 event.

Still, the Russians are resilient and their well of confidence will always assure one thing: they are an opponent that should never be taken lightly. In spite of the Olympic issue, the Russians barreled through the qualification tournament to regain their spot among Europe's elite. Despite being relegated again in 2007, they will surely bring bravado to any future qualifying event.

8

Sweden

To understand Swedish baseball requires an appreciation for a culture that emphasizes an active outdoor life. How else could you rationalize playing baseball 200 kilometers from the Artic Circle? Consider this: approximately half of Sweden's population ages seven to seventy are members of a sports club, with about 650,000 of the country's nine million residents engaging in competitive sports. Not only that, but more than two out of every three boys, ages seven to fifteen, belong to a sports club. All told there are some 22,000 sports clubs in towns and villages throughout Sweden. Quite simply, these Scandinavians love sports. So, while ice hockey reigns supreme — which is unsurprising in a country where very little light shines in the winter — even baseball benefits by this emphasis on athletics. In the summer months, the sun practically never sets on the game of baseball in Sweden.

An independent people, the Swedes originally took to baseball without the aid of Americans trying to export the game to them. Instead, locals were instrumental in the genesis of Swedish baseball at the dawn of the twentieth century. Initial reports of the sport in Sweden date back to 1904 in the southern town of Gothenburg, according to Swedish baseball federation president Mats Fransson. Six years later, baseball's first high-profile Swedish supporter would introduce the game in the north.

Born in 1870 on the Swedish island of Orust, Sigfrid Edström would become one of the most prominent Swedish sports figures of the first half of the twentieth century and a serious baseball supporter. A top-class sprinter at one time, Edström was instrumental in bringing the 1912 Olympics to Stockholm and would eventually become president of the powerful International Olympic Committee from 1942 to 1952. In addition to his sporting success,

Edström was a learned man. He attended the prestigious Chalmers Institute of Technology in Gothenburg and ultimately served as director of the prominent electrical engineering company ASEA from 1903 to 1933.[1] Augmenting his education at Chalmers, Edström spent time studying in both Switzerland and the United States. There's little doubt that his time in America instilled a deep affection for that country's national pastime because in 1910 he made a serious play for baseball. His launching ground for the game would be the home of his company ASEA — the town of Västerås, located about 100 kilometers from Stockholm. Edström helped set up a local team in Västerås and, according to one source, provided rules and equipment for games in the capital of Stockholm as well.[2]

By the time Stockholm was set to host the Olympics, Edström's baseball efforts had generated enough critical mass that he, along with other Swedish organizers, felt comfortable suggesting baseball as a great diversion during the Games. The obvious club to make it happen: Edström's Västerås team. Despite Edström's enthusiasm, his Västerås squad did not immediately jump at the

Sweden's first true baseball club (above) was based in the town Västerås, located about 100 kilometers from Stockholm. The team's central benefactor was Sigfrid Edström (number five in the photo). A former sprinter, Edström would not only support baseball but would also later serve as the president of the International Olympic Committee.

opportunity because they weren't sure they could compete. "As our club this year was in poor condition, on account of some of our best players being out on military duties, we hesitated at first, but then decided to risk it, knowing very well that whoever we would play against, they would not rub in to us too hard," wrote Västerås' Edwin Johnson just after the Olympics. "I knew, of course, that if the game could be played by two American teams, it would be a much better game than if our team took part, and told the Olympic Committee, and wanted to withdraw, but as they did not know for sure how it would be, told us to go ahead with arrangements just the same, and so we did, and by the time the [American Olympians] arrived, everything had been arranged for."[3]

The plan was to set up a game between Västerås and a U.S. squad on 10 July 1912 at the Ostermalm Athletic Grounds—site of the Games' equestrian events. Posters were printed advertising the baseball spectacular and even heralding a special guest. Future Hall-of-Famer George Wright, one of baseball's great early organizers and an excellent player in his own right, would be on hand to umpire the game. Unfortunately, when the Olympic athletes arrived, a change of plan was required. Concerned that baseball would distract the athletes from their primary events, the American Olympic Committee insisted that the game be shifted to 15 July. The move severely hurt the value of the contest as a demonstration. "Had the game been played as it was intended and advertised, on the 10th ... there would very likely have been a bigger crowd present, and the game would also have been more talked about in the papers, but ... we will have to be satisfied as it is," Johnson wrote.

As for the actual game, Johnson's fears about the disparity in talent between the Americans and the Swedish players would prove well-founded. Those representing the U.S. were top-notch athletes drafted from the country's track and field squad. In total, eight medalists from the Games of the Fifth Olympiad played in the Sweden baseball game for the Americans. The Swedes on the other hand had only experienced baseball for a couple of years and, with their ranks depleted, Västerås would need a little help to stay on the field with their American counterparts. To that end, the U.S. provided the Swedish club with a pitcher and a catcher from their squad. Wesley Oler, a high jumper from Yale University, was drafted to catch and Ben Adams, who had won a bronze a week earlier in the standing long jump, agreed to pitch for the Swedes.

No fools, the Swedes immediately installed Oler and Adams at the top of their lineup. But even with the addition, it would be a tough match for Västerås. The Americans were led by Abel Kiviat, who was the great Jim Thorpe's roommate on the voyage to Stockholm. Kiviat was a seasoned baseball player, having been an all-city baseball player in New York for Staten Island's Curtis High School. He would win a silver medal at the Stockholm games and play shortstop and bat third in the Västerås match-up. Other medal winners playing were Fred Kelly (gold medal in the 110 meter hurdles), George Bonhag (gold in the

3,000-meter relay), Richard Byrd (silver in the discus), Ira Davenport (bronze in the 800 meters), George Horine (bronze in the high jump) and Lawrence Whitney (bronze in the shot put).

The result of the six-inning game was never in doubt. The United States scored four in the first and another run in the second. The Swedish team did cut the lead to 5–2 in the fourth with two runs, but an eight-run American burst in the fifth ended any hopes. The final score: 13–3. The American pitching appeared to have overpowered their opponents. Västerås players struck out 10 times in the game. In addition, the Swedes were shaky on defense. The official Olympic Games report pointed out that the Swedes made five errors along with some other mistakes that were "excusable on account of nervousness, etc."[4] Nevertheless, the official report concluded that Västerås "did not at all make such a bad figure in the field."

One notable name missing from the roster was Thorpe himself. Undoubtedly, the best baseball player on the trip, Thorpe would go on to play parts of six seasons in the big leagues and would even return to Europe as part of a tour of professionals just two years later. But he was unable to compete against Västerås because the game conflicted with the final day of the decathlon — a discipline in which he would earn a gold medal in Stockholm.[5] Still, the indomitable Thorpe would enjoy a little baseball on Swedish soil the following day in an all–U.S. exhibition. Playing right field and batting ninth, he would connect for one hit in two at bats. It's quite possible that Thorpe's involvement gave the type of marquee figure necessary to get attention for baseball because — while the Sweden–United States game reportedly had "no great crowd of spectators, and those that were present were mostly Americans or Swedish Americans" — the all–American match "was a novelty to the Swedes, and a large crowd was present."[6]

No matter, the Västerås club was enthused by the baseball experience. In the run-up to the Olympics, the club translated a copy of Spalding's rules of baseball and distributed a few advanced copies at the Games. Following the event, the books were distributed by the firm Bjork & Boyeson and were made available in bookstores throughout Sweden, according to the club's organizer Johnson. They must have also been optimistic about how much the game would catch on because they even unofficially elected the future King Gustav VI (at the time he was a prince) as patron of Swedish baseball.[7] It's unclear whether the monarch took this post seriously (or was even aware of it).

Västerås continued to practice twice a week throughout the summer of 1912, and on August 24 gave an intra-squad exhibition wearing the uniforms made for the Olympic Games. Johnson was sanguine about the future. "Next year we intend to have our teams appear in the nearby cities around here, so as to give people a chance to see the game, and it will not be long before they will start it in Stockholm, so I think the game is bound to be popular here," he wrote.

The club endured over the next half decade. A photo in Spalding's 1917 baseball guide shows the Västerås club with ten players in uniform and a host of other finely dressed gentlemen, including Edström, the tallest man in the picture, standing solemnly in the back row. The club continued until at least 1920 and welcomed foreign teams, including a squad composed of players from the Bethlehem Steel Corporation.[8] The steel company was not the only American group to travel to Sweden in the name of baseball. When a St. Louis team corresponded with the Swedish Football Association in 1917 about playing in the Scandinavian country, the Swedes made one key request: they asked that the St. Louis squad be composed of players who could also play baseball. In 1916, an All–American soccer team had toured Sweden and offered a number of baseball exhibitions, which drew large attendances. "Apparently the Swedes enjoy the American pastime hugely, and the proposed trip by the St. Louis soccer eleven was immediately regarded as a good chance to provide more baseball," wrote the *New York Times*.[9] Led by Thomas W. Cahill, the secretary of the United States Football Association, U.S. soccer players would tour Sweden at least three times between 1917 and 1920 and on each occasion would also play baseball at the request of the Swedes. In the 1920 tour, baseball games were planned in the Olympic Stadium in Stockholm as well as in Västerås and Gothenburg.[10]

The shadow of time leaves no record of baseball activity over the next two decades or of what happened to Edström's involvement. Edström became a member of the IOC in 1920, which might have indicated a change in his focus. Still, one would expect that the interest shown by Swedes in the first twenty years of the twentieth century translated into pockets of baseball in the years leading up to 1940s. If that was the case, the play must have been sporadic. Following World War II, the sport did get back on track in Sweden. In the spring of 1945, the Swedish Air Force bought approximately 50 American surplus fighter planes—P-51 Mustangs—from the U.S. forces stationed in England. American pilots and mechanics came over with the shipment and were stationed at Stockholm-Bromma, a former international airport. Like most soldiers during this period, they brought baseball with them. The boys in the neighborhood took interest in the game and domestic play in the area ensued.[11]

Along with American military personnel who were playing ball, individual Swedes were also rediscovering the game throughout the country. Beyond the U.S. Air Force–inspired play, Stockholm also had three teams—Solna, Wasa and Presto—emerging just after the war, according to federation president Fransson. Two friends, Sune Lundberg and Willy Wåhlin, are credited with organizing the sport on a federation level. In fact, Wåhlin was the federation's first president when the organization was established in 1956.

In addition to the play in the capital, the game was making inroads throughout the country in some very unexpected places. In the tiny hamlet of Åsensbruk, an elementary-school teacher named John Erik Bangtsson took it

The 1912 Olympic Games featured a baseball exhibition between the local Västerås club and a team comprised of world-class U.S. athletes. Although the Americans gave the Swedes a pitcher and a catcher for the match-up, the United States won handily. (Above: an advertisement for the contest.)

upon himself to push baseball in the early 1950s. He'd heard a game broadcast on his short-wave radio and was inspired to scrape together some ad hoc equipment to outfit two youth squads. Impressed by his efforts, Earl J. Hilligan, the publicity director for the American League, sent Bangstsson a complete set of rules in 1951. Although the *Chicago Tribune* referred to Asensbruk as "[t]he cradle of baseball in Sweden,"[12] Bangstsson's efforts did not turn his village into a baseball mecca.

In contrast, the baseball labors of three brothers in the sports-crazy northern city of Leksand did have that kind of impact. In the mid–1950s, Ove, Rune and Kjell Leander got their hands on some baseball cards. The brothers were intrigued by the pictures and statistics and resolved to learn the game. They contacted some family members in the United States and were able to secure a copy of *Street and Smith's Baseball Yearbook*. By 1959, they'd set up a team, the Leksand Lumberjacks, and turned the club into one of the most successful baseball organizations in the country's history. As players the Leanders learned the game quite well. "Today," wrote long-time Atlanta Braves international scout Bill Clark in 1995, "their feats are legendary, like Babe Ruth, Lou Gehrig and Cy Young in the United States, but all in one family."[13] The Leander tradition continued into the 2000s as a current generation of family members—

Sweden entered the international baseball fray in 1962 at the European Championships in the Netherlands. While the Swedes would go on to win two bronze medals in Euros play, they placed last at their inaugural tournament. Above: Coach Bill Arce works with a player on hitting at a field in Amsterdam. (Courtesy Bill Arce.)

Rickard and David — both play among the country's elite. As for the Lumber-jacks, their history remains impressive: the team has spent more than 40 seasons in Sweden's top league, the Elite Series, and have captured 20 national titles,

Yet, even with the likes of the Leanders, marked development did not occur overnight. It wasn't until 1962 that Sweden entered a team in the European championships. Wisely, the Swedes reached out to American coaches to aid in their baseball education. In 1962, Bill Arce, who was instrumental in baseball development throughout Europe, became the first American to conduct clinics in Sweden. Glenn Gostick, a Minnesotan and former player for the University of Minnesota, was also an early coach. Throughout the modern history of baseball in Sweden, clubs and national programs have been very aggressive in securing the help of top-level American coaches. For example, Ron Brown, who coached for Chapman College, a strong California collegiate program, served as Sweden's national team coach from 1974 to 1976. More recently, college coaching legend Jerry Kindall worked with the national team in the early 2000s. As the skipper at the University of Arizona, Kindall, a former major-league player, won three NCAA Division I baseball championships. Not

Following the war, Willy Wåhlin (above, right) was instrumental in forming a Swedish baseball federation. Here he works with coach Bill Arce at a clinic. (Courtesy Bill Arce.)

surprisingly, Kindall, like Gostick, was a native of Minnesota and had personal ties to Sweden.

Sweden was getting the coaching, but the struggle to compete at a modest level was evident for the Scandinavians in the 1960s. For example, Ken Lindberg, who would go on to a long career both as a player and administrator in Sweden, was installed as the starting third baseman for the Bagarmossen club in the late '60s because he was the only player who could throw the ball to first base without a bounce, according to Braves scout Clark. Keep in mind that the Bagarmossen club, established in 1956, was one of the first formed in the country, so it should have had experience on its side. (In the club's defense, Bagarmossen would go on to win five national titles from 1973 to 1980.)

The national team was not doing much better, putting up a 2–17 record at the European championships during that decade. But the 1970s saw a spike in growth and an improvement in play. During that decade the number of clubs increased and the federation became a member of the Swedish sports confederation. This opened the way for government funding and meant that organizers "could start to work more seriously with the development of baseball in the country," Swedish federation president Fransson said.[14]

Not content with just increasing baseball's reach at home, Swedish baseball leaders also worked hard to bring the game to other Scandinavian countries. In the late–1970s and early 1980s, Sweden was instrumental in nudging Denmark and Finland into the European baseball community. Sweden was also central in organizing the Nordic Baseball Championships, which pits Scandinavian national teams against each other. As the most senior regional baseball player, Sweden dominated that event until it began sending its junior national team to the tournament.

Domestically, this far-flung development in the 1970s was best illustrated by the formation of the Skellefteå baseball club in 1971. Located just 200 kilometers from the Artic Circle, Skellefteå is so far north that the club would have to travel some 16 hours to take on teams from the southern part of the country in league games. Somehow the travel must not have gotten to the team because Skellefteå would develop into a consistent formidable contender for the national championship. In all, the club would win eight titles. (Most likely, the teams that had to travel up to Skellefteå probably thought differently about the impact of the travel.)

Along with clubs like Skellefteå emerging, baseball was also beginning to successfully recruit exceptional athletes from other sports. Peter Schöön was a talented ice hockey player who turned to baseball in the summer because his second-favorite sport, soccer, conflicted with his time on the ice. He represented Sweden for the first time in 1978 and would spend the next twenty years playing on behalf of his country.

Schöön would be among the leaders of a generation of Swedish baseball players who would earn the country much-deserved respect in the European baseball community. That group reached full maturation in the early 1990s and did it in grand style. In 1993, Sweden agreed to host the European Baseball Championships. While countries like Holland and Italy had the infrastructure to pull off the event without financial repercussions, the Swedes were taking a big risk by bringing the continent's biggest event home. The price turned out to be steep for the cash-light Swedish federation: a 350,000 SEK loss (about $50,000). Still it was worth every kronor as the Swedish team performed valiantly. The hometown boys made the semifinals and almost knocked off the heavily favored Italians, losing 8–5. Sweden then bounced back, beating France in two out of three games to earn the bronze medal.

The event and the Swedish squad's performance created a true groundswell of baseball support in the country. "It increased the game of baseball a lot with some TV coverage and other media," recalled Schöön, who was a member of the team.[15] Within two years following the tournament, baseball hit a high point in participation, with approximately 8,000 club members in structured baseball and countless other kids playing the sport.[16] Club baseball also became all the more competitive during this period as illustrated by Leksand's triumph at the 1996 Cupwinners Cup, becoming only the fourth country (along with Holland, Italy and Spain) to win the prestigious event.

Swedes make up the vast majority of players who compete in the country's top league, but the Elite Series has also proved to be an excellent place for American players to work on their game. On more than one occasion, players have headed off for a season or two in Sweden only to return to the States to play independent professional baseball. For example, pitcher Mark Randall won a title with Skellefteå before returning to the United States and posting a 1.77 ERA and eight saves in 1996 for the Allentown Ambassadors in the Northeast League. More recently, Eddie Aucoin spent two seasons (2001 and 2002) with Oskarshamn BSK in Sweden and then played three seasons of independent baseball in the Northeast, Northern and Can-Am leagues. Over three independent ball campaigns, he posted a 17–1 record and a 2.81 ERA.

Top Swedish players have also made the jump from their domestic circuit to the United States and Australia. Stockholm native Magnus Pilegard chose baseball over ice hockey and then started a journey that would have him playing club ball in Australia before playing junior-college baseball in Kansas and finally playing at the NCAA Division I University of North Carolina, Wilmington. Pilegard set the latter's consecutive-game hit-streak record in 2001. Although he didn't reach his goal of becoming the first Swedish-born and trained professional player, he's been a central part of the national team and Elite Series ever since. Other players such as Rickard Reimer (Belhaven College), Björn Johannessen (Santa Barbara City College) and Elias Sölveling (Riverland Community College) have also had stints in American programs.

All those players have had to overcome the minority nature of baseball in Sweden. "When people hear I'm from Sweden, they say, 'You don't play baseball in Sweden, do you?'" Pilegard told the *Morning Star* in Wilmington, in 2001. "Really, we don't. I can almost say that I know everybody that plays baseball on my level back home. Personally." Actually watching major-league baseball games live on TV in his youth was nearly impossible for Pilegard. "For awhile, they showed one game a week on TV. It was at 3 o'clock in the morning or something. I taped it every night, but nobody watched it, so they canceled it," he said.[17]

And yet each of those players found a way to compete at a reasonably high level in the States. Still, maybe it's the constant effort of having to fight uphill for your game that has caused Swedish baseball to experienced mixed results since the start of the millennium. The low came in 2001 when the Swedish national team suffered an embarrassing last-place finish at the European championships. Yet the turnaround was almost immediate: Sweden hosted a European qualifier the following year and won it, earning promotion back into Europe's elite pool. With players like Pilegard, Reimer, Johannessen and Sölveling on the roster, the biggest highlight was yet to come. At the 2003 European Championships in Holland, the Swedes shocked the Italians, beating them in the quarterfinals and assuring that Italy would not win a Euros medal for the first time since 1955.[18]

Like most players in European countries, development often requires spending some time abroad. Longtime Swedish national team member Björn Johannessen (above) played at both Santa Barbara (California) City College and in Australia to hone his skills.

The matchup between Italy and Sweden was a stark contrast in styles. The Italians are renowned for their fiery demeanor on the field. Mistakes and errors are followed with strong language and glove slapping. The Swedish approach to baseball is the exact opposite. There is a word, *lagom*, which is used to describe a Swedish philosophy to approaching life. The word, roughly translates to "in balance." There is a Swedish proverb, "Lagom är bäst," which means "Lagom is best." When you watch the Swedes play it's immediately apparent that so many of them live by this dictum. There is a calmness regardless of whether they are ahead or behind. For the most part, this approach is incredibly useful in the baseball world. After all, baseball is not a sport where aggression is valuable. Too much emotion can often lead to a breakdown in mechanics that in turn can cause failure. This *lagom* can also help fight nerves in close games. Emotional players might struggle when they're underdogs and have the lead because of a crush of excitement or the fear of failure. In those situations, the Swedes generally keep their cool.

The 2003 victory over Italy secured Sweden a spot at the 2005 World Cup in the Netherlands and, like a decade earlier, yielded some much-needed media attention. Alas, the Scandinavians couldn't capitalize on the stellar Euros performance. At the 2005 Euros, they placed eighth in the 12-team field and at the World Cup later that year finished sixteenth out of seventeen countries.

Leksand, which boasts an academy for young up-and-coming players, is a key center for Swedish player development. Above: Leksand's Niklas Melin delivers a pitch in a game against Karlskoga. (Courtesy Svenska Baseboll och Softbollförbundet)

Whereas the 1993 Euros performance caused a jump in baseball participation, numbers following the 2003 performance continue to drop. Only about
1,000 people were playing the game in 2006. Elite Series mainstay Skellefteå is
no longer there and the sway of so many other popular sports in Sweden — from
ice hockey and soccer to skiing and athletics — seems to be making baseball
ever more an afterthought. The quality of players has been "going up and down
over the years," said Schöön in 2007. "When I first started playing, most of the
players were athletes from other sports, whereas now most of the players are
only playing baseball. I think that the players were better athletes before, but
the players today are better baseball players."

In other words, players who do take up baseball really learn the game —
but not nearly enough are taking it up in the first place. The effort to develop
elite players appears to be in good hands. In 2006, Leksand opened a baseball
academy thanks in part to the assistance of Major League Baseball International. Thus, the country's best players are getting an opportunity to make the
most of their abilities. But are the days of teams playing each other from
Skellefteå in the far north all the way down to Gothenburg in the far south just
a memory?

In 2003, I played for Oskarshamn BSK, an Elite Series club in southeast
Sweden. The team had started modestly in early 1990s with a bunch of friends
from the area having discovered the game and looking for an outlet for their

Sweden has a handful of nice ballparks, including one in the town of Rättvik (above),
a small town north of Stockholm.

newfound passion. Over the years, the team progressed from the lower divisions and, with some ambition — they began to import player/coaches— eventually made it to the pinnacle of Swedish baseball. The club also convinced the town to put aside land for a proper baseball diamond. The Swedish government seems more open than most in Europe toward dedicating space for facilities. Beautiful parks exist in such small towns as Rattvik, Leksand and Karlskoga.

With some corporate support from the local electric company, Oskarshamn became increasingly competitive and, in the season I played, the club made the playoffs and the Swedish Cup finals for the first time. But over the years the players who had brought so much enthusiasm to the team had grown older and, by the time I was there, only one of the originals remained a regular player. Within a couple of years after my season there, the team had to fold. Quite simply, there was nobody left to carry the torch and raise the necessary money to keep the team running.

Oskarshamn's demise is a microcosm for both Swedish baseball and, in many ways, European baseball as a whole. The key is to figure out a way to maintain the enthusiasm. This will be a mandate that stewards of Swedish baseball will face for years to come.

9

$$\diamondsuit$$

France

In some ways, it's surprising that baseball isn't a major sport in France. Americans have made a dedicated effort — particularly in the years before and after World War I — to establish the game as a central part of that country's sports culture. Like the British and the Germans, the French even have sports antecedents to tie their country to baseball. Robert W. Henderson's 1947 book *Bat, Ball and Bishop — A History of Ball Games* describes a French bat-and-ball game called *la soule* dating back to medieval times.[1] In the nineteenth century, the French media would also point to a fifteenth-century game called *thèque*,[2] a sport similar to the English children's trifle rounders, as a predecessor to baseball.

Moreover, it's not that the French do not produce world-class athletes. While the country is better known for its artists, cuisine and architecture, it's the home of the likes of three-time Olympic skiing champion Jean-Claude Killy, who was one of the greatest of his era, and soccer stars Zinadine Zidane and Thierry Henry.

Finally, the French have not necessarily been adverse to embracing new sports. The Fédération Française de Basket-Ball was formed in 1932 and the sport has enjoyed a steady rise in the French sports world. Eight French players have been picked in the first round of the National Basketball Association draft — a sign of the country's strength in that sport.

And yet, baseball remains on the outskirts of France's sporting mainstream. The reasons for this are complicated. Possibly the timing of external efforts to promote baseball were wrong, or maybe it was the lack of persistence by locals to cultivate the sport. Perhaps, even with France's bat-and-ball heritage, baseball is just not compatible with the core of Gallic culture — after all the French also never took to cricket, either. As one French baseball federation document put it following World War II: "It is very difficult to become a good player after the age of twenty because of our total ignorance of a rather important action known as 'throwing the ball,' an athletic gesture not practiced in other sports. Certain players may have an inclination to throw with both arms."[3]

Despite all this, France's somewhat quiet baseball history has at least been sustained. The sport has consistently existed throughout the twentieth century in France. Its organizers played a role in formalizing a pan–European confederation. And its players have at times enjoyed periods in the upper tier of the continent's baseball-playing countries.

The fact that the sport is not bigger in France is not due to lack of effort by a handful of Frenchmen and some of America's most prominent baseball figures. A. G. Spalding, the great baseball entrepreneur and organizer who gave both the British and the Italians an early taste of baseball, did the same for the French. In 1874, when Spalding was a member of the first U.S. professional tour in Europe, he had pushed to play in Paris, according to author Mark Lamaster.[4] In the end, that first trip was confined to the British Isles. More than a decade later, in 1889, Spalding was in charge and he wasn't going to miss an opportunity to thrust baseball into the French public consciousness. Paris, in particular, was a potential gold mine for the sporting-goods magnate. With a wealthy population and a robust expatriate community, Paris baseball enthusiasts would have the means to purchase crateloads of Spalding baseball equipment.

Spalding's timing seemed fortuitous. In the early nineteenth century, recreational sports in France were a pleasure for the elites. But times were changing. Lamaster recounts that France's loss in the Franco-Prussian War in 1870–1871 humiliated the country and, as a result, there was "a movement to rehabilitate the French character, beginning with the body." With that in mind, French banker Henri Louis Bischoffsheim reportedly offered a thousand-dollar reward to the person who could introduce a new sport suitable for French schools and colleges.

Never one to back off a challenge, Spalding was game and he wrote a letter to Bischoffsheim, inviting him to the Spalding tour's exhibition in Paris. While in the French capital, he also set up a meeting with Paschal Grousset, who had founded La Ligue Nationale de l'Éducation Physique in 1888. His mission was to create more egalitarianism in sports throughout France. Spalding thought he would be the perfect ally. The American could confidently point out that baseball was a game of the masses in the United States. Many of the players on Spalding's tour had come from modest means and could serve as proof of the value baseball could have in democratizing sports in France.

The Paris contest was held on 8 March 1889 at the Parc Aérostatique, which was located next to the Trocadéro on the Quai de Billy (which today is the Avenue de New York). The early spring weather left the gravelly, makeshift sandlot quite muddy. Nevertheless, the crowd was a healthy size and even included Pierre de Coubertin, the father of the modern Olympic movement. The game, which like nearly all the games on the tour featured Spalding's Chicago ballclub against a mixed squad of big leaguers called All-America, was a close affair. The All-Americans won 6–3 thanks to the pitching performance of Ed Crane, who conceded just three hits.

Spalding had labored mightily to inculcate the Parisian media to the finer workings of baseball in the week leading up to the match, but the newspaper reports were mixed. *Revue des Sports*, a publication Spalding had particularly wooed, raved, "It's enough to say that batting, throwing, and fielding develops a superb musculature, and that the two teams demonstrated qualities of speed, precision and coordination that won the admiration of all." Still, the newspaper concluded that "few could understand the game or follow all of its phases and subtleties." Another publication, *Le Temps*, seemed to dismiss the sport as nothing more than a child's diversion. Pointing out the similarities between baseball and the old French game *thèque*— as well as the similarity to rounders— the paper patronizingly concluded that "[i]t's a very exciting and very amusing game that our school children practice in its French form with ardor in many schools in Paris and the Départments."

This backhanded compliment from *Le Temps* may have limited the impact of the Spalding trip in France. According to author James Elfers, Spalding did fund a small league in France "for years."[5] As late as 1913, there was a team based in the wealthy Paris suburb of Vésinet, called Spalding A.C.[6] Spalding's dogged interest in French baseball would make sense, as the sporting-goods magnate had the same interest in Great Britain for some time. But media coverage of these efforts was limited and what news of French baseball trickled into the American media by 1901 was farcical. In a light article that lacked all cultural sensitivity, the *Boston Globe* ran a story that reported "baseball has [now] been introduced officially in France." The article proceeded to satirize how a French player might argue with an umpire. The faux tale, complete with phonetic pidgen–English pronunciations, ended with the two players and the umpire "all bow[ing] extravagantly" and the two players "kiss[ing] each other on the cheek as they retire to the bench."[7]

To whatever extent Spalding was still involved, he was getting help in 1908, as an organized effort by expats in Paris was underway to firmly cement baseball in the City of Lights. That year, the Athletic Club of Paris began laying out a baseball diamond on their club grounds. Americans were driving the venture but "[m]any Frenchmen [were] in the new organization and they have become enthused over the great American game," a *Los Angeles Times* article reported.[8]

While these efforts likely created a small pocket of baseball-playing mainly among Americans, France needed a native to take up the cause of baseball. The first to do so was Emile Dubonnet. A successful balloonist (ballooning was a highly popular sport at the time), Dubonnet fell in love with baseball in 1911. "I am going to introduce baseball into France," he boldly proclaimed to the U.S. media. "The French are an excitable people and baseball will appeal to them. I believe it will be more popular even than it is here. Ballooning is the sport of France, but it can hardly be considered a real sport in the popular sense. They need something like baseball and I am going to introduce it to the nation."[9]

A year later, a league was being formed under the auspices of the French Baseball Union. A number of teams emerged during this period. There was a Paris circuit that included Ranelagh B.B.C. (Bagatelle), A.A. (Lyceum Condorcet), Racing Club de France, Pascal (free school), Spalding A.C. (Vésinet) and the Paris team (U.S. students). In addition a provincial division featured Normandie (College), U.S. du Berry (Bourges), Rugby Nantais, Olympique Seynois, A.S. Maconnaise and Evreux A.C. The Parisian Franz Messerly was named president and the *New York Times* announced the bold French expectation that the new circuit was promoting "the American game with the ultimate idea of providing a French competitor in [a] world's championship series."[10] These were grandiose plans as, at this point in time, there was nothing even close to resembling true international baseball competition. In fact, the first recognized world amateur championship, which pitted the United Kingdom against the United States, didn't take place until 1938. Still, these lofty aspirations indicated a buoyant enthusiasm or, at the least, a willingness to use the overblown rhetoric of a bold salesman. Regardless, in 1913, baseball was making progress behind the backing of the Racing Club of France, a respected organization founded in 1882. The club immediately built a field on its property outside of Paris and by 1914 was making plans to erect three more diamonds. Games were set up between club members and American boys living in the Latin Quarter, and contests were scheduled in a number of French towns, including Etretat and Havre. Elsewhere, a game between teams from Vésinet and Dieppe drew approximately 3,000 spectators, according to W. H. Burgess, president of the Vésinet baseball club (which was likely the Spalding club). It is worth noting that the French did bring their own culture to the game in that they eschewed the flannel uniforms traditional in the United States at the time, for "a lighter garb, resembling somewhat that of American track runners."[11]

Although A. G. Spalding's French exhibition a quarter of a century earlier had done little to push the game forward, he was now very sanguine about baseball's future in the Gallic country, encouraged by these small pockets of play. "The next baseball country will be France," proclaimed Spalding in New York on 9 January 1914. "The French took up boxing with enthusiasm and now they are getting into our national game. When they have been taught its delights there is no doubt that France will be second in baseball only to the Americans."[12]

Between Spalding's bluster and the seeming headway made by the Racing

Club of France, the time seemed right for a repeat French visit by major-league ballplayers. Indeed, New York Giants manager John McGraw and powerful Chicago White Sox owner Charlie Comiskey saw it just that way. In 1913, the pair took their respective teams, augmented by a few other big-league greats, on a world tour—à la Spalding's escapades in 1888–1889. On the schedule for February 1914 was a trip by the tourists to Nice and Paris. They arrived in France just one month after Spalding made his comments about a French baseball explosion. Unfortunately, the Americans had very little opportunity to build on any momentum. The first French matchup in Nice attracted far more expat Americans than natives. In addition, while the game was a good one (Chicago beat New York 10–9), author James Elfers suggested that "[d]iversions and sideshows nearly eclipsed the game."[13] The French aviator Lacrouse flew his monoplane before the game much to the delight of the crowd. Then the great Olympic athlete Jim Thorpe, baseball player on the tour, wowed the onlookers with a display of his shot-put and discus prowess. Baseball may have been a sideshow in Nice, but Paris would have likely given the major-league exhi-

bition its proper spotlight if it hadn't been for one serious hitch: the weather. For four days, the baseball teams waited for the rain to pass, but it never did. As a result, Parisians were deprived of seeing America's pastime played by its best. "The citizens in Paris were quite enthusiastic when we visited that city on the trip around the world," McGraw recalled two years after the tour. "[W]e would have drawn an immense throng but for a cold, heavy rain."[14]

Even if Comiskey, McGraw and their crews had of wowed audiences in Paris, their work would have certainly been forgotten quickly as the more pressing matter of war took center stage in the summer of 1914. France was to become a major proving ground of the Western Front between the Allies and the Germany-led Central Powers. No doubt, baseball would be a trifle during this period of tremendous bloodshed. "Had it not been for the outbreak of the war, I believe the French people would have taken up baseball very strongly," McGraw lamented in 1916. Nevertheless, baseball

Chicago White Sox owner Charles Comiskey (above) brought his team to France twice (in 1913 and 1924) to play in exhibitions. His work earned him a silver medal from French baseball's governing body.

would become a valuable diversion for American and Canadian soldiers stationed in France, who offered their game to the French from Paris to the countryside. In 1915, American League president Ban Johnson sent five gross of balls, fifty bats, six masks and six sets of catcher's gear to Canadian soldiers in France looking to "while away the intermissions between battles [by] playing the American national game," according to the *New York Times*. The *Times* would further crow that "baseball, introduced among the French and British soldiers by Canadian troops who learned the game at home, is taking a firm foothold back of the trenches. The French are described as enthusiastic rooters."[15]

The Canadians were just the first wave of baseball zealots to reach French soil. American GIs were also playing baseball throughout the country. By the summer of 1918, U.S. servicemen were enjoying games every Sunday at the Bois de Boulogne, the location of the Racing Club of France's prewar baseball facility just outside of Paris. The spread of American soldiers also meant a widening reach for the sport. For example, Rouen, the historical capital of Normandy located in France's northwest, became a baseball center. A crowd of nearly 20,000 watched a 4 July match-up between Americans there. (In the past two decades, Rouen has reestablished itself as a home for top-flight French baseball). By the end of the war, baseball was being played at the university level in Paris, Lyon, Nice, Dijon and Toulouse, among other places. The University of Toulouse actually boasted four teams in 1919.

One of the reasons for so much baseball enthusiasm was the large number of major leaguers fighting for the Allies in the war zone. They included future Hall-of-Famers like Christy Mathewson, Eppa Rixey, Grover Cleveland Alexander and Sam Rice, as well as such solid big leaguers as Hank Gowdy, Sherry Smith and George Kelly. But of all the ballplayers in France, it was Jonny Evers, the famous second baseman in the "Tinkers to Evers to Chance" ditty, who made the biggest effort to push baseball. Funded by Washington Senators owner Clark Griffith and the Knights of Columbus, Evers staged games throughout the country and supplied tons of equipment.

By the end of the war, the French were even producing their own bats. Searching for ways to assure that enough equipment was available, the YMCA approached French woodworkers about fashioning bats. Early attempts were somewhat feeble. "Their first efforts resembled the club affected by Jack the Giant Killer," wrote the *Boston Globe* on 18 August 1918. "They were too heavy for an ordinary man to lift and were shaped like George Moriarty's legs, which are formed so that you can tell the ankle from the calf only by noting which end the shoe is on." But the French would not be denied, and after some trial and error "they were turning out as neat a job as Louisville ever boasted. It was found that the bats could be made to sell for a franc, which is considerably less than a fair stick costs in America."

While the French were competent batmakers by the end of the war, a number of big-league players who served in the country were not as positive about the ballplaying abilities of the indigenous people. "I don't believe you could pick up a first-class catcher in all of France," lamented Christy Mathewson in a February 1919 edition of the *Washington Post*. "They're more afraid of a hard hit liner or grounder than they are of a hand grenade or a German 77 [artillery gun]."[16]

Bill Lange, who played seven seasons for the Chicago Cubs and boasted a .330 lifetime batting average, also didn't see the French as natural ballplayers. "The French ... can't seem to get the hang of American baseball, and the sport won't ever be the rage in France until the 10-cent ball and the 10-year-old kid are properly introduced," said Lange, who spent time during the war in France as a baseball coach for the YMCA. "It's a tough job to teach grown-up men the game. They figure that to learn the game they will have to make a show of themselves ... and a Frenchman fears ridicule more than anything else. The only way that baseball may be made a lasting and popular sport in France is to introduce it through the French children."

This pessimism was not held by everyone. The famed Giants manager McGraw, who seemed to have become a bit of a Francophile during his time in the country, defended the potential abilities of the French. "It would not be surprising to me to see France adopt the game [of baseball] at the close of hostilities as they are great natural sportsmen," proclaimed McGraw to the *Washington Post*.

Based on McGraw's attitude, it's understandable that within a decade of the end of the Great War, he and Comiskey were bringing major leaguers back to Paris. With the devastating hostilities behind the country, there was a residue of baseball throughout France, but it was still not a force. An *International Herald Tribune* article in August 1920 pointed out that French military were still playing the sport. The French Army's Eighth Engineer Regiment, which was stationed in the Loire Valley town of Tours, had organized a team and was searching for teams to play. "The sport might be said to be in the stage of the proverbial little acorn from which the great oak grows," the newspaper said.

In 1924, McGraw and Comiskey were looking to nurture that seed. Unlike their fruitless trip a decade earlier, McGraw and Comiskey would actually stage a Paris game this time around. While the trip was not a money-making venture, McGraw and Comiskey drew a lot of attention on their arrival in Paris. Following a series of exhibitions in England and Ireland, the Giants and the White Sox arrived in Paris at the *Gare du Nord* to an enthusiastic crowd, according to writer Miles Hyman, who wrote that "the next morning Paris newspapers announced their surprise at the fact that the 'Geants' were not giants at all, but medium-sized men." The paper concluded that they must be giant "in the quality of their exploits."[17] In total, three exhibition games were contested, with some 4,000 spectators per game, which were very respectable numbers.[18] The excitement garnered from these events would be so great that the *Federa-*

tion Francaise de Baseball, which in a slightly different form still exists today, was set up in its wake. This new organization would have substantial support. McGraw and Comiskey were named honorary vice presidents and awarded silver medals (as was Hughie Jennings) for "sowing seed from which the great game of baseball is expected to spring." More importantly, the federation would be headed by a prominent French sports figure, Frantz Reichel, who was the former secretary of the French Olympic Committee. Reichel, who had competed in both the 1896 and 1900 Olympic Games, was quick to assert the French roots of baseball. Recounting the statements made when Spalding came to Paris in 1889, Reichel claimed in 1924 that "baseball was played in France 50 years ago" in the form of *la grande théque.*[19] Reichel's efforts to tie baseball to France were not dissimilar to Spalding's efforts to establish baseball as a wholly American sport by dubbing Abner Doubleday the game's inventor. Quite simply, such a connection would increase national pride — and possibly interest — in baseball. The profile that Reichel brought to the game undoubtedly helped, but it's worth noting that Reichel wasn't a baseball fan per se. The man was a sports aficionado who had also been involved with the structuring of other athletic contests like rugby and boxing. More than anything he liked to see sports structured properly and that, according to French baseball organizers today, was the key reason for his involvement with America's pastime.[20]

Considering that Reichel lacked an evangelist's zeal for the game, he did affect progress for French baseball. The first championship took place in 1926, according to a French 1989 European Championships program. A.S. Transports beat Ranelagh B.C. 15–10. In 1929, United Press reported that the French Army was considering making baseball an "official" game following a baseball exhibition that was requested by the commandant of the French School of Physical Culture. "This is a great game," exclaimed one officer. "It requires just the right amount of coordination between mind and muscle that we wish to develop in our soldiers."[21] Even if baseball would be ulti-

Hall-of-Fame New York Giants manager John McGraw (above) was a vocal proponent of baseball in France. During World War I he optimistically told the press the French would take up baseball in earnest after the fighting.

mately adopted by the French Army, the sport seemed to be in a stasis in the 1930s. The biggest breakthrough in that decade was some formalized international play. The French had played informal games against Spain in the late 1920s, but set up a series of serious contests versus the Netherlands and Belgium in the mid–1930s. At the time, Belgium was relatively new to the game, while the Dutch had a history dating back to second decade of the twentieth century. With a length of time in baseball similar to France, Holland was a good barometer of how well the French had taken to the game. In the two country's first matchup in Paris, the Netherlands prevailed 9–5. The following year, Holland knocked off the French in a game in Amsterdam before France won in a closely contested 5–4 game in Paris on 20 June. While Holland and Belgium continued to compete until 1939, France bowed out of the three-way competitions after 1937, although it continued its matches into 1939 against Belgium, boasting a 2–1 record in their final three contests. Of course, by midsummer, France was occupied by the Germans in the north, while a Nazi collaborationist government ruled in the south. Baseball did continue in other occupied territories during World War II — most notably, the Netherlands — but it doesn't seem that the French had such an affinity for the game.

The sport would reemerge when the allies liberated France. Unlike Italy, where baseball exploded thanks to American influences after the war — or even Germany where baseball was used as a way to spread democratic ideals in German youth — soldiers in France mainly played among themselves. This led to some very good baseball. Still, it was just baseball between Americans. One of the best teams in France at the end of the war was the Thirteenth Division Blackcats. During the summer of 1945, the Blackcats, which featured New York Giants pitcher Dave Koslo and Chicago White Sox first baseman Merv Connors, played throughout France. They took on all comers in towns and cities like Auxerre, Paris, Sens and Compiegne — and they dominated. The team's overall record was 30–4 in France (they went 2–0 elsewhere). The French town of Rheims also hosted two games of the European Theater of Operations (ETO) World Series.

Baseball may have receded during the wartime period and received relatively less attention by liberating troops than elsewhere in Europe, but the sport in its French incarnation did persist. Parisian journalist Georges Bruni replaced Reichel as the president of France's baseball federation in 1931 and served as a worthy steward of the game until 1945. Bruni, who had been Reichel's second-in-command at the International Sports Press Association from 1924–1928, became a legitimate fan of baseball. The Giants–White Sox tour in 1924 had "kindled a latent sand-lot flame in Georges Bruni," explained writer Leslie Lieber in a 1946 edition of *Reader's Digest.*[22] Bruni's efforts with baseball had even earned the sport a $500 annual subsidy from the French Minister of Sport even though, joked Lieber, the minister had "no idea whether 'le baseball' resemble[d] bullfighting or tiddlywinks."[23]

In August 1945, the French proved they'd learned something from their prewar tilts against Belgium and the Netherlands when they beat a U.S. military team 5–3 despite wearing entirely inappropriate uniforms. "The second and third basemen were attired in blue baseball shorts, aviation goggles and coal miners' caps," Lieber recounted. "The pitcher wore the costume of an ice-hockey goalie, complete with heavily-padded shin guards. Two men, the shortstop and left fielder, donned steel helmets before assuming their positions."[24] Although Lieber's writing style was glib, there is nothing to suggest that the author wasn't being serious in the description of France's starting nine.

Regardless of the attire, it's clear that Bruni had helped France retain a baseball presence following the war. With this continuity, France earned some respect among the continent's baseball-playing nations, as evidenced by its important role in the formation of the European Baseball Federation. In April 1952, the five founding countries—Belgium, France, Italy, Germany and Spain—chose Paris as the site for its inaugural meeting. In addition, the articles of association made French the lingua franca of European baseball. Still, the depth of French baseball's involvement seems to have been limited. While the nascent organization's chairman was an Italian, the vice-chairman a Spaniard and the secretary a Belgian, there were no Frenchmen in positions of power. In fact, a news report mentioned that a there would be a French representative on the technical committee, but that person would not be an officer of the group and couldn't immediately be named.[25]

The reality—in spite of all of Bruni's efforts—is that baseball during this era was being kept afloat in part by those playing the game in France's decaying colonial empire. In the 1950s, Tunisia in North Africa was battling for independence; yet, détente still existed on baseball fields between France and her colony. In 1949, France and Tunisia squared off in Paris in their first international contest. Much to the chagrin of French imperialists, Tunisia prevailed 11–5 and won again in 1951, 21–13. These results indicated that domestic play in France was not strong. European baseball historian and official Roger Panaye underscored this fact when he wrote that "[i]n 1953, the baseball situation in France was far from brilliant and the Federation relied much on their contacts with Tunisia and Morocco."[26]

The French federation recognized these shortcomings, and, thanks to the work of a Tunisian local named Marcel Cohen, a French national team was formed in 1955 with "a number of players from the 'Ligue Tunisiennè." The additions didn't help very much as the French went 0–4 at the 1955 European Championships, playing tight games against Belgium and Germany, but falling to Spain 21–3 and Italy 16–1. France would be a sporadic participant in European Championships over the next two decades and when they did play, the results were not usually good. It didn't help that with the independence of Tunisia, the French could not rely on the North Africans to bolster their national team.[27] Between 1955 and 1983, the national team put up a dismal 2–39 record. Emblematic of this futility was a controversy involving the French at the 1962

F. F. B. B. T.
FÉDÉRATION FRANÇAISE DE BASE-BALL ET DE THÈQUE
Fondée en 1924

MEMBRE
DU COMITÉ NATIONAL
DES SPORTS

▼

SIÈGE SOCIAL:
134, rue de Charenton
PARIS-XII

•

Téléph. : DIDEROT 00-01

Le 27 AVRIL 1953

A PARIS, au Siège de la F.S.F. 5, Place Saint-Thomas d'Aquin, et grâce à la courtoisie des FEDERATIONS DE BASEBALL, d'Allemagne, de Belgique, d'Espagne, d'Italie, qui ont tenu à se réunir en FRANCE, geste dont la Fédération Française de Baseball remercie grandement ces Fédérations, a été fondée la :

" FEDERATION EUROPEENNE DE BASEBALL "

dont les règlements se trouvent dans nos status, et ceci en présence des Délègues dont les noms suivent :

Pour :		
l'ALLEMAGNE :	Monsieur N. SCHOFFERS	*Président* de la Fédération Allemande.
BELGIQUE	Monsieur PANAYE R.	Président
	Monsieur MARTIN H.	Vice-Président de la Fédération Belge.
ESPAGNE	Monsieur BARRIOS. L.	Président
	Monsieur ALVAREZ J.R	Commissaire de la Fédération Espagnole
ITALIE	Monsieur Le Prince Sténo Borghèse	Président
	Monsieur le Prof. UGO G.	Commissaire de la Fédération Italienne.
FRANCE	Mrs. BLANCHARD TH.	Président
	CHARRIER G.	Vice Président
	WAROT J.	Secrétaire Général
	COULKA R.	Président de l'Ile de France.

22

On 27 April 1953, French baseball hosted a pivotal event in the history of European baseball: the founding of the European Baseball Federation. The nascent organization's inaugural document (above) was signed by representatives of the five founding countries (Belgium, France, Germany, Italy and Spain) on French stationery. (Courtesy CEB.)

Euros. France was losing to Germany 30–0 when one of its players got into an argument with the team's captain and stormed off the field. The French were left with just eight players and had to forfeit the contest — the first known forfeit in Euros history. It was a sad state when a forfeit, which went in the books as a 9–0 loss, was a 21-run improvement over the real score.

Obviously, the loss of the Tunisian influence had an impact. But to explain the French struggles domestically, it's instructive to look at baseball's limited reach during this period. A pair of teams, the Paris Université Club (known as PUC — pronounced Pook) and Nice Université Club, dominated the national championship race for decades. Those two clubs combined to capture 26 of 28 contested French championships between 1955 and 1992. The level had devolved so greatly that by 1976, organizers saw what they were doing as essentially starting over. That year, just 21 clubs existed in the country. By 1987, 170 clubs were playing baseball. This period saw the founding of some of France's most successful clubs today, including Savigny-Sur-Orge Lions (1983), the Montpellier Barracudas (1985) and the Rouen Huskies (1986).

While baseball still does not compete with king soccer or even basketball or volleyball, why was there such a surge? Writer Miles Hyman, an American living in Paris in the 1980s, argued at the time that, in part, baseball — as the embodiment of Americana — was fashionable. "Baseball is, along with Apple Pie and Chevrolet, one of the cherished icons of the American Dream," wrote Hyman in a 1988 edition of *Giants Magazine*. "[A]nd in France, where one is likely to see more of Marilyn Monroe than Louis XIV, Napoleon and Charles de Gaulle *combined*, the American Dream is incontestably the hottest-selling thing." Admitted French baseball organizer Eric Tuffreaud to Hyman: "It may to some extent be baseball's 'exoticism' that appeals to the French."

If baseball was in vogue, then organizers were going to maximize the interest. In 1989, the French federation, which had now combined with softball to consolidate growth, hosted the European championships in Paris, Sarcelles and Savigny.[28] For the event, a brand new baseball field was constructed at the famous Bois de Vincennes park, while the fields in Sarcelles and Savigny were both renovated. The national team performed admirably, going 4–4. The four wins matched the country's total over the previous 35 years.

In the 1990s, French teams became more attentive at recruiting foreigners to increase their level of play. While overseas players were always available for a cosmopolitan team like PUC, other clubs had to seek out players more aggressively. For example, Steve Scagnetti, who had played for Kitchener in Canada's competitive InterCounty Baseball League, joined the Savigny-Sur-Orge Lions in France thanks to the recommendation of an old teammate. Scagnetti says he was paid $2,500 per month, which is a sizeable sum in European baseball.

The most high-profile recruit to French baseball in this period was Jeff Zimmerman. This Canadian native graduated from Texas Christian University

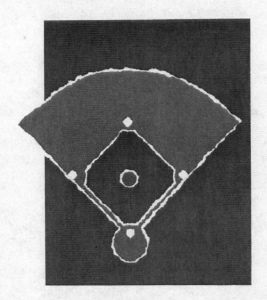

EUROBASEBALL 89
21ème CHAMPIONNAT D'EUROPE DE BASEBALL

EUROBASEBALL 89
P A R I S
S A R C E L L E S
S A V I G N Y
1 AU 10 SEPTEMBRE

PROGRAMME OFFICIEL 40 F

In 1989, France hosted the European Baseball Championships in Paris, Sarcelles and Savigny (above: program cover). The French national team put up a credible performance, going 4–4. In addition, the event led to a new baseball field and other facility renovations.

in 1993 and was looking for a baseball job when the Canadian National Team pitching coach suggested France. The following year, Zimmerman was pitching for Montpellier. While playing in France's top league, Zimmerman developed a slider that ended up being his ticket to bigger and better things. "The competition over there wasn't that good — kind of equal to junior college ball here in the States," Zimmerman told the *Palm Beach Post* in July 1999. "So I was able to experiment with the slider and not get hurt much.''

With the slider he'd developed in France, Zimmerman would play two seasons with the Canadian National Team and an additional year in the independent Northern League before getting a break with the Texas Rangers. In 1999, Zimmerman started the year as a Rangers middle reliever and at the season's midpoint he was named to the American League All-Star team thanks to an 8–0 record and a 0.86 ERA. Two years later, he would be installed as Texas's closer and would save 28 games. Although an injury would end his major-league career after 2001, Zimmerman would look back wistfully on his time in France. "It was a lot of fun, I had a blast up there," he concluded in an interview in 2000. "It was great for my ego, because I got to be Babe Ruth and Nolan Ryan all rolled up in one."[29]

France has an impressive record of developing some of the best pitching in Europe. Nicolas Dubaut (above) continued that tradition in 2007, posting a minuscule 0.66 ERA in 13.2 innings at the European Baseball Championships. (Photograph by Ezio Ratti/FIBS.)

One of the top baseball facilities in France, the ballpark in the town of Chartres (above) features a fine playing surface, lights, sunken dugouts, a clubhouse and an electronic scoreboard. (Photograph by David Young)

The improvement of French baseball was not left just to foreigners, as organizers also created a French baseball academy in the 1990s. The academy was established at INSEP (the Institut National des Sports et de l'Education Physique) in the Paris suburbs. Originally conceived for adult national-team members, the academy transitioned into focusing on younger players and has insured a core of solid baseball talent at the elite level. "France has been able to produce a small number of talented players who know how to play the game the right way," said Andrew Sallee, a former minor leaguer in the Philadelphia Phillies organization who spent nearly five years working with French baseball. "They practice twice a day, year round, at the Institute."[30]

The approach at INSEP illustrates that if players are given consistent and in-depth instruction at a young enough age they can develop — even in Europe. "We would attend local tournaments and practices and look for kids with athletic ability," Sallee recounted in 2007. "It didn't matter how well they knew the game, if they could run, or had good hands or a strong arm, we would follow them." To that end, the INSEP baseball program has turned, among others, a 15-year-old javelin thrower, who had never seen a major-league game, and a 16-year-old tennis player, who didn't know much about the sport, into important contributors in the national team structure.

Beyond player development, in 1997 the Federation also took on the responsibility for hosting a European championship for a second time. The home-field advantage certainly helped the local team as the French placed fifth out of twelve teams and boasted a sturdy 5–3 record. The French program was beginning to gain momentum that would culminate in a fantastic performance at the 1999 Euros in Italy. The tournament that year was the first to ban aluminum bats. This move helped the French squad, which had worked hard to develop its pitching. French hurlers would twirl three shutouts in the tournament and knock-off traditional powerhouse Spain 4–1 in the quarterfinals, en route to a bronze-medal-winning performance. The result was a sweet conclusion of more than a decade of development. It also qualified the squad for the World Cup in Chinese Taipei in 2001. Although the French finished that elite international event 0–7, their pitching did not let them down. In particular, Samuel Meurant shone. The 28-year-old right-hander would pitch 15⅔ innings without conceding an earned run. This included a complete game 3–1 loss to a Dominican Republic team that would beat a U.S. team 6–4 in another preliminary matchup. In a tournament that included such future major-league pitchers as Chris Capuano, Jose Contreras, Scott Cassidy, John Stephens and Chris Mears, Meurant took home the award for the pitcher with the best ERA.

Since the 1999 breakthrough, the French have consistently remained in the top half of the continent's baseball-playing nations at the European Championships. In addition, in 2007, Rouen became the first French club to make the finals of the European Cup club championships, falling to the Dutch team Corendon Kinheim in a tight 3–1 contest. Individual players continue to make headway as well. Frenchman Joris Bert, who first played in the town of Rouen and was later a member of the INSEP baseball academy, spent the 2007 season at Frank Phillips College in Texas. A speedy outfielder who swiped 42 bases in 49 games of junior-college baseball, Bert was selected by the Los Angeles Dodgers in the nineteenth round of the 2007 Major League Baseball draft, becoming the first Frenchman to be picked. While McGraw's expectations for the French baseball player may have been nearly nine decades too early, Bert and others may yet prove the Hall-of-Fame skipper right on his optimistic assessment of the country's baseball talent.

10

Czech Republic

In 1969, most Czechs had very little to celebrate. A democratic republic from 1918 to 1938, Czechoslovakia had suffered through World War II as an occupied state under Nazi rule and emerged after the war as a communist regime strongly influenced by the Soviet Union. But the 1968 Soviet invasion of their country — which occurred after a brief period of liberalization — was undoubtedly a crowning blow for many Czechs.

Maybe it shouldn't have been surprising then that when Bill Arce, athletic director and baseball coach at the Claremont Colleges in Southern California, came to Czechoslovakia that year with loads of equipment, a baseball was taken out of its box and put in a place of pride in the middle of a dinner table. It represented a small breath of freedom.

"The wife and the man I was going to eat dinner with unwrapped one of the balls and put it on the table as a centerpiece," recalled Arce just after the trip. "To them, the ball was like a chunk of gold. You'd have thought I had brought them half of Fort Knox."[1]

The plight of baseball enthusiasts in Czechoslovakia (and the Czech Republic following its split with Slovakia in 1989) is one of fits and starts. But it is also underscored by the same enthusiasm for baseball shown by Arce's hosts nearly four decades ago. The Czechs who have clung to baseball have shown noteworthy tenacity in their development of the sport.

Baseball's introduction to the country came a year after Czechoslovakia achieved independence in 1919. The Czech's original baseball missionary was named Joe First and he offered the locals in the town of Pilsen introductory courses in a number of sports, including baseball, basketball and archery, according to longtime Czech baseball player and organizer Jan Bagin. Identified by the *Prague Post* as an American resident in Prague, First continued his efforts a year later, setting up an exhibition game in Pilsen between YMCA branches from Prague and Pilsen.[2] In 1938, interest in the sport rose again. While the version of the game being played at the time was more of a hybrid of softball and baseball than true hardball, it could boast pockets of popularity. Such frivolities ended with the annexation of the Sudetenland and baseball disappeared during World War II. But the common story of American GIs playing the game following the war held true in Czechoslovakia. In 1945 and 1946, baseball began again in Prague and the western half of Czechoslovakia, which was occupied by U.S. troops. In addition, Joe First resumed his baseball work with a YMCA camp in 1948. But First's dogged efforts were for naught, as the emergence of a communist regime served as a massive stumbling block. In the same year as First's YMCA camp, the newly installed communist regime put an end to baseball, according to Bagin.

As a result, Arce's trip in the summer of 1969 represented a remarkable moment for baseball in a country where western ideas and cultural icons were being pushed aside. Softball had survived since the post–World War II period, but the number of players was minute. The first step toward sustained growth occurred in 1963, when an official Czech commission of "bat and glove games" was established. This paved the way for more softball and, in 1964, a Prague-based student's club called "Vojenske stavby" made the switch from softball to baseball, marking the official return of hardball. Two years later, Czech teams began traveling abroad to play clubs in Belgium, Holland, Italy and Poland. The early results indicated why instruction from the likes of Arce was necessary. For example, Prague's Slavia F.S. traveled to Antwerp in 1967 to play Belgium. The Czechs lost 19–3 in seven innings. According to longtime European baseball federation executive Roger Panaye: "The Czechs were at that time only beginning to play ball, a game they had learned with the university students from Cuba in Praha [Prague]."[3]

Arce's appearance offered a true coach's perspective. By the time he arrived in Czechoslovakia, Arce was a veteran of trips to Holland, where he'd successfully helped the Dutch develop a respectable standard of baseball. His reputation spread through the small European baseball fraternity and the coach was asked to travel to Prague to provide instruction.

"They had never had a bonafide baseball coach observe and work with their program," Arce said. "I finally decided it would be a unique opportunity for an individual to teach and promote a sport from a western culture behind the Iron Curtain. The Dutch were very understanding, and said they'd let me go. So I paid my way and went ahead."

The political climate in Czechoslovakia was not great for his sojourn — it was nearly one year to the day that the Soviets had invaded the country, setting up a federal republic consisting of the Czech Socialist Republic and the Slovak Socialist Republic. "The border guards couldn't figure out what the bats and helmets and things were," Arce said. "Fortunately, I had a letter telling the purpose of my trip." Arce immediately recognized that the game in Czechoslovakia was still in its infant stage. "They have no baseball field in Prague yet," he said just months after his visit. At the time, Prague had five baseball clubs and about 180 players, who all used the same inappropriate facility. "You would not believe it," Arce said. "It's bigger than Chicago's Soldier Field ... and is 350 to 400 yards wide. It's also very old, with a loose dirt and gravel surface. You get anything but an accurate bounce on ground balls. The backstop is 20 to 30 feet high."[4] Equipment was also incredibly scarce. Arce brought thirty-two bats. The Czechs only had twelve previously. Arce gave them six batting helmets. The Czechs were sharing just one helmet. Arce provided them with two and a half dozen balls. All told, they only had fifteen before he arrived. "The Prague Baseball Union shared everything," Arce said. "Gloves, bats, infield ball — not balls, but ball. One."

Substandard conditions did not stifle the players' enthusiasm. Arce had only four days in the country and it rained all afternoon one of the days. This did not deter the Czechs who insisted that training go on. They moved under an arcade and worked out for two and a half hours on the concrete. It was this attitude that understandably impressed Arce the most. "They were all totally unschooled in the basic fundamentals of the game," Arce said. "But [they] had a potentially innate ability to be successful at it in a very short time. Their movements were loose and their attention never waned. I gave one player an

In the mid–1970s, baseball in the Czech Republic fought the stigma of being an American sport. Nevertheless, those who played the game got to do so in one of the biggest sports venues in the world, Strahov Stadium (capacity: approximately 220,000). Here two Prague teams, Tempo and Kovo, square off. David Johanis is batting for Tempo. (Photograph courtesy of Jan Bagin.)

instructional book at 2 A.M. and at 9 the same morning he had it read and was back asking questions."

Arce's trip was part of a multi-pronged effort to establish baseball permanently in Czechoslovakia. In 1969, the Czechoslovakia Baseball and Softball Association became a temporary member of the Federation of European Baseball. The expectation was that it would become a full member, and external efforts were underway to help baseball burgeon in Czechoslovakia. At the time, South Africa was angling to become a member of the European federation. With the political pressures on the oppressive apartheid government, South African officials were looking for any way to ingratiate themselves with foreign sporting bodies. To that end, in early 1970 South Africa sent $100 to buy equipment for Czechoslovakian baseball.

But this push was short-lived. In March 1970, the Federation of European Baseball reported, "Czechoslovakia has cancelled its application for normal membership probably due to political circumstances." The federation was correct in its assessment. Many years later, Jan Bagin, who is the former executive

With very little support for baseball, facilities were not geared toward the game. Tempo's Richard Hauba, who was one of the best Czechoslovakian hurlers in the 1970s, pitches from flat ground in a game against Prague rivals Kovo. (Photograph courtesy of Jan Bagin.)

director of the Czech Baseball Association, becoming that organization's first full-time employee in 1993, elaborated. "When we had a Communist, or totalitarian system, they weren't interested in such sports as baseball because baseball came from the United States and they didn't like it on the Communist leaders' level," Bagin said. "They didn't like baseball or American sports in Czechoslovakia."[5]

The adversity baseball players were forced to face during this period became legendary. Long after the Iron Curtain fell, American coaches coming to Czechoslovakia would be floored by the tales of Czech players and coaches. One U.S. coach, Jim Jones, who spent more than a decade coaching and teaching baseball in the Czechoslovakia and the Czech Republic, heard them all. There was the story of players lacking the necessary papers who had to be hidden under equipment to get past border guards in order to play games internationally. Then there were the huge hurdles that had to be navigated in order to buy equipment. Czechoslovakia's communist leaders were always fearful of defection. As a result, they limited the amount of money people traveling outside the country could carry. Players desperate to bring cash abroad in order to purchase gear would unlace their gloves and stuff money in the padding or drill out a bat and put a roll of money in the hollowed stick — which clearly gave new meaning to the concept of corking a bat.

Worst of all, the Communist Party was constantly trying to place coaches with teams in order to spy on the players and their family. One of Jones's friends was approached a couple of times to join "the party" because he coached and worked with kids. Jones's comrade had turned them down each time, but the pressure was growing too great because the party would determine what schools his kids would go to and where his wife would do her medical practice. The man feared that if he was asked again, he would have no choice but to acquiesce. Luckily, they didn't come back, as this occurred near the end of the communist rule. Still, Jones knew others who could not refuse and when the list of collaborators came out after the end of the communist control, those who had joined the party were blacklisted by the baseball federation and clubs. "The ones I knew did not believe in the Communist Party but had to join to give their family a chance for a better life," Jones recalled.[6]

In spite of the obstacles, by the early 1980s baseball was making a comeback. In 1979, the first Czech champion — Tempo Praha — was crowned. The Czechs also resumed international play. In 1979, a Czechoslovakian team played eight games in Holland and the following season Czech clubs and three Dutch teams matched up for ten games in Prague.[7] Baseball gained even stronger footing in Eastern Europe on 13 October 1986, when the sport was adopted as an official Olympic medal event. At this point, it wasn't a crime to play baseball in Czechoslovakia, but it certainly wasn't encouraged in the same way the Soviets began pushing the game. "We were told it was not a good game for Czechs," said Jiri Votinsky, executive director of the Czech Baseball Association.[8]

Nevertheless, the tight grip of communist rule was beginning to weaken. That was enough for those smitten by the sport. The Czechs' baseball perseverance did begin to pay off internationally. For example, in October 1987, the first officially selected Czechoslovakian national team took three of four games from a Soviet team in Tbilisi, USSR.

The end of the Cold War was the final blow needed to unshackle Czech baseball leaders. In 1989, Czechoslovakia was able to do what had eluded them two decades earlier: the country became of a full member of the Confederation of European Baseball (CEBA). Led by the efforts of Jan and Daniel Bagin, Prague baseball organizers were particularly aggressive in development. The brothers began playing baseball in 1976 when they saw a local club Tempo Praha practicing at a nearby athletic track. Jan was 21 and Daniel was 16 at the time and the pair liked the looks of the bat-and-ball game. They had both had success in other sports like basketball and soccer and took to baseball immediately. Within a year, they were starting on the club's top team, with Jan patrolling the outfield and Daniel playing shortstop. Never lacking ambition, the Bagins and some of their teammates decided to start their own club in 1981, forming Sokol Krc. The clubs remains one of the country's top teams today. Trained as an atomic power engineer, Jan Bagin began living by the famed *Field of Dreams* credo, "If you build it they will come." He dreamed of a Prague facility that could rate with the best in Europe.

In 1983, he found the perfect location for his project in the southern part of Prague, a site which had been used as an illegal dump by construction companies. "The area looked horrible, but the size was big enough to fit our requirements," Bagin said. "Also, the location was excellent because it had easy access by public transportation and was only 15 minutes from downtown." Of course, in the byzantine bureaucracy of the Czechoslovakian state, it would take six years to get the necessary paperwork to move forward.

The loosening of travel restrictions in 1989 offered Bagin another avenue to reach his goal. The following year he embarked on his first trip to the United States to rally support for his idea of a multi-diamond facility, meeting informally with representatives of Major League Baseball International. Bagin's best selling point was that he could develop his dream fields at a reasonable cost. "In the United States, a small field would cost about $1 million," he told United Press International. "We could build a facility for about one-quarter of the expenses. We don't need a stadium, we just need one baseball field with bleachers for about 500 people." Within five years of that trip, the Bagin brothers' dream would become a reality.

Ironically, the Prague baseball facility might have been constructed faster if not for the liberalization after the Velvet Revolution in 1989. The Bagins had steered through the bureaucracy and were just a few rubber stamps away from getting the communist okay when changes in property, ownership and usage laws altered the situation. Still, they refused to give up. They finally got a lease

Jan Bagin's dream was to turn this field (above) into a first-class baseball facility. In 1989, this area was little more than an open field. In 2006, the complex — and the annual baseball tournament it hosts (Prague Baseball Week) — would be described as one of the world's top ten "Ultimate Baseball Experiences" by an ESPN.com writer. In this photo, Libor Rychetsky (Sokol Krc) is batting against Kovo. (Photograph courtesy of Jan Bagin.)

on the land and were able to keep costs down on the facility by getting baseball sponsors to donate their services. Some important construction elements like equipment and grading services were provided gratis. But the key maneuver came in the form of an ingenious way to raise money and get the necessary dirt to construct fields. "We offered an area of our complex as a dump again," Bagin said. "Companies were looking for a place to leave soil taken from their construction activities downtown. Our area had excellent advantages as it was a short distance from downtown and we could charge them a lower price than any other dumps available in Prague."[9]

Unwilling to stall until their facility was a reality, the Bagins' club also began hosting an 11-year-old event called Prague Baseball Week in 1992. Over the years, the festivities have become one of the most successful international tournaments in Europe. At the 1995 Prague Baseball Week, Johns Hopkins University's baseball coach Robert Babb, who had brought a team to Prague just three years earlier to play in the tournament, marveled at the Bagins' work. The difference between the new facility and the old field were "night and day," said Babb, whose Johns Hopkins program has a long history of success at the NCAA Division III level. He told the *Prague Post*, "I wouldn't mind having this setup at our place. It's ambitious and it will be beautiful [and] great for the game." Prague Baseball Week, which is played at the Bagins' beautiful facility, has become such an event that in 2006, respected ESPN.com writer Jim Caple named it one of his top ten "Ultimate Baseball Experiences." It placed seventh — just behind attending the famed Caribbean World Series.

Despite the value the Prague complex has had for Czech baseball, it came at a personal price to Jan Bagin. His club, Sokol Krc took on the main responsibility for construction of the site. This meant that members of the club were required to participate in Sokol's mandatory facility-building sessions. Several national team members opted to defect to other teams rather than do the work and, as a result, Sokol Krc was relegated from the Czech's top league in 1996. The organization would rebound. The next year the team qualified for the top league again where it continues to play today. The club is now known as Krc Altron (the team is sponsored by the electronics manufacturing company Altron) and has 455 members on 18 teams. All told, the baseball complex has five fields (two adult and three youth) with an automatic irrigation system, a clubhouse with eight locker rooms, a gym for off-season training, accommodation for visiting teams, a restaurant, a baseball shop and a club office. Two of the diamonds also have lights.

Along with facility improvements, Czech baseball has also focused heavily on player development. The split of the Czech Republic and Slovakia at the beginning of 1993 did little to deplete talent. At that time, the Czechs were already supplying all but one player on the joint Czechoslovakian national team. The country was improving, thanks in large part to an infusion of American coaches. Beginning in 1991 in the Netherlands, Major League Baseball International instituted an "envoy" program in which American high school and college coaches would travel to Europe and teach the game during the summer. The Czech Republic has taken full advantage of the program. In addition, teams were hiring American coaches to run their clubs. For example, Geoff Samuels, who had been drafted by the Montreal Expos and played at San Jose City College and Sacramento State in California, came to the Czech Republic as an envoy coach in 1993–1994. In 1995, he spent eight months of the year serving as a club coach in Brno. The town of Brno, the Czech Republic's second largest city, today overshadows Prague as the country's baseball hotbed. Indeed, Samuels' Draci club has won every national championship between 1995 and 2007.[10] "Prague authorities don't care about sports, as the city's focus is more on the fact that it is a very attractive tourist destination within Europe," said Bagin explaining Prague's second-city baseball status. "Also kids in Prague have many more options [than in Brno] as to which sports to play or what else to do besides sports."

One of the most important coaches to come to the Czech Republic was Jim Jones. Described in 1995 by Atlanta Braves international scouting director Bill Clark as one of the three people who had been key to the growth of Czech baseball, Jones first came to the Czech Republic in 1990. In the United States he had served as an assistant coach at Stanford University and at St. Mary's in California. "In 1990, the Czechoslovakian federation contracted with me to come over for three summers to get a consistent stream of information and to try to get the majority of club programs on the same page," Jones said. "I was able to continue my time there and follow up with — or correct — my earlier works there. Not many visiting coaches get that long of an opportunity to get their message across."

Jones is quick to point out that he did nothing "magical," but he did preach fundamentals. When he got there, Jones says the Czechs were obsessed with the long ball, but he worked on them learning how to play small ball, instructing the Eastern Europeans on the hit and run, bunting and stealing. "I was able to stress both defense and the multiple-offense approach in place of their love affair with the home run," Jones said. "When I first traveled to Czechoslovakia, they played on converted soccer fields with short fences — that combined with sub-par pitching, led to a lot of home runs in club competition. However, when they played internationally, they faced much stronger pitching and larger fields, putting them at a real disadvantage if they continued to swing for the fences as an offensive strategy."

The efforts of Jones and subsequent coaches did not lead to overnight success. In 1992, Czechoslovakia played in the International Baseball Federation's Merit Cup. The event was set up to give national teams in developing nations a chance to compete at the international level. The Czechs finished sixth in a seven-team field, placing ahead of only New Zealand.[11]

But signs of significant development were apparent by the mid–1990s. In 1996, the Czech Republic qualified for the top tier of the European Baseball Championships with a second-place finish in Hull, England, at a European championships qualifying event. The following year, the country's Pavel Budsky, a strapping power hitter, became the first Czech player to get signed by a major-league club, inking with the Montreal Expos. Budsky's signing was a huge accomplishment for Czech baseball. It gave other players something to shoot for and provided the Czech Baseball Association with an important benchmark to prove its progress. "We have no scouts [in the Czech Republic], but because of Budsky, there will be more scouts at European competitions," said former major-league manager Terry Collins, who was serving as the California Angels skipper in 1997.[12]

Jones also saw Budsky as a valuable inspirational figure for Czech players. "Pavel Budsky is a quality person, not just a good athlete," Jones said. "He was an inspiration to the other Czech players and showed that there were opportunities to play baseball outside of [the] Czech Republic."

Since then a number of players have competed at high levels in the United States. For example, pitcher Petr Pacas played for New Mexico State University and, in 2006, three players signed with big-league organizations: a catcher named Peter Cech with the Cincinnati Reds, and pitcher Jakub Toufar and shortstop Jakub Hajtmar with the Minnesota Twins. Other stars included Tomas Ovesny and Martin Duda, who both played at the collegiate level in the United States.

While these players went abroad they also continued to represent the Czech Republic with distinction in international competition. Aggressive travel overseas by Czech teams has further helped progress. In 2004, Draci Brno went to Florida and played against minor-league players from the Minnesota Twins organization. "I think they work hard, play hard," Twins director of baseball operations Rob Antony told the *News-Press* in Fort Myers.[13] Other Czech clubs as well as national teams of all age levels have gone abroad, including a group of 36 players sent to Florida by the Czech Baseball Association in April 2007 to play exhibition games against minor leaguers from the Minnesota Twins, Cincinnati Reds, Boston Red Sox and Pittsburgh Pirates.

The Czech Republic has been a fine ambassador of the game in international competition. Along with playing in the European Baseball Championships, the Czechs have represented Europe at both the World Cup and in the Olympic Test Event for the 2008 Games in China. Here Jan Rehacek pitches for the Czechs at the 2005 Euros. (Courtesy CEB.)

In European competition, the country has established itself as an upper-tier power at the national level. They finished a respectable seventh out of 12 at their first European Baseball Championships in 1997, going 4–4. After placing eighth at the Euros in 1999, the Czech team has come in fifth twice and sixth once. Although the team struggled mightily at the World Cup in 2005 (finishing 0–8), they did perform admirably in a qualifier for that event against the United States and Canada. In one game against the United States, the Czechs hung tough, ultimately losing 9–5. The Eastern Europeans even came close to securing a spot at the 2004 Athens Olympics. The national team placed third in the Olympic qualifier. Unfortunately, only the top two teams, Holland and Italy, qualified. After just missing out on the field, the Czechs filed a protest against the Italians, claiming the Italian roster included the illegal participation of some foreign players. (National team members must be lawful citizens of the country they represent.) The bureaucratic gambit did not work, but the fact that the Czechs were on the cusp of Olympic qualification is a sign of their marked development.

As the Czechs have improved on the field, they have also played a more active role as a host of major baseball events. By 1999, the Czech city of Brno was hosting European club events, but the country's biggest foray onto the international baseball stage came in 2005 when Prague and the towns of Chocen, Olomouc and Blansko hosted the European Baseball Championships.

This was no small undertaking. While Holland and Italy regularly pulled off hosting the event, smaller baseball nations had struggled with the cost of such a large undertaking. The Czech Baseball Association estimated that it would cost them $395,000 to put on the event. Major reconstruction jobs were done at the stadiums in all four cities. The work was evident. In Blansko, the small stadium was fitted with lights, beautiful seating and a number of hitting cages off the field's first-base side. Chocen's park would fit in nicely in a mid-sized NCAA Division I program in the United States. The picturesque field — complete with a railroad line running beyond the outfield fence —featured a great clubhouse area. Prague's facility, set up by the Bagins about a decade previously, remains the jewel. In 2003, the Prague site became the first in Europe to receive a grant from Major League Baseball's Baseball Tomorrow Fund. With the money, Bagin's club was able to expand its gymnasium, allowing for better off-season indoor use, as well as an area where visiting teams from outside Prague can stay.

The Czech Baseball Association raised about 60% to 70% of the budget they'd hoped for. Still, they were able to lure some big-name companies, Komerční Banka and the electronics giant Fujitsu-Siemens, as sponsors. "We were looking for a sport that would match with the requirements for IT business marketing. Baseball fulfilled the criteria.... It's a sophisticated game with complicated rules," Jan Manas, marketing communications manager for Fujitsu-Siemens, told the *Prague Post* that summer. In the end, bad weather probably limited attendance. While Czech games were broadcast on television,

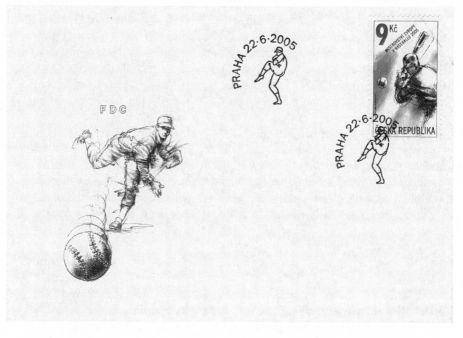

By the middle of the 2000s, baseball had earned a place of respect in the Czech sporting world. The country's president Vaclav Klaus made note of the values of the sport, a TV network was broadcasting domestic games and a stamp and commemorative envelope were even printed (above) in honor of the nation hosting the 2005 European Baseball Championships.

other matches between countries with smaller baseball followings were viewed by only a handful of onlookers. For example, the official attendance for the Ukraine–Great Britain game was 100 — although that might have been an overestimation. Nevertheless, the championship game was played on a beautiful day and it attracted 2,000 people. The results clearly emboldened Czech baseball leadership, as the country is hosting the fourth annual World University Baseball Championships in 2008.

At the beginning of the 2007 season, it was unclear how high the ceiling was for Czech baseball. The country's top circuit, the Extraliga, was established in 1993 and had a long history of recruiting strong overseas talent to complement its domestic players. Top players earn approximately $638 per month, according to Czech Baseball Association executive director Votinsky.[14] Still, the league is semiprofessional and discussions about fully professionalizing the league, which have been percolating since 2005, still remain just talk.

Part of the problem is that Czech baseball has been a victim of its own success. As Czech players develop, they go abroad or are lured to European leagues with more money, like Holland or Italy. For example, just before the

2007 campaign, Petr Baroch, who played in the Extraliga for Altron Krc in Prague, left to play in Holland's top division.

After the move, Richard Kania, who was the manager of Bagin's club at the time, was philosophical. "It's hard to find talented players," Kania told the *Prague Post*. "But the advantage of baseball is that you don't need to be extremely talented to become successful, so even the least talented can succeed."[15]

It's hard to believe that the Czechs will ever shun their beloved soccer or ice hockey for baseball, but the sport has shown a resiliency in the country — and has even won the recognition of some of its most powerful politicians. In 2005, Czech president Vaclav Klaus said that baseball in the Czech Republic has become "a certain lifestyle and also a social phenomenon. It has the possibility to address even those young people who might otherwise not find their way into sport. That is, in my view, the nicest thing about baseball."[16] A further sign of the sport's firm footing came in May 2007 when the Czech television network Channel 4 (Sport) announced it would broadcast 34 hours of Extraliga action during that season.

While Klaus's statement suggests that he may see baseball as merely a minor sport suitable for soccer and hockey outcasts, it is not the complete brush-off leaders in other European countries might give baseball. With the TV coverage, at the very least, it offers promise that the future of baseball will be more than just a table centerpiece in the Czech Republic.

11

Croatia

How important can a game be? To answer that question, you don't have to look any further than the development of baseball in Croatia. For a small band of brothers, the sport played a vital role in maintaining sanity and offering hope during a period of brutal violence.

First a quick summary is required on the modern history of Croatia. Geographically, Croatia is one of Europe's most stunning countries. Located on the Adriatic Sea, the coastal parts of the country compare to the French Riviera in terms of sheer beauty. The diversity is also breathtaking. To go along with their beaches, there are densely wooded mountains, picturesque lakes and rolling hills. In 2006, *National Geographic Adventure* magazine named Croatia its "destination of the year."

Despite all the nation's awe-inspiring physical wonders, the country has been marred by brutal violence in our lifetime. In 1991, Croatia declared its independence after being a part of Yugoslavia for 62 years. A long history of tension between Croats and Serbs quickly boiled over and for the next four years horrific bloodshed ensued. Thousands died and, according to Amnesty International, some 300,000 refugees were displaced by the conflict.[1]

In 1992, Aldo Vavra, a member of the Croatian Olympic Committee and at the time Croatia's national team head coach, described the dire situation in a letter to Carroll Land, the international director of the United States Baseball Federation:

There are so many things going on here, that it is almost impossible to concentrate on one alone.... Serbian Communist hardliners still believe they can make the great Serbia by taking Montenegro, Bosnia and Herzegovina, and two-thirds of Croatia. And they are fighting for that mercilessly, Nobody can stop them. They

186

Although it was ravaged by war, Croatia still remains one of the most beautiful locations in Europe. Dubrovnik (above) is located in the southern part of the country.
This region is also the home of Split, one of the first cities in the country to embrace
baseball. (Photograph by Jason Holowaty.)

> have all the jet fighters, all the battleships, all the tanks and rocket launchers and
> all the heavy artillery that [Yugoslavia] was buying for the past 45 years. The so-
> called Yugoslav army is now only Serbian and is acting brutally against all other
> nations. Unbelievable massacres are taking place.[2]

Strangely, these years were among the most formative for Croatian baseball. Through the shelling, violence and uncertainty in the early 1990s, baseball burgeoned. Before then, the sport had made appearances in Croatia dating
back to the early part of the century, but had difficulty sticking. During World
War I, U.S. sailors played the game on the Adriatic coast. Again, following
World War II, baseball was played briefly. Some interest after World War II was
strongly influenced by the Italians, who had taken quickly to baseball following the American liberation of Italy, according to author Peter Bjarkman.[3] In
1973, four clubs were established in the Croatian coastal town of Split due to
"intense contact with ... Italian clubs," wrote Roger C. Panaye in his short book
European Amateur Baseball: 25 Years.[4] This relationship continued for some
time, as an Italian squad reportedly toured Yugoslavia — including Split — in
1980.

But modern Croatian baseball was not mainly initiated by Italians. Aldo Vavra, who wrote the impassioned letter to Land and served as the Croatian Baseball Association's president, was an early driving force. In the summer of 1972, he served as a camp counselor in New Hampshire. He immediately fell in love with America's pastime. "Baseball, you have to think," Vavra explained in 2006. "Soccer, you don't think too much. It's a sport for the masses."[5] He immediately embarked on a campaign to convince his native country's masses that baseball was for them. He bought bats, balls and gloves and began working hard in the name of Croatian baseball.

Elsewhere in Croatia, there were others who were also gravitating to the sport for a variety of reasons. For Aleksandr Horvatic, the baseball inspiration came from the comic strip *Peanuts*. In 1983, Horvatic and a group of newly minted baseball enthusiasts commenced with their own baseball in the northern Serbian border town of Karlovac. "We all read the comics—Charlie Brown," Horvatic told a journalist in 2002. "They played baseball, so we thought we'd play too. It was a weird idea. It was such an American sport."[6]

All this enthusiasm began being channeled more efficiently when Ted Thoren, a longtime coach from the Ivy League's Cornell University, paid his own way to Yugoslavia to coach the sport in 1983. Thoren, whose grandmother was Croatian, was "the man responsible for laying a strong foundation for baseball" in Croatia, according to former Atlanta Braves international scout Bill Clark.[7] Every summer for more than a decade, he'd fly himself to Eastern Europe to teach the game. At first, he did this in Yugoslavia, but when Croatia split, he focused on his ancestral homeland.[8] In addition to teaching at Croatian training camps and coaching the national team, he also began hosting Croatian teams in Ithaca, New York. "Mr. Thoren has visited all the towns in Croatia where baseball is played and held clinics in all the places," Vavra wrote in 1992. "His experience in working with different levels and age groups, from teeball to the national team, was priceless. For us he is like the Godfather of Croatian baseball."

Thoren was one of a handful of American baseball men who saw firsthand the horrors of war in the 1990s and the amazing resilience of Croatian baseball and its players. In 1994, Thoren spent five weeks in Croatia, including some time in Karlovac. That September, he recounted his experiences to Syracuse, New York's newspaper the *Post-Standard*. Sleeping three miles from international forces, he learned not to jump at every bang he heard. He witnessed the bombed-out buildings and holes in the walls of churches and hospitals. "Whole towns and cities have been destroyed, communication links cut off, and overall inflation is unbelievable," Thoren said.[9] He told the newspaper that he took the job because he cared about Croatia and wanted the challenge. "I wanted to see how tough I was."[10]

While Thoren spent five weeks that summer in the war-torn country, Jimmy Summers spent a whole season the following year in Croatia—a choice that in many ways changed the direction of his life. Born in Sonora, Mexico, to a Mexican mother and a North American father, Summers grew up in Akron, Ohio. A crafty pitcher, the right-hander eventually played college baseball at Malone College in Canton, Ohio. A few summers before he graduated from college, Summers met a group of Croatians who had come to Ohio to play in a tournament. Among them were Kruno Karin and his son Damir.

Kruno Karin is one of the great figures in Croatian baseball history. For baseball to succeed in a European country there is always a Kruno who, through tireless effort and sheer will, moves the game along in some small corner of a country that otherwise likely wouldn't have sustained the sport.

Bill Percy, who has served as the Croatian National Team head coach since 1998, described Kruno in a blog he wrote for the Major League Baseball Web site, *Mlb.com*: "Our main baseball contact here is a man by the name of Krunoslav Karin and he is somewhat of a legend in these parts. Pure and simple the mastermind and chief organizer of baseball not only here but a driving force behind the movement nationwide. He could probably move to the States some day and do great as a promoter. Kruno knows how to raise money and promote this great game of ours in a passionately rich soccer and basketball country."

Clearly, Kruno was a great salesman because he convinced Summers to come to Karlovac to play for the local club, Karlovac Olimpija, in the summer of 1995 while the Croat-Serb conflict was still raging. Summers's payment for his services: $85 a month and the use of an apartment. He would stay for seven months that season. At the time of his arrival, Summers wasn't fully aware just how tough a place Karlovac was in the mid–1990s. Built in the sixteenth century, the ancient town was created to fortify the Austo-Hungarian Empire's defenses against encroachment from the Ottomans in the South. With ever evolving statecraft, by the 1990s, Karlovac, a town of roughly 70,000, happened to sit directly on the Croatian-Serbian boarder. It was literally on the front line of the war.

From the moment Summers stepped off the plane it was culture shock. "The country still felt so communist," Summers remembered in 2007. "There was communist architecture and everybody wore the same clothes. They all wore skin-tight Levi 501s and laughed at me because I wore Gap Jeans."[11]

The aesthetics were not the only surprise for the Ohio pitcher. Karlovac's field was a mere one and a half kilometers from the border. Although his teammates tried to reassure him that the worst years of the war were behind them, Summers was understandably a bit nervous. "Karlovac was the dividing line — on one side were the Croats and on the other side were the Serbs," he says. "What made it such a very difficult war was that everybody looked the same and talked the same. But what constantly amazed me was a guy would fight on the front line and do his shift and then after doing his shift, he would then go home put on his baseball gear and would come to baseball practice."

Early in the season, the baseball was quickly put in its proper perspective. One night in his first month in Karlovac, a teammate knocked on his door to warn him that there had been trouble elsewhere in Croatia and that there could be some bombing in Karlovac. Summers couldn't sleep. He sat up in his twelfth-story apartment waiting for the worst. At 3 A.M. he finally started to doze off when he heard a big bang. He remembered his teammate telling him to hunker down in the bathtub if the bombing did start. So he stayed in his porcelain tub until 7 A.M. Ragged, Summers did remember that there was supposed to be practice that day. There's no way it could be on, he thought, as he tried to reach his teammates but couldn't get any of them on the phone. Still, the committed ballplayer got up and trekked a nerve-wracking mile and a half to the field only to see the most unlikely of sights—all his teammates getting ready for practice.

Summers asked what had happened and the other players explained that it had only been a car bomb. "No big deal," they told him. In retrospect, Summers didn't fear death that night as much as he did later in the season. For the Croat players, bomb scares had become a part of life. On May 1, the big communist holiday of May Day, Karlovac had an important game scheduled. Warming up in the bullpen, Summers had baseball on his mind until he was told that there was going to be a bombing in fifteen minutes. He grabbed his gear and headed to Kruno and Damir Karin's basement bomb shelter. In what must have been the most surreal of situations, the Karins popped in a videotape of the 1986 World Series.

"I hated watching the tape because I'm a huge Red Sox fan," said Summers, remembering Boston's demise in the Series. "Then the first explosion hit about 300 yards from the basement where we were. I was so scared. I didn't think those bombs could be so loud. Damir then said, 'Let's go upstairs and watch.' But he warned me that you have to run up the steps because a bomb had previously hit there. You could see the tracer fire going back and forth. It was pretty scary. After a couple of days of being in the bomb shelter, I had post-traumatic stress. People would close a book and I would jump. The scariest thing is Kruno was our coach and he said not to worry because if anything serious were to happen, he'd be drafted and they'd send him to Zagreb. The next day he got drafted."

Kruno survived his return to military service and, of course, the baseball continued. Following the general alert, Karlovac began practicing again, even though Croatia was on the offensive in an effort to reclaim occupied land. "You could see rows of tanks from the field," remembered Summers.

While American players were leaving the country, Summers stayed. "I was 21 and I was dumb," he said. But that explanation sells short the real reason: he'd become too loyal to his teammates to leave them. Later in the season, the squad had progressed to the Croatian Cup finals. The championship game was being played in Split, the gorgeous town on the Croatian coast that used to be

Jimmy Summers (above) first came to Croatia during wartime in the 1990s and ended up becoming a major figure in the country's baseball history. In 1999, the right-handed pitcher went 21–2 in Croatia. He would also qualify for a Croatian passport and play for the national team. In 2007, he threw a 13-inning complete game victory against Ukraine at the European Baseball Championships.

a playground for Roman emperors and had Croatia's longest baseball lineage. The trip from Karlovac to Split in postwar Croatia would take three hours, but due to the hostilities it took Summers's team nine hours to make the journey. During the journey, two brothers, who were teammates of Summers, found out they had been drafted. Summers was set to pitch the climactic game, but the team had a little time before the dramatic contest. Summers was walking through the splendor of Split with one of the brothers, who made a request. "This could be the last game I ever see," he said. "You have to win this game for me." Summers did earn the victory and the next morning the brothers reported for service. The brothers survived the tour on the front line, but the experience put the importance of baseball in clear perspective. "[Years later], when I was going to pitch in the playoffs in Holland somebody asked me if I was nervous," said Summers recalling the stress of pitching in that Croatian Cup game. "After [pitching for somebody who was going off to war], how could I be nervous? That was real pressure."

Following that summer, Summers was hooked on Croatian baseball. He would return every year until 2000 when he got an offer to play in Holland in its top professional league. "In 1996, I was working in a pizza shop and as a carpenter in Ohio," says Summers about why he returned for a second season. "I had become closer to those guys [in Croatia] than anybody. We were so close because we'd been through so much together. They had respect for me because I didn't leave. No other Americans stayed. There is a lot of respect both ways."

Summers's second year in Croatia also marked the first full year without official hostilities and baseball played a role in mending relationships following the war. In August 1996, the Croatian National Team traveled to the northern England city of Hull to compete in the European Championships qualifying event. From a baseball perspective, the Croatia-Yugoslavia game was not a big matchup — in fact, Croatia won the game 14–4 — but from a political perspective this was the first athletic contest between Croatia and Yugoslavia. Yugoslavia, which would eventually devolve in 2002 into Serbia and Montenegro, was then the country of the Serbians who had attacked Croatia.

It was unclear before the game, how the two countries would react against each other. In fact, just two years earlier, Thoren told a story that did not augur well for a civilized encounter. At the 1994 B-pool championships, the Croatians said very little about the war with the Serbs, Thoren told the *Post-Standard*, the Syracuse newspaper. The war had heavily affected the national team program in a number of ways. Thoren had recalled four players who had trained with the Yugoslavian national team in 1989 and was informed that they were all casualties of the war. In addition, Croatian independence required players— Serbs and Croats— to choose sides. Thoren described one Serbian pitcher, who had been teammates with the Croatians in 1988, as "probably the best player in Croatia." But the war meant he had to move to Belgrade. Nevertheless, he showed up at the 1994 European (B-pool) Championships to watch his former teammates. He asked them longingly whether the Croatians might consider a series against some Serbs on a neutral field. The Croatians laughed at him, according to the *Post-Standard*.

Just two years later that very contest took place. Ken Krsolovic, an American of Croatian descent who was coaching the Croatian squad at the 1996 event, had his worries about the matchup. "I had told them if anybody gets out of line, they're out of the game.' We were not going to be an international incident," Krsolovic told *Newsday* in 1997. In the end, the players shook hands with their former opposition. "I had one fellow who had fought in the war and had some very bitter feelings," added the coach. "He said, I'm not going to shake hands and I said that was fine. But he did shake hands and said, 'You know, they weren't such bad guys.' I considered that a mini-triumph."

"The [Croatian team] wanted to beat them [Yugoslavia] bad. They really wanted to hurt them. [Can you] imagine playing a sport against people who bombed you?" said Summers, who had a number of Karlovac teammates on the 1996 Croatian team. "But one of my teammates said to me, 'I wanted to hate them, but they were so nice that I couldn't.'"

Although Croatia didn't qualify for Europe's top tier at the 1996 event, it was the start of marked improvement in the country's performance internationally. This development was helped by two straightforward factors: improved facilities and sustained good coaching.

The end of the war meant the Croatia government was eager to reinvest in infrastructure. Kruno Karin, the deft leader of baseball in Karlovac, anticipated that the local municipality would be willing to support even a minor sport like baseball if the alternative meant putting the war-torn city in a bad light. Thus, he took a big gamble: Karin bid and then won the right to host a European Cup club competition. With teams from other countries set to come to Karlovac, the town stepped up and invested money into the club's facilities. In 1998, that formula for support was employed again in Croatia. This time Karlovac cohosted the European Cupwinners Cup with Zagreb. Again, the pressure of teams coming from France, Holland, Italy, Spain and the Czech Republic earned the desired result: improvements to the field in Zagreb.

The changes were noticeable. "In 1995, you had to chase goats off the field in Zagreb," Summers said. Since then, Zagreb has won two national titles (1996 and 2001). They also won a championship in 1993. As for Karlovac, Croatian national team coach Bill Percy, who spent 30 years coaching at various levels in the state of Colorado wrote on *Mlb.com* that the "Karlovac field ... really is, by European standards, a decent set-up." This comment does not seem to do it justice. A look at photos of the park, with its finely cut grass, permanent fencing, solid pitchers mound and clay infield suggests that it might be a fine NCAA Division III facility.

In addition to fulfilling the "if you build it they will come" mantra, Croatia also benefited from additional foreign coaching help. With the war over, there was more reason to expect foreign coaches and players to come and stay for more than just brief visits. Karlovac was particularly helped by such a person. Rick Johnston, a former player and coach for the Canadian National Team and major-league scout, instituted a very professional approach to baseball in Karlovac when he arrived in 1997. "Johnston was tireless on the field," Summers said. "He was out there two sessions a day teaching hitting and fielding. He brought Karlovac to the next level." Indeed, Karlovac would enter a dynasty period with the arrival of Johnston, winning the national title seven straight years from 1997 to 2003.

These improvements percolated to the elite level and in August of 1998, Croatia earned promotion to Europe's elite level with a victory at the European B-pool Championships in Vienna, Austria. This outcome was not surprising, as Croatia had been on the cusp before, but what was improbable was that the team was led on the field by the Mexican-born, American-reared Jimmy Summers.

To be a member of a national team in an international baseball competition, a player must hold a passport from that country. The same Croatian pride that convinced the cities of Karlovac and Zagreb to improve their fields helped Summers get dual nationality in the Eastern European country. In his first season in 1995, Summers began working out with the national team and it was clear he could be an impact player, so the baseball powers began working toward getting him his proper papers. "You can get a passport if you have residence and can help a sports team," said Summers. "I didn't serve but I had to go through all the proper military channels. I even have a card that says that I was a sniper in the Croatian Army."

Summers's inclusion had immediate impact and the right-hander has been playing for the national team ever since. The success of Summers has led the Croatians to continue to recruit what Percy calls "tenth generation Croatians." Another notable national team member has been Tetsuhiro (Ted) Monna. Born in Shizuoka, Japan, Monna had an impressive career in Japan, spending time in 1993, 1994 and 1996 with the famed Yomiuri Giants. He pitched 44 games in the Japanese Major League, posting a 3.38 ERA.[12] But in 2000, at age 29, he took an offer to play in Holland. Monna met Summers and, according to Summers, the left-handed Japanese pitcher began spending his winters in Croatia. The two have provided Croatia with a formidable pitching staff that was bolstered at the 2005 European Championships with the arrival of a pitcher of Venezuelan extract. It's hard to blame Croatia for this level of recruitment. After all, every European country has drawn on players who are eligible for dual nationality but have learned the game in more established baseball countries like the United States, Australia or Canada.

Pride is a strong factor at all levels of Croatian baseball and it should never be underestimated in how they approach the game. For example, Summers explained that Split was known for their hometown umps who were very keen to assert their control. "There was an umpire there who was a cop and he would bring a gun and show it just to remind everybody who the boss was." There's little doubt that Split, which has been crowned national champions three times, takes its baseball seriously. Even as the war raged, baseball continued to grow in the coastal town, which was relatively isolated from the hostilities. Thoren reported that even in the midst of the war in 1992 interest spiked enough to earn "excellent" local radio, television and newspaper coverage during the Croatian championships.[13]

Along with pride, the Croatians also have a high level of tenacity on the field — surely in large part because of their experiences with the war. "Their approach was, 'We're going on with our lives,'" says Ken Krsolovic, who coached in Croatia in the mid–1990s. "There's a really impressive feeling about the game. There's a desire, an intensity to compete."

At the same time, the Croatians' passionate approach can lead to some letdown. "There is a 'Croatian way' and it's that they are very passionate people,"

One characteristic that exemplifies the Croats is their passion. Both Croatian baseball players and fans bring gusto to their sport. Here a fan shows his pride at the 2001
European Championships.

Summers said. "But for some reason there is an ability to choke in tough situations. It's crazy. I'm saying that as a guy who has choked as well." Summers
has played on Croatian teams that were leading continent heavyweights Holland and Italy very late in games, only to crumble in the end.

Maybe at times they want it too badly. Yet in other instances, baseball has
offered an environment to vent — just as long as they believe it won't hurt the
team's outcome. "It was harder to play there than anywhere else because the
guys on the team would say you're pitching tomorrow so I can get drunk tonight
and we'll be okay," Summers said. "That creates a problem when the person
saying they're going to get drunk is my catcher."

Despite all the improvements in Croatian baseball — from the fields to the
player development — the country's national team still remains, on paper, on
the fringes of the upper echelon of European baseball. Since earning promotion to the "A-pool" of the European Baseball Championships, Croatia's best
performance is an eighth-place finish in 2001 in Germany. In 2005 in the Czech
Republic, Croatia faltered badly, leading to relegation out of the top pool. The
proud Croats didn't lick their wounds for long, earning a return to the highest level the following summer with a strong qualifying performance. Summers is adamant that their performances have been marred by narrow losses
and some bad luck. For example, in 1999 the team fell in two 1–0 games at the

European Championships in Italy. Despite all the efforts of Kruno Karin, Croatia still remains a country with less money to spend than many of its European counterparts. As Croatian coach Bill Percy pointed out on the road to the 2005 championships: "The other eleven National Teams travel by plane or charter bus. Not us [we traveled by van]. I guess we just like the camaraderie and team chemistry that occurs when being so close. I think a very limited budget may have something to do with it also."

Regardless, the success of Croatian baseball can be better judged by what is happening domestically. Most notably, each season is marked by an Interleague competition, in which Croatian and Serbian teams compete on the baseball diamond. "The guys realize that it wasn't those guys (who created the war)," Summers said. Individual clubs are also bringing international hardware back home. In 2005, BK Zagreb knocked off clubs from Spain, Germany, Czech Republic, Russia and Sweden, among others, to win the CEB Cup.[14] The following summer, Kelteks Karlovac brought the title home for the second straight time. The victories made Croatia only the fifth country — along with Italy, Spain, the Czech Republic and Germany — to win the tournament, which was first organized in 1993.

As for Summers, he has moved on. In the 1999 season he went 21–2 in Croatia and decided he had nothing left to prove there on the diamond. Thanks to his Croatian passport, he got a job playing in Holland and spent six successful seasons in one of Europe's two most competitive leagues. In 2007, he took a job coaching at Columbus State (Ohio) College, but he has not totally left Croatia behind. At the 2007 European Championships in Spain, Summers logged an epic performance for the national team, pitching a 13-inning complete game en route to a 2–1 victory over the Ukraine team. Now, he'd also like to give Croatian players an opportunity to improve their baseball skills in the United States.

"I'm hopeful that I'll be able to bring some players over," said Summers, who recalled that during his time in Karlovac a McDonald's opened, becoming simultaneously one of the most exciting places to hang out and one of the best places to have a job. "I'd like to give these kids a chance to see the world. I've had such an incredible experience in Europe and I would like to reciprocate."

12

The Rest of Europe: A–K

Armenia

The former Soviet Republic of Armenia established its own federation in 1994. The area of Gugark in the northern part of the country offers the greatest interest in baseball with two teams—HBC Gugark and Gugark juniors—playing in the three-team top league as of 2006. Far from the center of Europe, Armenia has competed in just one European Confederation–sanctioned event. In 1998, an Armenian team placed last in the 12-team European Juvenile Championships.

Austria

Although Austria doesn't have a rich history in the upper level of European baseball, it is a country with a vibrant domestic league and improving national team. Much of the success must be attributed to Marlene Campbell, a native Austrian and longtime Baltimore Orioles fan, who was instrumental in founding the Austrian Baseball and Softball Association in the 1980s. Even by European standards, baseball was merely a blip in 1987 when only six teams played in the sport throughout the country. There were four in Vienna, one in Linz and one in Schwas (Tyrol). Within six years, there were more than 50 teams.[1] This period also included a facilities upgrade and improved coaching. In the late 1980s, Ted Thoren, then Cornell University coach, made multiple trips to Austria to conduct clinics. "The Linz field is by far the best in Austria, with raised mound, backstop and excellent turf," said Thoren in a 1989 interview.[2] A half-decade later, the federation celebrated the completion of Austria's first baseball field built to meet international specifications. Located in town of Stockerau, the field has hosted a number of European baseball events. According to the September 1994 program from the inaugural festivities, such baseball luminaries as Yogi Berra, Whitey Ford, Phil Rizzuto, Gaylord Perry and Enos Slaughter attended the opening.

Today, there are nearly 100 teams competing on approximately 26 fields. All told, nearly 2,500 people are playing the game. The top circuit, the Austrian Baseball League, features teams from throughout the country. Club teams have performed very well internationally. In 1998 and 2003, Austrian teams won qualifying club tournaments, which earned the country a spot in Europe's most prestigious club event, the European Cup. Austria has also had success in qualifiers for Europe's two other team championships: the Cupwinners' Cup and the CEB Cup. What's most promising is that it hasn't been just one Austrian team representing the country at these events. Clubs from Vienna, Kufstein and Dornbirn have all flown the Austrian banner internationally.

As for the national team, Austria has been a consistent competitor in second-tier competitions. The country has put a national team forward in senior events since 1990 and has shown progress. In 2006, Austria placed second at the European Championships qualifier event in Moscow. Austria went 2–1 in pool play and then beat up on Belarus in the semi-finals. But the chasm was apparent between the Austrians and Russia. The Russians, who have traditionally been in Europe's upper-echelon, beat Austria 12–2 in the preliminary round and 17–0 in the finals. Despite the Russian drubbing, Austria's overall performance paid off. When Greece announced it could not field a team at the 2007 European Championships in Spain, Austria filled the slot. At the younger levels, Austria has been able to break through to play among the elite countries, which should portend greater success for their adult national team over time.

Belarus

Belarus formed its own governing body in 1994 and not only has a competitive domestic league but also has been a keen competitor on the European competition circuit. Teams from Brest, Minsk and Skidel are traditionally the strongest in the country's top division, with the club Brest Zubrs being the country's preeminent squad. (They boast a purpose-built field, which was erected in 2005, and they've captured the Cup of Belarus six times as of 2007.) Making the most of their location, the landlocked country has set up numerous competitions against regional rivals Lithuania, Ukraine, Russia and Latvia. An "Interleague" was inaugurated in 2002 and while it has mainly been composed of squads from Belarus and Lithuania, representatives from the Ukraine, Russia and Latvia have also made appearances. It's worth noting that a Lithuanian team has won the Interleague every year (with the exception of an "Interleague Open" tournament in 2003, which was won by a Ukranian club).

Belarus baseball, as elsewhere in Eastern Europe, has focused on infrastructure. This field is located in the city of Brest. (Courtesy CEB.)

In addition to tilting with neighbors, a handful of teams from Belarus have consistently played in European events since 1999, while the national team entered a qualifier for the first time in 2000. In 2006, Belarus stormed through the preliminary phase of the European Championships qualifier in Moscow, going 3–0. Ultimately, they dropped two games in the play-offs to place fourth in the eight-team event.

Bulgaria

Although Bulgaria officially joined the Confederation of European Baseball in 1992, its history dates back to the late 1980s. When Jack Brenner, a University of Washington English professor, traveled to Bulgaria as a Fulbright lecturer in 1988, he was astonished to see a group of young men playing baseball on a soccer field in Sofia. By that time, the Akademik Baseball Club had already been formed and Brenner began working with the club led by Yuri Alkalay and Georgi Dimitrov, who had roughly translated the rules of the game into Bulgarian. Brenner's involvement must have been very welcomed, as Alkalay, Dimitrov and their teammates were using a vegetable crate as a catcher's mask before the American secured the group proper equipment.[3]

Baseball has not boomed since Brenner's seminal visit, but the sport continues to maintain a firm footing in Bulgaria. The Akademik club won the country's first three national championships from 1990 to 1992 and Sofia remains the country's baseball center with five of the seven teams in its top league hailing from the country's capital and largest city. Baseball has spread, as evidenced by the success of the Blagoevgrad Buffaloes. From 1993 to 2003 and again in 2005 and 2006, the club from the southwestern city about 100 kilometers south of Sofia hoisted the national championship trophy. The team also hosted European confederation club tournaments in 2005 and 2007. Its field includes sunken dugouts, a good-looking pitcher's mound, fencing around the whole field, and five rows of elevated stands that run from above the first base dugout to behind home plate.

Abroad, Bulgaria hasn't distinguished itself in any major European competitions, even though a senior national team first competed in a European qualifier in 1994. Still, the Bulgarians can boast at least one notable international victory. In 2005, they won the Balkan Tournament in Athens, Greece. Bulgaria finished the three-team event 3–1, beating Turkey twice and splitting two games against Greece.

Cyprus

Cyprus's baseball federation emerged in 1999 and the island country claims approximately 120 players. In a sign of the limited interest in the sport on the island, the federation reports only one field in the country.

Denmark

Although Denmark has a relatively long history with baseball — it organized in 1978 and joined the Confederation of European Baseball in 1979 — the country's bat-and-ball focus has been on a sister sport: fast-pitch softball. In particular, the Danish have had tremendous success in men's fast-pitch softball. Denmark has represented Europe in three men's fast-pitch World Championships (2000, 1996 and 1988) and has won a silver medal at the European Men's Fast-pitch Championships four times (2005, 1997, 1995 and 1993). Much of this action is centered on the island of Sjælland and in the greater Copenhagen metro area. As a result of this interest, a vast majority of the more than 2,000 members of its federation are softball players.

Denmark's baseball history may have been richer if not for tragedy. In 1988, the federation's first president and driving force Svend Eriksen died in an accident. Eriksen had been instrumental in building Danish baseball and, according to author Peter Bjarkman, he even had a "close personal friendship" with longtime Los Angeles Dodgers owner Peter O'Malley.[4] "He was the very active president of the Danish Federation he founded in 1978," a Confederation

Européene de Baseball Amateur (CEBA) publication explained in 1993.[5] "Europe will remember him as a good friend and an excellent comrade in sport."

Nevertheless, Denmark has fielded both a national baseball squad and has sent club teams to take on the rest of Europe. Most recently, a national team represented Denmark at the 2002 European Championships qualifier in Sweden. The Danish placed sixth out of eight teams. Domestically, the early dominant club was HBSK Hoersholm from Sjælland, which captured six national titles from 1978–1993. Since then Copenhagen teams have led the way, with the Copenhagen Fighters being the last Danish team to play in a European confederation event back in 1997.

One thing is clear: Denmark can produce some good ballplayers. In 2007, Frederik Terkelsen became the first Danish player to sign with a major-league club, inking with the Los Angeles Angels. What's remarkable about Terkelsen is that he had played less than twenty baseball games in his life when the Angels picked him up. Instead, he'd excelled at fast-pitch softball. A big kid (six-foot-four, 195 pounds), Terkelsen displayed a nice swing with the potential to develop power at Major League Baseball's European Academy.

Estonia

Reports of baseball in Estonia date back to 1923 when an Estonian club lost 11–7 in a matchup against a Lithuanian squad. While regional bat-and-ball games like *lapta* (see chapter 7) and *pesapallo* (see Finland entry below) were played in the decades that followed, American baseball apparently didn't reemerge until clinics were conducted as early as 1987 in the capital of Tallinn. The country showed some early baseball promise after forming a federation in 1992, but has since not delivered on it. At the second annual European Juvenile Championships in Italy in 1993, Estonia placed second behind Italy in its pool games and beat the Czech Republic, a far more developed baseball nation, to capture a bronze medal. After that, Estonia hasn't played in a single club- or national-team event. Keila, located in northwestern Estonia, was the game's center throughout most of the 1990s. In 2006, the country's federation reported a scant 171 players— of whom only fifteen were adults.

Finland

While a number of European countries claim that baseball is an offshoot of some earlier indigenous bat-and-ball sport, Finland is the one with a game that was initially based on baseball. Finnish baseball, which is called *pesapallo* (Finnish for "nest ball") was created by Professor Lauri Pihkala in 1922. Pihkala had spent time studying in the United States and when he saw baseball he deemed it too slow for the Finnish national temperament. Still, he saw enough that he liked and decided to modify baseball's rules and structure to appeal to his countrymen. "*Pesapallo* is a fast-paced version of baseball with skill, running speed and tactical brilliance counting more than strength," explained the *New York Times* in 1988.[6] A couple of the major differences between the two games: a pitcher in *pesapallo* is close to the hitter and offers a high lob instead of overhand pitch and the bases in the Finnish game are set up in a zig-zag line and are progressively farther apart. In the 1980s, the *Times* estimated that 300,000 people played *pesapallo* in Finland. In addition, small enclaves enjoy the sport in such varied countries as Japan, Estonia, Australia and Germany. In 1992, the first World Cup of *pesapallo* was contested.

Needless to say, this national game has surely hindered the development of America's pastime. Although Finland's American baseball federation was formed in 1980 in large part due to efforts from its Swedish neighbors,[7] less than 200 people were playing the American game in 2006. Some expansion was reported in 2007 as two new teams entered the country's "SM-sarja" league, bringing the total number of adult squads to seven. Baseball — American style — appears limited mainly to the capital, Helsinki, and Espoo, the country's second-largest city, which is located on Finland's southern coast close to Helsinki. One of two new teams, the U.S. Eagles, is composed of American embassy personnel, but the other was composed mostly of domestic players new to the game. This is an indication of progress. The country's top team is the Espoo Expos, which won four straight titles from 2003–2006.

Despite this limited play, there are signs that when the Finnish do take up the American game they have some skills. For example, at the 1986 European B-Pool Championships, Finland's Sakari Keskitalo led all hitters with a .438 batting average.[8] In addition, Finland bested both Norway and the Swedish Junior National Team to win the Nordic Baseball Championships in 2004, 2005 and 2007. Quite possibly, the *pesapallo* influence has helped those who have crossed over to the American game.

Georgia

When the Soviet Union embraced baseball in the late 1980s, Georgia was among the most eager of the communist states' republics. In 1987, *Tass* listed Georgia as one part of the Soviet Union where "there are baseball enthusiasts."[9] In fact, that year a Czechoslovakian team traveled to play in the Georgian capital of Tbilisi. Not surprisingly, an early president of the U.S.S.R. Baseball Softball Federation was Ramaz A. Goglidze, who was a high-ranking communist official from Tbilisi. "Baseball can be a big and beautiful bridge between our two countries," Goglidze told *Sports Illustrated* in 1988.[10] The following year, Goglidze was elected as a vice president of European baseball federation and, in 1990, Tbilisi hosted the CEBA Congress, with eleven countries attending. Goglidze held the top post in Soviet baseball until 1991. (He was replaced by the mayor of Moscow, Gavril Popov.)

By 1994, the Georgian junior national team boasted a roster with two pitchers who could throw more than 80 miles per hour, according to Basil Tarasko, who coached the Ukraine's team against Georgia at the European juniors qualifier.[11] Georgia would place second at the tournament and earn qualification into the top level of European baseball for those eighteen and under. Moreover, Georgia joined the Confederation of European Baseball in 1992 and sent a club team, Leliani, to a European club competition in 1993.

Unfortunately, that enthusiasm hasn't been sustained. Despite qualifying for the 1995 European junior championships with its performance in the Ukraine, Georgia didn't send a team, and in general the country's international play has been sporadic. In fact, no national team of any age level played in a confederation-sanctioned tournament between 2001 and 2005. In 2006, Georgia's adult national team competed in a European Championships qualifying event in Moscow, placing sixth in an eight-team field.

Greece

The history of Greek baseball is really a tale of two programs. One is the effort to create domestic baseball in Greece and the other is the push to put together the best team possible for the 2004 Olympic Games in Athens. While there was some overlap between the two, each is practically a separate story.

Before the 1997 announcement that Athens would host the Olympics in 2004, there had been limited baseball and softball in Greece. Tom Mazarakis's 27-page *The History of Baseball in Greece* offers a comprehensive account of the sparse early days.[12] American military personnel at the U.S. Air Force base at Hellenikon, near Glyfadas, played on two softball fields for years before Greeks starting competing in the sport in the early 1970s. A Greek Orthodox priest named Father Doumas established a Little League and successfully lobbied for the development of a baseball field on the grounds of the Aghia Kosma athletic center at Hellenikon. By 1972, four Little League teams were playing on the two baseball fields. A couple of the teams were made up of kids of U.S. military members and the other two squads were filled primarily by local Greeks. According to Mazarakis, one team was actually composed of boys from a local orphanage. Greek baseball proved successful, as an all-star team from the league won the European Little League championship and even competed in the 1974 Little League World Series in Williamsport, Pennsylvania. While the squad was almost entirely made up of children of Americans, one Greek boy, Sam Georgopoulos, was a member.

This brief spike of Greek baseball was quickly halted, as world politics got in the way. The Turkish invasion of Cyprus in 1974 led to tensions between Greece and the United States, as some believed that the United States was responsible. American military members continued to enjoy games of softball at the Hellenikon fields, but the two Greek Little League teams were disbanded. Even softball was a thing of the past by 1991 when the U.S. Air Force base shut down. The following year, Mazarakis, who was dubbed in 2004 as "the Abner Doubleday of Greek baseball" by ESPN.com's Jim Caple, founded the "Hellenic Baseball Association" in an effort to revive the game. He was able to muster three teams—all of whom were either U.S. military or diplomatic personnel or Greek-Americans. But this effort didn't last long and, with the exception of a softball league created by Mary Ann Ryder in 1994, the sport was moribund until the late 1990s. That's when the story of the Greek Olympic baseball movement begins.

In 1997, the International Olympic Committee chose Athens as the home of the 28th Games. As host of the competitions, Greece would receive an automatic entry into the Olympic baseball tournament—provided they could put together a competitive team. Led by Baltimore Orioles owner Peter Angelos, a Greek American, all efforts were made to make sure that the home team could stay on the field against the likes of Cuba and the United States. To that end, the Greeks tracked down players who had even tangential Greek lineage (players with great-grandparents who were Greek were deemed eligible). Angelos tabbed Rob Derksen, an international scout for the Orioles, to find these athletes. In 2002, a squad that included a number of Greek Americans made their first appearance in a European event successful. The squad earned promotion to European baseball's top tier with a victory at the European Championships qualifier in Hungary. The team, led by Erik Pappas, a three-season major-league veteran, breezed through the tournament, winning the championship game against Slovakia 21–0. Following that event, Derksen continued his effort to find Greek Americans. He scoured the minor leagues and colleges, and even wrote to Greek churches looking for help. "I'm like a lot of the guys on the team in that I'm not a real Greek," Pappas told Baseball America in 2004, "Rob did a great job finding a lot of guys who have Greek mothers. You never would know they were Greek."[13]

While the competition was ratcheted up at the 2003 European Championships, Greece would counter with more imports. The most notable was a young Nick Markakis, who would go on to slug 16 home runs in 2006 as a rookie with the Baltimore Orioles. The squad was strong, but even with former San Diego Padres pitcher Kevin Pickford on the mound for the finals, Greece would have to settle for the silver medal, falling to the Netherlands 2–0 in the championship game. Still, they proved that they would be competitive at the Olympics the following year.

But that ability to compete came at a price. The Hellenic Amateur Baseball Federation had been established in 1997 by Panagiotis Mitsiopoulos, and three years later six teams were battling it out for the first Greek national championship. Although the inaugural league champions, Marousi 2004, was made up of Greek Americans and Greek Canadians, the second-place team, coached by Mary Ann Ryder, who had started a Greek softball league six years earlier, was made up of locals who, according to Mazarakis, "had only been playing the game for a few weeks." That team, Spartakos Glyfadas, would go on to win the first Greek Cup Championship later that year.

While many of the players in the domestic league may have been dreaming of Olympic gold, they wouldn't have a shot at it. "No sport leadership is interested in ... a 'Jamaican Bobsled' scandal," Mazarakis wrote. This would lead to tensions when staffing the eventual Olympic squad. In the days leading up to the Olympics, coach Dimitris Goussios threatened to resign because the final 24-player squad contained just two home-based players. "I feel very bitter," Goussios told the BBC. "I've been used and I feel insulted as a person and as a coach."[14] It didn't help matters that Derksen, who had built so many bridges in his efforts to prepare Greece for the Olympics, died unexpectedly of a heart attack less than a month before the Olympics. Despite all the efforts to put together the best squad possible, the nearly exclusive Greek American and Greek Canadian squad finished 1–6, earning their only victory against Italy. Nevertheless, they did fulfill one goal: the team was competitive, losing close contests to Cuba (5–4) and Canada (2–0).

With the Olympics behind them, Greece's second story of baseball — the sport in Greece — returned to the forefront. The Olympic baseball stadiums were "left to just rot away," according to Mazarakis. But the practice fields were put in the care of the Hellenic Amateur Baseball Federation and are still being used. At the 2005 European Championships, the Greeks were able to retain a shell of their Olympic team, which allowed them to hold on to a spot in Europe's top level of baseball. But when a number of those Greek descendents from North America left near the end of the tournament, the chasm between domestic Greek players and the top level of European baseball came into focus. In a matchup against Sweden, the Greeks lost 25–2, a game ended in five innings due to the mercy rule. Further disappointment occurred in September 2005 when, due to financial difficulties, Greece had to pull out of the World Championships in Holland.

The future of Greek baseball was unclear as of Marazakis's writing in February 2006. "[B]aseball in Greece is on hold until the Hellenic Amateur Baseball Federation sorts out its differences with the Greek Ministry of Sports," he wrote. "The two organizations have been at odds with the Ministry trying to shut down the Federation entirely. We all await the outcome of this lose-lose situation." Marazakis's concerns have proved well-founded as the Greeks had to pull out of the 2007 European Championships just months before the event due to financial and personnel problems. Even worse, in September 2007 it was announced that the main stadium used for the Athens Games was being sold to the soccer club Ethnikos Piraeus. It will be reconfigured and used as a soccer training ground.[15] Still, some hope remains. In late 2007 and early 2008, organizers formed a mini Greek national league, which has kept prospects for the sport alive across the country.

Hungary

Like many Eastern European nations, Hungary began its modern baseball history in the early 1990s. Baseball has received the greatest attention in the capital of Budapest and its suburb Szentendre as well as the mid-sized city of Nagykanizsa, which is located in the southwestern part of the country. A team called the Budapest Islanders took Hungary's first four national titles. Since then, the Szentendre Sleepwalkers and the Nagykanizsa Ants have been consistent challengers for the crown, along with Obuda Brick Factory, a Budapest club.

In addition to domestic play, Hungarian teams play in one of the continent's most lasting inter-league competitions. Established in 1998, this inter-league has featured (at various times) teams from Hungary, Slovenia, Serbia and Croatia.

Ireland (and Northern Ireland)

Along with England and France, Ireland received the biggest baseball push from American professionals in the late nineteenth and early twentieth centuries. The result of these efforts is insubstantial: most denizens of the Emerald Isle today either are unaware that baseball is played on its shores or believe that the game's small but enthusiastic movement is a wholly new creation.

The first known game of baseball played in Ireland took place in Dublin on 24 August 1874. Following a 12-game tour of England, two of America's most prominent clubs—the Boston Red Stockings and the Philadelphia Athletics—traveled to Ireland to display the game. The squads split their two contests and also took on an All-Ireland team in cricket. Because of the great number of Irish-American baseball players, this leg of the trip was considered essential by Boston owner Harry Wright. In a letter to his Philadelphia counterpart before the trip, Wright wrote, "We must take Dublin in ... for with all our Mc's and O'R's, a game there would surely prove attractive and pay handsomely."[16] It's doubtful that the Ireland leg met Wright's expectation, as the whole trip lost money.

Despite this failure, A. G. Spalding, who had played a central role in the 1874 tour as both a player and an organizer, set out to conquer England and Ireland again in the name of baseball in 1889. This time, those countries would be part of a grander plan to bring the American pastime to countries around the world. Spalding's tour spanned the globe, including stops in such far-flung locales as Australia and Egypt before heading to Europe. Spalding brought his Chicago White Stockings club along with a combined squad of other big leaguers dubbed the All-Americas. Ireland would be the last overseas stop on the six-month sojourn. After eleven games in England and Scotland, the Emerald Isle was a welcome sight for the large contingent of ballplayers who were of Irish decent.

After a single game on the grounds of the North of Ireland Cricket Club in Belfast (in which the All-America club beat the Chicago team 9–8 thanks to a ninth-inning rally), the tourists headed to Dublin. Many of the players used a day off to visit Irish relatives. Chicago pitcher John Tener traveled to the Northern Ireland town of Londonderry to visit relatives, while his teammate, catcher Tom Daly, found family in County Kildare. All-America second baseman James Manning arrived to his ancestral home Callan in County Kilkenny to a hero's welcome. Author Mark Lamaster recounted the scene:

> When he arrived at the station there he was swarmed. Everyone had come out to meet the hero from abroad, and everyone had to shake his hand. A parade of jaunting cars delivered him to the house of a long-lost uncle, its walls covered with newspaper clippings and photos of the town's famous American son. How was life in America? Was baseball like [hurling], the local sport of choice? Could you really earn a living playing a child's game? Manning answered the questions, and with pleasure.[17]

Following these reunions, the Landsdowne Road Grounds hosted a baseball match on 27 March 1889. The crowd included a handful of luminaries, including Prince Albert of Saxe-Weimar, who was the commander of the English forces in Ireland, Lord Mayor Thomas Sexton of Dublin and Lord Londonderry. The game was a tight one, with pitchers Mark Baldwin (Chicago) and Ed Crane (All-America) throwing shutouts through six innings. Chicago took a late 3–1 lead, but the All-America squad won in dramatic style, with a four-run rally in the top of the ninth.

The players had put on a great Ireland performance and Spalding looked to back it with support. In 1890, he helped fund and organize a Great Britain and Ireland baseball association. This organization did lead to the formation of a brief professional league in England, but Ireland didn't appear to take to the game.

Why did baseball not receive a greater welcome? Some clues may be offered by the final major-league tour to grace the Emerald shores. In the fall of 1924, the Chicago White Sox and the New York Giants made stops in London, Liverpool, Birmingham, Dublin and Paris. The game played in Dublin was particularly unsuccessful, apparently attracting a group of just twenty spectators. Future Hall-of-Famer Sam Rice explained that baseball's Irish failure on the trip was a result of pure politics. "One clan was comprised of the newspapers which controlled the national sport of hurling ... and resented any intrusion of the American game [and] [t]he other faction, government heads and officials, desiring to win the approval of the Americans, practically demanded the contest be staged," Rice told the *Washington Post* on 2 December 1924. "It was, but before a meager crowd."

In England, baseball suffered because the elite were fearful of its potential encroachment of the indigenous sport of cricket. Quite possibly, some members of the Irish establishment feared that baseball would somehow hinder hurling, which is a far more physical game than baseball but has some vague similarities, in that both sports employ hitting a ball with a stick.

America's pastime did have a major presence in Northern Ireland during World War II. In July 1942, a contest in Belfast between the Thirty-Fourth Infantry Division Midwest Giants and the First Armored Division Kentucky Wildcats drew 7,500 spectators, including numerous local civilian onlookers. By May 1943 a 12-team league was playing at Belfast's Ravenhill Rugby Grounds. "I have fond memories of baseball over in Northern Ireland," U.S. veteran Orlando Langenfeld told author Gary Bedingfield. "The practices and games provided a welcome respite from the training and monotony of Army life, while our friendly rivalry always made the games interesting."[18] Some baseball must have been played after the war because, in 1966, the Federation of European Baseball reported that Ireland filed an application for membership "but in the years to come no actual result came from it."[19]

The seeds of modern Irish baseball began to take root at softball games in the early 1990s. For some of the players the competition from recreational co-ed slow-pitch softball was not enough. In 1995, they began informally play-

Ireland's national team made its international debut in 1996 and has steadily improved, reaching a European Championships qualifying tournament final in 2006. The squad has been led by dual-nationality players like Joe Kealty (above), who played NCAA Division I baseball at Boston College. (Photograph by Andrew Walker and Paul Brady.)

ing some hardball in Dublin. The group put up a makeshift backstop and cobbled together enough equipment to practice. Enjoying the workouts so much, they decided to take their game to the next level. In 1996, an Irish national team was formed from a group of about 30 players who hadn't done much more than scrimmage. The players found some financial backing and entered the 1996 European Championships qualifying tournament in Hull, England. This might have seemed like a stretch as most of their pitchers — if not all of them — had never thrown off a mound.

In their first game, Ireland's first batter, Gus Hernandez (a Mexican transplant to Ireland) rapped a single to right field, giving the Irish some hope that an upset could be in the making. It wasn't to be, as Ireland fell 23–2. The Irish dropped their next three games by lopsided scores, but were able to earn their first international victory in their final matchup, beating Yugoslavia 8–6.

The Irish returned home, buoyed by the Yugoslavian win. But a bigger victory off the field was in the making. During this period, Irish baseball official Ann Murphy met longtime Dodger owner Peter O'Malley. A big booster of international baseball and a proud Irish-American, O'Malley asked Murphy how he could best help the budding Irish baseball movement. Her answer: a proper baseball facility. True to his word, O'Malley was instrumental in the construction of the O'Malley Little League and Dodger Baseball Fields in Corcaigh Park in Dublin. U.S. Ambassador Jean Kennedy Smith threw out the ceremonial first pitch when the complex — which features one adult and one youth field — opened on 4 July 1998. The diamonds have served as a key training ground for the national program and an essential site for the country's domestic league, which started crowning champions in 1997. Three of the six teams in Ireland's adult league play at the Corcaigh Park site, which has also been dubbed the "Irish Field of Dreams."

Outside of Dublin, baseball has also sprung in Greystone and Belfast. In his 2006 documentary about Irish baseball called *The Emerald Diamond*, filmmaker John Fitzgerald eloquently tells how baseball served as a sports buffer in Belfast during the tense Protestant-Catholic sectarian clashes of the 1990s. "Baseball — because it's new to Ireland — it's a neutral sport," Ireland national team member John Dillon said in the documentary. "[Traditionally,] which sport you play ... indicates which side of the fence you're on." As a result, baseball teams in Northern Ireland have been a mix of Protestants and Catholics.

Since their victory over Yugoslavia, the Irish national team has continued to plug away at European Championship qualifiers and other events. Most notably, in 2001, Baseball Ireland raised £35,000 to send the Irish National Team and a youth all-star squad to New England. During that trip, the Irish had the once-in-a-lifetime opportunity to play at the Boston Red Sox field, Fenway Park, against the Rhode Island-based Slocum Baseball Club. In European competition, the country continues to make headway. There has been some solid development among Irish natives. In particular, John Dillon, a former rugby player who didn't pick up a baseball until he was 25, has been a very productive player for the national team since the team's inception in 1996. At the same time, Ireland has taken the same path as many other European countries by recruiting foreign-trained players with dual nationality. These players have included former Boston College players Joe Kealty and Chris Gannon and former University of West Virginia athlete Brendan Bergerson. The likes of Kealty, Gannon and Bergerson have helped Ireland's international performance, as the squad nearly earned promotion into European baseball's elite pool in 2006, making it to the finals of a European qualifying event in Belgium. With only one team being elevated from the tournament, the Irish had to settle for a silver medal at the event, as they fell in the finals to Croatia 12–2.

Looking forward, the demise of baseball as an Olympic sport has severely cut funding for Irish baseball. To continue to grow, Irish baseball will need sustained enthusiasm from its close-knit group of organizers.

Israel

As one story goes, baseball was first introduced in Israel on 4 July 1927 when the governess of the Sephardic Orphanage in Jerusalem handed out baseball equipment. The tale continues that the children examined the baseballs for a bit and then dropped them on the ground and began kicking them around like soccer balls.[20] That year, the Hebrew University of Jerusalem also played baseball with the university's first president Judah Magnes playing second base for the institution, according to Daniel Kurtzer, former United States ambassador to both Israel and Egypt.[21]

Whether those stories pinpoint the launch of baseball in the Holy Land or not, the recent history of the game began between 1979 and 1981, with the official formation of the Israel Association of Baseball (IAB) occurring in 1986.[22] From the start, one of the goals of the organization was to build bridges in a country and a region that is consistently rife with conflict. "The IAB is a fully integrated organization," the IAB website explains. "Religious and ultra orthodox youth, secular children, boys, girls, rich and poor, Kibbutz children, city dwellers, Jews, Christians and Arabs all play together on the same field and very often on the same team."[23]

To that end, some historic events have occurred on Israeli baseball fields. For example, the first sports contact between an Israeli and Saudi Arabian team took place in a Little League game. In 1994, Israel played Jordan in a youth contest just two days before the two countries signed a peace treaty. In Tel Aviv, a Jewish-Arab youth team was formed.

Israel's geographic location wouldn't suggest the nation would play in European competitions, but in 1995 the country was accepted into the Confederation of European Baseball. "We feel much at home in Europe," explained Israeli baseball official Sam Pelter at the time.[24] Israel formerly was a member of Asia's baseball federation, but Pelter told journalist Marco Stoovelaar that the large distances between Asian countries was the main reason for the switch into European play.

Since the move, Israel has been a regular participant in European events—particularly at the youth level. More than a dozen teams representing Israel have played from the juvenile level (12-and-under) to the adult level. The country's first appearance at the senior stage took place in 2004 in Germany. Paced by two American-based college pitchers, Dan Rotem (Georgia Southern University/Gardner–Webb University) and Shlomo Lipetz (University of California, San Diego), Israel earned victories over Hungary, Switzerland and Finland.[25]

Despite the national team's solid performance in 2004, adult baseball has lagged. In 2006, a mere 49 grown-up players were reported by the federation and the country's top league included just three senior teams along with the Israeli junior national squad. A central problem organizers have faced is substandard facilities. In 2006, the town of Bet Shemesh had a local youth league of about 600 children but were forced to play at a community amphitheater featuring a 30-degree slope. Before 2007, Jerusalem's only baseball field was an empty lot filled with thorns and thistles. In Ra'anana, which is located just north of Tel Aviv, the town's expansive baseball field also doubles as a grazing field for local horses.[26]

With this problem in mind, a Boston-based entrepreneur named Larry Baras has looked to change the country's baseball landscape and, in turn, quickly catapult Israel into the realm of major baseball-playing countries. In March 2006, the Israel Baseball League (IBL) announced a joint venture with the Jewish National Fund to develop community baseball fields throughout the country. The following year, the IBL opened a professional league. With players from the United States, Canada, the Dominican Republic, Australia and Israel (not all the players are Jewish), the six-team league began play on 24 June 2007. (Games are never played on the Jewish Sabbath and all ballpark food is kosher.) The players received $1,500 each in the first season and some prominent baseball names joined the endeavor, including former Boston Red Sox and Montreal Expos general manager Dan Duquette, who served as director of baseball operations in 2007, and former major leaguers Ken Holtzman, Ron Blomberg and Art Shamsky, who all signed on to manage teams in the inaugural campaign. (Even Major League Baseball commissioner Bud Selig was on the league's advisory board.)

Would the circuit succeed? Baras told the *Chicago Tribune* that the league's target audience was the more than 120,000 Israelis who immigrated to Israel from the United States, along with curious American tourists and students on study abroad programs. At the same time, he remained optimistic on the eve of the league's opening about the broader appeal of baseball in the country.

"The biggest goal of all is to give Israelis a true respite," Baras told the

In 2007, a professional circuit called the Israel Baseball League opened with former Jewish-American major leaguers Ron Blomberg, Art Shamsky and Ken Holtzman serving as managers for teams. Here Petach Tikva Pioneers skipper Holtzman (far right) greets player Ryan Crotin during the pre-game ceremony at the league's inaugural contest on June 24. (Photograph by Clive Russell.)

Tribune. "I don't consider fast-paced spectator sports any kind of relaxation. At a baseball game you can sit back and talk to friends; there's something well-paced about it that fits the way life should be. In Israel, everyone's on edge, jostling and honking, ears to the radio. They really would benefit from just being able to relax a couple of hours at a game."[27]

Early signs were good for the league. Nine IBL games were broadcast on Arutz Sport, Israel's leading all-sports television network, and the season's opening contest between the Modiin Miracles and the Petach Tikva Pioneers drew an announced attendance of more than 3,000. But the league quickly began to unravel, according to the 29 May 2008 issue of the *Jerusalem Post.* The newspaper said there were "financial and organizational problems—from missed player payments to games canceled early because of inadequate lighting." Petach Tikva manager Holtzman quit with one week left in the season because he was frustrated with the operation, and a number of the circuit's star-studded advisory board also resigned, including New York Yankees president Randy Levine. With money still owed to Israeli creditors from the first campaign, a 2008 IBL season was extremely unlikely. Nevertheless, Israeli baseball officials still hold out hope that the league (or some other like it) can resume at a later date.

13

The Rest of Europe: L–Z

Latvia

Latvia had a brief flirtation with baseball in 1920, according to the October 10th edition of the *New York Times* that year. The paper recounted a game in Riga featuring members of the American Red Cross Commission of Western Russia and the Baltic States that garnered high-level political attention. "During the third inning," the paper wrote, "the Prime Minister of Latvia drove onto the field. [The fielding team] whooped with joy, thinking that here was a worthy player to match [the other club's star]. Instead, the Minister-President took our first baseman away with him."

Today, Latvia's baseball movement is minuscule — even by European standards. With about 80 players in the mid–2000s, the country had four teams in its top league in 2006. BK Riga was the class of the group, going 11–1 and even fielding a second team. BK Riga also won the national title in 2005 with an identical 11–1 record.

Lithuania

Long before it was a Soviet republic, Lithuania was a baseball-playing nation. The sport was first introduced to the country in 1922 by Steponas Darius, a Lithuanian who grew up in Chicago.[1] Born in 1896 in Lithuania, Darius moved to the United States in December 1907. An athlete who played baseball, basketball and football, among other sports, he fought for the United States in World War I, earning a Purple Heart for injuries sustained on the battlefields of France. After the war, he studied at the University of Chicago and helped organize the Alliance of Lithuanian-American Soldiers.

In 1920, Darius returned to the newly independent Lithuania (the country had formerly been under the thumb of the Austrian Empire) and brought with him his love for sports. Among the games he introduced, basketball enjoyed the greatest success, as Lithuania is a top hoops nation today. Still, Darius made a vigorous play for baseball as well. In 1922, he organized the first Lithuanian baseball league, with a club called "Lietuvos Fizinio Lavinimois Sajunga" from the city of Kaunas winning the first championship. The following year a Lithuanian team called Aviacijos took the country's first international victory, beating a squad from Estonia 11–7. In 1924, Darius took the essential step of translating the rules of baseball from English to Lithuanian.

Unfortunately, Darius's initial efforts were not enough and even he recognized that baseball wasn't taking hold. Still, he was optimistic about the sport's future in his native land. In 1933, Darius, a pilot by trade, was planning a transatlantic flight from the United States to Lithuania. Before the sojourn, he confidently told a newspaper reporter: "[I]f I succeed in flying to Lithuania and conquer the Atlantic in Lithuania's name, my goal will be to bring Lithuanian-Americans and the youth in Lithuania closer through the sport of baseball."[2] Tragically, Darius's transatlantic flight ended in disaster: he and another pilot died in a crash just three hours before they were to have reached Lithuania. Darius's death marked a long hiatus for Lithuanian baseball.

In the late 1980s, Lithuania, like all the Soviet republics, accepted baseball. In 1986, Vidas Šapamis, an ice-hockey lecturer at the Kaunas Physical Culture Institute, conducted Lithuania's first baseball seminar since the days of Darius. During this period the Soviets were searching throughout their lands for established athletes to help springboard the country's baseball program to an elite level. Lithuanian Edmundas Matusevičius was one of those picked to join the baseball ranks. A high-level javelin thrower, Matusevičius became a pitcher on the USSR national team. In 1989, during the first Soviet baseball tour in the United States, Matusevičius pitched relief in the opening game against the United States Naval Academy. (The USSR lost that game 21–1.)

The first Lithuanian team — made up of Lithuanians as well as a few Latvian players—competed in the inaugural all–Soviet tournament in April 1987. Following that event, Atletas was formed in Kaunas. It was the first purely Lithuanian squad and it was quickly followed by another club in Kaunas (Banga) and two squads from Vilnius (Elektronas and Zalgirietis). Atletas was the class of this first group of teams, taking home the Vilnius Cup in August 1987 and the first Lithuanian Cup the following month. The next year, despite restrictions on Americans in the Soviet Union, a team of 14- and 15-year-olds from Illinois traveled to Lithuania. The Americans handily defeated Lithuanian opponents in three straight games— despite the fact that no Lithuanian on the field was younger than 18.

Baseball continued to make headway in the early 1990s. With its independence restored in 1991, Lithuanian baseball players began traveling throughout the world. Teams played in Sweden, France and the United States. The Kaunas Sports Institute also included in its curriculum a baseball course.

These positive steps have been blunted by the constant need for money. At the 1996 European B-pool Baseball Championships in Great Britain, the Lithuanian national team was forced to camp out behind one of the diamonds, presumably because they couldn't afford better accommodations. In Lithuania, facilities are also limited. "Games are often played on abandoned soccer fields or on simple grass fields where you will not find a pitching mound or backstop anywhere in sight and where the foul lines are wood chips instead of chalk," wrote authors John J. Chernoski and Arvydas Birbalas in 2003. "Team uniforms often consist of hand-me-down gifts from America. Baseball gloves, balls and other equipment are not readily available in Lithuania and, if available, are very costly."

Hope remains for future baseball development in Lithuania. There are now some proper baseball diamonds in the country, and in 2007 talks were underway to erect an international-grade facility in Vilnius. Such a move would bring to Lithuania the type of baseball development lost all those years ago with Darius's tragic death.

Luxembourg

Founded in 2002, the Federation de Baseball Luxembourg (FBL) describes itself as being in the "development phase" of its growth.[3] With less than 500,000 residents, Luxembourg is among the continent's smallest countries and its baseball play reflects its size. The country has only four teams and a national squad. The clubs play a domestic competition, which has been dominated by the Beckerich Hedgehogs. That squad has won every national championship since the FBL was formed. In addition, beginning in 2006, Luxembourg and Belgium have competed in a cross-border "Bellux" circuit. In practice, this circuit integrates Luxembourg's teams into Belgium's third division. A national team also participates in international competitions. In 2007, Luxembourg played in the 24th annual Eifel Cup in Germany. The national squad, which was competing against clubs, mainly from lower divisions, hailing from such countries as Great Britain, Holland, Germany and Switzerland, placed last out of ten teams.[4]

Malta

Malta has a small baseball community but those who play the game there do so with vigor. Malta received its first taste of baseball on 29 April 1890 when teams from Boston and Atlanta played a "hotly contested match on the Malta polo grounds," according to Spalding's 1891 Official Base Ball Guide. "A large attendance mainly of Great Britain's naval and military officers— many of high rank — accompanied by their wives and daughters, witnessed the game."

Concluded the guide: "The Englishmen seemed very much mystified all through the game, but the ladies enjoyed it very much."[5]

A more lasting introduction to the game came nearly a century later when the archipelago's Italian neighbors offered instruction. The Italians announced their first trip to Malta in 1979 and according to a European baseball confederation booklet this is "where the basis was laid for local baseball activity."[6] Four years later, Malta became an official member of the Confederation Européene de Baseball Amateur (CEBA). The Malta-Italy relationship remains close. In 2007, Italy's baseball federation supplied two umpires per game during the first two months of the season in order to help train Maltese officials. (The Italians also provided uniforms for Malta's local umpiring corps.) Historically, the country's top team has been the Mellieha Northenders, who have won seven national championships since 1994. The Gozo Tornadoes and the Marsa Mustangs have each captured three titles through 2006.

Moldova

Moldova's baseball history seems in many ways typical of the nascent programs from the former Soviet Republics — a brief burst to begin with and then a whole lot of treading water. In 1991, just before the breakup of the Soviet Union, a Moldovan team from Tiraspol had the funding to travel to the Cocoa Expo facility in Florida to play at the Expo Internationale. As was the case throughout the USSR, the Tiraspol club was comprised of athletes with little baseball know-how but tons of athletic experience. There were former decathletes, soccer players, handball players and volleyball players. The team's manager Vladislav Telpyakov was a former national team rugby player with no previous baseball experience. In what would have led to cringing from any baseball coach in the West, the Moldovan squad relied heavily on one pitcher Alexander Pasisnichenko. The former star javelin thrower hurled 21 innings in six days. Despite this lack of experience and a clear overuse of Pasisnichenko, the team managed to win two games in the seven-game affair, including one victory against the tournament's runner-up. "(Tiraspol) is playing at a better level than their national team was a year ago," tournament director Kevin Russell told Florida's *St. Petersburg Times.*[7]

At the same time, baseball was also sprouting in the capital of Kishinev, which today is known as Chişinău. This early growth led to immediate results. In 1993 and again in 1994, Moldova captured the silver medal at the European Cadet (13- to 15-year-olds) Baseball Championships, placing just behind Italy at both tournaments. The future should have been bright for baseball in the country, but following Moldova's independence from the USSR in 1991, the economic difficulties of becoming a free state, which included energy shortages and ambitious efforts to liberalize the economy, eventually had some trickle-down effect on baseball. For example, Abator, a baseball club in

Chişinău, enjoyed immediate success when it was founded in 1992, winning the country's first national championship the following year. But by 1995, problems with financing the team meant the club no longer trained on a regular basis and could only take part in tournaments sporadically.[8] In spite of its woes, Abator continues to play and has even captured two national championships (2001 and 2005) since its maiden triumph.

Chişinău remains Moldova's baseball center today, but Tiraspol, the home of that team that traveled to Florida during the Soviet era, also maintains a baseball tradition. In 2006, Kvint Tiraspol earned the national title, marking the second time in three years the club has taken those honors. With less than 500 players in the country, the hope is that the game somehow resonates with the Moldovan youth. One positive note to that end: in the country's seven-team 115-player top league in 2006, the average player's age was 22. Moreover, in June 2007, Moldova's baseball federation, in conjunction with volunteers from the Peace Corps USA, hosted a President's Cup, which attracted about 70 children, of ages 13–15 years.

Norway

Baseball has been regularly played in Norway since the early 1990s, but it hasn't made much of an impact on the country's sporting scene. Americans serving as part of a NATO base in Oslo and U.S. oil workers from the Trondheim area brought baseball to Norway, according to European baseball journalist Marco Stoovelaar.[9] Throughout the intervening years, clubs have popped up in such locales as Oslo, Bekkestua, Osterøy, Porsgrunn, Bergen and Haugesund. As far as performance goes, one team has clearly dominated: the Oslo Pretenders. The club has captured the vast majority of national championships since the event's inception in 1991. In fact, between 2001 and 2006, the club boasted an aggregate record of 112–12 in the Norwegian Baseball League. Yet, to give a sense of where Norwegian baseball stands on the European scene, when the Pretenders played in the European Cup qualifiers during that same period the club went 6–21.[10]

Poland

There's a Polish baseball legend that the country's first baseball glove was purchased from the Czechs for a bottle of vodka. While this story is likely apocryphal, as various sources date this famous exchange in the early 1980s or late 1970s, and forms of baseball were played in Poland before that, it does indicate how far the sport has come in the intervening years.[11] The country now has one of Europe's most impressive baseball complexes and is considered by the Confederation of European Baseball's president, Martin Miller, to be one of the most promising baseball nations on the continent. "Poland has great

Norway's harsh weather for large stretches of the year has forced local baseball organizers to come up with some inventive ways to play the game. The Nordic Baseball Challenge (pictured here in 2003) has been played in an indoor soccer facility during February in the outskirts of the city of Fredrikstad.

potential," Miller said in an interview in 2007. "The country has 40 million people and the [baseball] infrastructure just keeps getting better."

Baseball made its Polish debut on 30 May 1919 in a town near Warsaw called Modlin, according to a 2002 article in the *Warsaw Voice*. This matchup probably featured American or Canadian military personnel competing in a post–World War I contest. The occurrence raised little attention. Poland, after all, had its own similar game and the interest in an alternative might not have created a stir. Poland had played its own traditional bat-and-ball game — particularly in the areas of Upper Silesia and the Opole District — dating back centuries and, by the 1920s, the game of *palant* had a popular following.

Palant and baseball do have similarities — enough so that some have argued that *palant*, brought to the United States by Polish and German immigrants, was the inspiration for baseball. Both games are played with a ball that is approximately the same size (a baseball is a bit heavier); baseball bats are similar to a *palant* bat — albeit longer; and the goal in both sports is for a batter is to hit the ball and eventually return to his starting point.[12] Of course, the sports differ as well. *Palant* is played on a rectangular field (approximately 164 feet by 82 feet) and it's a game of mainly power hitting, in which "strikers" try to slug the ball as far as possible and run to a designated point and back. Instead of baseball's structure of innings, *palant* is a played for forty minutes with a five-minute break.

Between 1923 and 1963, *palant* was popular enough to set up a national league with teams in such locales as Rybnik, Zory and Boguszowice. Curiosity about baseball eventually got to these *palant* ball players and, in 1960, a Polish Palant-ball and Baseball Federation was formed.[13] This effort to start baseball was a gutsy one. The sport was perceived as wholly American and most Eastern Bloc countries strongly shunned baseball during the height of the Cold

War. "Through the years of communism, baseball was treated as the imperialist sport and the enemy of the system," Polish Baseball Association president Ireneusz Wyszomirski told the publication *Warsaw Voice* in 2002. "It was not in good taste to promote baseball and the journalists who were brave enough to mention the sport were severely criticized for doing so."[14] With this problem in mind, European Baseball Federation president Steno Borghese attempted to minimize the political tension of baseball behind the Iron Curtain when the nascent Polish baseball organization joined the EBF in 1960. Prince Borghese said flatly in a press interview: "We are interested in baseball and are not involved in politics."[15] Those efforts to make it just about the game must have failed because the baseball federation quickly disappeared from the Polish sporting landscape.

Still, the game — in the form of softball — continued under the radar in the Upper Silesia area in the 1960s and 1970s. Baseball's close cousin was brought to Poland from Czechoslovakia in 1962 and games and tournaments between the two countries were often conducted. During this period, baseball was still played by at least one team, Silesia Rybnik, and the sport seemed to be gaining a toehold in 1976 when Japan's baseball federation provided a gift of baseball equipment. At that time, teams in Boguszowice, Bytom and Cyprzanow had all tried baseball.

The 1980s brought the trade-unionist Solidarity movement to Poland, which began the process of eroding communist power. During this era, baseball began to make inroads. In 1983, a Dutch team called Foresters Heilo traveled to Poland and played the country's first international baseball match. The following season, the first official Polish baseball championships were held. Silesia, a team from the town of Rybnik, which had long been a baseball/softball haven, emerged winners. In the late 1980s, the Polish communist government was crumbling and baseball was chosen as an Olympic sport — two factors that paved the way for even more baseball development. In 1987, the sport received a number of big boosts. The Polish Baseball Federation was finally registered with the country's ministry of sports; Rawlings, the famed baseball equipment manufacturer, donated $50,000 worth of gear to Polish baseball; and St. Louis Cardinals Hall-of-Famer Stan Musial visited Poland. The Polish-American Musial, who would be a great advocate for Polish baseball, was given the title of "honorary chairman" of the Polish Baseball and Softball Federation.

Along with those events, 1987 also marked the beginning of discussions with Little League Baseball about developing a facility in Poland. These talks would end up being very fruitful as an expansive Little League complex was eventually built in the town of Kutno. But that monumental construction was still years off. On the field, Polish players in the late 1980s remained a long way from becoming serious ballplayers. A 1987 *Los Angeles Times* article recounts how little players in Kutno grasped the game when Juan Echevarria, a Cuban coach, began working with them. "I had to teach team how to throw the ball, then I had to teach them not to knock it down with their heads," said Echevarria, referring to his players' penchant for applying soccer skills to baseball.[16]

Strides have since been made by Polish players, but they still remain in the continent's second tier of baseball-playing countries. The national team competed in its first European Championship qualifier in 1990, losing all three of its games by a combined score of 54–6. Things have since gotten better for the squad. In 2002, the Poles earned a bronze medal at the European Championships qualifier in Stockholm, Sweden. At the club level, Polish teams have fared similarly, with no club having earned promotion to the top level of European club competition. (Poland's best club finish is a second-place showing by SKRA Warszawa at the Cupwinners Cup qualifier in France in 1993.)

Nevertheless, Poland's relationship with Little League baseball has the country on track to become a true baseball nation. Polish Little League began in 1989 almost by chance. When U.S. President George H. W. Bush planned a visit to the country, officials thought he'd like to see Polish children playing an American game, so a baseball exhibition was set up. The showing was such a success that kids started playing regularly and the country became the first former Soviet-bloc country to receive a Little League charter. The relationship between Little League and Poland was taken to new heights when the youth baseball organization agreed to make its biggest capital investment outside the United States in Kutno, Poland. The $6-million facility, which includes numerous playing fields (with dimensions for all age groups), lighting for night games, dormitories, office space and many other amenities, is easily amongst the best on the continent.

Not surprisingly, the quality of the Kutno complex, which is officially called the Little League European Leadership Training Center, has led to a boom in both numbers and performance by younger Polish teams. In 2004, Kutno's Little League team played in the Little League Baseball World Series in Williamsport, Pennsylvania, after winning the Europe, Middle East and Africa Region (EMEA) Tournament. Although, the Kutno kids didn't win a single game at the World Series, they did go 6–0 at the EMEA tournament, outscoring its opponents 79–10. The following year, Poland's national team in the 12-and-under age group earned a bronze medal at the European Juvenile Baseball Championships. With nearly 2,000 players in Poland, a number greater than such top-level European baseball countries as Spain and Sweden, CEB president Miller's expectations for Polish baseball appear to be well-founded.

Portugal

Unlike their Spanish neighbors who have benefited greatly from the Spanish-speaking Latin American baseball world, Portugal has not enjoyed a sus-

Polish baseball got a big boost when Little League decided to open a facility in the town of Kutno. Polish-American Hall-of-Famer Stan Musial has visited the field and is the namesake for the complex's adult-sized diamond. (Above: scoreboard).

tained baseball history until recently.[17] The first known game of baseball in Portugal dates back to 1919 when a group of U.S. sailors played in Lisbon while their ship was docked in the port. There were a couple of mentions of baseball in the Portuguese media in the 1920s and one passing reference to the sport being played in Portugal in a 15 April 1934 *New York Times* article, but for the most part locals did not take to the game. Decades later, an effort to revive the game was spurred by Markus van Hooff, a Dutch physical education teacher, and some baseball was played in Lisbon.[18] During that decade baseball also quietly emerged in the town of Coimbra. Brothers Sergio and Bruno Medeiros brought baseball gear to Portugal and began teaching the sport. In 1989, Sergio Medeiros founded the Black Tigers in Coimbra.

Even with these efforts, baseball was not gaining traction, and the 1990s began with the sport's main practitioners, according to one source, being Venezuelans living in the country.[19] In March 1993, Portugal formed a baseball and softball federation — although it wouldn't become a fully recognized federation in Portugal until February 1996. Still, Portugal's baseball governing body became a member of the European confederation in 1994. That season also marked the start of the Associacao Académica de Coimbra's involvement with the sport. The students' union of the University of Coimbra features several sports and cultural sections as well as autonomous organizations. These independent organizations include a professional soccer team, a long-running club that has primarily played at the highest level of Portuguese soccer (also known as Académica de Coimbra), and an eponymous baseball club that was an offshoot of the Black Tigers. Elsewhere during the early and mid–1990s, teams were forming in such diverse cities as Loulé (Tigres de Loulé B.C.), Seixal (the Pioneers), Oliveira de Azeméis (the Peloteros and Paz BC) and Porto (Porto Baseball Club). Baseball was also continuing in Lisbon with the Lisbon Baseball Club (formerly known alternatively as the Old Stars and then the Astros) serving as the capital's main team.

In the first two recognized championships, Paz from Oliveira de Azeméis earned the national championship, but Associacao Académica de Coimbra dominated through the late 1990s, winning four championships between 1996 and 2000. (The club won a fifth in 2004). The country's other top power has been the Tigres de Loule B.C., who have captured six championships (1998, 2001–2003, 2005–2006).

Abroad, Portugal has not been a massive player. In 1998, the country made its first appearance at a European qualifying competition in Vienna, Austria. Portugal won its first international game against Finland 14–6. But, as of 2006, the country hadn't returned a national team to a major competition. That should all change in the coming years with the construction of an impressive baseball complex in city of Abrantes in 2006. The facility has a nice press box, fencing around the whole field and a fine surface. It could easily serve as a solid municipal-park facility in a U.S. city and it should be an excellent site for international competition. Already, in 2007, the Abrantes complex hosted a European Cup qualifying event. Clubs from Sweden, Belgium, Switzerland, Norway and Finland played in the event, with the Tigres de Loule finishing fourth out of six teams.

The field should also give additional momentum for the country's national squad. At the opening of the field in Abrantes, the Portuguese national team took on a collection of players from Germany's top league. Portugal lost 13–3 but their efforts portended more action from a Portuguese representative team in the future.

Romania

Baseball is not the first game of its kind to be played inside Romania's borders. The country's indigenous bat-and-ball sport *oina* dates back to the fourteenth century. Like baseball, two teams compete with one team "at bat" and the other "at catching" (the equivalent of being in the field). Hitters in *oina* also use a bat (albeit a longer and slimmer one than ones employed in baseball) and the ball in the Romanian game is approximately the same weight as a baseball. Differences include eleven players in the lineup and a time limit on *oina* contests (30 minutes). As for the American version of the game, Dinamo Bucureşti is the class of the country. The club has won every

Opened in 2006, the baseball field in Abrantes (above) has given Portugal a venue to host international baseball events. (Courtesy CEB.)

national championship since 2000 and has even distinguished itself in international competition. In 2004, the club won the Cupwinners Cup qualifying tournament in Kufstein, Austria, breezing through the competition with a 5–0 record.

San Marino

Although San Marino is completely surrounded by Italy, the country has been able to carve out its own baseball identity. According to San Marino's baseball federation, baseball first took hold in this country of only 30,000 people in the 1960s when local residents returning from the United States began expressing a passion for the game.[20] The country joined Europe's federation in 1971 and immediately made a splash at the European championships in Italy, placing fifth out of nine countries. San Marino knocked off both Great Britain and Spain at the event, which proved to be an auspicious debut. While a local competition does occur annually, all the country's teams also play at various levels in Italy's leagues. The top club is T&A San Marino. Boasting an incredibly picturesque stadium, T&A plays in Italy's top league Serie A1. The club brought home some serious hardware in 2006, winning the continent's most prestigious club event, the European Cup.

Serbia (Formerly Yugoslavia and Serbia and Montengro)

Although the former Yugoslavia included, among other republics, the baseball-playing nations of Croatia and Slovenia, it is Serbia, home of the country's elite ruling class and location of Yugoslavia's federal capital of Belgrade, that's been most closely identified with the former nation. The region that made up Yugoslavia received a lot of exposure to baseball in the twentieth century. After both world wars, American personnel located in the area did play some baseball.

The game stuck to some extent in the 1970s, largely due to the influence of the Italians, according to writer Peter Bjarkman. By 1973, games were being played by local clubs against visiting Italians and, in 1979, a Yugoslavian team of 13- to 15-year-olds played in the European Cadet Baseball Championships. (The team finished in last place in the six-team field but did lose a close 16–13 slugfest to France.) The Italian involvement continued into the 1980s, as clubs from Italia traveled to the Croatian town of Split and the Slovenian Ljubljana in Yugoslavia in the early part of that decade.

Still, the sport was not officially recognized by Yugoslavia's communist regime until the mid–1980s. Performances by Serb teams were not always impressive during this period. For example, Partizans, a new Serbian team from Belgrade, allowed fifteen runs— all scored on walks— in a 15–8 loss to a Slovenian club in 1989. "Their desire to learn and eagerness to play after only eight months of practice is highly motivating," said Partizan's Bolt Morre, an American businessman from Detroit who was living in Belgrade at the time. "During indoor winter practices I showed the players video tapes of last year's World Series," Moore said, blaming his pitchers' base-on-balls problems to their attempts to imitate the pitching style of Los Angeles Dodgers ace Orel Hershiser.[21]

Baseball was still going in the waning days of a unified Yugoslavia. In 1990, the country's last national team, including Croatians and Slovenians, put up a credible performance at the European Championships qualifier, placing fourth in a seven-team field in Italy. At the time, there were twenty-five clubs competing in one federal and two local leagues, according to the *Washington Post*.[22]

The following year, Croatia and Slovenia declared their independence from Yugoslavia and bitter violence ensued. The war created much hardship, and for many — although not all — baseball became at most an afterthought. (See the chapter 11 for more on this period). Still, baseball continued to exist in what was left of Yugoslavia. The country's first national championship was contested in 1993, with the Partizans, now split into two teams, competing against clubs from Batajnica (a Belgrade suburb), Kragujevac (located 60 miles from the capital) and an international team made up mainly of U.S. and Canadian diplomats. In 1996, Beograd '96 was formed and has since been Serbia's most consistent performer both at home and abroad. The club has won more national titles than any other team, with the most recent crowns coming in 2005 and 2006. In addition, the club captured the countries first-ever international trophy, winning the CEB Cup qualifier in Belgrade in 2006.

Even with this success, the Beograd '96 club is realistic about Serbia's baseball place in the region. "Serbian baseball is not as developed as Croatia or Slovenia," explains the Beograd website. "We are doing our best to catch up — although we are behind them, it is very possible to make all of these national leagues equal in a few years."[23] To help reach that goal, teams from Serbia, Croatia, Slovenia and Hungary compete in an interleague. (In 2006, Beograd placed fourth in the seven-team circuit.) Proof that development may be occurring: a Serbia and Montenegro national team placed a solid fourth at the nine-team 2004 European qualifier in Sweden.

Slovakia

To appreciate where Slovakia stood regionally in the baseball world when it became an independent state in 1992, you just have to look at the final Czechoslovakian national team. That squad only included one Slovakian player, with the Czech Republic supplying the rest. Since then Slovakia has made great strides, and while the country cannot yet compete with the Czechs, it has enjoyed some minor success on the international stage.

Improvement did not happen overnight, and Slovakia struggled in its 1994 debut at the European qualifiers, finishing second to last out of thirteen teams in Slovenia. But in the new millennium there have been triumphs. Most notably, Slovakia won the 2002 European (18-and-under) junior qualifying tournament, outclassing more developed countries Sweden and Great Britain, among others. That year, the senior national squad almost earned promotion into the continent's top pool. The Slovakians placed second in a qualifier and might have been a winner in another year but had the misfortune of facing Greece — which had a squad packed with Greek-Americans in anticipation for the 2004 Olympics — in the finals. The Greeks prevailed by a lopsided 21–0 score.

Two cities dominate Slovakian baseball: the capital of Bratislava and the western Slovakian town of Trnava, which is located approximately 28 miles from the capital. Every national champion has come from one of these two locations. Trnava has also excelled internationally. In 2003, Slovakia hosted a qualifying event for the Europe's most prestigious club trophy, the European Cup, and the local club TJ STU Trnava prevailed, besting seven other clubs from throughout Eastern Europe. This was TJ STU Trnava's second piece of European hardware. The club also won a Cupwinners Cup qualifier in 1998.

Slovenia

In professional baseball, players who are too good to play in the minors (the highest being triple–A) but can't quite cut it at the major-league level are called "four–A players." If European baseball were to have a four–A country, it would have to be Slovenia. It has tasted competition at Europe's highest club and national team levels, but has never been able to retain a spot among the elite. Slovenia joined the Confederation of European Baseball in 1993. Its national team promptly qualified for the top-tier European championships the following year and between 1995 and 1999 yo-yoed between the "A-pool" and the qualifying level. Slovenia club teams have experienced similar occurrences.

After Yugoslavia's communist government recognized baseball in the mid–1980s, the Slovenian part of the country showed particular acumen. In 1987 and 1988, the Ljubljana club Gunclje won Yugoslavian titles. "[They] would be sorely tested by an average U.S. high school team," wrote the Associated Press in describing the Gunclje's performance level in 1989.[24] Surely, even that standard was helped by Italian teams that visited the Slovenian capital in the early part of the 1980s.

Following the nation's independence, baseball retained a small presence in Slovenia — 560 players were registered in 2006. Nevertheless, some vital support from U.S. sources has helped those who have taken up the game. In 1994, John Vodenlich, a former player at University Wisconsin-Whitewater, went with former UW-W teammate Jay Wojcinski to Slovenia to play for the Ljubljana club Zajcki. Vodenlich, who comes from Slovenian heritage and had relatives in the country, was a two-time All-American in college. In 2003, he also became head coach at Wisconsin-Whitewater. Not only did he bring his baseball acumen to the country, but he also arranged a U.S. tour for the Zajcki team in 1995.[25] The trip had games scheduled throughout seven states and into Canada. The tour must have been fruitful as Zajcki has captured eight national titles — half of which were won after the trip.

One positive recent sign of development: in 2005, Rok Vadas, a left-handed pitcher, became the first Slovenian invited to Major League Baseball's exclusive European Baseball Academy.

Switzerland

Swiss baseball has a long history that cannot claim great player development but does have a solid domestic league. Swiss baseball got its start in 1981, with Zurich being a popular place for the sport. The Zurich Challengers, who took the first Swiss championships, have won nine national titles. As a sign that there is nationwide interest, teams from a variety of cities have enjoyed success in the national league. The Bern Cardinals took the crown in 2001, 2005 and 2006 and the Therwil Flyers have also taken home multiple championships.

Although Switzerland has not broken into the top tier of European baseball, its domestic league has enjoyed a consistent level of competitiveness for more than two decades. Schweiz (above) has been one location where there's been sustained baseball interest. (Courtesy CEB.)

Baseball teams also exist in Geneva, Sissach, Hünenberg and Reussbühl, among other places. Not surprisingly, as Switzerland is one of the epicenters of international banking, some teams have had enough financial wherewithal to recruit foreign professionals to augment locals. While this isn't uncommon in countries with more developed baseball, it's a valuable resource for a country of Switzerland's baseball level. In a sign that there may be increasing local interest in the sport, plans to broadcast a domestic league baseball game on Swiss television (StarTV!) were set for 2008.

Internationally, Switzerland has often entered national teams in various age groups and had club teams represent in European events. The country's best performance at the adult level include a first-place performance by the Bern Cardinals at the 2008 European Cup qualifier in the Czech Republic and the national team's fourth-place finish at the European Championships qualifier in 2006. The Cardinals' 2008 triumph was the first for a Swiss team in more than forty European confederation–sanctioned qualifying events.

Turkey

Before a formal federation was created in Turkey, baseball was played on such university campuses as the Orta Dogu University and Bilkent University in Ankara. The sport attracted a lot of interest, with more than fifty students coming out to practices at some universities, according to Turkish baseball official Alper Bozkurt. Unfortunately, with limited access to equipment and minimal organizational support from the universities, the Turkish baseball community remained small.

The sport officially organized in 2001 with the founding of the Turkish Baseball and Softball Federation. "The reason for the founding ... was simple," Bozkurt explained. "Turkey was competing in the race to host the Olympic Games in 2012. Therefore, all Olympic sports had to be organized including baseball and softball."[26] Coaching clinics and baseball camps ensued and in 2005 organizers decided to form a senior national team. They believed that a senior team would be the best way to maximize public interest, according to Bozkurt. Although no domestic league play was occurring, the national squad began competing in March 2005. The team played an exhibition game against a German squad in Mainz and then entered tournaments in Austria and Greece. In the summer of 2006, Turkey made its debut in a Confederation of European Baseball competition, finishing in last place at the European championships qualifier in Moscow. The squad, which was comprised of players in Europe who had Turkish citizenship, did play a number of close games, losing 8–5 to Lithuania and 16–13 to Georgia.

Following the Moscow performance, the federation decided that a different approach should be taken. Instead of a national team with no local players, the organization would focus on in-country activity. A Turkish academy for kids ages 15 and under has been a central part of this development as has a 12-and-under program at Kent State College in Istanbul.

Turkish baseball's biggest break came in 2007 when the first proper baseball facility was built in the Southern Turkish town of Antalya at the Arcadia Golf & Sports Complex. "The baseball field is part of a good-looking sports complex in Antalya, which also has soccer fields and a golf course," wrote longtime European baseball journalist Marco Stoovelaar after viewing the new baseball field. The diamond had a successful opening event in March 2007, when a two-day tournament between 16-and-under national teams from Bulgaria, Germany and Turkey competed. In addition, top Dutch club Corendon Kinheim played against Russian champion Tornados Balashikha.

Ukraine

With the exception of Russia, no other former Soviet Republic has had as much baseball success as the Ukraine. From the start, Russia and the Ukraine showed the most baseball skill in the former USSR. In June 1987, the Tass News Agency reported that Moscow's Aviation Institute defeated the Ukraine's Kiev Spartak club to win the first Soviet national baseball tournament. The following summer, *Sports Illustrated* writer Steve Wulf traveled to Moscow and had this to say about the Ukrainian team competing in a national tournament:

> Most of the players on the team representing the Ukraine are from the capital city of Kiev. They have the best baseball uniforms in all of the U.S.S.R., red with nuclear blue trim and the leaf of the beriozka (birch) tree, native to the Ukraine, over the heart. The Ukrainians have become one of the better teams in the Soviet Union with the help of Cuban, Nicaraguan and Ukrainian-American advisers and under the whip of their blustery coach, Victor Pyanikh, known affectionately to his players as Attila the Hun. He looks a bit like San Diego Padres manager Jack McKeon.[27]

Kiev was a key spot when touring foreigners came to the Ukraine. When a squad from the Eastern League, a Double-A minor league circuit, toured the Soviet Union in fall 1989, Kiev was its first stop. That sort of interest helped spur the development of a permanent field in 1990. "Because there is no grass, what should be the infield diamond blends into the outfield," wrote Glenn Nelson in a 1990 *Seattle Times* article about the Kiev facility named after the mercurial Ukrainian coach Victor Pyanikh. "The field has such unusual touches— by Soviet standards, that is— as an outfield fence, foul poles and backstop. Pyanikh Field also features the first pitching mound ever used in a Soviet tournament."[28]

The collapse of the Soviet Union — and Ukraine's independence in 1991— offered many newfound freedoms, but for those in the Soviet baseball world the change was not for the better. "I'm only sorry that baseball came here so

Top: Fifteen-year-old Ismail Kilinc (above) throws the first pitch in Turkey by a national team player on 30 March 2007. (Courtesy Alper Bozkurt.) *Bottom*: Despite often being under-funded, Ukraine has proved to be a tenacious competitor at the European Baseball Championships. Here a Ukrainian hitter bats against Great Britain at the 2001 Euros.

late," said Vladimir Bogatyrev, a key figure in Russian baseball in 1992. "The teams from Ukraine are playing in a separate league now. There are very good players in Ukraine. It's so terrible that the Soviet Union split up. This will stop the growth of sports."[29]

The dilution of talent has required the Ukrainians to work hard on creating more depth. In 1994, Basil Tarasko, a baseball coach from City College in Bayside, New York, took the Ukrainian national team to a European baseball championships qualifier in Slovenia. The Ukrainians were still learning, as evidenced by the fact that in one game, Tarasko reported that six of his players missed signs, costing runs. Still, the Ukrainians earned promotion to the elite level. While they have been relegated since then, they have also earned promotion on two other occasions—1995 and 2005. (In 2007, the national team placed ninth and will have to hope to requalify again.)

Club teams have also performed admirably in Europe. Ukrainian clubs have won qualification tournaments in all three of the European federation cups—the European Cup (1999, Gorn Kirovograd), the Cupwinners Cup (1995, Gorn Kirovograd) and the CEB Cup (1997, Foton Simferopol). The gloss of that success must be tempered by the fact that financial constraints—particularly with baseball's Olympic status—will have on player and facility development.

14

European Baseball Championships

When national pride is on the line, Europeans take their baseball very seriously. The European Baseball Championships is where this tension is at its greatest. First contested in 1954, the European Baseball Championships is the only event that pits the best players from one country against each other. In contrast, Europe's baseball federation holds club competitions (most notably, the European Cup) in which clubs can utilize the skills of non-nationals.

Not surprisingly, the Netherlands and Italy have dominated the Euros— both on and off the field. The two nations have won all but two of the 29 events and, in one of those two years, neither squad competed (1967) due to federation politics. The dominance of those two counties also extends beyond their on-field performance. As the two most developed baseball nations, Italy and the Netherlands have hosted more than half of all the European Championships. Only Spain, which has put on the event six times, comes close. This isn't surprising because the Euros are a costly event that has caused financial stress for less developed baseball-playing countries. In 1969, for example, Germany's baseball federation reported "financial difficulties" while preparing to host the European Championships in Wiesbaden.[1] Nearly three decades later, France's governing body faced an even graver situation when it ran the 1997 Euros in Paris. "Shortly after the conclusion of the European Championships, CEB [the Confederation of European Baseball] suspended the French baseball federation, due to financial problems," according to the October–December 1997 issue of *International Baseball Rundown* magazine. "As long as this suspension is in place, no national baseball teams from France can participate in international tournaments." France was able to solve its problems, as it was back at the next Euros in 1999. (Since 1958, the tournament has been played every other year.[2] The bottom line: cost has meant that only a handful of countries—seven in total—have hosted a Euros.

Exclusivity is not limited to hosting, as the championships also feature only the top tier of European baseball. In a process similar to European soccer, the event has a relegation-promotion system. The bottom two finishers at the Euros are banished from the top echelon of European baseball, while winners of qualification tournaments are promoted to the elite.[3] (Following the 2007 Euros, this setup changed with more countries being relegated, increasing the number of qualifiers.) The number of teams that make up this upper echelon of European baseball has varied over the years.

As government support and even private sponsorship can hinge on a place in this top group, it's not surprising that countries have labored hard to find the best talent to represent their nation. Throughout the history of European baseball this has meant pushing the rules to field the best "national team." From the founding days of the European Baseball Federation, a number of countries have faced questions about the true nationality of their nation's representative side. Spain was the first country to deal with controversy over its rostering. At the 1955 European championships, allegations were leveled that the team's star pitcher Bernardo José Luis Menéndez was carrying a false passport and was actually Venezuelan. The accusations were never substantiated, but this did come a year after the Spanish admitted to using a Puerto Rican player in a Federation-sanctioned exhibition against Italy.

During this time, France was also relying heavily on its relationship with Tunisia. At the 1955 Euros, the French national team included a number of Tunisians—from the North African territory that was still a colony of France at the time. No one questioned this recruiting, likely because France was not a top competitor at the event. But a similar use of a territory led to tensions in the 1960s and early 1970s between the Netherlands and Italy. In 1967, the Dutch included a number of West Indies players on its national team during a head-to-head series with Italy. This was not the first time that players from the Dutch Antilles had been used, but the talented group at this event led the Netherlands to four straight victories, including a 19–1 pasting of the Italians. In 1969, five Antilleans were on the Dutch national team and this must have been too much for the Italians as they filed a formal protest with the Europe's baseball federation.[4] The Italians' hectoring became so bad that the Royal Dutch Baseball Association wrote the following on 14 March 1970 to the Federation of European Baseball: "Today's general meeting of our association has authorized us to inform you that the Netherlands will abstain from all international activities as long as you have the regulation that players born outside Europe are not allowed to play for their country even when they possess the nationality of that country 100%. We don't accept such discrimination for [any of] our players."

The Netherlands went on to suggest that "this regulation is an absolute violation of the rules of the IOC [International Olympic Committee] and FIBA [international baseball's governing body]." This strenuous objection must have done the trick, as the Dutch were back at the Euros in 1971. Along with the players from the West Indies, Holland has also used a player born and trained neither in the Netherlands nor the Antilles on their national team. In 2000, the Dutch pulled off one of the biggest upsets in international baseball history, beating Cuba 4–2. Who was the pitcher on the mound for the Netherlands? Oregon native Ken Brauckmiller. Brauckmiller was not an American mercenary. The former San Francisco Giants farmhand played in Holland's top league for more than a decade before his Cuban performance. Still, he was not a product of the Dutch youth baseball systems.

Ironically, Italy has had its own issues with using foreign-born players. In the past few decades, the Italians have utilized lax passport rules to regularly bring Italian-Americans onto the national team. For example, former major leaguer Tom Urbani, who was born in Santa Cruz, California, found himself being called "Tommaso" Urbani as a member of the Italian national team in 1999. Four years later an even greater potential controversy occurred when the Italians were questioned by the Czech Republic for using players who the Czechs claimed were not legally Italian. On the line was a spot at the 2004 Athens Olympics. In the end, Italy prevailed in the dispute.

Even for countries that have not become mired in disagreement, this issue has become less of a question about *whether* to take Americans, Canadians, South Africans or Australians with local family ties, but how many to take. For example, Great Britain has stocked its roster with players who grew up outside the British Isles and Croatia has found passports for top players born and trained in such faraway places as Japan and the United States.

With the advent of the World Baseball Classic, the use of non–Europeans to represent a European country may become even more prevalent. After all, Italy's WBC squad featured Mike Piazza, who had Italian lineage but had little connection to Italian baseball. The Olympics also led to a similarly skewed lineup, with Greece's national team. A controversy erupted at the 2004 Olympic Games, when coach Dimitris Goussios threatened to resign. He was angry that just two home-based players were chosen for the 24-man squad picked for the Olympics. The vast majority of players on the squad were of Greek heritage but from the United States or Canada. "I feel very bitter," Goussios told the media at the time. Although a compromise was ultimately negotiated, the Greek approach underscored the tensions between putting the best team forward and choosing a club that represents play within the country.

This national-team issue has been one that has vexed Martin Miller, former head of the German baseball federation and current president of the Confederation of European Baseball. He says that one of his biggest goals during his time running Germany's governing body was to make sure that the national team phased out the use of players who did not learn their baseball in Germany. Whether other countries will follow suit, remains to be seen.

Today, nearly every squad at the European Championships does have enough home-grown talent to offer some sense of baseball development throughout Europe. While Holland still dominates, some countries have shown massive progress in recent years. In 2001, Russia finished second beating both the Netherlands and Italy at the tournament. Great Britain, Germany and Sweden have also had impressive surprise performances in the past decade. Moreover, these tournaments are increasingly drawing both corporate support and media interest. When countries like Germany, the Czech Republic and Spain hosted the Euros, there was television coverage and financial sponsorship from big companies like Motorola and Fujitsu Siemens. The pan–European Eurosport broadcast games from the 2007 tournament in Spain. The success of the championships offers more than a bellwether of the development of individual European baseball playing countries— it also offers a bellwether of the overall growth of the sport on the continent.

Here is a year-by-year look at Europe's premier event. It includes a short summary of each Euros, standings, scores and individual awards (as available).

1954
June 26–27
Antwerp, Belgium

The inaugural Euros was a small affair, as four of the five founding members of the Federation of European Baseball squared off in Belgium. (France was not present.) These early games were sloppy, as the four matches averaged more than ten errors a game. Italy prevailed, beating Spain in the final game 7–4. Not surprisingly, Spain's eight errors made the difference. "Although this first championship was really a try-out, one could speak of a considerable success, looking at the moderate financial resources and the lack of experience," longtime European baseball official Roger Panaye wrote in 1978.

1. Italy (2–0)
2. Spain (1–1)
3. Belgium (1–1)
4. Germany (0–2)

Scores: Bel.-Italy 1–6; Ger.-Spain 4–10; Bel.-Ger. 12–5; Italy-Spain 7–4.

1955
July 5–10
Barcelona, Spain

On its home turf, Spain dominated, posting three shutouts and winning its other game 21–3 against France. Although Italy put in a disappointing performance — this would be the last time the Italians would finish off the podium for nearly a half-century — they did give the Spanish their toughest match-up. The two teams finished their contest in a 0–0 tie. Spain did have to weather controversy involving its star pitcher's nationality (it was claimed he was actually Venezuelan). France, which utilized a number of Tunisian players, struggled in its first Euros.

1. Spain (3–0–1)
2. Belgium (3–1)
3. Germany (2–2)
4. Italy (1–2–1)
5. France (0–4)

Scores: Bel.-Ger. 10–2; Spain-France 21–3; Italy-Bel. 4–9; Ger.-Spain 0–9; Bel.-France 4–1; Italy-Ger. 4–5; France-Ger. 4–5; Spain-Italy 0–0; France-Italy 1–16; Bel.-Spain 0–2.

1956
July 10–15
Rome, Italy

The Netherlands made an auspicious debut at the European Championships, going undefeated and winning the tournament. The road to the top was not easy, as the Dutch won three of their games by two runs or less. Surprisingly, the team's one blowout victory was against the Italians by a score of 13–2. The two countries' most celebrated pitchers of that era: Han Urbanus (Netherlands) and Giulio Glorioso (Italy) squared off in that contest. Years later, Urbanus, who was the victor, allowing just five hits in the triumph, would call this game one of the most memorable moments of his illustrious international career. One team notably missing from the championships: France. The country had to pull out, according to the 10 July 1956 edition of the *Chicago Tribune*, because "apparently ... so many [French] players ha[d] been called up for North African service."

1. Netherlands (4–0)
2. Belgium (3–1)
3. Italy (2–2)
4. Spain (1–3)
5. Germany (0–4)

Scores: Bel.-Ger. 10–2; Neth.-Italy 13–2; Bel.-Spain 14–3; Italy-Ger. 7–3; Bel.-Neth. 0–1; Ger.-Spain 4–5; Spain-Neth. 4–6; Bel.-Italy 3–2 (10); Neth.-Ger. 3–2; Spain-Italy 5–7.

1957
July 7–13
Mannheim, Germany

Cosponsored by the U.S. Army in Europe, the championships saw the Netherlands dominate. Besides a 3–1 win over Italy, the Dutch won their other three games by a combined score of 33–1. The event was sparsely attended, according to a 13 July 1957 edition of the *New York Times*. "The weeklong tournament ... attracted little attention," the paper wrote. "Baseball is unknown to most Europeans." The *Washington Post* wrote on 11 July: "The European baseball championships currently under way here have failed to arouse interest in the game among the sports-loving Germans."

1. Netherlands (4–0)
2. Germany (3–1)
3. Italy (2–2)
4. Spain (1–3)
5. Belgium (0–4)

Scores: Bel.-Ger. 5–16; Bel.-Spain 9–12; Neth.-Ger. 9–0; Bel.-Italy 2–8; Spain-Ger. 7–8; Neth.-Italy 3–1; Italy-Ger. 2–8; Spain-Italy 3–7; Bel.-Neth. 0–14; Neth.-Spain 10–1.

1958
June 5–12
Amsterdam, Netherlands

Although the Dutch won their third straight European title, they had to work hard to get there. The Netherlands prevailed in two extra-inning affairs— beating Italy 6–5 in 12 innings and Germany 4–3 in 10 innings. The hard-fought victory against Germany had a lasting impact on Holland, as the Dutch hired Germany's head coach Ron Fraser following the event. Fraser would later go on to become one of the greatest coaches in college baseball history, winning 1,271 games and two national collegiate titles as head coach at the University of Miami (Florida). The tournament did attract fans, with some 10,000 spectators on hand for the tournament's finals between Holland and Italy.

1. Netherlands (3–0)
2. Italy (4–2)
3. Germany (1–2)
4. Belgium (1–2)
5. Spain (1–2)
6. France (0–2)

Scores: Bel.-Italy 1–3; France-Spain 4–29; Spain-Ger. 0–5; Italy-Neth. 5–6 (12); Bel.-France 17–2; Spain-Italy 3–14; Neth.-Ger 4–3 (10); Italy-Bel. 8–2; Ger.-Italy 2–6; Neth.-Italy 5–2.

1960
September 22–25
Barcelona, Spain

United States President Dwight Eisenhower was recognized at these Euros, having been recently named honorary president of the Spanish baseball federation. The support of the former general didn't help the Spanish, as they finished third in a field of only four. The Netherlands won it all. The key game: a 1–0 Dutch triumph over the Italians at the start of the event. With this tournament, Barcelona became the first city to host the Euros twice.

1. Netherlands (3–0)
2. Italy (2–1)
3. Spain (1–2)
4. Germany (0–3)

Scores: Neth.-Italy 1–0; Ger.-Spain 1–5; Ger.-Neth. 1–12; Italy-Spain 7–1; Spain-Neth. 0–11.

1962
July 21–29
Amsterdam, Netherlands

In the largest field to date, seven teams vied for the European crown. The Netherlands won and Sweden made its debut, finishing 0–4. (The Swedes' closest contest: a 14–11 loss to France). The tournament was also distinguished by the first forfeit in Euros history. During the France-Germany game, a French player got into a disagreement with the team's captain and stormed off the field. The departure left the French with just eight players, forcing them to forfeit. The default actually improved the French situation in the game: they had been losing 30–0 before the game was called and officially recorded a 9–0 contest.

1. Netherlands (5–0)
2. Italy (3–1)
3. Spain (3–2)
4. Belgium (1–3)
5. Germany (2–2)
6. France (1–3)
7. Sweden (0–4)

Scores: Bel.-Italy 1–15; France-Neth. 1–20 (7); Spain-Neth. 2–7; France-Swe. 14–11; Italy-Ger. 16–0 (7); Spain-Swe 16–0 (8); Ger.-Bel. 3–13; Spain-France 20–6 (7); Swe.-Ger. 5–11; France-Ger. 0–9 (forfeit); Bel.-Spain 8–11; Spain-Italy 0–8; Bel.-Neth. 2–8; Neth.-Italy 9–4.

1964
August 29–September 6
Milan, Italy

The chasm between the established and the developing European baseball nations was very apparent at the eighth European championships. Seven of the ten contests were won by more than 10 runs, with the Netherlands taking the biggest victory — a 30–0 pasting of France. Sweden earned their first Euros victory, beating the struggling French 5–0. This tournament also featured the dedication of a new stadium in Milan, by Milan mayor Pietro Bucalossi. The facility, dedicated to slain U.S. President John F. Kennedy, was "designed principally for a sport, that of baseball, which is popular overseas and loved also by the late president." A crowd of 6,000 watched the Netherland beat Italy in the finals. Not surprisingly, the gold-medal-winning Dutch also swept the individual awards for best pitcher, hitter, catcher and coach, as well as Most Valuable Player, which was given to Boudelwijn Maat.

1. Netherlands (4–0)
2. Italy (3–1)
3. Spain (2–2)
4. Sweden (1–3)
5. France (0–4)

Scores: Swe.-Italy 1–19; Neth.-Spain 10–0; Italy-France 18–0; France-Spain 6–16; Swe.-Neth. 4–19; France-Swe. 0–5; Spain-Italy 1–13; Neth.-France 30–0; Spain-Swe. 9–6; Italy-Neth. 1–3.

Awards: Best hitter: Boudewijn Maat (Neth.), Best pitcher: Hoffman (Neth.), MVP: Boudewijn Maat (Neth.).

1965
August 29–September 5
Madrid, Spain

The Netherlands put in their most dominating performance, going 4–0 with a combined score of 57–0. Even the Italians were no match for the Dutch, who won that always anticipated match-up 16–0. Holland's big star was Hamilton Richardson, a player from the Dutch Antilles, who batted lead-off in the tournament and captured the Most Valuable Player award. Probably in light of Richardson's performance, the Italians protested the use of Antilleans in the years to come.

1. Netherlands (4–0)
2. Italy (3–1)
3. Germany (2–2)
4. Spain (1–3)
5. Sweden (0–4)

Scores: Spain-Ger. 5–8; Italy-Swe. 30–1; Spain-Neth. 0–19; Ger.-Italy 0–9; Neth.-Spain 15–0; Spain-Swe. 14–6; Swe.-Ger. 0–10; Neth.-Italy 16–0; Ger.-Hol. 0–7; Italy-Spain 14–9.

Awards: Best pitcher: Herman Beidschat (Neth.), MVP: Hamilton Richardson (Neth.)

1967
August 6–12
Antwerp, Belgium

Thanks to European baseball politics, neither the Netherlands nor the Italians sent a team to these Euros. (The controversy revolved around the election process for the European federation's president.) As a result, the Belgians won their one and only European title. They were paced by hitter Edgard Vaerendonck who batted .346 and pitcher Edmond Van Trichtveldt, who was named the tournament's best pitcher. Great Britain, which was making its inaugural Euros appearance, captured the silver — its first of two Euros medals to date. Germany, led by tournament MVP Roland Hoffmann, took the bronze medal.

1. Belgium (4–0)
2. Great Britain (3–1)
3. Germany (2–2)
4. Spain (2–2)
5. Sweden (0–4)

Scores: Spain-Bel. 0–11; GB-Spain 10–4; Bel.-Swe. 18–6; Ger.-Swe. 18–1; Bel.-GB 13–2; Swe.-GB 2–3; Spain-Ger. 1–3; Swe.-Spain 2–16; GB-Ger. 11–9; Ger.-Bel. 3–8.

Awards: Best hitter: Edgard Vaerendonck (Bel.), Best pitcher: Edmond Van Trichtveldt (Bel.), MVP: Roland Hoffmann (Ger.)

1969
July 27–August 3
Wiesbaden, Germany

In an effort to split the elite and second tier of European baseball, the seven-team field at these championships was broken into two groups. Group A was composed of 1967 champ Belgium along with the Netherlands and Italy, both of whom had returned after their spat with Europe's governing body. Group B featured Spain, Germany, Sweden and France. Americans played a large role in the event, as the Euros were held at the Lindsey Air Station. As a result, the military squad, the Wiesbaden Flyers, played an exhibition game midway through the tournament. A squad from South Africa was also in attendance, although they did not play in the official competition. Interestingly, the teams in Group B were allowed to each use two foreign players. Spain played with a Cuban and a Puerto Rican, while Germany had two Americans. Sweden and France didn't have any foreigners and complained. This use of foreigners did not occur again. Even in the A-pool, the foreign specter could not be avoided. Five Antilleans were on the Dutch team, which led to a bitter protest from the Italians.

1. Netherlands (3–0 — group A)
2. Italy (2–1— group A)
3. Spain (3–0 — group B)
4. Germany (3–1— group B/classification)
5. Belgium (0–5 — group A/classification)
6. Sweden (1–2 — group B)
7. France (0–3 — group B)

Scores: *Group A:* Italy-Bel. 9–2; Neth.-Bel. 9–0; Bel.-Italy 3–7; Neth.-Bel. 9–3; Italy-Neth. 5–9. *Group B:* France-Swe. 6–11; Ger.-Spain 2–6; Swe.-Ger. 8–19; France-Spain 5–17; Swe.-Spain 2–16; France-Ger. 2–5. *Classification game:* Ger.-Bel. 6–3.

1971
September 5–12
Parma and Bologna, Italy

The Netherlands may have captured yet another European title, but Dutch blood had finally been drawn at a Euros. For the first time, Holland lost a game in this event, falling to the Italians 1–0 in the second game of a finals series between the two countries. Italy's ace pitcher Giulio Glorioso was at his best at this event, twirling an 11-strikeout no-hitter against Germany. San Marino, the small principality within Italy's borders, delivered a solid performance in its first appearance. The squad won two games, beating both Great Britain and Spain. "The Championship was a tremendous success thanks to the perfect organization by the Italian Federation," Panaye wrote in 1978. The drama for the championship went down to the final game, as Holland and Italy split in their first two contests. The third game started in the drizzling rain and had to be stopped for one hour after the fifth with Holland leading 4–3. The crowd waited patiently as the organizers decided whether to continue the game despite a sustained downpour. The decision was made to continue and in the seventh, the Dutch tacked on three more runs. The game finally ended around midnight, with Holland emerging the winner.

1. Netherlands (6–1)
2. Italy (4–2)
3. Germany (4–1)
4. Belgium (3–3)
5. San Marino (2–2)
6. Spain (2–3)
7. Great Britain (1–3)
8. Sweden (1–4)
9. France (0–4)

Scores: Spain-Neth. 1–7; Bel.-France 12–3; Italy-SM 24–0; France-Swe. 12–15; Ger.-GB 12–3; Neth.-Bel. 20–1; GB-Italy 0–21; Bel.-Spain 8–5; Swe.-Neth. 0–14; Neth.-France 21–0; SM-GB 13–10; Spain-Swe. 5–2; Ger.-Italy 0–10; Swe.-Bel. 5–0; SM-Ger. 5–6; France-Spain 2–12; Ger.-Bel. 12–1. *Finals:* Neth.-Italy 4–2; Italy-Neth. 1–0; Italy-Neth. 3–7. *Bronze-medal:* Bel.-Ger. 1–6. *5th-6th:* SM-Spain 6–4. *7th-8th:* GB-Swe. 10–7.

1973
June 30–July 8
Haarlem, Netherlands

The epic battle between the Netherlands and Italy continued at these championships. In pool play, the two squads played a dramatic contest. Holland went up 4–0 through two innings only to see the Italians score six in the third. But a young Dutch pitcher named Wim Remmerswaal entered the game and threw 6 2/3 innings of spectacular relief. He would yield no runs and only two hits and two walks. He also struck out nine as the Netherlands prevailed 7–6. Interestingly, this preliminary game was not supposed to occur, but Germany pulled out of the tournament at the last moment, requiring a schedule change. As for Remmerswaal, his performance was only a sign of things to come for the right hander. In 1979 he would pitch for the Boston Red Sox becoming the first born-and-trained European player to make the major leagues. The Holland-Italy finals were a bit anticlimactic: the Dutch took a 6–0 lead by the fourth and would cruise to the 6–2 win. Among the notables in attendance: Major League Baseball commissioner Bowie Kuhn.

1. Netherlands (5–0 prelims/3–0 1st–4th round)
2. Italy (4–1 prelims/2–1 1st–4th round)
3. Spain (3–2 prelims/1–2 1st–4th round)
4. Belgium (1–4 prelims/0–3 1st–4th round)
5. Sweden (1–4/2–0 5th–6th place)
6. France (1–4/0–2 5th–6th place)

Scores: Swe.-France 7–8; Spain-Neth. 0–7; Bel.-Italy 2–20; Spain-Swe. 7–1; Neth.-Bel. 16–0; France-Italy 1–14; France-Bel. 4–19; Italy-Spain 11–2; Swe.-Neth. 1–16; Neth.-France 21–0; Swe.-Italy 0–25; Bel.-Spain 0–1 (5); Bel.-Swe. 3–4; France-Spain 1–4; Italy-Neth. 6–7; France-Swe. 7–10; Spain-Italy 5–9; Bel.-Neth. 0–8; Swe.-France 5–6; Neth.-Spain 10–2; Italy-Bel. 17–1; Spain-Bel. 11–3; Neth.-Italy 6–2.

Awards: Best hitter: Hamilton Richardson (Neth.), Best pitcher: Win Remmerswaal (Neth.); MVP: Richardson (Neth.)

1975
July 25–August 3
Barcelona, Spain

The Dutch stranglehold on the European title was finally broken at these championships hosted by Barcelona for the third time. Great pitching by the Italians was the difference as they won their second European title. Deadlocked one game apiece in the finals series, Italy beat the Netherlands 5–1, thanks to the mound work of Federico Martone, who allowed just three hits and struck out 14. The Dutch came back to even the series, but the final was dominated by Italy's Michele Romano who delivered two hits at the plate and went the distance on the mound in a 9–4 triumph. All told, the Italian pitchers boasted a minuscule 1.35 earned run average. Bill Arce coached the Italians to victory, becoming the only skipper to lead two countries to a European Championships title. (He also led Holland to the crown in 1971.)

1. Italy (2–0 prelims/3–2 Gold-medal finals)
2. Holland (2–0/2–3 Gold-medal finals)

3. Germany (1–1/2–2 Bronze-medal finals)
4. Spain (1–1/2–2 Bronze-medal finals)
5. Sweden (0–2/3–0 5th-6th place)
6. France (0–2/0–3 5th-6th place)

Scores: Swe.-Ger. 3–6; Italy-Spain 9–0; Neth.-Ger. 9–3; Italy-France 13–0; Neth.-Swe. 12–1; Spain-France 11–1; Ger.-Spain 7–1; Neth.-Italy 2–0; France-Swe. 4–8; Neth.-Italy 1–7; Ger.-Sapin 9–4; Swe.-France 6–1; Spain-Ger. 6–2; Italy-Neth. 5–1; France-Swe. 6–11; Spain-Ger. 4–9; Neth.-Italy 9–4; Spain-Ger. 3–6; Italy-Neth. 9–4.

1977
July 23–31
Haarlem, Netherlands

Longtime Los Angeles Dodgers owner Peter O'Malley was on hand to witness another classic Dutch-Italian battle. For the second tournament in a row, Italy hoisted the European championship trophy. Holland won 6–5 when the two teams met in the preliminary rounds, but Italy had made a furious comeback in that game in the ninth inning, scoring three runs. This portended success for Italy in the finals. Holland had its own comeback in the first game of the best-of-five series, scoring runs in the seventh and eighth innings to win 2–1. After that, it was all Italy as *la nazionale azzura* never trailed the Dutch again in the tournament, winning three straight. Italy dominated both at the plate (a .362 batting average) and on the hill (a 1.10 ERA). For the second time, Germany pulled out of the tournament on the eve of the event. All told, more than 40,000 attended these Euros.

1. Italy (3–1 prelims/3–1 Gold-medal finals)
2. Netherlands (4–0 prelims/1–3 Gold-medal finals)
3. Belgium (2–2 prelims/2–0 3rd–5th place group)
4. Sweden (0–4 prelims/1–1 3rd–5th place group)
5. Spain (1–3 prelims/0–2 3rd–5th place group)

Scores: Spain-Neth. 1–30; Italy-Swe. 29–0; Neth.-Bel. 12–2; Italy-Spain 22–0; Spain-Bel. 14–1; Neth.-Swe. 10–1; Bel.-Italy 0–27; Swe.-Spain 3–8; Swe.-Bel. 1–2; Neth.-Italy 6–5. *Gold-medal finals:* Italy-Neth. 1–2; Neth.-Italy 4–7; Italy-Neth. 4–1. Italy-Neth. 1–0. *3rd–5th place group:* Spain-Swe. 0–2; Bel.-Swe. 7–6; Bel.-Spain 6–4.
Awards: Best hitter: Riccardo Landucci (Italy), Best pitcher: Bertil Haage (Neth.), MVP Ted Alfieri (Italy).

1979
August 11–19
Trieste and Ronchi dei Legionari, Italy

The Italian dynasty was completed in 1979 with its third straight Euros triumph. Italy dominated, handing the Netherlands an embarrassing 14–1 loss in the best-of-five finals, which the Italians won three games to one. Dario

Borghino was a master on the mound, throwing 10 scoreless innings and allowing just one single and one walk. The Most Valuable Player was Davide DiMarco, who batted .385 and drove in 12 runs in just six games. The four-team event had the fewest countries in attendance in nearly two decades.

1. Italy (3–0 prelims/3–1 Gold-medal finals)
2. Netherlands (2–1 prelims/1–3 Gold-medal finals)
3. Belgium (1–2 prelims/1–1 Bronze-medal finals)
4. Sweden (0–3 prelims/1–1 Bronze-medal finals)

Scores: Italy-Swe. 6–0; Neth.-Bel. 14–0; Swe.-Neth. 0–9; Bel.-Italy 5–21; Swe.-Bel. 4–5; Neth.-Italy 2–3. *Gold-medal finals:* Italy-Neth. 14–1; Neth.-Italy 0–5; Italy-Neth. 8–4; Neth.-Italy 8–5. *Bronze-medal finals:* Bel.-Swe. 13–11; Swe.-Bel. 7–5.

Awards: Best hitter: Giuseppe Del Sardo (Italy), Best pitcher: Dario Borghino (Italy), MVP: Davide DiMarco (Italy).

1981
July 11–19
Haarlem, Netherlands

In front of a home crowd, the Dutch reclaimed their crown, with only four teams vying for the European championship. The Dutch, who were led by Harvard University coach Jim Stoeckel, went 5–0 in the preliminaries. After a surprisingly tight 6–5 win over Sweden and a hard fought 5–4 victory against Italy, Holland cruised the rest of the way. The closest margin of victory in their final seven games was five runs. Charles Urbanus was the tournament's top hitter, logging a .522 batting average. Sweden took two out of three from Belgium in the bronze-medal finals to pick up its first Euros medal. Fan support was strong at the tournament, with a total 55,000 attending games, including Prince Claus of the Netherlands, who was present at the opening ceremonies.

1. Netherlands (5–0 prelims/3–0 Gold-medal finals)
2. Italy (4–1 prelims/0–3 Gold-medal finals)
3. Sweden (1–4 prelims/2–1 Bronze-medal finals)
4. Belgium (1–4 prelims/1–2 Bronze-medal finals)

Scores: Neth-Swe. 6–5; Bel.-Italy 0–5; Neth.-Italy 5–4; Bel.-Swe. 4–3; Neth.-Bel. 19–1; Swe.-Italy 0–16; Italy-Bel. 20–6; Neth.-Swe. 14–2; Italy-Swe. 25–0; Bel.-Neth. 1–13; Bel.-Swe. 4–5. *Gold-medal finals:* Italy-Neth. 3–8; Neth.-Italy 11–7; Neth.-Italy 8–1. *Bronze-medal finals:* Swe.-Bel. 2–8; Bel.-Swe. 2–12; Swe.-Bel. 2–3 (11).

Awards: Best hitter: Charles Urbanus (Neth.), Best pitcher: Jan Hijzelendoorn (Neth.), MVP: Paul Smit (Neth.)

1983
July 28–August 7
Catiglione della Pescaia, Firenze, Grosseto, Lucca, Italy

Italy enjoyed one its most dominant performances at these Euros. In the preliminaries, the Italians won by such extravagant scores as 21–1 (against

Sweden), 24–0 (against Spain) and 32–0 (against France). The offensive juggernaut continued into the finals as Italy topped Holland 14–1 and 12–2 in the first two games of the best-of-five series. Holland would take one game but Italy would take the gold with a 10-inning 3–2 win. Pitchers Luigi Colabello, David Farina and Michele Romano each won two games apiece for *la nazionale azzura* and Roberto Bianchi was the tournament's best hitter, sporting a .487 batting average with three home runs and 15 runs batted in.

1. Italy (5–0 prelims/3–1 Gold-medal finals)
2. Holland (4–1 prelims/1–3 Gold-medal finals)
3. Belgium (3–2 prelims)/3–0 3rd–6th group)
4. Spain (1–4 prelims/2–1 3rd–6th group)
5. Sweden (2–3 prelims/1–2 3rd–6th group)
6. France (0–5 prelims/0–3 3rd–6th group)

Scores: Neth.-Italy 5–9; Spain-France 7–3; Swe.-Bel. 0–5; Spain-Neth. 0–12; France-Bel. 0–25; Bel.-Italy 0–7; Neth.-France 36–0; Swe.-Spain 23–13; France-Swe. 5–15; Neth.-Bel. 21–0; Italy-Spain 21–0; Bel.-Spain 3–2; Italy-France 32–0; Swe.-Neth. 0–17. *Gold-medal finals:* Italy-Neth. 14–1; Neth.-Italy 2–3; Italy-Neth. 8–2; Italy-Neth. 4–14. *3rd–6th group:* Spain-Swe. 11–8; Bel.-France 12–11; Swe.-France 18–6; Spain-Bel. 3–13; Bel.-Swe. 15–2; France-Spain 1–11.

1985
July 6–14
Haarlem, Eindhoven, Netherlands

The European title moved back to the low country in 1985. In typical fashion, the Dutch and the Italians easily navigated through the preliminary rounds. The home-town crowd came out to support the Dutch: In their preliminary game against Italy, 6,000 fans were "singing and chanting in unison" throughout the game, according to Dutch head coach Harvey Shapiro.* (Holland would win 5–4.) In the end, it was all Holland as they swept four straight games in the finals, which saw crowds as large as 7,500. Charles Urbanus was a star in the finals, collecting four hits in one of the games and three in another. Bronze-medalist Belgium had two standout individual performances. Frank Lauwers was named best pitcher. He threw 17 innings, yielding just nine hits and no earned runs, going 2–0. Belgian hitter Oswald Boermans led the tournament in hitting with a .583 batting average.

1. Netherlands (5–0 prelims/4–0 Gold-medal finals)
2. Italy (4–1 prelims/0–4 Gold-medal finals)
3. Belgium (3–2 prelims/3–0 3rd–6th group)

*See Harvey Shapiro, "Holland: An American Coaching Honkbal," in Baseball Without Boards: The International Pastime, edited by George Gmelch (Lincoln: University of Nebraska Press: 2006), 259-260.

4. Sweden (2–3 prelims/2–1 3rd–6th group)

5. Spain (1–4 prelims/1–2 3rd–6th group)

6. San Marino (0–5 prelims/0–3 3rd–6th group)

Scores: Neth.-Swe. 31–2; SM-Bel. 1–9; Spain-Italy 1–11; Italy-Neth. 4–5; Bel.-Spain 7–2; SM-Swe. 8–9; Swe.-Italy 2–12; Spain-SM 10–4; Neth.-Bel. 11–1; Spain-Neth. 1–12; Swe.-Bel. 12–16; Italy-SM 12–1; Bel.-Italy 2–9; SM-Neth 7–18; Swe.-Spain 1–0. *Gold-medal finals:* Neth.-Italy 6–4; Italy-Neth. 4–12; Neth.-Italy 11–8; Italy-Neth. 6–8. *3rd–6th group:* Bel.-Swe. 18–0; SM-Spain 2–6; Swe.-SM 13–9; Spain-Bel. 5–6; Bel.-SM 10–0; Spain-Swe. 2–3.

Awards: Best hitter: Judsel Baranco (Neth.), Best pitcher Frank Lauwers (Bel.), MVP: Marcel Joost (Neth.).

1987
July 17–26
Barcelona and Saint Boi, Spain

Because of the continued dominance of the Netherlands and Italy, European baseball looked to stratify the top and the bottom of this tournament. After a brief preliminary round, the top four teams played for medals while the bottom three competed for classification. Holland's 7–6 10-inning win against Italy in the early rounds proved a key, as the victory carried over to the finals. The two countries would each earn two victories in the finals so the early Dutch victory meant they took home their second straight title. Future major leaguer Rik Faneyte (San Francisco Giants) was the event's Most Valuable Player.

1. Netherlands (3–0 prelims/2–0 1st–4th group*/2–2 Gold-medal finals†)

2. Italy (2–0 prelims/1–1 1st–4th group*/2–2 Gold-medal finals†)

3. Spain (2–1 prelims/1–1 1st–4th group*/2–2 Bronze-medal finals†)

4. Belgium (1–1 prelims/0–2 1st–4th group*/2–2 Bronze-medal finals†)

5. Sweden (1–2 prelims/2–1 5th–7th group*)

6. France (0–3 prelims/2–1 5th–7th group*)

7. Germany (0–2 prelim/1–3 5th–7th group*)

Scores: Neth.-Swe. 11–1; France-Spain 3–13; Italy-Bel. 41–2; Spain-Neth. 0–22; Swe.-France 27–12; Bel.-Ger. 14–1; Ger.-Italy 0–11; Swe.-Spain 0–9; France-Neth. 0–27. *1st–4th group:* Spain-Italy 2–7; Neth.-Bel. 19–4; Bel.-Spain 2–4; Italy-Neth. 6–7 (10). *5th–7th group:* France-Ger. 3–5; Ger.-Swe. 0–11; France-Swe. 15–13; Ger.-France 6–8; Swe.-France 14–3 *Gold-medal finals:* Neth.-Italy 7–4; Italy-Neth. 13–4; Neth.-Italy 4–5; Italy-Neth. 1–16. *Bronze-medal finals:* Spain-Bel. 1–4; Bel.-Spain 1–12; Spain-Bel. 1–7; Bel. Spain 3–11.

Awards: Best hitter: Marcel Kruyt (Neth.), Best pitcher: Pedro Valarezo (Spain); MVP: Rikkert Faneyte (Neth.)

Records in classification stage represent just games played during that stage. Additional head-to-head games were carried over from the preliminary stage to determine final placements.

†*Head-to-head performances in the group stage carried over to the gold- and bronze-medal finals.*

1989
September 1–10
Paris, Sarcelles and Savigny, France

France hosted its first European championships, joining Italy, Holland, Germany, Belgium and Spain as countries to have put on the event. Italy reclaimed the European title with a series of closely contested wins in the finals against its long-standing rivals, the Netherlands. Although Italy won the title, a Dutchman claimed the top individual trophy: Robert Niggebrugge was named Most Valuable Player. The eight countries in the tournament represented the largest field since 1971. The number of teams has not dropped below that total since.

1. Italy (3–0 prelims/1–1 1st–4th group*/2–1 Gold-medal finals)
2. Netherlands (3–0 prelims/2–0 1st–4th group*/1–2 Gold-medal finals)
3. Spain (2–1 prelims/1–1 1st–4th group*/2–1 Bronze-medal finals)
4. Sweden (2–1 prelims/0–2 1st–4th group*/1–2 Bronze-medal finals)
5. France (1–2 prelims)/3–2 5th–8th group*)
6. Belgium (1–2 prelims/3–2 5th–8th group*)
7. Great Britain (0–3 prelims/3–2 5th–8th group*)
8. Germany (0–3 prelims/1–4 5th–8th group*)

Scores: Italy-Spain 7–0; Ger.-France 9–10; GB-Bel. 7–8; Swe.-Neth. 1–16; Bel.-Neth. 0–3; Spain-France 14–1; GB-Swe. 4–5; Ger.-Italy 4–24; Swe.-Bel. 6–5 (11); Spain-Ger. 22–4; Neth.-GB 35–0; France-Italy 3–15. *1st–4th group:* Swe.-Italy 0–12; Spain-Neth. 1–14; Spain-Swe. 8–3; Swe.-Spain 6–11; Neth.-Italy 15–2. *5th–8th group:* Ger.-Bel. 8–18; GB-France 4–14; France-Bel. 3–2; GB-Bel. 9–5; France-GB 16–6; Bel.-Ger. 12–2; GB-Ger. 8–6; Bel.-France 20–6; France-Bel. 7–6. *Bronze-medal finals:* Spain-Swe. 5–4; Swe.-Spain 12–11; Swe.-Spain 9–18. *Gold-medal finals:* Italy-Neth 6–10; Neth.-Italy 6–8; Neth.-Italy 5–7

Awards: Best hitter: Claudio Cecconi (Italy), Best pitcher: Peter Callenback (Neth.), MVP: Robert Niggebrugge (Neth.)

Records in classification stage represent just games played during that stage. Additional head-to-head games were carried over from the preliminary stage to determine final placements.

1991
August 2–11
Nettuno, Caserta, Montefiascone, Italy

Eager to match its success in other sports with a stellar performance in baseball, the USSR completed a rather steady rise into the top tier of European baseball at this tournament. After qualifying the previous year, the Soviets made their debut with the continent's best baseball countries. Although the communist superpower went 0–3 in the preliminary rounds, they impressed in the classification stage, going 4–1 by beating more established teams Belgium, Sweden and Great Britain. At the top of the pile, Italy prevailed with a three games to zero drubbing of the Netherlands in the finals. Italian Guglielmo Trinci was named Most Valuable Player driving in 13 runs and batting .459.

1. Italy (3–0 prelims/2–0 1st–4th group*/3–0 Gold-medal finals)
2. Netherlands (3–0 prelims/1–1 1st–4th group*/0–3 Gold-medal finals)
3. Spain (2–1 prelims/1–1 1st–4th group*/2–1 Bronze-medal finals)
4. France (2–1 prelims/0–2 1st–4th group*/2–1 Bronze-medal finals)
5. Belgium (1–2 prelims/4–1 5th–8th group*)
6. USSR (0–3 prelims/4–1 5th–8th group*)
7. Sweden (1–2 prelims/2–3 5th–8th group*)
8. Great Britain (0–3 prelims/0–5 5th–8th group*)

Scores: Italy-France 15–1; Italy-Swe. 26–6; Italy-USSR 10–0; France-Swe. 10–9; France-USSR 11–10; Swe.-USSR 7–4; Neth.-Spain 10–5; Neth.-Bel. 4–0; Neth.-GB 10–0; Spain-Bel. 7–5; Spain-GB 10–2; Bel.-GB 4–2. *1st–4th group:* Italy-Neth. 12–3; Italy-Spain 7–1; Neth.-France 10–0; Spain-France 8–1. *5th–8th group:* Bel.-USSR 4–3; Bel.-Swe. 15–15; Bel.-GB 20–2; Bel.-USSR 5–14; Bel.-Swe. 7–5; USSR-Swe. 6–4; USSR-GB 7–6; USSR-GB 14–4; Swe.-GB 10–0; Swe.-GB 15–8; *Gold-medal finals:* Neth-Italy 1–12; Italy-Neth. 9–2; Neth.-Italy 1–3; *Bronze-medal finals:* France-Spain 7–8; Spain-France 11–1; France-Spain 21–13.

Awards: Best batter: Roberto Bianchi (Italy), Best pitcher: Xavier Camps (Spain); MVP: Guglielmo Trinci (Italy).

Records in classification stage represent just games played during that stage. Additional head-to-head games were carried over from the preliminary stage to determine final placements.

1993
July 9–18
Alby, Skarpnack, Sundbyberg, Sweden

Sweden celebrated its first opportunity to host a European championship by winning the bronze medal. The Swedes showed that a second-tier European baseball country could pull off a heavily logistical event like the Euros. The three fields used in the event were substantially improved and the event garnered solid press coverage. In addition, the tournament was credited with spurring increased baseball interest in Sweden. Holland won the gold medal, beating Italy three to one in a best-of-five series, but it was the bronze-medal finals between Sweden and France that attracted the most attention. Sweden won the series three game to two in a tightly contested series. Sweden's Johan Hasselstrom was named the event's best hitter, batting .517 with a home run and 10 RBI.

1. Netherlands (3–0 prelims/1–0 semis/3–1 Gold-medal finals)
2. Italy (3–0 prelims/1–0 semis/1–3 Gold-medal finals)
3. Sweden (2–1 prelims/0–1 semis/ 3–2 Bronze-medal finals)
4. France (2–1 prelims/0–1 semis/2–3 Bronze-medal finals)
5. Spain (1–2 prelims/4–1 5th–8th group*)
6. Belgium (1–2 prelims/3–2 5th–8th group*)

7. Germany (0–3 prelims/2–3 5th–8th group*)
8. Russia (0–3 prelims/1–4 5th–8th group*)

Scores: Italy-France 15–5; Italy-Bel. 14–1; Italy-Ger. 11–0; France-Bel. 21–18; France-Ger. 10–4; Bel.-Ger. 10–9; Neth.-Swe. 12–5; Neth.-Spain 9–1; Neth.-Russia 6–2; Swe.-Spain 11–1; Swe.-Russia 19–5; Spain-Russia 17–6; *Semifinals:* Italy-Swe. 8–5; France-Neth. 2–10; *5th–8th group:* Spain-Bel. 5–9; Spain-Ger. 11–4; Spain-Bel. 12–3; Spain-Ger. 13–3; Spain-Russia 8–5; Bel.-Ger. 9–4; Bel.-Russia 3–1; Bel.-Russia 8–11; Ger.-Russia 9–8; Ger.-Russia 4–1. *Gold-medal finals:* Italy-Neth. 1–7; Neth.-Italy 7–2; Italy-Neth. 2–11; Neth.-Italy 7–21; Italy-Neth. 0–11; *Bronze-medal finals:* Swe.-France 5–6; France-Swe. 2–3; Swe.-France 11–9; France-Swe. 4–7; Swe.-France 5–14.

Awards: Best hitter: Johan Hasselstrom (Swe.), Best pitcher: Patrick Klerx (Neth.), MVP: Marcel Joost (Neth.).

Records in classification stage represent just games played during that stage. Additional head-to-head games were carried over from the preliminary stage to determine final placements.

1995
July 7–16
Haarlem, Hemsteede, Netherlands

The Dutch captured their fifteenth European title in style, dispatching their opponents with tremendous offensive potency. In the preliminary stage, the Netherlands put up double-digit scores in each of its games, including a 23–3 thrashing of Spain — a team that would end up fourth in the tournament. The steamrolling continued in the semis with a 10–0 victory over Belgium. The finals included a 19–4 triumph over the Italians. Belgium won the bronze, thanks in large part to the pitching of Frank Mathijs. This was the first Euros to feature ten teams.

1. Netherlands (4–0 prelims/1–0 semis/3–1 Gold-medal finals)
2. Italy (4–0 prelims/1–0 semis/1–3 Gold-medal finals)
3. Belgium (3–1 prelims/0–1 semis/3–2 Bronze-medal finals)
4. Spain (3–1 prelims/0–1 semis/2–3 Bronze-medal finals)
5. France (2–2 prelims/3–0 5th–10th group*)
6. Germany (2–2 prelims/2–1 5th–10th group*)
7. Sweden (1–3 prelims/2–1 5th–10th group*)
8. Russia (1–3 prelims/1–2 5th–10th group*)
9. Ukraine (0–4 prelims/1–2 5th–10th group*)
10. Slovenia (0–4 prelims/0–3 5th–10th group*)

Scores: Neth.-Spain 23–3; Neth.-France 15–8; Neth.-Russia 11–3; Neth.-Ukraine 10–0; Spain-France 4–0; Spain-Russia 8–2; Spain-Ukraine 11–2; France-Russia 17–3; France-Ukraine 17–5; Russia-Ukraine 11–1; Italy-Bel. 6–3; Italy-Ger. 15–1; Italy-Swe. 11–0; Italy-Slovenia 17–1; Bel.-Ger. 12–3; Bel.-Swe. 15–4; Bel.-Slovenia 7–4; Ger.-Swe. 13–7; Ger.-Slovenia 18–0; Swe.-Slovenia 14–0; *Semifinals:* Neth.-Bel. 10–0; Italy-Spain 13–2; *5th–10th group:* France-Ger. 18–2; France-Swe. 10–7; France-Slovenia 23–2; Ger.-Russia 7–4; Ger.-Ukraine 12–1; Swe.-Russia 5–3; Swe.-Ukraine 17–5; Russia-Slovenia 8–0; Ukraine-

Slovenia 11–10; *Gold-medal finals:* Neth.-Italy 4–2; Ital-Neth. 2–7; Neth.-Italy 19–4; Italy-Neth. 15–5; *Bronze-medal finals:* Bel.-Spain 12–3; Spain-Bel. 6–8; Bel.-Spain 11–14; Spain-Bel. 15–11; Bel.-Spain 8–6.

Awards: Best hitter: Johnny Balentina (Neth.); Best pitcher (ERA): Carlos Ros (Spain), Best pitcher (W-L) Frank Mathijs (Bel.), MVP: Balentina.

*Records in classification stage represent just games played during that stage. Additional head-to-head games were carried over from the preliminary stage to determine final placements.

1997
August 30–September 7
Paris, France

For the first time, the Confederation of European Baseball expanded the field for the top-tier European Championships to 12 ("B-pool" qualifiers continued for other European nations). In this last tournament to feature aluminum bats, Italy took the title. It was clear that the potent Italian lineup would miss the ping of metal, as they put up slow-pitch-softball-like scores against many of their opponents, including two 20-run–plus outbursts. With the crumbling of the communist East, this tournament saw the debuts of a number of Eastern European nations: the Czech Republic, Ukraine and Slovenia. While Ukraine and Slovenia faltered, the Czechs were impressive in their first outing at the top. They finished seventh and almost beat Italy, falling by a score of 6–5.

1. Italy (5–0 prelims/3–0 classification rounds)
2. Netherlands (5–0 prelims/2–1 classification rounds)
3. Spain (3–2 prelims/2–1 classification rounds)
4. Russia (3–2 prelims/1–2 classification rounds)
5. France (3–2 prelims/2–1 classification rounds)
6. Belgium (3–2 prelims/1–2 classification rounds)
7. Czech Republic (3–2 prelims/1–2 classification rounds)
8. Sweden (2–3 prelims/0–3 classification rounds)
9. Great Britain (0–5 prelims/2–0 9th–12th place group*)
10. Germany (2–3 prelims/1–1 9th–12th place group*)
11. Ukraine (1–4 prelims/1–1 9th–12th place group*)
12. Slovenia (0–5 prelims/0–2 9th–12th place group*)

Scores: Neth.-Spain 9–2; Neth.-Russia 19–1; Neth.-France 13–3; Neth.-Ukraine 28–0; Neth.-GB 28–2; Spain-Russia 8–9; Spain-France 14–4; Spain-Ukraine 12–2; Spain-GB 19–4; Russia-France 7–10; Russia-Ukraine 11–2; Russia-GB 17–5; France-Ukraine 11–1; France-GB 12–0; Ukraine-GB 7–5; Italy-Bel. 21–4; Ital-Czech 6–5; Italy-Swe. 12–0; Italy-Ger. 11–1; Italy-Slovenia 25–8; Bel.-Czech 12–0; Bel.-Swe. 10–3; Bel.-Ger. 6–7; Bel.-Slovenia 21–2; Czech-Swe. 11–2; Czech-Ger. 12–2; Czech-Slovenia 23–6; Swe.-Ger. 16–10; Swe.-Slovenia 16–6; Ger.-Slovenia 8–3; *9th–12th group:* GB-Ger. 5–3; GB-Slovenia 9–7; Ger.-Ukraine 15–5; Ukraine-Slovenia 11–1; *Quarterfinals:* Neth.-Swe. 10–3; Spain-Czech 14–4; Italy-France 17–12; Bel.-Russia 7–12; *Semifinals:* Neth.-Spain 14–4; Russia-Italy 5–15; France-Swe. 12–2;

Czech-Belgium 5–6; *7th–8th place:* Swe.-Czech 5–15; *5th–6th place:* Bel.-France 4–19; *Bronze-medal:* Spain-Russia 7–2; *Gold-medal:* Neth.-Italy 2–4.

Awards: Best batter: Tony Verhart (Bel.), Best pitcher: Michael Leys (Bel.), MVP Randolph Balentina (Neth.)

Records in classification stage represent just games played during that stage. Additional head-to-head games were carried over from the preliminary stage to determine final placements.

1999
July 23–31
Bologna, Parma, Reggio Emilia, Italy

In order to get in line with the Olympic baseball tournament, the Confederation of European Baseball reintroduced wooden bats for the first time in more than a decade. The shift changed the dynamics at the event, as scores were down in comparison to years past. There were twelve shutouts in 1999 compared to four at the previous Euros. Both the Dutch and the Italians appeared ready for the change, as they both went 5–0 in the preliminaries. That said, the margins of victory for the two traditional powerhouses were down. In a one-game final, the Netherlands were winners over Italy in a 3–0 shutout. This event also served as an Olympic qualifier, with the top two finishers—Italy and Holland—earning spots at the 2000 Games in Sydney, Australia.

1. Netherlands (5–0 prelims/3–0 classification rounds)
2. Italy (5–0 prelims/2–1 classification rounds)
3. France (4–1 prelims/2–1 classification rounds)
4. Russia (3–2 prelims/1–2 classification rounds)
5. Spain (3–2 prelims/2–1 classification rounds)
6. Belgium (2–3 prelims/1–2 classification rounds)
7. Sweden (2–3 prelims/1–2 classification rounds)
8. Czech Republic (4–1 prelims/0–3 classification rounds)
9. Great Britain (1–4 prelims/2–0 9th–12th group*)
10. Germany (1–4 prelims/1–1 9th–12th group*)
11. Croatia (1–4 prelims/1–1 9th–12th group*)
12. Slovenia (0–5 prelims/0–2 9th–12th group*)

Scores: Italy-France 5–0; Italy-Russia 8–3; Italy-Swe. 10–3; Italy-GB 13–0; Italy-Croatia 22–1; France-Russia 4–0; France-Swe. 7–0; France-GB 9–8; France-Croatia 1–0; Russia-Swe. 6–2; Russia-GB 11–5; Russia-Croatia 2–4; Swe.-GB 3–2; Swe.-Croatia 1–0; GB-Croatia 10–0; Neth.-Czech 9–0; Neth.-Spain 8–1; Neth.-Bel. 9–1; Neth.-Ger. 8–1; Neth.-Slovenia 15–2; Czech-Spain 7–4; Czec-Bel. 11–1; Czech-Ger. 2–1; Czech-Slovenia 18–10; Spain-Bel. 10–0; Spain-Ger. 3–1; Spain-Slovenia 8–0; Bel.-Ger. 5–2, Bel. Slovenia 4–3; Ger.-Slovenia 14–4; *9th–12th group:* GB-Ger. 4–2; GB-Slovenia 6–4; Ger.-Croatia 8–3; Croatia-Slovenia 7–6; *Quarterfinals:* Italy-Bel. 17–1; Neth.-Swe. 6–0; France-Spain 4–1; Czech-Russia 3–5; *Semifinals:* Italy-France 10–0; Neth.-Russia 7–0; Bel.-Swe. 3–2; Czech-Spain 2–12; *7th–8th place:* Swe.-Czech 6–5; *5th–6th place:* Bel.-Spain 0–12; *Bronze-medal:* Russia-France 3–8; *Gold-medal:* Neth.-Italy 3–0.

Awards: Best hitter: Daniel Newman (Italy), Best pitcher (ERA): Robin Roy (France), Best pitcher (W-L): Carlos Ros (Spain), MVP: Daniel Newman (Italy).

Records in classification stage represent just games played during that stage. Additional head-to-head games were carried over from the preliminary stage to determine final placements.

2001
July 28–August 5
Bonn, Cologne and Solingen, Germany

In a sign that parity might be creeping into European baseball, the Netherlands and Italy did not finish one-two for the first time ever in a tournament they both played in. The Russians were the Cinderella squad of the event. They knocked off the Netherlands in the preliminary rounds, but it looked like a fluke, as Russia also lost to Great Britain and Spain in that round. Yet, in the semifinals, the Russians shocked everyone, knocking off the Italians 2–0. The Russian victory over the Dutch was historic: In some 100 contests against nations other than Italy at the Euros, Holland had never lost a game until then. Although Holland beat the Russians 4–0 in the finals, the event suggested that maybe the Netherlands-Italy monolith that had dominated for decades was finally becoming a little unsteady.

1. Netherlands (4–1 prelims/3–0 classification rounds)
2. Russia (3–2 prelim/2–1 classification rounds)
3. Italy (5–0 prelims/2–1 classification rounds)
4. France (4–1 prelims/1–2 classification rounds)
5. Czech Republic (3–2 prelims/2–1 classification rounds)
6. Spain (2–3 prelims/1–2 classification rounds)
7. Germany (2–3 prelims/1–2 classification rounds)
8. Croatia (2–3 prelims/0–3 classification rounds)
9. Belgium (2–3 prelims/2–0 9th–12th place group*)
10. Great Britain (2–3 prelims/1–1 9th–12th place group*)
11. Ukraine (1–4 prelims/1–1 9th–12th place group*)
12. Sweden (0–5 prelims/0–2 9th–12th place group*)

Scores: Neth.-Russia 3–4; Neth.-Czech 5–1; Neth.-Spain 6–3; Neth.-GB 27–0; Neth.-Ukraine 6–0; Russia-Czech 8–6; Russia-Spain 3–8; Russia-GB 5–6; Russia-Ukraine 13–2; Czech-Spain 9–7; Czech-GB 6–2; Czech-Ukraine 19–9; Spain-GB 16–11; Spain-Ukraine 7–14; GB-Ukraine 5–4; Italy-France 7–2; Italy-Ger. 14–5; Italy-Croatia 6–5; Italy-Bel. 10–1; Italy-Swe. 11–1; France-Ger. 18–6; France-Croatia 14–0; France-Bel. 9–5; France-Swe. 7–3; Ger.-Croatia 3–2; Ger.-Bel. 9–0; Ger.-Swe. 8–6; Bel.-Swe. 1–0. *9th–12th group:* Bel.-GB 4–3; Bel.-Ukraine 8–0; GB-Swe. 13–7; Ukraine-Swe. 11–4; *Quarterfinals:* Neth.-Croatia 8–7; Italy-Spain 6–4; France-Czech 5–3; Russia-Ger. 10–4; *Semifinals:* France-Neth. 1–5; Italy-Russia 0–2; Croatia-Czech 0–14; Spain-Ger. 3–2; *7th–8th place:* Croatia-Ger. 4–10; *5th–6th place:* Czech-Spain 4–0; *Bronze-medal:* Italy-France 3–0; *Gold-medal:* Neth.-Russia 4–0.

Records in classification stage represent just games played during that stage. Additional head-to-head games were carried over from the preliminary stage to determine final placements.

2003
July 11–19
Haarlem, Amsterdam and Rotterdam, Netherlands

These Euros had a healthy dose of big-league experience. Due to a family tragedy, Holland's manager and former New York Yankee Robert Eenhoorn was unable to attend this event. But he was replaced by former major-league manager Davey Johnson, who won a World Series with the New York Mets in 1986. Johnson's Dutch team would face more former big leaguers than they were accustomed to. For the first time, Greece fielded a team in the Euros. The reason for their involvement: as hosts of the 2004 Athens Games, the Greeks were given a spot in the Olympic baseball tournament. To assure that the team would be competitive, Greek-American Baltimore Orioles owner Peter Angelos scoured the United States for players of Greek heritage. The best ones were then given Greek passports. Among the former or future major leaguers who represented Greece: Erik Pappas (St. Louis Cardinals), Kevin Pickford (San Diego Padres) and Nick Markakis (Baltimore Orioles). Despite the firepower, the Greeks lost their opener to Spain but rebounded, making it to the finals, only to lose 2–0 to the Dutch. The biggest surprise of the tournament came from Sweden. Relegated at the 2001 European championships (the bottom two teams must requalify for this tournament), Sweden not only won its qualifier but also stunned Italy in the quarterfinals 4–2. It was the first time since 1955 that Italy entered a European Championships and didn't win a medal.

1. Netherlands (5–0 prelims/3–0 classification rounds)
2. Greece (4–1 prelims/2–1 classification rounds)
3. Spain (4–1 prelims/2–1 classification rounds)
4. Sweden (2–3 prelims/1–2 classification rounds)
5. Italy (4–1 prelims/ 2–1 classification rounds)
6. Czech Republic (3–2 prelims/1–2 classification rounds)
7. France (2–3 prelims/1–2 classification rounds)
8. Russia (2–3 prelims/0–3 classification rounds)
9. Great Britain (1–4 prelims/2–0 9th–12th place group*)
10. Croatia (2–3 prelims/ 1–1 9th–12th place group*)
11. Belgium (1–4 prelims/1–1 9th–12th place group*)
12. Germany (0–5 prelims/0–2 9th–12th place group*)

Scores: Neth.-Czech 6–0; Neth.-Swe. 10–0; Neth.-France 1–0; Neth.-Croatia 5–3; Neth.-Bel. 7–0; Czech-Swe. 1–0; Czech-France 5–3; Czech-Croatia 3–2; Czech-Bel. 1–2; Swe.-France 7–1; Swe.-Croatia 4–6; Swe.-Bel. 10–2; France-Croatia 4–0; France-Bel. 9–1; Croatia-Bel. 5–0; Greece-Italy 2–1; Greece-Spain 0–1; Greece-Russia 11–4; Greece-GB 10–1; Greece-Ger. 11–0; Italy-Spain 5–1; Italy-Russia 6–0; Italy-GB 7–5; Italy-Ger. 10–2; Spain-Russia 5–4; Spain-GB 9–2; Spain-Ger. 5–2; Russia-GB 4–1; Russia-Ger. 7–6; GB-Ger. 5–3; *9th–12th place group:* GB-Croatia 10–2; GB-Bel. 6–5; Croatia-Ger. 5–3; Bel.-Ger. 8–0. *Quarterfinals:* Neth.-Russia 8–0; Greece-France 11–1; Czech-Spain 5–9; Italy-Swe. 2–4; *Semifinals:* Swe.-Neth. 0–21; Greece-Spain 10–0; Italy-Russia 9–3; Czech-France 2–0; *7th–8th place:*

France-Russia 5–0; *5th–6th place:* Czech-Italy 1–2; *Bronze-medal:* Spain-Swe. 5–2; *Gold-medal:* Neth.-Greece 2–0.

Awards: Best hitter: Sharnol Adriana (Neth.), Best pitcher (ERA): Patrick Beljaards (Neth), Best pitcher (W-L): Tetsuhiro Monna (Croatia), MVP: Javier Civit (Spain).

*Records in classification stage represent just games played during that stage. Additional head-to-head games were carried over from the preliminary stage to determine final placements.

2005
July 7–17
Prague, Blansko, Chocen and Olomouc, Czech Republic

Boasting support from none other than Czech Republic president Vaclav Klaus, the Czech Baseball Federation successfully hosted its first European championships. Weather threatened to dampen the Czech efforts and required some teams to play doubleheaders in the preliminary rounds. But warm weather and good play as the tournament progressed assured a smooth result. As with Russia and Sweden in the two previous Euros, Germany was the surprise in the Czech Republic. The Germans had been relegated two years earlier, but requalified and squeaked through to the second round in this event, thanks to a 4–3 victory over Great Britain. In the 1st-place through 6th-place round, the Germans excelled, beating the Czechs and the French to earn a spot in the bronze-medal finals. Although they didn't get hardware, they did qualify for the World Championships, with a fourth-place finish. As for the top of the pile, the Dutch rolled, roughing up the Italians—who made it back to the finals for the first time since 1999—15–0.

1. Netherlands (5–0 prelims/3–0 1st–6th group*/1–0 Gold-medal finals)
2. Italy (4–1 prelims/3–0 1st–6th group*/0–1 Gold-medal finals)
3. Spain (5–0 prelims/1–2 1st–6th group*/1–0 Bronze-medal finals)
4. Germany (2–3 prelims/2–1 1st–6th group*/0–1 Bronze-medal finals)
5. Czech Republic (4–1 prelims/0–3 1st–6th group*)
6. France (3–2 prelims/0–3 1st–6th group*)
7. Great Britain (2–3 prelims/2–1 7th–12th group*)
8. Sweden (1–4 prelims/2–1 7th–12th group*)
9. Greece (2–3 prelims/1–2 7th–12th group*)
10. Ukraine (1–4 prelims/2–1 7th–12th group*)
11. Russia (1–4 prelims/1–2 7th–12th group*)
12. Croatia (0–5 prelims/1–2 7th–12th group*)

Scores: Neth.-Italy 4–1; Neth.-Ger. 15–4; Neth.-GB 4–0; Neth.-Swe. 2–0; Neth.-Russia 11–1; Italy-Ger. 8–5; Italy-GB 12–0; Italy-Swe. 5–3; Italy-Russia 5–4; Ger.-GB 4–3; Ger.-Swe. 6–3; Ger.-Russia 2–7; GB-Swe. 8–2; GB-Russia 10–1; Spain-Czech 10–1; Spain-France 5–3; Spain-Greece 9–3; Spain-Ukraine 12–2; Spain-Croatia 10–5; Czech-France 10–5; Czech-Greece 14–0; Czech-Ukraine 9–1; Czech-Croatia 7–4; France-Greece 12–2; France-Ukraine 10–0; France-Croatia 2–0; Greece-Ukraine 3–2; Greece-Croatia 7–2; Ukraine-Croatia 7–1;

7th–12th group: GB-Greece 9–1; GB-Ukraine 2–3; GB-Croatia 13–3; Swe.-Greece 25–2; Swe.-Croatia 0–2; Greece-Russia 6–5; Ukraine-Russia 7–1; Russia-Croatia 8–0; *1st–6th group:* Neth.-Spain 12–0; Neth.-Czech 3–0; Neth.-France 17–1; Italy-Spain 7–1; Italy-Czech 6–1; Italy-France 11–1; Spain-Ger. 10–2; Ger.-Czech 11–2; Ger.-France 2–0. *Bronze-medal:* Spain-Ger. 7–3; *Gold-medal:* Neth.-Italy 15–0.

Awards: Best hitter: Ian Young (GB), Best pitcher (ERA): Samuel Meurant (France), Best pitcher (W-L) Javier Civit (Spain), MVP: Ivanon Coffie (Neth.).

*Records in classification stage represent just games played during that stage. Additional head-to-head games were carried over from the preliminary stage to determine final placements.

2007
September 7–16
Barcelona (Montjuic, Sant Boi, Viladecans), Spain

These Euros served as evidence that greater parity has come to European baseball. While the Netherlands captured its fifth straight championships, there were signs that some historic also-rans were becoming contenders. The changing world order at the Euros was best exemplified by the performances of Great Britain and Italy. The British, who hadn't placed higher than seventh at this event since 1967, were this tournament's Cinderella story, winning the silver medal behind the MVP performance of Brant Ust, a Triple-A player in the Seattle Mariners organization. Ust batted a blistering .613 with two home runs and 11 runs batted in. In contrast, Italy faltered in a historic manner. For just the third time in its 29 appearances at the Euros, Italy failed to win a medal. Its seventh place performance was its worst ever. This was bad timing for the country as this tournament served as the qualifying event for the final Olympic baseball tournament at the 2008 Games in China.

Although the Netherlands swept through the championships undefeated, there were some signs on the margins that its hegemony may be challenged one of these days. In a key medal-round game, Spain held a 5–2 lead through six innings against the Dutch. Holland would battle back and have to go 11 innings to earn a hard-fought 10–8 victory over the Spanish.

    1. Netherlands (5–0 prelims/3–0 medal round)*
    2. Great Britain (4–1 prelims/1–2 medal round)*
    3. Spain (4–1 prelims/2–1 medal round)*
    4. Germany (4–1 prelims/2–1 medal round)*
    5. France (3–2 prelims/1–2 medal round)*
    6. Sweden (3–2 prelims/0–3 medal round)*
    7. Italy (3–2 prelims/1–0 7th–8th-place game)
    8. Croatia (1–4 prelims/1–0 9th–10th-place game)
    9. Ukraine (1–4 prelims/0–1 9th–10th-place game)
    10. Russia (0–5 prelims/1–0 11th–12th-place game)

11. Austria (0–5 prelims/0–1 11th–12th-place game)
12. Czech Republic (0–6 by forfeit; 2–3 prelims/0–1 7th–8th-place game)†

Scores: GB-Spain 12–8; Swe.-Ger. 1–9; Czech-Croatia 4–1†; Ukraine-Italy 0–13; Austria-Neth. 0–22; France-Russia 4–2; Croatia-Swe. 2–11; Spain-Ukraine 5–4; Ger.-Austria 10–0; Italy-France 1–5; Neth.-Czech 11–0†; Russia-GB 7–10; Neth.-Swe. 14–2; France-Ukraine 6–2; Czech-Austria 6–2†; Spain-Russia 4–0; Ger.-Croatia 8–7; Italy-GB 6–0; Neth.-Ger. 6–3; France-GB 3–4; Austria-Croatia 3–8; Ukraine-Russia 4–3 (11); Czech-Swe. 1–2†; Italy-Spain 4–6; Ger.-Czech 6–1†; Russia-Italy 2–7; Croatia-Neth. 0–13; GB-Ukraine 9–0; Swe.-Austria 4–1; Spain-France 6–2; *7th-place game:* Czech-Italy 2–7†; *9th-place game:* Ukraine-Croatia 1–2 (13); *11th-place game:* Russia-Austria 7–2; *Medal round:* Swe.-GB 7–10; Neth.-France 18–0; Ger.-Spain 3–11; Swe.-France 0–10; GB-Ger. 5–7; Spain-Neth. 8–10 (10); Ger.-France 7–1; Neth.-GB 6–1; Swe.-Spain 5–8.

Awards: Best hitter: Brant Ust (GB), Best pitcher (ERA): Nicolas Dubaut (France), Best pitcher (W-L): Stephen Spragg (GB), MVP: Ust (GB).

*Records in medal round stage represent just games played during that stage. Additional head-to-head games were carried over from the preliminary stage to determine final placements.

†Czech Republic was forced to forfeit all its games due to its improper handling of its professional players. As a result, the official score for all the Czech games was 9–0 in favor of its opponent. The actual scores of the contests are listed here.

Appendix 1

A Brief History of European Baseball's Governing Body

The European Baseball Confederation (CEB) has changed names three times and has had five presidents during its more than half-century of existence. Here is a brief timeline explaining the organization's name changes and listing the dates of CEB presidents' tenures.

1953— From 27–29 April, representatives from five countries— Belgium, Germany, France, Italy and Spain — met in Paris to form a pan-European governing body for baseball. The result was the *Fédération Européenne de Baseball* (FEB) or European Baseball Federation. Two European countries actively playing baseball did not attend. England reportedly could not afford the cost of sending delegates, while the Netherlands took a wait-and-see approach to the nascent body. The constitution accepted French as the organization's official language and placed the annual subscription fee at 100 Swiss Francs. Prince Steno Borghese of Italy was named FEB president.

1971— Italian Bruno Beneck replaced Steno Borghese as president of FEB.

1972— FEB changed its name to the *Confederation Européene de Baseball Amateur/ European Amateur Baseball Federation* (CEBA). At the time, the Olympics were still a wholly amateur sport. The name change was made to reflect Europe's support of the *Federación Internacional de Béisbol Amateur* (FIBA), which was pursing baseball's recognition as an Olympic event.

1985— The Netherlands' Guus van der Heyden assumed the position of CEBA president, replacing Beneck who resigned after 14 years of European and international activity.

1987—Aldo Notari took over as CEBA president following the death of van der Heyden. Notari would go on to not only serve as president of the European federation but also as president of the International Baseball Federation (IBAF), a position he would hold from 1993 to 2006. Notari was the first European to assume the IBAF's top post.

1994—Europe's baseball federation dropped the "Amateur" part to its name to reflect a shift in the Olympic movement toward using professionals in the Games. The new name: *Confederation Européene de Baseball/ European Baseball Confederation* (CEB).

2005—Martin Miller replaced Notari as CEB president. Miller, a German who was previously president of his country's federation, is the first non–Dutch or -Italian head of the European organization.

Sources: "Five Nations Form New European Baseball Federation" in *Baseball News* (UK), 6 June 1953; *European Amateur Baseball: 1979–1993* by Gaston Panaye, published by CEBA (1993); and Daniel Bloyce.

Appendix 2

Player Participation in Europe

The total number of players taking up baseball in Europe has taken a dynamic rise in the past three decades. The most notable growth has occurred in Germany, which, as of 2006, was the continent's largest baseball-playing nation. Gains have also been made in Eastern Europe. Still, participation in some of the more established baseball countries has deteriorated over the past decade. The totals below come from Confederation of European Baseball (CEB) documents.

Overall (players)

1970: 18,133
1977: 41,518
1992: 70,023
2006: 96,790

Country-by-Country

	1992	2006
Armenia	N/A	126
Austria	1,027	2,412
Belarus	N/A	455
Belgium	2,211	1,712
Bulgaria	560	2,317
Croatia	358	490
Cyprus	N/A	120
Czech Republic*	2,265	2,629
Denmark	110	1,106

	1992	*2006*
Estonia	215	171
Finland	210	190
France	11,165	5,750
Georgia	199	387
Germany	10,545	27,884
Great Britain	1,197	5,718
Greece	N/A	1,465
Hungary	N/A	620
Ireland	N/A	450
Israel	N/A	623
Italy	18,178	14,047
Latvia	N/A	77
Lithuania	494	866
Luxembourg	N/A	91
Netherlands	11,165	13,515
Norway	N/A	612
Malta	N/A	114
Moldova	N/A	469
Poland	509	1,916
Portugal	N/A	785
Slovakia*	N/A	1,094
Slovenia	1,015	560
San Marino	128	196
Serbia	N/A	213
Spain	1,383	1,513
Sweden	1,308	1,090
Switzerland	1,200	932
Turkey	N/A	310
Romania	367	930
Russia	2,820	2,045
Ukraine	N/A	790

*The 1992 numbers for Czech Republic represent Czechoslovakia, which includes both the Czech Republic and Slovakia.

Source: Confederation of European Baseball (CEB)

Appendix 3

Medals at the European Baseball Championships

In 2007, European baseball held its thirtieth continental championships. In thirty events only ten different countries have placed in the top three. Below is the breakdown of awards, as well as the number of Euros in which each country has participated (through 2007). Note that these rankings were used in the ordering of the chapters in this book with the exception of Greece, which was covered in the "A–K" chapter. Czech Republic (six appearances; no medals) and Croatia (five appearances; no medals) were also covered in full chapters. Ukraine (with five), Slovenia (three), San Marino (twice) and Austria (once) are the only other countries to have qualified for the event.

Country	Gold	Silver	Bronze	Total
Netherlands (27)	20	7	0	27
Italy (29)	8	15	3	26
Spain (28)	1	1	12	14
Belgium (24)	1	2	6	9
Great Britain (10)	0	2	0	2
Germany (21)	0	1	6	7
Russia (9)*	0	1	0	1
Greece (2)	0	1	0	1
Sweden (25)	0	0	2	2
France (20)	0	0	1	1

*Includes one appearance by the USSR in 1991.

Appendix 4

European Club Competitions

    Along with the European Baseball Championships, which is a national team competition, European baseball's governing body also sanctions club events. These tournaments do not require that all members of the clubs participating hold the passport of the team's home country. The oldest and most prestigious of these events is the European Cup. The Cupwinners Cup is considered the next most high-profile tournament followed by the CEB Cup. The Confederation of European Baseball (and its predecessors) have organized other cups such as the North European Cup, the Mediterranean Cup, the Latin Cup and the Super Cup (between Holland and Italy), but the most enduring and regionally inclusive are the three listed above. It is worth noting that in late 2007, CEB announced plans to consolidate its club competitions, offering just the European Cup in 2008. Nevertheless, below are lists of the all-time winners at each event.

European Cup

1963: Picadero Jockey Club (ESP)
64: Piratas Madrid (ESP)
65: Simmenthal Nettuno (ITA)
66: Haarlem Nicols (NED)
67: Piratas Madrid (ESP)
68: Picadero Damm (ESP)
69: Europhon Milano (ITA)
70: Europhon Milano (ITA)
71: Milano Baseball Club (ITA)
72: Glen Grant Nettuno (ITA)
73: Amaro Montenegro Bologna (ITA)
74: Nettuno Baseball Club (ITA)
75: Haarlem Nicols (NED)
76: Derbigum Rimini (ITA)
77: Germal Parma (ITA)
78: Germal Parma (ITA)
79: Derbigum Rimini (ITA)
80: Parmalat Parma (ITA)
81: Parmalat Parma (ITA)
83: Parmalat Parma (ITA)

84: World Vision Parma (ITA)
85: Be. Ca. Carni Bologna (ITA)
86: World Vision Parma (ITA)
87: World Vision Parma (ITA)
88: World Vision Parma (ITA)
89: Ronson Lenoir Rimini (ITA)
90: Haarlem Nicols (NED)
91: SCAC Nettuno (ITA)
92: Cariparma Angels (ITA)
93: Levi's Neptunus (NED)
94: Levi's Neptunus (NED)
95: Cariparma Angels (ITA)
96: Tropicana Neptunus (NED)
97: Caffè Danesi Nettuno (ITA)
98: C.U.S. Cariparma (ITA)
99: C.U.S. Cariparma (ITA)
00: Neptunus Rotterdam (NED)
01: Door Neptunus Rotterdam (NED)
02: Neptunus Rotterdam (NED)
03: Door Neptunus (NED)
04: Door Neptunus (NED)
05: Grosseto Orioles (ITA)
06: T&A San Marino (SMR)
07: Corendon Kinheim (NED)

Cupwinners Cup

1990: Neptunus Rotterdam (NED)
91: Mediolanum Milano (ITA)
92: Mediolanum Milano (ITA)
93: Levi's Neptunus (NED)
94: Planet Kinheim (NED)
96: Leksand Tumberjack (SWE)
97: Cariparma Angels (ITA)
98: Tropicana Neptunus (NED)
99: Neptunus Rotterdam (NED)

00: Mr. Cocker HCAW (NED)
01: Kinheim Haarlem (NED)
02: Kinheim Haarlem (NED)
03: Hoofddorp Pioniers (NED)
04: Rojos de Tenerife (ESP)
05: Rojos de Candelaria (ESP)
06: Minolta Pioniers (NED)
07: Door Neptunus (NED)

CEB CUP

1993: CFC Nettuno (ITA)
94: Telemarket Rimini (ITA)
95: Caffè Danesi Nettuno (ITA)
96: Juventus Torino (ITA)
97: Papalini Grosseto (ITA)
98: GB Ricambi Modena (ITA)
99: GB Ricambi Modena (ITA)
00: Caffè Danesi Nettuno (ITA)
01: Technika Brno (CZE)
02: Sokol K.R.C. Praga (CZE)
03: Cologne Dodgers (GER)
04: Marlins Puerta Cruz (ESP)
05: BK Zagreb (CRO)
06: Kelteks Karlovac (CRO)
07: FC Barcelona (ESP)

Abbreviations

CRO — Croatia
CZE — Czech Republic
ESP — Spain
GER — Germany
ITA — Italy
NED — Netherlands
SMR — San Marino
SWE — Sweden

Appendix 5

European Countries in World Events

Beginning with the first-ever recognized World Cup in 1938, Europe has been a participant on the wider international baseball scene. Below are country-by-country results for European national teams in internationally recognized events.

Belgium

1978: *World Cup* (in Italy) — last place out of eleven teams (Record: 0–10)
1986: *World Cup* (in Netherlands) — last out of twelve teams (Record: 1–10)

Czech Republic

2004: *Olympic Test Event* (in Greece) — last out of four teams (Record: 2–3)
2005: *World Cup Qualifier* (in USA) — last out of three teams (Record: 0–3)
2005: *World Cup* (in Netherlands) — ninth out of nine teams (Record: 0–8)*
2007: *Olympic Test Event* (in China) — last out of four teams (Record: 1–4)

*At the 2005 World Cup there were no classification games for teams that did not qualify for the quarterfinals. Record and standing reflects performance in pool play.

France

1991: *Intercontinental Cup* (in Spain) last place out of ten teams (0–9)
1993: *Intercontinental Cup* (in Italy) last out of ten teams (Record: 0–9)
1994: *World Cup* (in Nicaragua) — last out of sixteen teams (Record: 0–7)
1997: *Intercontinental Cup* (in Spain) — seventh out of eight teams (Record: 1–6)
2001: *World Cup* (in Chinese Taipei) — last of eight teams in pool play (Record: 0–7)*

2003: *World Cup* (in Cuba) — last out of eight teams in pool play (Record: 0–7)*
2007: *Olympic Test Event* (in China) — third out of four teams (Record: 1–4)

*At the World Cup in 2001 and 2003 there were no classification games for teams that did not qualify for the quarterfinals. Record and standing reflects performance in pool play.

Germany

1972: *World Cup* (in Nicaragua) — last out of sixteen teams (Record: 0–15)
1973: *World Cup (II)* (in Nicaragua) — last out of eleven teams (Record: 0–11)
2007: *World Cup* (in Chinese Taipei) — seventh out of eight teams in pool play (Record: 1–6)*
2008: *Final Olympic Qualification Tournament* (in Chinese Taipei) — sixth out of eight teams (Record: 2–5)

*At the World Cup in 2007 there were no classification games for teams that did not qualify for the quarterfinals. Record and standing reflects performance in pool play.

Great Britain

1938: *World Cup* (in Great Britain) — first place out of two teams (Record: 4–1)

Greece

2004: *Olympic Test Event* (in Greece) — first out of four teams (Record: 3–2)
2004: *Olympic Games* (in Greece) — seventh out of eight teams (Record: 1–6)

Italy

1970: *World Cup* (in Colombia) — tenth place out of twelve teams (Record: 1–9)
1971: *World Cup* (in Cuba) — eighth out of ten teams (Record: 2–7)
1972: *World Cup* (in Nicaragua) — fifteenth out of sixteen teams (Record: 3–12)
1973: *Intercontinental Cup* (in Italy) — sixth out of eight teams (Record: 3–4)
1974: *World Cup* (in USA) — fourth out of nine teams (Record: 3–5)
1975: *Intercontinental Cup* (in Canada) — seventh out of eight teams (Record: 2–5)
1978: *World Cup* (in Italy) — sixth out of eleven teams (Record: 5–5)
1980: *World Cup* (in Japan) — sixth out of twelve teams (Record: 5–6)
1982: *World Cup* (in South Korea) — last out of ten teams (Record: 2–7)
1984: *World Cup* (in Cuba) — eleventh out of thirteen teams (Record: 3–7)
1986: *World Cup* (in Netherlands) — sixth out of twelve teams (Record: 5–6)
1987: *Intercontinental Cup* (in Cuba) — last out of ten teams (Record: 1–7)
1988: *World Cup* (in Italy) — ninth out of twelve teams (Record: 4–7)
1989: *Intercontinental Cup* (in Puerto Rico) — last out of seven teams (1–5)
1990: *World Cup* (in Canada) — tenth out of twelve teams (Record: 3–5)
1991: *Intercontinental Cup* (in Spain) seventh out of ten teams (Record: 4–5)
1992: *Olympic Games* (in Spain) seventh out of eight teams (Record: 1–6)
1993: *Intercontinental Cup* (in Italy) eighth out of ten teams (Record: 2–7)
1994: *World Cup* (in Nicaragua) — seventh out of sixteen teams (Record: 4–4)

1995: *Intercontinental Cup* (in Cuba)—fifth out of six teams in pool play (Record: 1–4)*

1996: *Olympic Games* (in USA)— sixth out of eight teams (Record: 2–5)

1997: *Intercontinental Cup* (in Spain)— sixth out of eight teams (Record: 2–5)

1998: *World Cup* (in Italy)—fourth out of sixteen teams (Record: 4–6)

1999: *Intercontinental Cup* (in Australia)— sixth out of eight teams (Record: 2–5)

2000: *Olympic Games* (in Australia)— sixth out of eight teams (Record: 2–5)

2001: *World Cup* (in Chinese Taipei)— sixth out of eight teams in pool play (Record: 2–5)†

2002: *Intercontinental Cup* (in Cuba)— seventh out of eleven teams (Record: 2–6)

2003: *World Cup* (in Cuba)— sixth out of seven teams in pool play (Record: 1–5)†

2004: *Olympic Games* (in Greece)—last out of eight teams (Record: 1–6)

2006: *Intercontinental Cup* (in Chinese Taipei)— sixth out of eight teams (Record: 3–6)

2006: *World Baseball Classic* (in USA)§— tenth out of sixteen teams (Record: 1–2)

2007: *World Cup* (in Chinese Taipei)— sixth out of eight teams in pool play (Record: 3–4)†

*At the 1995 Intercontinental Cup there were no classification games for teams that did not qualify for the quarterfinals. Record and standing reflects performance in pool play.
†At the World Cup in 2001, 2003 and 2007 there were no classification games for teams that did not qualify for the quarterfinals. Record and standing reflects performance in pool play.
§The 2006 World Baseball Classic was played at a number of venues. Italy played its games in Florida.

Netherlands

1956: *Global World Series* (held in USA)— last place (Record: 0–2)

1970: *World Cup* (in Colombia)— last out of twelve teams (Record: 1–10)

1973: *World Cup (I)* (in Cuba)— last out of eight teams (Record 0–14)

1976: *World Cup* (in Colombia)— last out of eleven teams (Record 1–9)

1978: *World Cup* (in Italy)— seventh out of eleven teams (Record: 4–6)

1980: *World Cup* (in Japan)— last out of twelve teams (Record: 1–10)

1982: *World Cup* (in South Korea)— sixth out of ten teams (Record: 3–6)

1983: *Intercontinental Cup* (in Belgium) fourth out of seven (Record: 3–6)

1984: *World Cup* (in Cuba)— last out of thirteen teams (Record: 1–8)

1986: *World Cup* (in Netherlands)— ninth out of twelve teams (Record: 5–6)

1988: *World Cup* (in Italy)— tenth out of twelve teams (Record: 2–9)

1990: *World Cup* (in Canada)— ninth out of twelve teams (Record: 3–5)

1994: *World Cup* (in Nicaragua)— tenth out of sixteen teams (Record: 3–4)

1995: *Intercontinental Cup* (in Cuba)—fifth out of six teams in pool play (Record: 2–3)*

1996: *Olympic Games* (in USA)—fifth out of eight teams (Record: 2–5)

1998: *World Cup* (in Italy)— sixth out of sixteen teams (Record: 5–5)

1999: *Intercontinental Cup* (in Australia)— last out of eight teams (Record: 0–7)

2000: *Olympic Games* (in Australia)—fifth out of eight teams (Record: 3–4)

2001: *World Cup* (in Chinese Taipei)— seventh out of sixteen teams (Record: 5–5)

2002: *Intercontinental Cup* (in Cuba)— eighth out of eleven teams (Record: 2–3)

2003: *World Cup* (in Cuba)—fifth out of eight teams in pool play (Record: 3–3)†

2004: *Olympic Games* (in Greece)— sixth out of eight teams (Record: 2–5)

2005: *World Cup* (in Netherlands)—fourth out of eighteen teams (Record: 8–3)

2006: *Intercontinental Cup* (in Chinese Taipei)— second out of eight teams (Record: 6–3)

2006: *World Baseball Classic* (in Puerto Rico)§—eleventh out of sixteen teams (Record: 1–2)

2007: *World Cup* (in Chinese Taipei)—fourth out of sixteen teams (Record: 6–4)

*At the 1995 Intercontinental Cup there were no classification games for teams that did not qualify for the quarterfinals. Record and standing reflects performance in pool play.
†At the 2001 World Cup there were no classification games for teams that did not qualify for the quarterfinals. Record and standing reflects performance in pool play.
§The 2006 World Baseball Classic was played at a number of venues. Italy played its games in San Juan, Puerto Rico.

Russia (formerly Soviet Union)

1991: *Intercontinental Cup* (held in Spain) ninth out of ten teams (1–8)

1998: *World Cup* (in Italy)—last out of sixteen teams (Record: 0–7)

2001: *World Cup* (in Chinese Taipei)—seventh out of eight teams in pool play (Record: 1–6)*

2003: *World Cup* (in Cuba)—last out of seven teams in pool play (Record: 1–5)*

2004: *Olympic Test Event* (in Greece)—second out of four teams (Record: 3–2)

*At the World Cup in 2001 and 2003 there were no classification games for teams that did not qualify for the quarterfinals. Record and standing reflects performance in pool play.

Spain

1955: *Global World Series* (held in United States)—last place (Record: 0–2)

1988: *World Cup* (in Italy)—last out of twelve teams (Record: 0–11)

1991: *Intercontinental Cup* (in Spain) eighth out of ten teams (2–7)

1992: *Olympic Games* (in Spain) last out of eight teams (Record: 1–6)

1993: *Intercontinental Cup* (in Italy) ninth out of ten teams (Record: 2–7)

1995: *Intercontinental Cup* (in Cuba)—last out of six teams in pool play (Record: 0–5)*

1997: *Intercontinental Cup* (in Spain)—last out of eight teams (Record: 0–7)

1998: *World Cup* (in Italy)—fourteenth out of sixteen teams (Record: 2–5)

2005: *World Cup* (in Netherlands)—seventh out of nine teams (Record: 2–6)†

2007: *World Cup* (in Chinese Taipei)—seventh out of eight teams (Record: 2–5)†

2008: *Final Olympic Qualification Tournament* (in Chinese Taipei)—seventh out of eight teams (Record: 1–6)

*At the 1995 Intercontinental Cup there were no classification games for teams that did not qualify for the quarterfinals. Record and standing reflects performance in pool play.
† At the 2005 and 2007 World Cup there were no classification games for teams that did not qualify for the quarterfinals. Record and standing reflects performance in pool play.

Sweden

1994: *World Cup* (held in Nicaragua)—fifteenth out of sixteen teams (Record: 1–6)

2004: *Olympic Test Event* (in Greece)—third out of four teams (Record: 2–3)

2005: *World Cup* (in Netherlands)—eighth out of nine teams in pool play (Record: 1–7)*

*At the 2005 World Cup there were no classification games for teams that did not qualify for the quarterfinals. Record and standing reflects performance in pool play.

Appendix 6

Country-by-country National Champions and Federations

The following is a country-by-country catalog of national champions along with the countries' governing bodies (as of 2007) and website addresses (as available). Primary sources for these lists were the International Baseball Federation (IBAF), the Confederation of European Baseball (CEB) and domestic federations (when possible). Discrepancies are noted when two organizations reported different champions.

Armenia

Armenian Baseball Federation

1994 BC Taron — Vanadzor
1995 BC Taron — Vanadzor
1996 HBC Gugark — Darpas
1997 HBC Gugark — Darpas
1998 Dodgers — Stepanavan
2000 Vanadzor — Vanadzor
2002 BC Taron — Vanadzor
2004 BC Taron — Vanadzor
2005 HBC Gugark — Darpas
2006 HBC Gugark — Darpas

Austria

Österreichischer Baseball & Softball Verband (ÖBSV)

www.baseballaustria.com

1985 WBV Homerunners
1986 WBV Homerunners
1987 WBV Homerunners
1988 WBV Homerunners
1989 WBV Homerunners
1990 Vienna Wanderers
1991 Sportunion wien Vienna Bulldogs
1992 WBV Homerunners Vienna Lions
1993 Sportunion Wien Vienna Bulldogs
1994 WBV Homerunners Vienna Lions

1995 SC Schwaz Tigers
1996 WBV Homerunners Vienna Lions
1997 Sportunion Wien Vienna Bulldogs
1998 SC Schwaz Tigers
1999 Dornbirn Indians
2000 Vienna Bulldogs
2001 Hard Bulls
2002 Kufstein Vikings
2003 Dornbirn Indians
2004 Kufstein Vikings
2005 Vienna Metrostars
2006 Vienna Metrostars
2007 Vienna Metrostars

Belarus

Belarus Baseball & Softball Federation (BBSF)

www.baseballminsk.com

1999 Sdusor 1—Minsk
2000 Brest Zubrs
2001 Sdusor 1—Minsk
2002 Brest Zubrs/Sdusor 1—Minsk*
2003 Brest Zubrs
2004 Brest Zubrs
2005 Brest Zubrs
2006 Minsk
2007 Brest Zubrs

*The Confederation of European Baseball (CEB) lists Brest Zubrs as the 2002 champion, while the International Baseball Federation (IBAF) lists Sdusor 1- Minsk.

Belgium

Koninklijke Belgische Baseball en Softball Federatie (KBBSF)

Fédération Royale Belge de Baseball et Softball (FRBBS)

www.kbbsf.be

www.lfbbs.be (Ligue Francophone Belge de Baseball et de Softball)

1947 General Motors
1948 General Motors
1949 General Motors
1950 Luchtball
1951 Spalding Kendalls
1952 GM Giants
1953 Brussels Senators
1954 Spalding Haecht
1955 Borgerhout Squirrels
1956 Luchtball Greys
1957 Borgerhout Squirrels
1958 Brussels Senators
1959 Brussels Senators
1960 Berchem Cristals
1961 Luchtbal Greys
1962 Pioneers
1963 Luchtbal Greys
1964 Luchtbal Greys
1965 Luchtbal Greys
1966 Luchtbal Greys
1967 Luchtbal Greys
1968 Luchtbal Greys
1969 Brasschaat
1970 Pioneers
1971 Luchtbal Greys
1972 Luchtbal Greys
1973 Luchtbal Greys
1974 Luchtbal Greys
1975 Luchtbal Greys
1976 Luchtbal Greys
1977 Luchtbal Greys
1978 Luchtbal Greys
1979 Luchtbal Greys
1980 Berchem
1981 Berchem
1982 Berchem
1983 Antwerp Eagles
1984 Antwerp Eagles
1985 Antwerp Eagles
1986 Antwerp Eagles
1987 Antwerp Eagles
1988 Antwerp Eagles
1989 Luchtbal Greys
1990 Luchtbal Greys
1991 Antwerp Eagles
1992 Brasschaat Braves
1993 Brasschaat Braves

1994 Brasschaat Braves
1995 Brasschaat Braves
1996 Brasschaat Braves
1997 Brasschaat Braves
1998 Namur Angels
1999 Brasschaat Braves
2000 Mortsel Stars
2001 Brasschaat Braves
2002 Brasschaat Braves
2003 Brasschaat Braves
2004 Brasschaat Braves
2005 Royal Greys
2006 Royal Greys
2007 Royal Greys

Bulgaria

Bulgarian Baseball Federation

1990 Academic Sofia
1991 Academic Sofia
1992 Academic Sofia
1993 Buffaloes Blagoevgrad
1994 Buffaloes Blagoevgrad
1995 Buffaloes Blagoevgrad
1996 Buffaloes Blagoevgrad
1997 Buffaloes Blagoevgrad
1998 Buffaloes Blagoevgrad
1999 Buffaloes Blagoevgrad
2000 Buffaloes Blagoevgrad
2001 Buffaloes Blagoevgrad
2002 Buffaloes Blagoevgrad
2003 Buffaloes Blagoevgrad
2004 Devils Dupnitza
2005 Buffaloes Blagoevgrad
2006 Buffaloes Blagoevgrad

Croatia

Croatian Baseball Association (Hrvatski Baseball Savez) (HBS)

www.baseball-cro.hr

1992 Nada Split
1993 Zagreb
1994 Olimpija Karlovac
1995 Olimpija Karlovac

1996 Zagreb
1997 Olimpija Karlovac
1998 Olimpija Karlovac
1999 Olimpija Karlovac
2000 Olimpija Karlovac
2001 Hask Zagreb/Kelteks Karlovac*
2002 Kelteks Karlovac
2003 Kelteks Karlovac
2004 Nada S.S.M. Split
2005 Nada S.S.M. Split
2006 Kelteks Karlovac
2007 Kelteks Karlovac

*CEB lists Hask Zagreb as the 2001 champion, while the IBAF lists Kelteks.

Czech Republic

Czech Baseball Association (Ceská Baseballová Asociace) (CBA)

www.baseball.cz

1979 Tempo Praha
1980 Tempo Praha
1981 Sokol Krc
1982 Sokol Krc
1983 Kovo Praha
1984 Kovo Praha
1985 Kovo Praha
1986 Kovo Praha
1987 Kovo Praha
1988 Sokol Krc
1989 Kovo Praha
1990 Technika Brno
1991 Technika Brno
1992 Kovo Praha
1993 Technika Brno
1994 Technika Brno
1995 Draci Brno
1996 Draci Brno
1997 Draci Brno
1998 Draci Brno
1999 Draci Brno
2000 Draci Brno
2001 Draci Brno
2002 Draci Brno
2003 Draci Brno

2004 Draci Brno
2005 Draci Brno
2006 Draci Brno
2007 AVG Draci

Denmark

Danish Baseball Softball Federation (Dansk Baseball Softball Forbund) (DBSF)

www.dbasof.dk

1978 HBSK Hoersholm
1979 HBSK Hoersholm
1980 HBSK Hoersholm
1981 Munkene Gentofte
1982 HBSK Hoersholm
1983 HBSK Hoersholm
1992 Copenhagen Fighters
1993 HBSK Hoersholm
1994 Ballerup Vandals
1995 Copenhagen Fighters
1996 Copenhagen Fighters
1997 Copenhagen Fighters
1998 Copenhagen Fighters
1999 Copenhagen Fighters
2000 Warriors (Copenhagen)
2001 Warriors (Copenhagen)
2002 Copenhagen Fighters
2003 Copenhagen Fighters
2004 Copenhagen Fighters

Estonia

Estonian Baseball & Softball Federation (EBSF)

1989 Estonians Tallinn
1990 Estonians Tallinn
1991 Estonians Tallinn
1992 Kairos Keila
1993 Kairos Keila
1994 Kairos Keila
1995 Kairos Keila
1996 Kairos Keila
1997 Kairos Keila

1998 Baseball Club of Keila
1999 Baseball Club of Keila

Finland

Finnish Baseball & Softball Federation (FBSF)

www.baseballfinland.com

1981 Hawks
1982 Wranglers
1983 Puumat (Helsinki)
1984 Puumat (Helsinki)
1985 Kintaro
1986 EBSC
1987 Puumat (Helsinki)
1988 Devils
1989 Devils
1990 Devils
1991 Puumat (Helsinki)
1993 Puumat (Helsinki)
1994 Piraijat (Riihimaki)
1995 Puumat (Helsinki)
1996 Athletics (Espoo)
1997 Athletics (Espoo)
1998 Athletics (Espoo)
1999 Puumat (Helsinki)
2000 Athletics (Espoo)
2001 Athletics (Espoo)
2002 Helsinki Icebreakers
2003 Espoo Expos
2004 Espoo Expos
2005 Espoo Expos
2006 Espoo Expos
2007 Espoo Expos

France

Fédération Française de Baseball et Softball (FFBS)

www.ffbsc.org

1926 A.S. Transports
1968 CSF Cagnes-sur-Mer
1969 Pirates de Paris
1970 Paris UC (PUC)

1971 Nice UC
1972 Paris UC (PUC)
1973 Paris UC (PUC)
1974 Nice UC
1975 Paris UC (PUC)
1976 Paris UC (PUC)
1977 Paris UC (PUC)
1978 BC Nippon et Nice UC
1979 Nice UC et BC Nippon
1980 Paris UC (PUC)
1981 Paris UC (PUC)
1982 Paris UC (PUC)
1983 Paris UC (PUC)
1984 Paris UC (PUC)
1985 Paris UC (PUC)
1986 Paris UC (PUC)
1987 Paris UC (PUC)
1988 Paris UC (PUC)
1989 Paris UC (PUC)
1990 Paris UC (PUC)
1991 Paris UC (PUC)
1992 Paris UC (PUC)
1993 Montpellier-Castelnau
1994 Montpellier-Castelnau
1995 Montpellier-Castelnau
1996 St. L_
1997 St. L_
1998 Savigny-sur-Orge
1999 Savigny-sur-Orge
2000 Paris UC (PUC)
2001 Savigny-sur-Orge
2002 Savigny-sur-Orge
2003 Les Huskies de Rouen
2004 Savigny-sur-Orge
2005 Les Huskies de Rouen
2006 Les Huskies de Rouen
2007 Les Huskies de Rouen

Georgia

Baseball Softball Federation of Georgian Republic (BSFG)

1997 Iveria Tbilisi
1998 Iveria Tbilisi
1999 Iveria Tbilisi
2000 Iveria Tbilisi

Germany

Deutscher Baseball und Softball Verband (DBV)

www.baseball-softball.de

1951 Baseball Club Stuttgart
1952 Frankfurt Juniors
1953 Frankfurt Juniors
1954 Mannheimer Baseball Club
1955 Frankfurt Juniors
1956 MEV Munchen
1957 Mannheimer Baseball Club
1958 Mannheimer Baseball Club
1959 Mannheimer Baseball Club
1960 TB Germania Mannheim
1961 TB Germania Mannheim
1962 TB Germania Mannheim
1963 TB Germania Mannheim
1964 TB Germania Mannheim
1965 VFR Mannheim
1966 VFR Mannheim
1967 Darmstadt Colt 45
1968 Darmstadt Colt 45
1982 Mannheim Tornados
1983 Mannheim Amigos
1984 Mannheim Tornados
1985 Mannheim Tornados
1986 Mannheim Tornados
1987 Mannheim Tornados
1988 Mannheim Tornados
1989 Mannheim Tornados
1990 Köln Cardinals
1991 Mannheim Tornados
1992 Mannhel Amigos
1993 Mannheim Tornados
1994 Mannheim Tornados
1995 Trier Cardinals
1996 Trier Cardinals
1997 Mannheim Tornados
1998 Köln Dodgers
1999 Paderborn Untouchables
2000 Lokstedt Stealers
2001 Paderborn Untouchables
2002 Paderborn Untouchables
2003 Paderborn Untouchables
2004 Paderborn Untouchables

2005 Paderborn Untouchables
2006 Solingen Alligators
2007 Mainz Athletics

Great Britain

British Baseball Federation (BBF)

www.britishbaseball.org
www.baseballsoftballuk.com
(Baseball SoftballUK)

1890 Preston North End
1892 Middlesborough
1893 Thespian London
1894 Thespian London
1895 Derby
1896 Wallsend-On-Tyne
1897 Derby
1898 Derby
1899 Nottingham Forest
1906 Tottenham Hotspur
1907 Clapton Orient
1908 Tottenham Hotspur
1909 Clapton Orient
1910 Brentford
1911 Leyton
1934 Hatfield Liverpool
1935 New London
1936 White City (London)
1937 Hull Baseball Club
1938 Rochdale Greys
1939 Halifax
1948 Liverpool Robins
1949 Hornsey Red Sox
1950 Burtonwood Bees
1951 Burtonwood Bees
1959 Thames Board Mills
1960 Thames Board Mills
1961 Liverpool Tigers
1962 Liverpool Tigers
1963 East Hull Aces
1964 Hull Aces
1965 Hull Aces
1966 Stetford Saints
1967 Liverpool Yankees
1968 Hull Aces
1969 Watford — Sun Rockets

1970 Hull Royals
1971 Liverpool Tigers
1972 Hull Aces
1973 Burtonwood Yanks
1974 Nottingham Lions
1975 Liverpool Tigers
1976 Liverpool Trojans
1977 Golders Green Sox
1978 Liverpool Trojans
1979 Golders Green Sox
1980 Liverpool Trojans
1981 London Warriors
1982 London Warriors
1983 Cobham Yankees
1984 Croydon Blue Jays
1985 Hull Mets
1986 Cobham Yankees
1987 Cobham Yankees
1988 Cobham Yankees
1989 London Warriors
1990 Enfield Spartans
1991 Enfield Spartans
1992 Leeds City Royals
1993 Humberside Mets/Bedford Chick-
    sands Indians
1994 Humberside Mets
1995 Humberside Mets
1996 Menwith Hill Patriots
1997 London Warriors
1998 Menwith Hill Patriots
1999 Brighton Buccaneers
2000 London Warriors
2001 Brighton Buccaneers
2002 Brighton Buccaneers
2003 Windsor Bears
2004 Croydon Pirates
2005 Croydon Pirates
2006 Richmond Flames
2007 London Mets

Greece

Hellenic Amateur Baseball Federation (EABF)

www.baseballgreece.com
(Baseball in Greece, unofficial site)

2000 Athletics Maroussi 2004
2001 Athletics Maroussi 2004
2002 Athletics Maroussi 2004
2003 Athletics Maroussi 2004
2004 Spartakos Glyfadas
2005 Spartakos Glyfadas

Hungary

Hungarian National Baseball & Softball Federation (Magyar Országos Baseball és Softball Szövetség) (MOBSS)

www.baseball.hu

1992 Budapest Islanders
1993 Budapest Islanders
1994 Budapest Islanders
1995 Budapest Islanders
1996 Nasskanizsa Ants Thùry
1997 Nasskanizsa Ants Thùry
1998 Szentendre Sleepwalkers
1999 Szentendre Sleepwalkers
2000 Szentendre Sleepwalkers
2001 Torony Szönyeghaz Thúry
2002 Torony Szönyeghaz Thúry
2003 Torony Szönyeghaz Thúry
2004 Obuda Brick Factory
2005 Obuda Brick Factory
2006 Szentendre Sleepwalkers
2007 Szentendre Sleepwalkers

Ireland

Baseball Ireland

www.baseballireland.com

1997 Dublin Hurricanes
1998 Dublin Panthers
1999 Dublin Spartans
2000 Dublin Spartans
2001 Dublin Panthers
2002 Dublin Spartans
2003 Dublin Hurricanes
2004 Dublin Spartans
2005 Dublin Hurricanes

2006 Dublin Spartans
2007 Dublin Spartans

Israel

Israel Association of Baseball

www.iab.org.il

1996 Sharon District
1997 Shefla District
1998 Jerusalem District
1999 Shefla District
2000 Moshav Zofit
2001 Moshav Zofit
2001 Shefla District
2002 Shefla District
2003 Shefla District
2005 Maccabia
2006 Jerusalem Seniors
2007 Bet Shemesh Blue Sox (Israel Baseball League)

Italy

Federazione Italiana Baseball Softball (FIBS)

www.baseball-softball.it

1948 Libertas Bologna
1949 Firenze (Lib)
1949 Lazio (Fibs)
1950 Libertas Roma
1951 Nettuno BC
1952 Nettuno BC
1953 Nettuno BC
1954 Nettuno BC
1955 Lazio
1956 Chlorodont Nettuno
1957 Chlorodont Nettuno
1958 Cus Milano
1959 Coca Cola Roma
1960 Seven Up Milano
1961 Europhon Milano
1962 Europhon Milano
1963 Simmenthal Nettuno
1964 Simmenthal Nettuno
1965 Simmenthal Nettuno

1966 Europhon Milano
1967 Europhon Milano
1968 Europhon Milano
1969 Montenegro Bologna
1970 Europhon Milano
1971 Glent Grant Nettuno
1972 Montenegro Bologna
1973 Glent Grant Nettuno
1974 Montenegro Bologna
1975 Cercosti Rimini
1976 Germal Parma
1977 Germal Parma
1978 Biemme Bologna
1979 Derbigum Rimini
1980 Derbigum Rimini
1981 Parmalat Parma
1982 Parmalat Parma
1983 Barzetti Rimini
1984 Beca Bologna
1985 World Vision Parma
1986 Grohe Grosseto
1987 Trevi Rimini
1988 Lenoir Rimini
1989 Mamoli Grosseto
1990 Scac Nettuno
1991 Parma Angels
1992 Telemarket Rimini
1993 CFC Nettuno
1994 Cariparma
1995 Cariparma
1996 Danesi Nettuno
1997 Cus Cariparma
1998 Danesi Nettuno
1999 Semenzato Rimini
2000 Semenzato Rimini
2001 Danesi Nettuno
2002 Semenzato Rimini
2003 Italeri Bologna
2004 Prink Grosseto
2005 Italeri Bologna
2006 Telemarket Rimini
2007 Monte Paschi Grosseto

Latvia

Latvijas Beisbola Federacija

www.beisbols.lv

2005 BK Riga
2006 BK Riga
2007 Riga Diamonds

Lithuania

Lithuanian Baseball Association (LBA)

www.beisbolas.lt

1922 LFLS Kaunas
1988 Auda (Lituanica) Kaunas
1989 Auda (Lituanica) Kaunas
1990 _algiris (Juodasis vikingas) Vilnius
1991 Panerys-Deka (Juodasis vikingas) Vilnius
1992 Panerys (Juodasis vikingas) Vilnius
1993 Klevas Vilnius
1994 FBK Kaunas (Lituanica)
1995 Klevas Vilnius
1996 Juodasis vikingas Vilnius
1997 Juodasis vikingas Vilnius
1998 FBK Kaunas (Lituanica)
1999 Juodasis vikingas Vilnius
2000 Juodasis vikingas Vilnius
2001 Juodasis vikingas Vilnius
2002 Lituanica Kaunas
2003 Lituanica Kaunas
2004 Juodasis vikingas Vilnius
2005 Lituanica Kaunas
2006 Lituanica Kaunas
2007 Lituanica Kaunas

Luxembourg

Fédération de Baseball Luxembourg (FBL)

*http://membres.lycos.fr/
fbluxembourg/*

2003 Beckerich Hedgehogs
2004 Beckerich Hedgehogs

2005 Beckerich Hedgehogs
2006 Beckerich Hedgehogs
2007 Beckerich Hedgehogs

Malta

Maltese Baseball & Softball
Association (MABS)

www.baseballsoftballmalta.org

1994 Marsa Slammers
1995 Mellieha Northenders
1996 Marsa Mustangs
1997 Mellieha Northenders
1998 Mellieha Northenders
1999 Marsa Mustangs
2000 Mellieha Northenders
2001 Gozo Tornadoes
2002 Gozo Tornadoes
2003 Gozo Tornadoes
2004 Mellieha Northenders
2005 Mellieha Northenders
2006 Mellieha Northenders
2007 Mellieha Northenders
2008 Gozo Tornadoes

Moldova

Baseball and Softball Association
Republic of Moldova

www.moldbaseball.com
(Clubul Sportiv Abator)

1993 Abator Kishinev
1994 Sucess Kishinev
1995 Sucess Kishinev
1998 Sucess Kishinev
1997 Sucess Kishinev
1998 Sucess Kishinev
1999 Sucess Kishinev
2000 Sucess Kishinev
2001 Abator Kishinev
2002 Scorpion Chisinau
2003 Scorpion Chisinau
2004 Kvint Tiraspol
2005 Chisinau Abator
2006 Kvint Tiraspol

Netherlands

Koninklijke Nederlandse Baseball
en Softball Bond (KNBS)

www.knbsb.nl

1922 Quick Amsterdam
1923 Blauw-Wit Amsterdam
1924 Ajax Amsterdam
1925 Quick Amsterdam
1926 AGHC Amsterdam
1927 AGHC Amsterdam
1928 Ajax Amsterdam
1929 SC Haarlem Haarlem
1930 SC Haarlem Haarlem
1931 Blauw-Wit Amsterdam
1932 Blauw-Wit Amsterdam
1933 VVGA Amsterdam
1934 SC Haarlem Haarlem
1935 Quick Amsterdam
1936 HHC Haarlem
1937 Blauw-Wit Amsterdam
1938 Blauw-Wit Amsterdam
1939 Seagulls Amsterdam
1940 SC Haarlem Haarlem
1941 SC Haarlem Haarlem
1942 Ajax Amsterdam
1943 Blauw-Wit Amsterdam
1944 Blauw-Wit Amsterdam
1945 Blauw-Wit Amsterdam
1946 Blauw-Wit Amsterdam
1947 Schoten Haarlem
1948 Ajax Amsterdam
1949 OVVO Amsterdam
1950 OVVO Amsterdam
1951 OVVO Amsterdam
1952 OVVO Amsterdam
1953 OVVO Amsterdam
1954 EHS Haarlem
1955 OVVO Amsterdam
1956 Schoten Haarlem
1957 Schoten Haarlem
1958 EDO Haarlem
1959 EHS Haarlem
1960 Schoten Haarlem
1961 Schoten Haarlem
1962 EHS Haarlem

1963 Sparta Rotterdam
1964 Sparta Rotterdam
1965 Haarlem Nicols Haarlem
1966 Sparta Rotterdam
1967 Sparta Rotterdam
1968 Haarlem Nicols Haarlem
1969 Sparta Rotterdam
1970 Haarlem Nicols Haarlem
1971 Sparta Rotterdam
1972 Sparta Rotterdam
1973 Sparta Rotterdam
1974 Sparta Rotterdam
1975 Haarlem Nicols Haarlem
1976 Tetramin Nicols Haarlem
1977 Tetramin Nicols Haarlem
1978 Wera Kinheim Haarlem
1979 Amstel Tijgers Amsterdam
1980 Amstel Tijgers Amsterdam
1981 Kok Juwelier Neptunus Rotterdam
1982 Haarlem Nicols Haarlem
1983 Haarlem Nicols Haarlem
1984 Haarlem Nicols Haarlem
1985 Haarlem Nicols Haarlem
1986 Cleo Tijgers Amsterdam
1987 Detach Pirates Amsterdam
1988 Opel Nicols Haarlem
1989 Opel Nicols Haarlem
1990 Tas Detach Pirates Amsterdam
1991 Levi's Neptunus Rotterdam
1992 Install Data ADO Den Haag
1993 Levi's Neptunus Rotterdam
1994 Boom Planeta Kinheim Haarlem
1995 Levi's Neptunus Rotterdam
1996 Mr. Cocker HCAW Bussum
1997 Minolta Pioniers Hoofddorp
1998 Mr. Cocker HCAW Bussum
1999 Door Training Neptunus Rotterdam
2000 Door Training Neptunus Rotterdam
2001 Door Training Neptunus Rotterdam
2002 Door Training Neptunus Rotterdam
2003 Door Training Neptunus Rotterdam
2004 Door Training Neptunus Rotterdam
2005 Door Training Neptunus Rotterdam
2006 Corendon Kinheim
2007 Corendon Kinheim

Norway

Norges Softball og Baseball Forbund (NSBF)

www.soft-baseball.no

1991 Oslo Pretenders BBK
1992 Oslo Pretenders BBK
1993 Oslo Pretenders BBK
1994 Oslo Pretenders BBK
1995 Oslo Pretenders BBK
1996 Oslo Ballkam Alligators
1997 Bekkestua Dragons
1998 Oslo Ballkam Alligators
1999 Oslo Ballkam Alligators
2000 Oslo Pretenders BBK
2001 Oslo Pretenders BBK
2002 Oslo Pretenders BBK
2003 Oslo Ballkam Alligators
2004 Oslo Pretenders
2005 Oslo Pretenders
2006 Oslo Pretenders
2007 Oslo Pretenders

Poland

Polish Baseball and Softball Federation (Polski Zwiazek Baseballu i Softballu)

www.baseball.pl

1984 KS Silesia Rybnik
1985 KS Silesia Rybnik
1986 KS Silesia Rybnik
1987 KS Silesia Rybnik
1988 Stal Kutno
1989 Stal Kutno
1990 RKS Skra Warszawa
1991 Stal Kutno
1992 Stal Kutno
1993 RKS Skra Warszawa
1994 RKS Skra Warszawa
1995 MKS Kutno
1996 MKS Kutno
1997 MKS Kutno
1998 BK Jastrzebie

1999 BK Jastrzebie
2000 BK Jastrzebie
2001 BK Jastrzebie
2002 MKS Kutno
2003 MKS Kutno
2004 DEBY Osielsko (KS Hirshpol Deby)
2005 MKS Kutno
2006 MKS Kutno
2007 MKS AMZ Kutno

Portugal

Federação Portuguesa de Beisebol e Softbol (FPBS)

www.fpbsweb.org

1994 Paz B.C.
1995 Paz B.C.
1996 Associaçao Academica de Coimbra
1997 Associaçao Academica de Coimbra
1998 B.C. Tigres
1999 Associaçao Academica de Coimbra
2000 Associaçao Academica de Coimbra
2001 B.C. Tigres de Loulé
2002 B.C. Tigres de Loulé
2003: B.C. Tigres de Loulé
2004: Associaçao Academica de Coimbra
2005: B.C. Tigres de Loulé
2006: B.C. Tigres de Loulé

Romania

Federación Rumana de Béisbol y Softbol

www.frbs.ro

1995 CSS Roman
1996 LPS CSS Roman
1997 LPS CSS Roman
1998 CSS Nr.6 Bucharest
1999 CSS Nr.6 Bucharest
2000 Dinamo Bucharesti/Sportiv Club Bucharest*
2001 Dinamo Bucharesti/Sportiv Club Bucharest*
2002 Dinamo Bucharesti/Sportiv Club Bucharest*

2003 Dinamo Bucharesti
2004 Dinamo Bucharesti
2005 CS Dinamo Bucharesti
2006 Dinamo CSS Bucharesti

*CEB lists Dinamo Bucharesti as the 2000–2002 champions, while the IBAF lists Sportiv Club Bucharest.

Russia

Russian Baseball Federation

www.baseballrussia.ru

1992 Krasniye Diavoly Moscow
1993 Krasniye Diavoly Moscow
1994 Krasniye Diavoly Moscow
1995 Krasniye Diavoly Moscow
1996 CSKA PVO Balashilha, Moscow oblast
1997 CSKA PVO Balashilha, Moscow oblast
1998 CSKA PVO Balashilha, Moscow oblast
1999 VATU of Zhukovskiy Moscow
2000 CSKA PVO Balashilha, Moscow oblast
2001 CSC WS Balashikha
2002 Tornado MGU Moscow
2003 Tornado Balashikha
2004 Tornado Balashikha
2005 Tornado Balashikha
2006 CSC VVS Balashikha
2007 Tornado Balashikha

San Marino

Federazione Sanmarinese Baseball Softball (FSBS)

www.tradecenter.sm/cons

1997 Caravantours San Marino BC
1998 Factory Outlet San Marino BC
1999 Factory Outlet T & A San Marino BC
2000 T & A San Marino BC
2001 T & A San Marino BC
2002 T & A San Marino BC
2003 T & A San Marino BC

2004 T & A San Marino BC
2005 T & A San Marino BC
2006 T & A San Marino BC

Serbia (Formerly Yugoslavia and Serbia-Montenegro)

Baseball Savez Srbije (BSS)

www.baseball.org.yu

1993 Belgrade Kings
1994 Belgrade Dogs
1995 Belgrade Dogs
1996 Belgrade Dogs
1997 Beograd 96
1998 Beograd 96
1999 Beograd 96
2000 Belgrade Dogs
2002 Vojvode
2004 Beograd 96
2005 Beograd 96
2006 Beograd 96
2007 Beograd 96

Slovakia

Slovak Baseball Federation (Slovenská Basebullová Federácia)

www.sbf.sk

1991 Ekonom Indians Bratislava
1992 White Angels Trnava
1993 STU Tronet Spiders Bratislava
1994 STU Tronet Spiders Bratislava
1995 STU Tronet Spiders Bratislava
1996 STU Tronet Spiders Bratislava
1997 STU Tronet Spiders Bratislava
1998 STU Tronet Spiders Bratislava
1999 TJ STU White Angels Trnava
2000 TJ STU White Angels Trnava
2001 TJ STU White Angels Trnava
2002 TJ STU White Angels Trnava
2003 TJ STU Angels Trnava
2004 BK Apollo Bratislava

2005 STU Angels Trnava
2006 BK Apollo Bratislava
2007 TJ STU Angels

Slovenia

Baseball & Softball Association of Slovenia (Zveza za Baseball in Softball Slovenije) (ZBSS)

www.slobaseball.org

1991 Golovec, Ljubjana
1992 Golovec, Ljubjana
1993 Zajcki, Ljubjana
1994 Zajcki, Ljubjana
1995 Mibex Group Zajcki Ljubjana
1996 BSD Zajcki Ljubjana
1997 BSD Zajcki, Ljubjana
1998 Jezica Ljubjana
1999 Kranjski Lisjaki (Kranj)
2000 Cetrta pot Kranjski Lisjaki (Kranj)
2001 Cetrta pot Kranjski Lisjaki (Kranj)
2002 Jezica Ljubljana
2003 Jezica Wilson Ljubljana
2004 BSD Zajcki Ljubljana
2005 Kranjski Lisjaki
2006 Zajcki Ljubljana

Spain

Real Federación Española de Béisbol y Sóftbol (RFEBS)

www.rfebeisbolsofbol.com

1944 R.C.D. Espanyol
1945 Real Madrid
1946 F.C. Barcelona
1947 F.C. Barcelona
1948 Real Madrid
1949 Atlético de Madrid
1950 Real Madrid
1951 Atlético de Madrid
1952 Atlético de Madrid
1953 R.C.D. Espanyol
1954 Hércules Les Corts
1955 Real Madrid

1956 F.C. Barcelona
1957 Picadero C.B.
1958 Hércules Les Corts
1959 Real Madrid
1960 Real Madrid
1961 Real Madrid
1962 Picadero B.C.
1963 Real Madrid
1964 Picadero B.C.
1965 El Corte Inglés
1966 B.C. Piratas
1967 B.C. Piratas
1968 El Corte Inglés
1969 El Corte Inglés
1970 Rayo Vallecano
1971 Condepols M.B.C
1972 Condepols M.B.C.
1973 Condepols M.B.C.
1974 Condepols M.B.C.
1975 Condepols M.B.C.
1976 Johnson & Johnson
1977 Catalunya B.C.
1978 Condepols M.B.C.
1979 Condepols M.B.C.
1980 Condepols M.B.C.
1981 B.C. Piratas
1982 C.B. Viladecans
1983 C.B. Viladecans
1984 C.B. Viladecans
1985 C.B. Viladecans
1986 C.B. Viladecans
1987 C.B. Viladecans
1988 C.B. Viladecans
1989 C.B. Viladecans
1990 C.B. Viladecans
1991 C.B. Viladecans
1992 C.B. Viladecans
1993 C.B. Viladecans
1994 C.B. Viladecans
1995 C.B. Viladecans
1996 C.B. Viladecans
1997 C.B. Viladecans
1998 C.B. Viladecans
1999 C.B. Viladecans
2000 C.B. Viladecans
2001 C.B. Viladecans
2002 C.B. Viladecans

2003 C.B.S. Sant Boi
2004 Rojos de Tenerife B.C.
2005 Marlins P.C. Tenerife
2006 Marlins P.C. Tenerife
2007 Marlins P.C. Tenerife

Sweden

Svenska Baseboll och Softboll Förbundet (SBSF)

www.baseboll-softboll.se

1963 Solna
1964 Leksand
1965 Wasa
1966 Wasa
1967 Leksand
1968 Leksand
1969 Leksand
1970 Leksand
1971 Leksand
1972 Leksand
1973 Bagermossen
1974 Bagermossen
1975 Leksand
1976 Bagermossen
1977 Bagermossen
1978 Leksand
1979 Leksand
1980 Bagermossen
1981 Leksand
1982 Leksand
1983 Leksand
1984 Sundbyberg
1985 Sundbyberg
1986 Sundbyberg
1987 Leksand
1988 Leksand
1989 Skellefteå
1990 Skellefteå
1991 Skellefteå
1992 Skellefteå
1993 Skellefteå
1994 Skellefteå
1995 Skellefteå
1996 Leksand

1997 Leksand
1998 Leksand
1999 Skellefteå
2000 Alby
2001 Rättvik
2002 Rättvik
2003 Sundbyberg
2004 Leksand
2005 Leksand
2006 Sundbyberg
2007 Karlskoga

Switzerland

Swiss Baseball and Softball Association (Suisse Baseball and Softball Federation) (SBSF)

www.swiss-baseball.ch
(Schweizerischer Baseball and Softball Verband)

1983 Zürich Challengers
1984 Ceresio
1985 Zürich Lions
1986 Zürich Challengers
1987 Zürich Lions
1988 Therwil Flyers
1989 Zürich Lions
1990 Geneve Hound Dogs
1991 Therwil Flyers
1992 Therwil Flyers
1993 Therwil Flyers
1994 Therwil Flyers
1995 Therwil Flyers
1996 Zürich Barracudas
1997 Zürich Barracudas

1998 Zürich Challengers
1999 Zürich Challengers
2000 Zürich Challengers
2001 Bern Cardinals
2002 Zürich Challengers
2003 Therwil Flyers
2004 Zürich Challengers
2005 Bern Cardinals
2006 Bern Cardinals
2007 Bern Cardinals

Turkey

Turkish Baseball Federation (Turkiye Beyzbol ve Softbol Federasyonu)

www.tbsf.org.tr

Ukraine

Ukrainian Baseball Softball Federation

1993 Alliance Kiyiv
1994 Alliance Kiyiv
1996 Gorn Kirovograd
1997 Gorn Kirovograd
1998 Gorn Kirovograd
1999 Gorn Kirovograd
2002 TechUniversity KDTU
2003 KDTU Kirovograd
2005 TechUniversity Kirovograd
2006 KNTU-OSVSM Kirovograd
2007 KNTU-OSVSM Kirovograd

Appendix 7

European-born Major Leaguers

Nearly 200 European-born players have competed at baseball's highest level. The following is a list of those players sorted by country. Additional information includes their cities of birth (as available), the years they played in the big leagues and brief backgrounds on their careers. As many of these players competed in the late 1800s, the definition of "major leagues" includes such circuits as the American Association, National Association, Union Association, Players League and Federal League.

Austria (also Austria-Hungary)

Joe Koukalik (N/A) 1904: Pitched a single game for the National League's Brooklyn Superbas; got the start on September 1 and allowed just one earned run in eight innings of work but still suffered a loss.

Kurt Krieger (Traisen) 1949, 1951: Appeared in one game in 1949 and two in 1951 for St. Louis Cardinals; nicknamed "Dutch."

Frank Rooney (Podebrady) 1914: First baseman went 7 for 35 (.200 batting average) in 12 Federal League games for the Indianapolis Hoosiers; hit one home run and drove in eight runs.

Jack Quinn (Stefurov) 1909–33: Great control pitcher, he won 247 games and registered a career 3.29 ERA with eight different teams in 23 years; pitched in three World Series ('21, '29, '30).

Belgium

Brian Lesher (Wilrijk) 1996–98, 2000, 2002: First baseman-outfielder played for Oakland A's, Seattle Mariners and Toronto Blue Jays; hit nine homers in 108 career games.

Czech Republic (also Czechoslovakia)

Amos Cross (N/A) 1885–87: Played three seasons for American Association's Louisville Colonels; career average: .268.

Joe Hovlik (N/A) 1909–11: Played for Washington Senators and Chicago White Sox, posting a 2–0 record with a 3.62 ERA.

Carl Linhart (Zborov) 1952: A left-handed hitter, he had two at bats (no hits) in three games for Detroit Tigers.

John Stedronsky (N/A) 1879: Went 1 for 12 in four games for NL's Chicago White Stockings.

Elmer Valo (Rybnik) 1940–43, 1946–61: A .282 hitter over 20 seasons, he finished in the top-10 in AL stolen bases seven times.

Denmark

Olaf Henriksen (Kirkerup) 1911–17: Backup outfielder appeared in three World Series (1912, 1915, 1916) with Boston Red Sox; nicknamed "Swede."

Finland

John Michaelson (Taivalkoski) 1921: Pitched two games for the Chicago White Sox on 28 and 30 August; worked $2\frac{2}{3}$ innings and allowed three runs.

France

Bruce Bochy (Landes De Bussac) 1978–80, 1982–87: Best known as a successful manager, winning NL Manager of the Year award in 1996 with San Diego Padres.

Ed Gagnier (Paris) 1914–15: Spent two seasons in the Federal League with Brooklyn Tip-Tops and Buffalo Blues.

Claude Gouzzie (N/A) 1903: Had no hits in one at bat for the St. Louis Browns.

Steve Jeltz (Paris) 1983–90: Defensive-minded middle infielder played nearly his whole career with Philadelphia Phillies.

Charlie Lea (Orleans) 1980–88: A 1984 All-Star with the Montreal Expos, he won 16 games for the Canadian club in 1983.

Duke Markell (Paris) 1951: Threw $21\frac{1}{3}$ innings for St. Louis Browns, recording a 1–1 record in only season.

Larry Ressler (N/A) 1875: Batted .194 for National Association's Washington Nationals; scored 17 runs in 27 games.

Joe Woerlin (Trenheim) 1895: Went 1 for 3 at shortstop in lone game for NL's Washington Senators.

Germany (also West Germany)

Jeff Baker (Bad Kissagen) 2005–07: Utility player made his debut with the Colorado Rockies on 4 April 2005.

Heinz Becker (Berlin) 1943, 1945–47: Manned first base in 151 games for the Chicago Cubs and Cleveland Indians.

Rob Belloir (Heidelberg) 1975–78: Middle infielder played parts of four seasons for NL's Atlanta Braves.

Mike Blowers (Wurzburg) 1989–99: Played for four teams in 11 seasons, hitting career-high 23 home runs for 1995 Seattle Mariners.

Fritz Buelow (Berlin) 1899–1907: Logged 431 games in Detroit (Tigers), Cleveland (Indians) and St. Louis (Cardinals and Browns).

Bob Davidson (Bad Kurznach) 1989: Pitched one inning for New York Yankees, allowing two runs on one hit and one walk.

Pep Deininger (Wasseralfingen) 1902, 1908–09: Played 55 of his career 58 games for 1909 Philadelphia Phillies.

Ed Eiteljorge (Berlin) 1890–91: Pitched nine games for NL's Chicago Colts (1890) and American Association's Washington Statesmen (1891).

Fred Gaiser (Stuttgart) 1908: Pitched 2⅓ innings (two runs allowed) in only game for St. Louis Cardinals.

Ron Gardenhire (Butzbach) 1981–85: Followed playing career (.232 lifetime hitter) with success as manager for Minnesota Twins.

Charlie Getzein (N/A) 1884–92: Captured 145 wins in nine NL seasons; placed in the top ten in wins four times.

George Heubel (N/A) 1871–72, 1876: Batted .255 in parts of three seasons in the National Association and NL.

Glenn Hubbard (Hahn Air Force Base) 1978–89: A 1983 All-Star with Atlanta Braves, he led the NL in sacrifice hits (20) in 1982.

Edwin Jackson (Neu Ulm) 2003–07: Pitcher for Los Angeles Dodgers and Tampa Bay Devil Rays; youngest player in the NL in 2003 and 2004.

Jack Katoll (N/A) 1898–99, 1901–02: Best season: 11 wins and 2.81 ERA for 1901 Chicago White Sox.

Steve Kent (Frankfurt) 2002: Made 34 relief appearances on the mound for the Tampa Bay Devil Rays.

Ben Koehler (Schoerndorn) 1905–06: A regular for the 1905 St. Louis Browns, playing 142 games and driving in 47 runs.

Marty Krug (Koblenz) 1912, 1922: Ten years after MLB debut, appeared in 127 games for 1922 Chicago Cubs, hitting .276.

Bill Kuehne (Leipzig) 1883–92: Ten-year journeyman played for six different teams in various major leagues.

Craig Lefferts (Munich) 1983–94: Reliever finished in top ten in saves in '90 and '91 and had total of 101 saves for career.

David Lenz (N/A) 1872: Made brief appearance for National Association's Brooklyn Eckfords, registering one hit in 12 at bats.

Tom McCarthy (Lundstahl) 1985, 1988–89: Made 40 MLB relief appearances for Boston Red Sox and Chicago White Sox.

George Meister (Dorzbach) 1884: Batted .194 in 34 games for American Association's Toledo Blue Stockings.

Bill Miller (Bad Schwalbach) 1902: Connected for one hit in five NL at bats (two RBI) for the Pittsburgh Pirates.

Joe Miller (N/A) 1872, 1875: Appeared in the National Association for the Washington Nationals, Keokuk Westerns and Chicago White Stockings.

Fritz Mollwitz (Coburg) 1913–19: Placed seventh in NL in stolen bases (23) and second in sacrifice hits (30) in 1918 for Pittsburgh Pirates.

Will Ohman (Frankfurt) 2000–01, 2005–07: Chicago Cubs relief pitcher averaged more than a strikeout per inning in first five years.

Dave Pavlas (Frankfurt) 1990–91, 1995–96: 2–0 with 2.65 ERA in 34 games with Chicago Cubs and New York Yankees.

Reggie Richter (Dusseldorf) 1911: Posted a 3.13 ERA and had one win and two saves for Chicago Cubs.

Skel Roach (Danzig) 1899: Earned a complete-game victory for Chicago Orphans in only big-league appearance.

Dutch Schesler (Frankfurt) 1931: Threw 17 games in relief for the Philadelphia Phillies.

Dutch Schliebner (Berlin) 1923: First baseman appeared in 146 games for Brooklyn Robins and St. Louis Browns in only season.

Mickey Scott (Weimar) 1972–73, 1975–77: Tenth in AL in pitching appearances (50) in 1975 for California Angels; 8–7, 3.72 ERA for career.

Gus Shallix (Paderborn) 1884–85: Won 17 games in two campaigns for American Association's Cincinnati Red Stockings.

Frank Siffell (N/A) 1884–85: Represented the American Association's Philadelphia Athletics in ten games over two seasons.

Joe Straub (N/A) 1880, 1882–83: Played in 38 games for NL's Troy Trojans and American Association's Philadelphia Athletics and Columbus Buckeyes

Marty Swandell (Baden) 1872–73: Among the oldest player in the National Association during his two big-league years.

Bun Troy (Bad Wurzach) 1912: Pitched 6⅔ innings in only start for Detroit Tigers; suffered the loss, allowing four runs.

Tony Welzer (N/A) 1926–27: 10–14 with a 4.78 ERA in two campaigns for Boston Red Sox.

Stefan Wever (Marburg) 1982: Made one start for New York Yankees, allowing eight earned runs in 2⅔ innings.

Bill Zimmerman (Kengen) 1915: Outfielder hit .281 in one season with NL's Brooklyn Robins.

Great Britain (England)

Dave Brain (Hereford) 1901, 1903–08: Played seven seasons for six different teams; career .252 hitter.

Tom Brown (Liverpool) 1882–98: Led the American Association in steals in 1891 (106) and the National League in 1893 (66).

Walter Carlisle (Yorkshire) 1908: Played three games for the Boston Red Sox, logging one hit and one stolen base.

Bobby Clack (N/A) 1874–76: Spent two seasons with the National Association's Brooklyn Atlantics and one with the National League's Cincinnati Reds.

Ed Cogswell (N/A) 1879–80, 1882: Ranked sixth in the National League in hitting (.322 batting average) in 1879.

Danny Cox (Northampton) 1983–88, 1992–95: Pitched in three World Series; won a championship with the 1993 Toronto Blue Jays.

Ned Crompton (Liverpool) 1909–10: Made brief appearances for the St. Louis Browns (1909) and Cincinnati Reds (1910).

Hobe Ferris (Trowbridge) 1901–09: Second baseman for AL's Boston Americans on team that won first-ever World Series in 1903.

Dennis Fitzgerald (N/A) 1890: Saw action in two games (two hits in eight at bats) for the American Association's Philadelphia Athletics.

George Hall (Stepney) 1871–77: Placed second in NL batting race (.366 batting average) for Philadelphia Athletics in 1876.

Jim Halpin (N/A) 1882, 1884–85: Youngest player in the National League in 1882 (18 years old).

Charlie Hanford (Tunstall) 1914–15: Finished fifth in the Federal League in hits (174) in 1914.

Pete Hasney (N/A) 1890: Played two games in the outfield for the American Association's Philadelphia Athletics.

Dick Higham (N/A) 1871–76, 1878, 1880: Utility player tallied a .307 lifetime batting average in 372 career games.

Marty Hogan (Wednesbury): 1894–95: Played parts of two seasons for Cincinnati Reds and St. Louis Cardinals.

Sam Jackson (Ripon) 1871–72: Played for National Association's Brooklyn Atlantics (1871) and Boston Red Stockings (1872).

Keith Lampard (Warrington) 1969–70: Second-round draft pick by Houston in 1965; played 62 career games for the Astros.

Al Lawson (London) 1890: Started three games on the mound and lost all three contests, walking 14 in 19 innings.

Tim Manning (Henley-On-Thames) 1882–85: Middle infielder appeared in 200 games in American Association and NL.

Paul Marak (Lakenheath) 1990: Threw 39 innings, posting a 3.69 ERA for Atlanta Braves in only big-league season.

Al Nichols (Worcester) 1875–77: Saw action with three teams in brief career in National Association and NL.

Lance Painter (Bedford) 1993–2001, 2003: Won 25 career games with Colorado Rockies, St. Louis Cardinals, Milwaukee Brewers and Toronto Blue Jays.

Al Reach (London) 1871–75: Top player but most famous for off-field work; one of the founders of the Philadelphia Phillies.

Les Rohr (Lowestoft) 1967–69: Went 2–3 with a 3.70 ERA in parts of three seasons with the New York Mets.

Al Shaw (Burslem) 1901, 1907–09: Played 181 games for four teams in four seasons; made debut for the Detroit Tigers at 28 years old.

Harry Smith (Yorkshire) 1901–10: Catcher logged 1004 at bats in 10 seasons, mainly with the Pittsburgh Pirates.

Klondike Smith (London) 1912: Hit .187 in seven games in the outfield for the New York Yankees in only big-league season.

Phil Stockman (Oldham) 2006: Made major-league debut in 2006 with the Atlanta Braves, throwing a scoreless inning against the Florida Marlins.

Al Thake (Wymondham) 1872: Hit .295 in 19 games for the Brooklyn Atlantics in only season in the National Association.

Ed Walker (Cambois) 1902–03: Made four appearances as a pitcher for the Cleveland Indians.

Sam White (Kinsley) 1919: A catcher who had one at bat for the Boston Braves.

Harry Wright (Sheffield) 1871–77: A Hall-of-Famer who was one of baseball's first great organizers; a .272 hitter as a player.

Jim Wright (Hyde) 1927–28: Pitched in four games for the St. Louis Browns; recorded a 1–0 record with one complete game.

Great Britain (Scotland)

George Chalmers (Aberdeen) 1910–16: Posted a 3.41 ERA over seven seasons for the Philadelphia Phillies.

Mike Hopkins (Glasgow) 1902: Had a perfect 1.000 batting average (2-for-2) in brief stint with Pittsburgh Pirates.

Mac MacArthur (Glasgow) 1884: Pitched six complete games in six starts for the American Association's Indianapolis Hoosiers.

Jim McCormick (Glasgow) 1878–87: Won 265 games, including a 45-win campaign for the NL's Cleveland Blues in 1880.

Mike McCormick (N/A) 1904: Batted .184 in 105 games during only big-league season with the Brooklyn Superbas.

Hugh Nicol (Campsie) 1881–90: Appeared in 888 NL and American Association games before the start of the twentieth century.

Bobby Thomson (Glasgow) 1946–60: Three-time All-Star is best known for his "shot heard 'round the world" homer.

Tom Waddell (Dundee) 1984–85, 1987: Won 15 games and saved 15 in three seasons for the Cleveland Indians.

Great Britain (Wales)

Jimmy Austin (Swansea) 1909–29: Placed 20th in 1911 AL MVP voting; served as St. Louis Browns player-manager for parts of 1913, 1918 and 1923 seasons.

Ted Lewis (Machynlleth) 1896–1901: Won more than 20 games for Boston Beaneaters twice (1897, 1898); 94–64 career record.

Peter Morris (Rhuddlan) 1884: Appeared in one game (0-for-3) for Union Association's Washington Nationals.

Greece

Al Campanis (Kos) 1943: Longtime major-league executive for Los Angeles Dodgers; saw action as a player in seven big-league games.

Ireland (also Northern Ireland)

Jimmy Archer (Dublin) 1904, 1907 1909–18: Finished in top 25 in MVP voting in '11, '12, '13 as a member of Chicago Cubs.

Tommy Bond (Granard) 1874–82, 1884: Earned 234 victories and had three 40-win seasons, mainly for NL's Boston Red Caps.

Hugh Campbell (N/A) 1873: Went 2–16 on the mound in only season with National Association's Elizabeth Resolutes.

Mike Campbell (N/A) 1873: Brother of Hugh Campbell; also played only season with the Resolutes, hitting .145.

Joe Cleary (Cork) 1945: Pitched ⅓ of an inning for the Washington Senators; struck out a hitter but gave up 7 runs.

Bill Collins (Dublin) 1887, 1889–91: Played in five games in four seasons in the NL and American Association.

Tony Cusick (Limerick) 1884–87: Recorded 15 RBI in 95 big-league games; mostly played for the NL's Philadelphia Quakers.

Pete Daniels (County Cavan) 1890, 1898: Nicknamed "Smiling Pete," he won two contests and posted a 4.79 ERA in 14 career appearances.

Pat Deasley (N/A) 1881–88: Catcher batted .244 over 402 NL and American Association games.

Patsy Donovan (County Cork) 1890–1907: Longtime player and manager, he sported a .301 career batting average and went 684–879 as a skipper.

Tom Dowse (Mohill) 1890–92: In his best season, he drove in 22 runs in 55 games for American Association's 1891 Columbus Solons.

Conny Doyle (N/A) 1883–84: Hit .294 for American Association's 1884 Pittsburgh Alleghenys.

Jack Doyle (Killorglin) 1889–1905: A lifetime .299 hitter; the 17-year veteran finished in top ten in NL stolen bases five times.

Ed Duffy (N/A) 1871: Chicago White Stocking player placed tenth in National Association stolen bases race (11) in only season.

Jocko Fields (Cork) 1887–92: Clouted nine home runs for the 1890 Pittsburgh Burghers (Players League) and drove in 86 runs in 126 games.

Mike Flynn (County Kildare) 1891: Hitless in two at bats in only game for American Association's 1891 Boston Reds.

Curry Foley (Milltown) 1879–83: Finished in top ten in NL batting race twice (1880, 1882); lifetime .286 hitter.

Jimmy Hallinan (N/A) 1871, 1875–78: His three homers in 1875 for the New York Mutuals were good enough for fourth in the National Association.

Mike Hines (N/A) 1883–85, 1888: Played 120 games for four different clubs in various big league circuits.

John Horan (N/A) 1884: Recorded a 3–6 record in only season with the Chicago/Pittsburgh club of the Union League.

Andy Leonard (County Cavan) 1871–80: Smacked 761 career hits, primarily for Boston franchises in NL and National Association.

Con Lucid (Dublin) 1893–97: Posted a 23–23 record for four NL clubs; lifetime ERA: 6.02.

Reddy Mack (N/A) 1885–90: As member of American Association's 1887 Louisville Colonels was tenth in league in RBI (87).

Fergy Malone (N/A) 1871–76, 1884: Placed ninth in RBI for 1871 Philadelphia Athletics in National Association.

Charlie McCullough (Dublin) 1890: Went 5–23 in one year, splitting time between American Association's Brooklyn Gladiators and Syracuse Stars.

John McGuinness (N/A) 1876, 1879, 1884: At 17 was third-youngest player in the NL in 1876 for New York Mutuals.

Irish McIlveen (Belfast) 1906, 1908–09:

Played 44 games as an outfielder for the 1908 New York Yankees.

Barney McLaughlin (N/A) 1884, 1887, 1890: An infielder who could also pitch, he appeared in 178 games in Union Association, NL and American Association.

Mike Muldoon (Westmeath County) 1882–86: While with the Cleveland Blues in 1882, his six homers were good for second in NL.

Tony Mullane (Cork) 1881–94: Won 284 games, leading either the American Association or NL in wins and ERA seven times each.

Sam Nichol (County Antrim) 1888, 1890: An outfielder who registered ten hits in 78 career at bats (.128 batting average).

Johnny O'Connor (Cahirciveen) 1916: Appeared in one game at catcher for the Chicago Cubs but never got a major-league at bat.

Paddy O'Connor (County Kerry) 1908–10, 1914–15, 1918: Played in one game for the Pittsburgh Pirates in the 1909 World Series.

Jack O'Neill (Maam) 1902–06: Eighth in the NL in hit by pitches (11) in 1905 with the Chicago Cubs; career average: .196.

Mike O'Neill (Maam) 1901–04, 1907: Posted a 32–44 record with a 2.73 ERA in four seasons with the St. Louis Cardinals.

Cyclone Ryan (Cappagh White) 1887, 1891: A pitcher and first baseman, he made brief appearances in the NL and American Association.

Bill Sullivan (N/A) 1878: An outfielder, he went 1-for-6 in two games for the Chicago Cubs.

Ted Sullivan (County Clare) 1884: As player-manager, led the 1884 St. Louis Maroons to the Union Association championship.

Thomas Sullivan (N/A) 1881–84: Nicknamed "Sleeper," he mainly served as a catcher for franchises in the American Association, Union League and NL; for career hit .184 in 97 games.

John Tener (County Tyrone) 1885, 1888–90: Won 15 games for the 1889 Chicago Cubs, throwing 28 complete games.

Jimmy Walsh (Kallila) 1912–17: Appeared in the World Series in 1914 (with Philadelphia Athletics) and in 1916 (with Boston Red Sox).

Italy

Rugger Ardizoia (Oleggio) 1947: Pitched two innings in one big-league appearance for the New York Yankees.

Reno Bertoia (St. Vito Udine) 1953–62: An infielder who played parts of ten seasons, mainly with the Detroit Tigers.

Hank Biasatti (Beano) 1949: Played first base, connecting for two doubles in 24 at bats for the Philadelphia Athletics.

Julio Bonetti (Genoa) 1937–38, 1940: Posted a 6–14 pitching record for the St. Louis Browns and Chicago Cubs.

Marino Pieretti (Lucca) 1945–50: Won 14 games in his rookie season with the Washington Senators; overall record: 30–38.

Lou Polli (Baveno) 1932, 1944: Pitched two games for the St. Louis Browns in 1932, then returned 12 years later for New York Giants.

Netherlands

Bert Blyleven (Zeist) 1970–92: A workhorse with a devastating curveball (287–250 lifetime record); placed in the top ten in AL Cy Young Award voting four times.

Robert Eenhoorn (Rotterdam) 1994–97: Starting second baseman behind Dwight Gooden when pitcher threw no-hitter for Yankees on 14 May 1996.

Rikkert Faneyte (Amsterdam) 1993–96: Played 80 games in outfield for San Francisco Giants and Texas Rangers.

John Houseman (N/A) 1894, 1897: Saw action with NL's Chicago Colts and St.

Louis Browns; hit six triples for 1897 Browns.

John Otten (N/A) 1895: Primarily a catcher, batted .241 in 87 games with the St. Louis Browns.

Win Remmerswaal (The Hague) 1979–80: First born-and-trained Dutchman to play in the majors; 3–1 in two seasons pitching for Boston Red Sox.

Rick VandenHurk (Eindhoven) 2007: Made big-league debut on 10 April 2007; winning pitcher in 2007 Futures All-Star Game at AT&T Park in San Francisco.

Rynie Wolters (Schantz) 1871–73: Hit .370 and led National Association in RBI (44) for 1871 New York Mutuals.

Netherlands (Aruba)

Radhames Dykoff (Paradera) 1998: Pitched one big-league inning in 1998 for Baltimore Orioles; allowed two runs on two hits and one walk while striking out one batter.

Eugene Kingsale (Solito) 1996, 1998–2003: Saw action with four big league teams; best year: 2002 when he drove in 28 runs in 89 games for San Diego Padres.

Calvin Maduro (Santa Cruz) 1996–97, 2000–02: Pitched for Baltimore Orioles and Philadelphia Phillies, compiling a 10–19 record with 5.78 ERA.

Sidney Ponson (Noord) 1998–2007: Won 17 games for the Baltimore Orioles and San Francisco Giants in 2003; led the American League in complete games in 2004.

Netherlands (Dutch Antilles)

Wladimir Balentien (Willemstad) 2007: Connected for two hits (a double and a home run) in three at bats as a 22-year-old for the Seattle Mariners.

Ivanon Coffie (Klein) 2000: Played in 23 games for the Baltimore Orioles in only MLB season.

Yurendell DeCaster (Brevengat) 2006: Appeared in three games for Pittsburgh Pirates, going hitless in two at bats.

Andruw Jones (Willemstad) 1996–2007: A six-time All-Star and nine-time Gold Glove outfielder through 2007.

Jair Jurrjens (Willemstad) 2007: Debut for Detroit Tigers on 15 August made him the first player from Curacao to pitch in the Majors.

Hensley Meulens (Willemstad) 1989–93, 1997–98: Nicknamed "Bam Bam," hit 15 home runs for three big-league teams in 182 games.

Ralph Milliard (Willemstad) 1996–98: A middle infielder, he scored 12 runs in 42 appearances for Florida Marlins and New York Mets.

Randall Simon (Willemstad) 1997–99, 2001–04, 2006: Hit a career-high 19 home runs for Detroit Tigers in 2002; the first baseman registered a career .283 batting average.

Norway

John Anderson (Sarpsborg) 1894–1908: Placed in top ten in homers four times; played for seven teams in NL and AL, posting a career .290 average.

Art Jorgens (Modum) 1929–39: New York Yankees backup catcher; appeared in 307 career games.

Jimmy Wiggs (Trondheim) 1903–06: 3–4 with a lifetime 3.81 ERA with Detroit Tigers and Cincinnati Reds.

Poland

Moe Drabowsky (Ozanna) 1956–72: Ranked in top ten in AL saves in 1967; career: 88–105 record and 3.71 ERA.

Nap Kloza (N/A) 1931–32: Had brief stints as an outfielder for St. Louis Browns, playing 22 games in two seasons.

Henry Peploski (Garlin) 1929: Played in six

games (2-for-10) for Boston Braves; tallied one RBI and one run.

Johnny Reder (Lublin) 1932: First baseman had five hits (one double) in 37 at bats for Boston Red Sox.

Russia

Eddie Ainsmith (N/A) 1910–24: Placed in AL's top ten in triples twice ('18 and '19); hit 13 homers for 1922 St. Louis Cardinals.

Victor Cole (Leningrad) 1992: Went 0–2 with 5.48 ERA in eight games for Pittsburgh Pirates.

Jake Gettman (Frank) 1897–99: Swiped 32 bases for NL's 1898 Washington Senators; lifetime .278 hitter.

Jake Livingstone (St. Petersburg) 1901: Pitched 12 innings over two games in only season for New York Giants.

Rube Schauer (Kamenka) 1913–17: Led the NL in wild pitches in 1915; pitched for New York Giants and Philadelphia Athletics.

Spain

Al Cabrera (Canary Islands) 1913: Played shortstop and registered two at bats (no hits) for St. Louis Cardinals in only major-league game.

Bryan Oelkers (Zaragoza) 1983, 1986: Went 3–3 with a save for 1986 Cleveland Indians; pitched for Minnesota Twins in 1983.

Al Pardo (Oviedo) 1985–86, 1988–89: Catcher played with Baltimore Orioles and Philadelphia Phillies; hit .132 in 53 career games.

Danny Rios (Madrid) 1997–98: Pitched in

relief in seven games for New York Yankees ('97) and Kansas City Royals ('98).

Sweden

Charlie Bold (Karlskrona) 1914: As a 19-year-old saw action in two games for AL's St. Louis Browns.

Eric Erickson (Goteborg) 1914, 1916, 1918–22: Finished tenth in AL ERA (3.62) in 1921 for Washington Senators; 34–57 with 3.85 ERA during career.

Charlie Hallstrom (Jonkoping) 1885: Nicknamed the Swedish Wonder, suffered a complete-game loss in only start (and appearance) for NL's Providence Grays.

Axel Lindstrom (Gustavsberg) 1916: Earned a save for Philadelphia Athletics in only big-league game.

Switzerland

Otto Hess (Bern) 1902, 1904–08, 1912–15: Won 20 games for AL's 1906 Cleveland Naps; finished top ten in wins, ERA and saves that season.

Ukraine

Bill Cristall (Odessa) 1901: Threw a shutout and five complete games in six appearances for AL's Cleveland Blues.

Reuben Ewing (Odessa) 1921: Played three games for St. Louis Cardinals, seeing action in one game at shortstop.

Izzy Goldstein (Odessa) 1932: Went 3–2 with 4.47 ERA for Detroit Tigers; threw two complete games in six starts.

Note: The primary source for birth location and statistics in this appendix was *www.baseball-reference.com*.

Appendix 8

Major Leaguers in European Domestic Baseball Leagues

Not only has Europe been the birthplace for numerous major leaguers but the pipeline has also flowed in the other direction. At least 145 major leaguers have played in various domestic leagues in Europe. A vast majority have competed in Italy (and, to a lesser degree, the Netherlands), where the circuit is most professionalized. The following list includes the European teams the players competed for as well as MLB teams, brief personal histories and big-league years of service. While this list is not exhaustive, it covers the greater part of players who have crossed over.

Belgium

Tom Magrann (Brasschaat) Went hitless in 10 at bats in nine Major League games as a September call-up. Cleveland Indians (1989)

Joel McKeon (Brasschaat) Former first round draft pick logged a 4–3 record with one save in 43 Big League relief appearances. Chicago White Sox (1986–87)

France

Jeff Zimmerman (Montpellier) Named an All-Star in 1999; eighth in AL in saves (28) in 2001. Texas Rangers (1999–2001)

Germany

Mike Hartley (Heidenheim Heideköpfe) Career numbers: 19–13 with four saves and 3.70 ERA. LA Dodgers, Phil. Phillies, Min. Twins, Balt. Orioles (1989–93, 1995)

Great Britain

John Foster (Brighton Buccaneers) 4–2 lifetime record with one save in 90 appearances. Atlanta Braves, Milwaukee Brewers (2002–03, 2005)

Roland Gladu (West Ham) Batted .242 with one home run in 60 games. Boston Braves (1944)

Italy (and San Marino)

Manny Alexander (Rimini) Logged 594 games as infielder in 11 seasons. Six teams incl. Balt. Orioles, Chi. Cubs, SD Padres (1992–1993, 1995–2000, 2004, 2005–2006)

Kim Andrew (Diavia Bollate) Went one for two in two games as a second baseman. Boston Red Sox (1975)

Randy Asadoor (San Marino) Infielder batted .364 (20-for-55) in 15 major-league games. San Diego Padres (1986)

Don August (Rimini) Went 13–7 in his rookie season — good enough for ninth in the AL in won-loss percentage in 1988; sported a 3.09 ERA that year. Milwaukee Brewers (1988–91)

Matt Beech (Rimini) Struck out 266 in 295 Big League innings but posted an 8–22 record and 5.37 ERA. Philadelphia Phillies (1996–98)

Tim Birtsas (Rimini) Tenth in AL in win-loss percentage (10–6 record); struck out 231 in 328⅔ career innings. Oakland A's, Cincinnati Reds (1985–86, 1988–90)

George Canale (Nettuno) Connected for four home runs and 13 RBI in 44 games as a first baseman and designated hitter. Milwaukee Brewers (1989–91)

Willie Canate (Modena and Parma) Member of 1993 World Series champion Toronto as back-up outfielder; played in 38 games. Toronto Blue Jays (1993)

Chuck Carr (Rimini) Led the NL in stolen bases (58) and finished fourth in Rookie of the Year voting in 1993. Five teams, including Florida Marlins (1990–97).

Giovanni Carrara (Nettuno) Compiled a 28–19 record over parts of ten seasons; best year: 5–2, 2.18 ERA in 2004. Five

teams, including Los Angeles Dodgers (1995–97, 2000–06).

Steve Carter (Nettuno) Played 14 games over two seasons, registering three hits (.143 batting average) including a homer and a double. Pittsburgh Pirates (1989–90)

Carlos Casimiro (Paterno and San Marino) Had a double and three RBI in eight major-league at bats. Baltimore Orioles (2003)

Ray Chadwick (Novara and Rimini) Made seven appearances, recording a 0–5 record with 7.24 ERA. California Angels (1986)

Harry Chappas (Grosseto and Castiglione) Five-foot-three middle infielder hit .245 over 72 big-league games. Chicago White Sox (1978–80)

Anthony Chavez (Nettuno) Registered a 0.93 ERA in 9⅔ innings of work, striking out ten batters over seven games. Anaheim Angels (1997)

Rocky Childress (San Marino) Career: 2–3 with 4.76 ERA; registered 2.98 ERA in 32 games for 1987 Houston Astros. Philadelphia Phillies, Astros (1985–89)

Daryl Cias (Nettuno) Hit .333 (6-for-18) with a double, a run, an RBI and a stolen base in only season. Oakland A's (1983)

Marty Clary (Parma) Made 32 career starts; posted a 3.15 ERA with 4–3 record in 1989. Atlanta Braves (1987, 1989–90)

Cristobal Colon (Caserta) Shortstop went 6-for-36 (.167 batting average) with five runs and one RBI in 14 games. Texas Rangers (1992)

Jason Conti (Bologna) An outfielder who connected for 100 major-league hits in 420 at bats (.238) with six home runs. Four teams including Arizona Diamondbacks (2000-2004)

Glen Cook (Nettuno) Started seven games in nine big-league pitching appearances (2–3 record). Texas Rangers (1985)

Nelson Cruz (Nettuno) Went 15-23 with two saves and 5.04 ERA over six seasons. Four teams including Detroit Tigers, Houston Astros (1997, 1999–2003)

Todd Cruz (Fortitudo Bologna) Slammed 16 home runs and drove in 57 runs for 1982 Seattle Mariners. Six teams including Mariners and Baltimore Orioles (1978–80, 1982–84)

Tom Dettore (Grosseto) Went 8–11 in 68 major-league games; struck out 106 in 179²⁄₃ career innings. Pittsburgh Pirates, Chicago Cubs (1973–76)

Tom Dunbar (Bologna) In 91 games, outfielder batted .231 with three home runs and 18 RBI. Texas Rangers (1983–85)

Gary Eave (Grosseto) Was 2–0 with 1.31 ERA in three starts for 1989 Atlanta Braves; Career: 2–3, 3.56 ERA in 16 games. Braves, Seattle Mariners (1988–90)

Brian Edmondson (Rimini) Went 9–12 with one save in 121 major-league relief appearances. Atlanta Braves, Florida Marlins (1998–99)

Angel Escobar (Macerata) Went 1 for 3 with a run scored against the Philadelphia Phillies in only major-league game. San Francisco Giants (1988)

Horacio Estrada (San Marino) Posted a 4–1 record in 15 appearances over three campaigns. Milwaukee Brewers, Colorado Rockies (1999–2001)

Dave Falcone (Rimini) Won 12 games twice (1975, 1976); 70 career wins with 4.07 ERA in 325 appearances. San Francisco Giants, St. Louis Cardinals, New York Mets, Atlanta Braves (1975–84)

Joe Ferguson (Scavolini Pesaro) Veteran major leaguer who played in two World Series; Finished 21st in 1973 MVP voting. Four teams, including Los Angeles Dodgers (1970–83)

Anthony Ferarri (Grosseto) Left-handed pitcher saw action on the mound in four relief appearances. Allowed three runs

in four innings of work. Montreal Expos (2003)

Tony Ferreira (Fortitudo Bologna) Struck out five batters in 5²⁄₃ innings in two relief appearances. Kansas City Royals (1985)

Tony Fiore (Rimini) Top campaign: 10–2 with a 3.16 ERA for Minnesota Twins in 2002; 87 total career appearances. Tampa Bay Devil Rays and Twins (2000–03).

Willie Fraser (Parma) 38–40 lifetime record with seven saves. Five teams including California Angels (1986–91, 1995–96)

Alejandro Freire (Nettuno) Hit .246 with a home run and four RBI in 25 Big League contests. Baltimore Orioles (2005)

Mark Funderburk (Rimini) Batted .314 with two homers and 13 RBI in 23 games for 1985 Minnesota Twins; .294 career average. Twins (1981, 1985)

Jay Gainer (Grosseto) Career: .171 batting average (7-for-41) with three homers, six RBI and one stolen base in 23 games. Colorado Rockies (1993)

Bob Galasso (Nettuno) Went 4–8 with four saves in 55 big-league appearances. Seattle Mariners, Milwaukee Brewers (1977, 1979, 1981)

Amaury Garcia (Rimini) A second baseman who saw action in 10 games, knocking six base hits (including 2 home runs) in 24 at bats. Florida Marlins (1999)

Miguel Garcia (Fiorentina) Left-handed reliever saw action in 14 games over parts of three seasons. California Angels, Pittsburgh Pirates (1987–89)

Brian Giles (Milano) Middle infielder stole 17 bases and drove in 27 runs in 400 at bats for the 1983 New York Mets. Four teams, including Mets (1981–83, 1985–86, 1990)

Beiker Graterol (Rimini) Roughed up by New York Yankees in only start — allowed seven runs in four innings pitched. Detroit Tigers (1999)

Drew Hall (Fortitudo Bologna) Saved five career games, including three for 1990 Montreal Expos. Chicago Cubs, Texas Rangers, Expos (1986–90)

Mike Hartley (Nettuno) *See Germany entry for MLB background.* Made his first foray into domestic European baseball in Italy, when he pitched for Nettuno in 1998.

Kelly Heath (Milano) Hitless in one at bat against the Detroit Tigers on 20 April 1982. Kansas City Royals (1982)

Don Heinkel (Rimini) Pitched 21 games in relief for 1988 Detroit Tigers, earning a save and posting a 3.96 ERA in 36⅓ innings of work. Tigers, St. Louis Cardinals (1988–89)

Wilson Heredia (Grosseto) Pitched 16 games, logging a 1–1 record and a 3.41 ERA. Texas Rangers (1995, 1997)

Ubaldo Heredia (Macerata) Started two games (0–1) allowing six runs in 10 innings while striking out six. Montreal Expos (1987)

Brad Holman (Parma) Went 1–3 with three saves and a 3.72 ERA in only major-league season. Seattle Mariners (1993)

Randy Hunt (Parma) Catcher hit two home runs and drove in six runs in 35 games. St. Louis Cardinals, Montreal Expos (1985–86)

Tim Ireland (Nettuno) Played four different positions (1B, 2B, 3B, OF) in 11 major-league games. Kansas City Royals (1981–82)

Greg Jelks (Rimini) Hit a double for only major-league hit (1-for-11); saw action in ten games, scoring two runs. Philadelphia Phillies (1987)

Steve Kiefer (Rimini) Infielder's best season: five home runs and 17 RBI in 28 games for 1987 Milwaukee Brewers. Oakland A's, Brewers, NY Yankees (1984–89)

Mike Kinnunen (Verona and Parma) Left-handed pitcher made 48 appearances in the major leagues. Minnesota Twins, Baltimore Orioles (1980, 1986–87)

Brad Komminsk (Rimini) Hit 23 homers and knocked in 105 runs in 376 career games. Six teams including the Atlanta Braves (1983–87, 1989–91)

Randy Kramer (Grosseto) Logged a 5–9 record with one shutout and two saves for 1989 Pittsburgh Pirates. Pirates, Chicago Cubs, Seattle Mariners (1988–90, 1992)

Les Lancaster (Fortitudo Bologna) Durable reliever went 41–28 with 22 saves in seven-year career. Chicago Cubs, Detroit Tigers, St. Louis Cardinals (1987–93)

Rick Lancellotti (Parma) Played 36 games, hitting two home runs and registering 11 RBI. San Diego Padres, San Francisco Giants, Boston Red Sox (1982, 1986, 1990)

Stephen Larkin (Parma) Brother of Cincinnati Reds great Barry Larkin; went one for three in only major-league game. Cincinnati Reds (1998)

Jack Lazorko (Parma) Earned five wins and two saves in 69-game career. Milwaukee Brewers, Seattle Mariners Detroit Tigers, California Angels (1984–88)

Terry Lee (Rimini) Big first baseman drove in 3 runs and scored a run in 15 games (4-for-25). Cincinnati Reds (1990–91)

Dave Leeper (Parma) University of Southern California product knocked in four runs on three hits (3-for-34) in 19 games. Kansas City Royals (1984–85).

Cole Liniak (Nettuno) Third baseman played in 15 games over two seasons; hit .219 (7-for-39) with two RBI and three runs. Chicago Cubs (1999–2000)

Brian Looney (Rimini, San Marino) Got two starts in seven major-league appearances (0–1 record); 11 strike outs in 12⅔ innings. Montreal Expos, Boston Red Sox (1993–95)

Andrew Lorraine (Godo) Left-handed pitcher made 56 appearances in parts of seven seasons, finishing with a 6–11 record. Seven teams including Oakland

A's, Chicago Cubs (1994-1995, 1998-2000, 2002)

Dwight Lowry (Grosseto) Batted .307 with three home runs and 18 RBI in 150 at bats for 1986 Detroit Tigers; career average: .273. Tigers, Minnesota Twins (1984, 1986–88)

Willie Lozado (Rimini) Infielder hit .271, one home run, 20 RBI in 105 at bats in only major-league season. Milwaukee Brewers (1984)

Jose Malave (Rimini) Outfielder smacked four home runs (17 RBI) in 102 at bats for 1996 Boston Red Sox; lifetime average: .226. Red Sox (1996–97)

Greg Martinez (Grosseto) Scored two runs and stole two bases in 13-game major-league stint. Milwaukee Brewers (1998)

Pascual Matos (Parma) Catcher registered one hit in eight at bats in six major-league games. Atlanta Braves (1999)

Kirk McCaskill (Fiorentina) Placed in top ten in AL ERA and shutouts three times apiece; won 106 career games. California Angels, Chicago White Sox (1985–96)

Paul McClellan (Nettuno) Went 3–6 with a complete game in 13 appearances (12 starts) for 1991 San Francisco Giants; career ERA: 5.26. Giants (1990–91)

Rusty Meacham (Grosseto) Fifth in AL winning percentage in 1992 (10–4); 23–14 lifetime with 4.43 ERA. Five teams including Kansas City Royals (1991–96, 2000–01)

Rafael Medina (Parma) Started 12 games on the hill for the 1998 Florida Marlins; career numbers: 3–7, 5.96 ERA, 32 games. Marlins (1998–99)

Juan Melo (Rimini) Registered one hit and one RBI in 13 at bats over 11 games as a second baseman in his single September call-up. San Francisco Giants (2000)

Carlos Mendoza (San Marino) Outfielder scored six runs in 15 games for 1997 New York Mets; hit .182 in 28 career contests. Mets, Colorado Rockies (1997, 2000)

Frank Menechino (Nettuno) Played in three post seasons with the Oakland A's during a seven year career; hit .240 with 36 home runs and 149 RBI during tenure. A's, Toronto Blue Jays (1999–2005)

Lemmie Miller (San Marino) Went 2 for 12 with a run scored in eight-game major-league stint. Los Angeles Dodgers (1984)

Craig Minetto (Bologna) Earned one win (1–7 record) and one save in 55 career games. Oakland A's (1978–81)

Charlie Mitchell (Bologna) Posted a 2.76 ERA in 16⅓ innings for 1984 Boston Red Sox; career ERA in 12 games: 4.00. Red Sox (1984–85)

Dale Mohorcic (Fortitudo Bologna) Finished sixth in the AL in saves (16) in 1987; lifetime 16–21, 33 saves, 3.49 ERA. Texas Rangers, New York Yankees, Montreal Expos (1986–90)

Rafael Montalvo (Fortitudo Bologna) Threw one inning against the Atlanta Braves on 13 April 1986; allowed one run on one hit and two walks. Houston Astros (1986)

Jeff Moronko (Grosseto) Saw action in 14 big-league games going 4-for-30 (.158) with three RBI. Cleveland Indians, New York Yankees (1984, 1987)

Jim Morrison (Milano) Ranked in top ten in doubles in AL in 1980 (40) and NL in 1986 (35); Slammed 112 career homers. Five teams, including Pittsburgh Pirates (1977–88)

Sean Mulligan (Parma) Former University of Illinois standout got one at bat in two major-league games. San Diego Padres (1996)

Jaime Navarro (Grosseto) Won 15 games or more three times; in 1995 placed in NL top ten in wins and ERA. Milwaukee Brewers, Chicago Cubs, Chicago White Sox, Cleveland Indians (1989–2000)

Dave Nilsson (Rimini) A major-league All-Star in 1999; finished sixth in AL hitting

(.331 average) in 1996; 105 career home runs. Milwaukee Brewers (1992–99)

Chris Nyman (Roma) Batted .251 with two home runs and six RBI in 93 lifetime at bats. Chicago White Sox (1982–83)

Francisco Oliveras (Nettuno) Amassed a 11–15 record with five saves, one complete game and 3.71 ERA in 116 games. Minnesota Twins, San Francisco Giants (1989–92)

Jorge Orta (Parma) Two-time All-Star won a World Series ring with 1985 Kansas City Royals; 1,619 career hits. Five teams including Chicago White Sox and Royals (1972–87)

Johnny Paredes (Parma) Career numbers: 60 games, .211 average (26-for-123), a homer, six stolen bases, 11 RBI, 12 runs. Montreal Expos, Detroit Tigers (1988, 1990–91)

Bob Pate (Grosseto) Outfielder hit .267 with five RBI and three runs in 31 games. Montreal Expos (1980–81)

Dave Pavlas (Parma) Had solid season with 1996 World Series champion New York Yankees: 2.35 ERA, one save in 16 games. Chicago Cubs, Yankees (1990–91, 1995–96)

Elvis Pena (Rimini) A middle infielder who made 25 appearances logging 12 hits in 49 at bats (.245). Colorado Rockies, Milwaukee Brewers (2000–2001)

Jesus Pena (Nettuno and Grosseto) Lefthander went 2–1 with a save in 48 appearances. Chicago White Sox, Boston Red Sox (1999–2000)

Jeff Peterek (Crocetta — PR) Pitched in seven games, going 0–2 with a 4.02 ERA; struck out 13 in 31⅓ innings. Milwaukee Brewers (1989)

Jeff Pico (Rimini) Threw four-hit complete-game shutout in MLB debut against Cincinnati Reds; career stats: 13–12, five saves, 4.24 ERA. Chicago Cubs (1988–90)

Carlos Quintana (Grosseto) Batted .295 with 11 HRs and 71 RBI as Boston Red Sox starting first baseman in 1991; Red Sox (1988–91, 1993)

Lenny Randle (Nettuno, Fortitudo Bologna, Milano) Top 25 in 1974 AL MVP voting; top ten in triples in AL (1975) and NL (1978). Six teams, including Texas Rangers (1971–82)

Jeff Ransom (Nettuno) Catcher was NL's second-youngest player (20) in 1981; played in 26 major-league games. San Francisco Giants (1981–83)

Jessie Reid (Nettuno) Outfielder's only major-league hit was a solo home run. San Francisco Giants (1987–88).

Win Remmerswaal (Parma, Nettuno, San Marino) Struck out 36 in 55⅔ innings; 3–1 career record. Boston Red Sox (1979–80)

Liu Rodriguez (Grosseto and Rimini) Middle infielder went 22 for 93 (.237) in 39 games with a home run, two double, two triples and 12 RBI. Chicago White Sox (1999)

Mel Rosario (Parma) A catcher who went hitless in three at bats in a September call up. Baltimore Orioles (1997)

Mike Saipe (Rimini) Made two big-league starts; pitched effectively in the first, giving up three runs in six innings. Colorado Rockies (1998)

Angel Salazar (Collecchio) Middle infielder played 383 games, batting .212 (188-for-886) with 59 RBI and 69 runs. Montreal Expos, Kansas City Royals, Chicago Cubs (1983–84, 1986–88)

Manny Sarmiento (Roma and Fortitudo Bologna) 5–1 with 2.06 ERA for 1976 World Series winner Cincinnati Reds. Reds, Seattle Mariners, Pittsburg Pirates (1976–80, 1982–83)

Benj Sampson (Nettuno) Registered a 3–2 record over 88⅓ innings, striking out 72 batters. Minnesota Twins (1998–99)

Jeff Schulz (Bologna) Logged a .244 (19-for-79) batting average with six extra-base hits. Kansas City Royals, Pittsburgh Pirates (1989–90)

Jeff Schwarz (Rimini) Went 2–2 with a 4.17 ERA in 54 career games. Chicago White Sox, California Angels (1993, 1994)

Jim Scranton (Fortitudo Bologna) Short-stop went hitless in six major-league at bats; scored one run. Kansas City Royals (1984–85)

Tom Shopay (Fortitudo Bologna) Out-fielder played 232 games over parts of seven seasons. New York Yankees, Baltimore Orioles (1967, 1969, 1971–72, 1975–77)

Doug Simons (Rimini) Left-handed pitcher was 2–3 with a save in 43 major-league appearances. New York Mets, Montreal Expos (1991–92)

Jason Simontacchi (Rimini) Top ten in NL winning percentage twice (2002, 2003); ninth in 2002 Rookie of the Year voting; St. Louis Cardinals, Washington Nationals (2002–04, 2007)

Daryl Smith (Milano) Made one start in a total of two major-league pitching appearances; registered a 4.05 ERA. Kansas City Royals (1990).

Ken Smith (Nettuno) Hit .291 (12-for-41) in 48 games for the 1982 Atlanta Braves. Braves (1981–83)

Tommy Smith (Firenze) Outfielder's best season: .256 with eight stolen bases and two homers in 55 games for 1976 Cleveland Indians. Indians, Seattle Mariners (1973–77)

Mark Souza (Santarangelo) A former first-round pick by the Kansas City Royals; pitched five games in relief for Oakland A's in 1980. A's (1980)

Craig Stimac (Grosseto, San Marino) Mainly a catcher who saw action in 29 major-league games. San Diego Padres (1980–81)

Les Straker (Bologna) Started two games on the mound in the 1987 World Series for the winning team (Minnesota Twins). Twins (1987–88)

Andres Thomas (Grosseto) Hit 13 homers in back-to-back seasons ('88 and '89)

as Atlanta Braves' starting shortstop. Braves (1985–90)

Rich Thompson (Grosseto) Recorded five saves for 1985 Cleveland Indians; logged a 2.18 ERA in 33 innings in 1989 for Montreal. Indians, Montreal Expos (1985, 1989–90)

Tony Torcato (Grosseto) Former first-round draft pick hit .298 in 47 career at bats. San Francisco Giants (2002–05)

Luis Ugueto (Nettuno) Connected for six hits in 28 at bats (.214) but scored 23 runs and stole 10 bases. Seattle Mariners (2002–2003)

Tom Urbani (Rimini) Left-handed pitcher saw action in 81 games, compiling a 10–17 record. St. Louis Cardinals, Detroit Tigers (1993–96)

Dave Van Gorder (Grosseto) Catcher was a Cincinnati Reds second-round pick; drove in 38 run in 183 major-league games. Reds, Baltimore Orioles (1982, 1984–87)

Jim Vatcher (Rimini) Outfielder hit .248 with a home run and 11 RBI in 87 games. Philadelphia Phillies, Atlanta Braves, San Diego Padres (1990–92).

Ed Vosberg (Novara) Won a World Series ring with 1997 Florida Marlins; pitched in 266 career games. Eight teams, including Texas Rangers (1986, 1990, 1994–97, 1999–2001)

Rick Waits (Rimini and Parma) Lifetime 79–92 record with 4.25 ERA in 317 games; won 16 contests in 1979. Texas Rangers, Cleveland Indians, Milwaukee Brewers (1973, 1975–85)

Jim Walewander (Milano) Infielder hit .215 with a homer and 14 RBI in 242 big-league at bats. Detroit Tigers, New York Yankees, California Angels (1987–88, 1990, 1993)

Netherlands

Stan Bahnsen (Harlem Nicols) 1968 AL Rookie of the Year winner; won 21 games in 1972. Six teams, including New York Yankees, Chicago White Sox, Montreal Expos (1966, 1968–82)

Ivanon Coffie (Almere '90) Infielder had five extra-base hits (four doubles, one triple) and six RBI in 60 career at bats. Baltimore Orioles (2000)

Robert Eenhoorn (Neptunus) Former second-round draft pick hit one home run and drove in 10 runs in 37 games. New York Yankees, California/Anaheim Angels (1994–97)

Rikkert Faneyte (Amsterdam Pirates) Connected for 23 hits in 132 lifetime at bats (.174 average). San Francisco Giants, Texas Rangers (1993–96)

Eugene Kingsale (Almere '90 and Neptunus) Career: .251 batting average, three homers, 53 RBI in 211 games. Four teams, including Baltimore Orioles (1996, 1998–2003)

Calvin Maduro (HCAW) Struck out 140 batters in 260 innings pitched. Philadelphia Phillies, Baltimore Orioles (1996–97, 2000–02)

Ralph Milliard (HCAW) Middle infielder played in 47 games over three seasons. Florida Marlins, New York Mets (1996–98)

Eddie Oropesa (Sparta/Feyenoord) Lefthander went 8–4 in 125 games, striking out 78 in 92 innings. Philadelphia Phillies, Arizona Diamondbacks, San Diego Padres (2001–04)

Note: In a few cases with the Italian entries, players' names and dates were matched from *www.baseball-reference.com* to the Italian baseball site *www.fibs.it*. Efforts were made to confirm every player's status in the major leagues and Italian baseball.

Appendix 9

International Glossary of Baseball Terms

One country's baseball (United States and elsewhere) is another country's honkbal (Netherlands). Here's a glossary of some baseball terms from a sampling of countries in the Confederation of European Baseball.

Hitting

Base hit

Dutch: Honkslag
French: Coup sûr
Hebrew: (single) חבטת יחידה
Italian: Battuta valida
Spanish: Batazo de una base, limpio, base hit

Bat

Dutch: Knuppel, slaghout, hout
French: Batte
Hebrew: מחבט
Italian: Mazza
Spanish: Bate, garrote, palo, macana, manopla
Swedish: Slagträ

Batter

Dutch: Slagman
French: Frappeur
German: Schlaeger
Hebrew: חובט
Italian: Battitore
Spanish: Bateador
Swedish: Slagman

Bunt

Dutch: Stoolslag
French: Amortie
Hebrew: באנט \ נקיטה
Italian: Smorza
Spanish: Toque, plancha, bont

Double

Dutch: Tweehonkslag
Hebrew: חבטה כפולה
Italian: Doppio

Spanish: Un doble, hit double
Swedish: Dubbel

Fly ball

Dutch: Hoge bal
French: Chandelle
Hebrew: כדור גובה
Italian: Volata
Spanish: Bolea, flay
Swedish: Lyra

Foul ball

Dutch: Foutslag
French: Hors ligne
Hebrew: בול פאול / פאול כדור
Italian: Volata faul
Spanish: Bolea a fao, flay de fao (faul, foul)
Swedish: Foul boll

Ground ball

Dutch: Grondbal
French: Balle au sol
Hebrew: כדור קרקע
Italian: Radente
Spanish: Pelota por el suelo, rolin
Swedish: Markboll

Hit (a)

Dutch: Slag (een)
French: Frappe
Hebrew: חבטה
Italian: Battuta
Spanish: Batazo bueno, hit, incogible hit limpo

Hit (to)

Dutch: Slaan (naar)
French: Frapper
Italian: Battere
Spanish: Batear
Swedish: Slag

Home run

Dutch: Home run, ronde
French: Un circuit
Hebrew: הום רון

Italian: Quattro basi, fuori campo, home run
Spanish: Batazo de 4 bases, Jonron, home run
Swedish: Home run

Sacrifice bunt

Dutch: Opofferings-stoolslag
French: Amortie sacrifice
Hebrew: נקיטת הקרבה
Italian: Smoozata di sacrificio
Spanish: Toque de sacrificio

Steal

Dutch: Gestolen honk
French: Vol
Hebrew: לגנוב גניבה
Italian: Rubata
Spanish: Robo, ladron de bases

Swing

Dutch: Zwaai
German: Schwung
Hebrew: הנפה
Italian: Sventolare
Swedish: Sving

Pitching

Balk

Dutch: Schijn
French: Faute irrégulière
Hebrew: הטעיה
Italian: Bolk
Spanish: Verro, engano, boc

Ball (as in "ball or strike")

Dutch: Wyd
French: Balle
Hebrew: בול
Italian: Bool
Spanish: Bola
Swedish: Boll

Base on balls

Dutch: Vrije loop naar eerste honk
French: But sur balle
Hebrew: ארבעה בולים
Italian: Base gratis
Spanish: Base por bolas

Change-up

Dutch: Vertraagde worp
French: Changement de vitesse
Italian: Cambio di velocita
Spanish: Cambio de velociadad

Count (balls and strikes on a batter)

Dutch: Stand
French: Compte
Hebrew: ספירה
Italian: Conto
Spanish: Cuenta
Swedish: Räkningen

Curveball

Dutch: Curve, bocht, kromming
French: Courbe
Italian: Curva
Spanish: Curva
Swedish: Kurva

Fastball

Dutch: Snelle bal
French: Rapide
Italian: Lancio veloce
Spanish: Tiro rapido

Fat pitch (an easy-to-hit pitch)

Dutch: Mooie slag
French: Grosse balle
Italian: Lancio in mezzo all 'area di straik
Spanish: Strike facil

Knuckleball

Dutch: Knuckle bal (door pitcher met knokkels gegooide bal)

Italian: Lancio effettuato con le nocche delle dita
Spanish: Bola nudillos

Mound

Dutch: Werpersheuvel
French: Monticule
Hebrew: גבעת המגיש
Italian: Pedana
Spanish: Monticulo, loma
Swedish: Kulle

No-hitter

Dutch: Wedstrijd, waarin de werper de tegenpartiij geen enkele honkslag toestaat
Italian: Partita in cui il lanciatore non concede battute valide
Spanish: Sin hits

Pitcher

Dutch: Werper
French: Lanceur
Hebrew: מגיש
Italian: Lanciatore
Spanish: Lanzador, picher, tirador
Swedish: Kastare

Screwball

Dutch: Schroefbal
Italian: Lancio a vite
Spanish: Bola de tornillo

Shutout

Dutch: Voor nul aan de kant
Italian: Partita in cui gli avversari non segnano
Spanish: Juego sin carrera, blanqueo

Slider

Dutch: Slider, Kleine afwijking aan gerworpan bal
French: Glissante
Italian: Slaider, Lancio sinile alla curva ma piu veloce e con minore scarto
Spanish: Eslaider, Lazamiento similar a la curva, pero mas rapido y con menos desarrollo

Strikeout

Dutch: Slag uit
French: Retrait sur prise
Hebrew: (strike) סטרייק
Italian: Straik out
Spanish: Ponchado, aut

Defense

Bases

Dutch: Honken
Hebrew: תחנה / בסיס
Italian: Basi
Swedish: Baser

Catch (a)

Dutch: Vangbal
French: Attraper
German: Fang
Hebrew: תפיסה
Italian: Presa
Spanish: Cogida
Swedish: Lyra

Catch (to)

Dutch: Vangen
French: Rattraper
German: Fangen
Hebrew: תפיסה
Italian: Ricevere
Spanish: Coger
Swedish: Fånga

Catcher

Dutch: Achtervanger
French: Receveur
Hebrew: התוף
Italian: Ricevitore
Spanish: Receptor, catcher

Defense

Dutch: Verdediging
French: Défense
German: Verteidigung

Hebrew: הגנה
Italian: Difesa
Spanish: Defensa
Swedish: Försvar

Double play

Dutch: Dubbelspel
French: Double jeu
Hebrew: פסילה כפולה
Italian: Doppio gioco
Spanish: Doble jugada, doble play

Error

Dutch: Veldfout
French; Erreur
German: Fehler
Hebrew: פישול
Italian: Errore
Spanish: Error
Swedish: Misstag

Field (to)

Dutch: Fielden
French: Ramasser
Italian: Raccogliers
Spanish: Recoger, "fildear"

Fielding position

Dutch: Veld positie
French: Position de défense
Hebrew: (fielder) הגנה שחקן
Italian: Posizione di difesa
Spanish: Posicion en el campo jardinero

First base

Dutch: Eerste honk
French: Première base
Italian: Prima base
Spanish: Primera base, base clave
Swedish: Första bas

Glove

Dutch: Handschoen
French: Gant
German: Handschuh
Hebrew: כפפה

Italian: Guanto
Spanish: Guante
Swedish: Handske

Infield

Dutch: Binneveld
French: Champ interieur
Hebrew: (החצר) חצר פנימי
Italian: Campo interno
Spanish: Campo interior o cuadro infield

Infielder

Dutch: Binnenvelder
Hebrew: שחקן חצר פנימי
Italian: Interno
Spanish: Jugador del cuadro, infildear, jardin centro
Swedish: Infield spelare

Left field

Dutch: Linkshandig
French: Champ gauche
Hebrew: (Left fielder) שחקן שדה שמאל
Italian: Esterno sinistra
Spanish: Exterior jardin izquierdo

Out

Dutch: Uit
French: Retrait
German: Aus
Hebrew: פסול / פסילה
Italian: Eliminato
Spanish: Eliminado, aut
Swedish: Bränning

Outfielder

Dutch: Buitenvelder
French: Champ extérieur
Hebrew: שחקן חצר חיצוני
Italian: Esterno
Spanish: Exterior, fil, filder, jardinero

Right field

Dutch: Rechtsveld
French: Champ droit
Hebrew: (right fielder) שחקן שדה ימין

Italian: Esterno destro
Spanish: Exterior derecho, jardin derechio

Second base

Dutch: Tweede honk
French: Deuxième base
Italian: Seconda base
Spanish: Segunda base
Swedish: Andra bas

Shortstop

Dutch: Korte stop
French: Arrêt-court
Hebrew: קשר / שורטסטופ
Italian: Interbase
Spanish: Medio, shortstop

Third base

Dutch: Derde honk
French: Troisième base
Italian: Terza base
Spanish: Tercera base
Swedish: Tredje bas

Miscellaneous

Baseball

Dutch: Honkbal
French: Base-ball
Hebrew: בייסבול
Italian: Pallabase, basebol, baseboll
Spanish: Baseball, pelota base, béisbol
Swedish: Baseboll

Field (a)

Dutch: Speelveld
French: Un terrain
German: Feld/Spielfeld
Hebrew: Hebrew: (Fair territory) כדור תחום פעיל
Italian: Campo
Spanish: Campo, jardin
Swedish: Plan

Game

Dutch: Wedstryd
French: Un match
German: Spiel
Italian: Partita
Spanish: Juego o partido
Swedish: Match

Umpire

Dutch: Scheidsrechter
French: Un arbitre
German: Schiedsrichter
Hebrew: פסילה משולשת

Italian: Arbitro
Spanish: Arbitro, umpaiar
Swedish: Domare

Sources: *Glossary of International Baseball Terms*, compiled by Danny Litwhiler (an official publication of the United States Baseball Federation, 1980); the Israel Baseball League website (*http://www.israelbaseballleague.com/baseballinisrael/glossary/*); Deutscher Baseball und Softball Verband; Svenska Baseboll och Softbollförbundet; and Fédération Française de Baseball et de Softball.

Chapter Notes

Introduction

1. It is documented that Spalding lost money on his efforts to start a league in Great Britain. There are also signs that he was involved with attempts to push baseball in France. There is less information on his French efforts but it's pretty safe to assume that any funds he put forward in that country were lost, as the French league never became fully established.

2. M. E. Travaglini, "Olympic Baseball 1936: Was es Das?" *The National Pastime* 4, no. 2 (Winter 1985), 48.

3. Gary Bedingfield, *Baseball in World War II Europe* (Charleston, SC: Arcadia Publishing,1999), 124.

4. Caroline Camp Leiser, "Babe Ruth Club: Baseball Becomes a German Sport," *Information bulletin* no. 158 (May 1949), 9–10. From Berlin, Germany: Office of Military Government for Germany (U.S.), Control Office, APO 742, US Army. *http://digital.library.wisc.edu/1711.dl/History.omg1949n 160* (accessed December 5, 2007).

5. Daniel Bloyce, "That's Your Way of Playing Rounders, Isn't It? The Response of the English Press to American Baseball Tours to England, 1874–1924," *Sporting Traditions* 22, no. 1 (November 2005), 83.

6. Ibid., 86.

7. Daniel Bloyce, "John Moores and the 'Professional' Baseball Leagues in 1930s England," *Sport in History* 27, no. 1 (March 2007), 66.

8. Associated Press, "U.S. Defines Baseball for Russia with Let-Up Pitch of Lyric Prose," *New York Times*, November 19, 1956, 33.

9. Stefan Szymanski and Andrew Zimbalist, *National Pastime: How Americans Play Baseball and the Rest of the World Plays Soccer* (Washington, DC: Brookings Institution Press) 49.

10. Interview with Ian Young, August 31, 2007.

11. Jenkins, Bruce, "Baseball Opener in Japan Evokes Mixed Messages," *San Francisco Chronicle*, March 29, 2000.

12. Associated Press, "Baseball Chiefs Plan Conquest of Europe," *Taipei Times*, March 18, 2003, 20.

13. Stephen Wilson, "IOC has suggestions for baseball, softball," Associated Press, July 10, 2005.

Chapter 1

1. See *Brief History of Baseball in The Netherlands* by Marco Stoovelaar. This four-page article was given to international baseball sources in the run-up to the 2004 Athens Olympic Games.

2. Associated Press, "U.S. Sailors Teach Dutch Baseball; Game is Called Ideal Summer Sport," *Washington Post*, June 9, 1928, 17.

3. Stoovelaar, Marco, *Mr. Cocker Honkbalgids 2000* (M. Stoovelaar, 2000), 351.

4. "Belgium Likes Baseball: Brussels Wins Pennant in Seven-Club Circuit Overseas," *New York Times*, September 14, 1919.

5. The Football Association or FA Cup was effectively the same as winning England's national championship at the time.

6. Ajax also sporadically used the Olympic Stadium.

7. *IBAF News*, week 17, 2007, no. 461, 1.

8. Kabout wrote a brief history of Dutch baseball for the website Baseball Fever (www.baseball-fever.com). In correspondence with the author he said his history is a combination of materials gleaned from a March 8,1988, article in the Dutch magazine *Inside* and recollections of his father, who was born in 1927 and, like Kabout, was a baseball player in Holland.

9. Associated Press, "U.S. Sailors Teach Dutch Baseball; Game is Called Ideal Summer Sport," *Washington Post*, June 9, 1928, 17.

10. E-mail correspondence with the author dated May 25, 2007.

11. Gershen, Marty, "Take Me Out to the *Honkbal* Game," *Stars and Stripes* (European edition), September 2, 1961.

12. Associated Press, "American Baseball Fans Assist Dutch Amateurs," *New York Times*, June 8, 1948, 30.

13. Roger C. Panaye, *European Amateur Baseball: 25 Years* (CEBA, 1978), 27.

14. The inaugural members of the European Baseball Federation were Belgium, Germany, France, Italy and Spain.

15. Associated Press, "Netherlands Nine Wins," *New York Times*, July 16, 1956, 25.

16. "Honkballer from Holland," *Time*, February 25, 1952.

17. "Hannie Hurls 'Em," *Time*, September 8, 1952.

18. E-mail correspondence with the author, May 2007.

19. It is worth noting that Urbanus was not monolithic in his success on the mound during this era. Roel De Mon was also such a dominating figure as a pitcher that Kabout joked, "When you managed to get a hit against [De Mon], you had a starting spot in the Dutch national team."

20. Associated Press, "Tigers Teach Dutchman 'Honkbal,'" *Washington Post*, March 21, 1965, C2.

21. Shirley Szelkowski, "Honkbal!" *Grand Rapids Press*, September 19,1982; quoted in *International Baseball Rundown*, October 1992, 4.

22. Stoovelaar. *Mr. Cocker Honkbalgids 2000*, 186.

23. Steve Wulf, "A Last Hurrah; Ron Fraser's Final Coaching Mission is to Take Team USA to the Gold Medal," *Sports Illustrated*, July 22, 1992,150.

24. Charles Maher, "Baseball in Dutch," *Los Angeles Times*, February 12, 1970, D2.

25. *International Baseball Rundown*, February 1995, 6.

26. This quote comes from a letter written by the Dutch federation's M. Bremer to the Federation of European Baseball, April 4, 1970.

27. In 2005, 14 of the 30-member Dutch national team came from either Curaçcao or the Netherlands Antilles.

28. Email correspondence with author, March 2007.

29. Interview with Jimmy Summers, March 2007.

30. Harvey Shapiro, "An American Coaching Honkbal," in *Baseball without Borders: The International Pastime*, edited by George Gmelch (Lincoln: University of Nebraska Press, 2006), 247–262.

31. Jeff Archer, *Strike Four* (Lafayette, CO: White-Boucke Publishing, 1995), 163.

32. Pitching great Bert Blyleven was born in Zeist, Netherlands, but grew up in Southern California. He still has family in the Netherlands but has not returned there since 1993, as of 2007. Still, in a February 2007 interview, he described himself as "one proud Dutchman."

33. Joe Connor, *A Fan's Guide to the 2006 World Baseball Classic!* (Modernerabaseball.com, 2005–2006).

34. "Baseball America's Daily Dish," August 19, 2005, http://www.baseballamerica.com/today/minors/050419dish.html (accessed December 5, 2005).

35. Shapiro, "An American Coaching Honkbal."

Chapter 2

1. Bill Barich, "Going to the Moon," in *The Greatest Baseball Stories Ever Told*, ed. Jeff Silverman, (Guilford, CT: Lyons Press, 2001), 97.

2. "Sports Buzz." *Birmingham News* (quoting the *Akron Bee*), October 17, 2000.

3. According to Igino Scafella in his paper "Evoluzione e sviluppo di uno sport d'importazione: Il caso del baseball in Italia," two U.S. naval teams squared off in February 1884 at the Livorno port. (Scafella's paper was presented in the 2000–2001 academic year at the Universita degli Studi di Roma to the faculty of the motor sciences department.

4. Mark Lamaster, *Spalding's World Tour: The Epic Adventure That Took Baseball Around The Globe — And Made It America's Game* (New York: Public Affairs, 2006), 190–191.

5. Ibid., 195–196.

6. Ibid., 197.

7. *Spalding's 1891 Official Base Ball Guide*, 37. Because I had only a part of this guide and the complete version was not readily available, it is possible that this anecdote actually comes from the 1890 edition. (Whichever edition, the page number is accurate.)

8. James Elfers, *The Tour to End All Tours: The Story of Major League Baseball's 1913–1914 World Tour* (Lincoln: University of Nebraska Press, 2003), 198–216.

9. G. W. Axelson, "Comiskey Rallies and Allays Fears," *Chicago Record-Herald*, February 11, 1914.

10. "Teach Italians Baseball," *Washington Post*, December 2, 1918, 8.

11. Scafella, 5.

12. Federazione Italiana Baseball Softball, *Un Diamante Azzuro: Personaggi e Storie* (Macron Team Uniforms, 2006), 3.

13. Frank Cerabino, "Baseball Italiano; the Great American Pastime — Translated," *Palm Beach Post*, March 18, 2007, p.1A.

14. Blake Ehrlich, "Slide, Luigi Slide!" *Los Angeles Times*, September 6, 1953, F11.

15. Ibid.

16. Bob Addie, "Nats Diplomatic Rookies from Italy See Drill, Are Amazed at Skill of Players," *Washington Post*, March 20, 1955, C2.

17. Associated Press, "Italians Ban Catcher; Too Slow Getting Home," *New York Times*, March 11, 1956.

18. Christopher P. Winner, "Italians Cheer Sluggers from Afar," *USA Today*, September 8, 1998, 1A.

19. Associated Press, "DiMaggio Takes Batting Practice; Result: Sore Back," *Washington Post*, June 17, 1957, A14.

20. According to Italian baseball's official history, Morgan was well on his way to a big-league career when an injury cut it short. In 1952, as a teammate of Hank Aaron's on the Eau Claire (Wisconsin) Bears of the Northern League, Morgan hit .300 and slugged 14 home runs.

21. See Stephen Hall, "Baseball in Italy No Work of Art," *Washington Post*, July 11, 1977, D1.

22. Author Peter Carino wrote in 2006 that a lawsuit by foreign basketball players against their league had led to a relaxation of the foreigner rule. See his chapter "Italy: No Hotdogs in the Bleachers" in *Baseball without Borders: The International Pastime*, ed. George Gmelch (Lincoln, NE: University of Nebraska Press), 229–246.

23. Joe Garagiola, "Baseball in Italy: As easy as I, II, III," *New York Times*, July 15, 1975, S2.

24. Carino, "Italy: No Hotdogs in the Bleachers," 234.

25. E-mail correspondence with the author, June 3, 2007.

26. Stephen Hall, "Baseball in Italy No Work of Art," *Washington Post*, July 11, 1977, D1.

27. Steve Dolan, "U.S. Players Add a Touch of Spice to Italian Olympic Baseball Team," *Los Angeles Times*, July 26, 1984, SD B6.

28. E-mail correspondence with author, September 23, 2007.

29. Gordon Edes, "Baseball — Now that's Italian; When in Rome, Ardor Exceeds Ability to Turn the Double Play," *Sun-Sentinel* (Fort Lauderdale, Florida), February 21, 1996, 1C.

30. Alan M. Klein, *Growing the Game:*

The Globalization of Major League Baseball (New Haven, CT: Yale University Press, 2006), 175.

Chapter 3

1. Milton H. Jamail and Larry Dierker, *Full Count: Inside Cuban Baseball* (Carbondale: Southern Illinois University Press, 2002), 15–16.

2. Wikipedia, "Cuban League," http://en.wikipedia.org/wiki/Cuban_League (accessed December 7, 2007).

3. Jamail and Dierker, 15–16.

4. Fernando Garrido, "Primeros Pasos Del Bééisbol Por Barcelona," Secció ó de Bééisbol del Fc Barcelona, *http://www.galeon.com/fguillen/fernandogarrido.htm.*

5. "Baseball in France: Game Booming There and Organized Effort Being Made to Popularize Sport," *Washington Post*, March 15, 1914 SP2.

6. "Spanish Baseball Team Winner, 22 to 12," *Christian Science Monitor*, May 2, 1918, 10.

7. Roger C. Panaye, *European Amateur Baseball: 25 Years* (C.E.B.A., 1978), 15.

8. FC Barcelona baseball history from Garrido.

9. Today the federation is known as La Real Federación Españñola de Bééisbol y Sóófbol. Because of the organization's long history it has received the "Real" (Royal) title.

10. Roger C. Panaye, 15.

11. Ibid., 32–33.

12. The Spanish were crushed in their two games at the Global World Series, losing to Hawaii 23–0 and Japan 8–0.

13. John Kernaghan, "Baseball, Olympic-style; 'Bééisbol' in Barcelona: using base paths to make inroads," *Hamilton Spectator*, July 11, 1992, E2.

14. Mike Preston, "Barcelona '92 Olympics: Spain Still Playing Catch-Up Against Team USA," *Baltimore Sun*, quoted from *Los Angeles Times*, July 27, 1992, C11.

15. Jim Myers, "King of Spain reigns mainly at the Games," *USA Today*, August 4, 1992, 11E.

16. E-mail correspondence with author, April 2, 2007.

17. "Q&A with Grizzlies Forward Pau Gasol," *Sporting News*, January 27, 2006, 35.

Chapter 4

1. "Belgium Likes Baseball: Brussels Wins Pennant in Seven-Club Circuit Overseas," *New York Times*, September 14, 1919.

2. Quotes from Gaston Panaye come from correspondence with the author from December 2006 through April 2007.

3. Roger C. Panaye, *European Amateur Baseball: 25 Years* (C.E.B.A.,1978), 6.

4. During this period, Belgium and France also played a series of international games. Between 1937 and 1939, the two countries split four games. The games were close, with Belgium winning two by the scores of 5–4 and 8–4 and the French taking a pair both by the identical count of 9–8.

5. The Dutch used a modified ball in their domestic competitions during the war. Still, they continued to play baseball.

6. E-mail correspondence with the author, March 2007.

7. When the team was no longer allowed to play at Bell Telephone's complex, they changed their name and moved to the town of Hoboken, where they secured their own field.

8. E-mail correspondence with the author, May 25, 2007.

9. Wat remt onze sport?" *Baseball: Officieel Orgaan Der Belgische Baseball Federatie*, July/August/September 1954, 1. The original text was in Flemish — it's translated here by Peter Janssen.

10. Ibid.

11. The European Cup events are club competitions as opposed to the European Championships, which pit each country's national team against each other.

12. The Greys are today known as the Royal Greys. The "Royal" moniker is offered to clubs and federations in Belgium after 25 years of official registration.

13. Ian Thomsen, "Baseball, the Belgian Pastime," *International Herald Tribune*, August 23, 1994.

14. According to Peter C. Bjarkman's *Diamonds Around the Globe: The Encyclopedia of International Baseball*, the Intercontinental Cup was established in 1973 when a group of baseball countries broke away from the sport's main international governing body. Ostensibly, the event was going to be an alternative World Championship, but

when the two competing bodies reformed, the cup continued as an elite international baseball event.

15. Along with the Francophone league, some Francophone Belgian teams also play interleague contests with clubs from Luxembourg.

Chapter 5

1. This chapter is adapted from Josh Chetwynd, "Great Britain: Baseball's Battle for Respect in the Land of Cricket, Rugby, and Soccer," in *Baseball Without Borders: The International Pastime*, ed. George Gmelch (Lincoln: University of Nebraska Press, 2006), 263–287.

2. Daniel Bloyce, "That's Your Way of Playing Rounders, Isn't It? The Response of the English Press to American Baseball Tours to England, 1874–1924," *Sporting Traditions* 22, no. 1 (November 2005), 82.

3. Ibid., 83.

4. Newton Crane, *Baseball: The All-England Series* (London: George Bell & Sons, 1891), 13.

5. Patrick Carroll, "Baseball in Graceland," *SABR (UK) Examiner*, July 2001, 5.

6. Crane, 16.

7. Peter Levine, *A.G. Spalding and the Rise of Baseball* (New York: Oxford University Press, 1985), 105.

8. Bloyce, "That's Your Way," 87.

9. James Elfers, *The Tour to End All Tours: The Story of Major League Baseball's 1913–1914 World Tour* (Lincoln: University of Nebraska Press, 2003), 227.

10. Ibid., 229–230.

11. Ibid., 229.

12. *Daily News and Leader*, February 27, 1914, 10.

13. From Wilson Cross scrapbook, courtesy of Mike Ross and SABR (UK). The article from which the quote was taken was published in the *Evening Standard*, November 4, 1924.

14. Dean's involvement with baseball should not be a surprise. He likely had a close relationship with John Moores and, after his playing career worked for Moores' Littlewoods company.

15. John Keith, *Dixie Dean: The Inside Story of a Football Icon* (London: Robson Books, 2001), 119–120.

16. Teams in the 1935 North of England League: Oldham Greyhounds, Bradford Northern, Rochdale Greys, Salford Reds, Manchester North End Blue Sox, Belle Vue Tigers, Hurst Hawks and Hyde Grasshoppers.

17. *Liverpool Echo*, May 4, 1935, 7.

18. *Ashton-under-Lyne Reporter*, June 15, 1935, 15.

19. In the future, this problem would be somewhat stemmed, as most professional teams ultimately played on the better-kept grass of greyhound stadiums.

20. *Ashton-under-Lyne Reporter*, May 2, 1936, 18.

21. Ibid., August 10, 1935.

22. The inaugural teams in the Yorkshire League: Greenfield Giants, Hull Baseball Club, Wakefield Cubs, Bradford City Sox, Sheffield Dons, Leeds Oaks, Scarborough Seagull and Dewsbury Royals. The 1936 London Major League teams: White City, West Ham, Hackney Royals, Harringay, Romford Wasps and Catford Saints. The Streatham and Mitcham Giants were also a founding member but folded weeks into the first season.

23. Interview with author, February 1, 2003.

24. Ian Smyth, "The History of Baseball in the North of England," Master's thesis, Leeds Polytechnic Faculty of Cultural and Education Studies, 1992.

25. *Daily Mirror*, May 29, 1937, 27; quoted in Daniel Bloyce, "John Moores and the 'Professional' Baseball Leagues in 1930s England," *Sport in History* 27, no. 1 (March 2007) 75.

26. Interview with author, August 11, 2002.

27. "The Overseas Influence" (editorial), *Baseball News*, July 16, 1953, 2.

28. Jeff Archer, *Strike Four: Adventures in European Baseball* (Lafayette, CO: White Bouke, 1995), 19.

29. Interview with author, December 2, 2002.

30. Interview with author, September 5, 2007.

Chapter 6

1. David Block, *Baseball Before We Knew It: A Search for the Root of the Game* (Lincoln: University of Nebraska Press, 2005), 67–68.

2. E-mail correspondence with the author, August 1, 2007.

3. Roger C. Panaye, *European Amateur Baseball: 25 Years* (CEBA,1978), 12. Panaye wrote: "The possibility exists ... that this game was exported to America with the early colonists and later came back to [Europe] as baseball."

4. Josh Chetwynd and Brian A. Belton, *British Baseball and the West Ham Club: History of a 1930 Professional Baseball Team in 1930s East London* (Jefferson, NC: McFarland, 2006).

5. Louis Jacobson, "Herman Goldberg: Baseball Olympian and Jewish-American," in *Baseball History 3: An Annual of Original Baseball Research,* ed. Peter Levine (Westport, CT: Meckler, 1990), 71–88. Quotes from Goldberg in this chapter come from Jacobson's piece unless otherwise indicated.

6. Phil Elderkin, "History of Olympic Baseball," and Loel Schrader, "Former Baseball Olympians," 1984 Olympic Baseball program. As late as early August, Mann was publicly saying that ten countries would be playing baseball at the Olympics: the United States, Japan, Mexico, Chile, China, England, Netherlands, Belgium, France and Canada. See "Push Olympic Baseball," *New York Times,* August 1, 1936, 6.

7. M. E. Travaglini, "Olympic Baseball 1936: Was es Das?" *National Pastime: A Review of Baseball History,* Winter 1985, 46–55.

8. Stuart McIver, "Big Hit at the Hitler Games: Hometown Hero 'Rabbit' McNeece Stood Tall at the Plate When the World Was Watching the '36 Olympics in Germany," *Sunshine Magazine* (Fort Lauderdale *Sun-Sentinel*), May 1, 1994, 16.

9. Telephone interview with the author, May 1, 2005.

10. See Travaglini (53–54) for Goldberg's quote and other descriptions on the game conditions.

11. For material on prisoner of war baseball, see Tim Wolter, *POW Baseball in World War II: The National Pastime Behind Barbed Wire* (Jefferson, NC: McFarland, 2002).

12. It's worth mentioning Stalag Luft III because it was so iconic as a Nazi POW camp. Nevertheless, Stalag Luft III was actually located in Poland near the town of Sagan, approximately 100 miles southeast of Berlin.

13. Gary Bedingfield, *Baseball in World War II Europe* (Charleston, SC: Arcadia Publishing, 1999), as well as Bedingfield's website "Baseball in Wartime" (http://www.garybed.co.uk) for histories of major leaguers and military games in Germany.

14. Blackwell's team represented the Seventy-First Infantry Division. Along with Blackwell, other established or future big leaguers on the club were the Pittsburgh Pirates' Johnny Wyrostek, Maurice Van Robays and Ken Keintzelman, the St. Louis Cardinals' Harry Walker, the Cincinnati Reds' Benny Zientara and the New York Giants' Bill Ayers

15. The OISE All-Stars represented the Overseas Invasion Services Expedition force.

16. From a U.S. Army document called *The U.S. Armed Forces German Youth Activities Program, 1945–1955* (1956); http://digital.library.wisc.edu/1711.dl/History.GerYouth.

17. *Information bulletin,* no. 158 (April 1949) from Berlin, Germany: Office of Military Government for Germany (U.S.), Control Office, APO 742, US Army; http://digital.library.wisc.edu/1711.dl/History.omg1949n158.

18. *Weekly Information Bulletin,* No. 46 (June 1946) from U.S. Army Office of the Assistant Chief of Staff, G-5 Division USFET, Information Branch, http://digital.library.wisc.edu/1711.dl/History.omg1946n046.

19. Caroline Camp Leiser, "Babe Ruth Club: Baseball Becomes a German Sport," *Information Bulletin,* no. 158 (May 1949) from Berlin, Germany: Office of Military Government for Germany (U.S.), Control Office, APO 742, US Army, http://digital.library.wisc.edu/1711.dl/History.omg1949n160.

20. Telephone interview with the author, April 2007.

21. Alan M. Klein, *Growing the Game: The Globalization of Major League Baseball* (New Haven, CT: Yale University Press, 2006), 181. Beyond the Helmig brothers' minor league stint, Klaus Helmig also told Klein that he and his brother played on a Negro Leagues team called the Baltimore Elite Stars for a few months in 1956. What this team was is unclear as the Negro Leagues Baseball Museum does not recog-

nize such a club and, by 1956, the Negro Leagues were basically extinct. That said, the club might have been some sort of barnstorming offshoot of the Baltimore Elite Giants, which folded in 1950.

22. Panaye, *European Amateur Baseball: 25 Years*, 36–37.

23. Klein, *Growing the Game*, 182.

24. E-mail correspondence with author, March 25, 2007.

25. Klein, *Growing the Game*, 185.

Chapter 7

1. Although *The Comrades of Summer* is not a memorable piece of cinematic history, it's worth noting that the movie's writer Robert Rodat was later nominated for an Academy Award for his work on *Saving Private Ryan* (best screenplay written directly for the screen). He lost to the writers from *Shakespeare in Love*, Marc Norman and Tom Stoppard.

2. Kim Steven Juhase and Blair A. Ruble, "Soviet Baseball: History and Prospects," *National Pastime: A Review of Baseball History*, no. 12 (1992), 45.

3. Irving G. Gutterman, "Baseball, Played Abroad, Gaining Wide Popularity," *New York Times*, April 15, 1934.

4. "Ambassador to Start Baseball in Russia," *Washington Post*, April 20, 1934, 23.

5. Juhase and Ruble, 46.

6. Most of the facts on Starffin's life come from Richard Puff's excellent article "The Amazing Story of Victor Starffin," *National Pastime: A Review of Baseball History*, no. 12 (1992), 17.

7. United Press International, "Introduction of Baseball In Russia Suggested," *New York Times*, September 10, 1945. 8.

8. Associated Press, "Russia May Get Baseball," *Washington Post*, August 31, 1946, 8.

9. Associated Press, "U.S. Defines Baseball for Russia With Let-Up Pitch of Lyric Prose," *New York Times*, November 19, 1956, 33.

10. The basic rules of Lapta, according to the October 23, 2003, edition of the *St. Petersburg* (Russia) *Times*, go something like this: It's played on a field about half the size of a soccer pitch and the team on defense has five players in the field and one "server,"

who is effectively the pitcher. The server stands next to the opposing hitter and lobs a ball up underhand to the batter. The batting team has six-person lineup and each hitter has two attempts to knock the ball over a 10-meter line. If that's done, runners can advance to an endline on the other side of the field. Runners who make it back and forth between the two endlines get two points. Games are played in two 30-minute halves.

11. Bill Keller, "In Baseball, The Russians Steal All the Bases," *New York Times*, July 20, 1987, 1.

12. United Press International, "DiMag Strikes Out as Moscow Celebrity," *Los Angeles Times*, May 22, 1962, 4.

13. Jeff Elijiah, "How Did It Happen? A Russian Baseball Chronology," *International Baseball Rundown*, May 17, 1992, 3.

14. According to Elijiah in ibid., the claim that the October 7, 1986, game was the inaugural "official" contest "is a matter of much dispute."

15. Steve Wulf, "The Russians Are Humming; Now That Baseball Is an Olympic Sport, the Soviets are Starting to Fall in Love with the American Pastime," *Sports Illustrated*, July 25, 1988, 38.

16. Thom Shanker, "Soviets Step up to Home Plate: Russians Wind up for Pitch at Bezbol in '92 Olympics," *Chicago Tribune*, August 23, 1987, 3.

17. The professionals weren't the first U.S. team to compete in the Soviet Union in the modern era. From May 28–June 12 1988, Johns Hopkins University's baseball team played games in Moscow and Leningrad.

18. Kim Palchikoff, "Baseball: Diamond in the Rough," *New York Times*, July 24, 2001, 2D.

19. The quality of other fields has led to some tricky ground rules. For example, at a ballpark in Balashika, the short right-field fence led to inclusion of a "home run pole" placed 250 feet from home plate. All balls hit in fair territory to the right of the pole are ground rule doubles while shots to the left are home runs.

20. According to John Gilmore, who led a number of tours to Russia in the early 1990s, the team had considered the name the "Red Square Devils," but the moniker was "vetoed" by the KGB. See "SABR Nine: John

Gilmore and the Foreign Devils," SABR-ZINE, http://www.sabr.org/sabr.cfm?a=cms,c,898,34,0 (accessed December 7, 2007).

21. See untitled sidebar in *International Baseball Rundown*, May 17, 1992, 2.

22. History of the Russian League comes from Russian statistician Sergei Borisov's Russian Baseball League website, http://www.geocities.com/s_borisov/index.html. As of August 2007, Borisov's site was no longer up and running.

23. John Lehr, "California Angels Abandon Russian Friends," *International Baseball Rundown*, January 1994, 4.

Chapter 8

1. ASEA merged with the Swiss company BBC Brown Boveri in 1988 to form ASEA Brown Boveri. It survives today as a holding company for the ABB Group.

2. Peter C. Bjarkman, *Diamonds Around the Globe: The Encyclopedia of International Baseball* (Westport, CT: Greenwood Press, 2005), 407.

3. *Spalding's 1913 Official Base Ball Guide*, 19–22.

4. Peter Cava, "Baseball in the Olympics," *National Pastime: A Review of Baseball History*, no. 12 (1992), 2–4.

5. Thorpe's gold medals at the Stockholm Games were famously stripped in 1913 because he was deemed a professional athlete. In 1982, his awards were reinstated.

6. Cava, 4. The first quote is attributed to "the organizing committee report" from the Stockholm Games and the second to the *New York Times*.

7. Roger C. Panaye, *European Amateur Baseball: 25 Years*, 12.

8. In 1978, Oscar Johansson discussed his time with the Väästeråås club from 1919 to 1920. At that time, the 87-year-old had kept a Spalding baseball bat, a baseball with the signature of the captain of the Bethlehem Steel Baseball Club, an old glove and an old instruction book on fielding. See ibid., 16.

9. "Sweden Wants Baseball," *New York Times*, April 8, 1917, S3.

10. "Soccer Players to Sail: Will Play Baseball as Well as Football in Sweden," *New York Times*, July 4, 1920, 19.

11. This piece of history was provided by Lars Aberg, information secretary of Sweden's baseball federation in 1978. See Panaye's *European Amateur Baseball: 25 Years*, 16–17.

12. Dick Joiner, "Baseball Invades Sweden — in Smorgasbord Fashion," *Chicago Tribune*, December 10, 1951, E4.

13. Bill Clark, "Sweden's Lindberg Family: Baseball the Way It Should Be," *International Baseball Rundown*, January 1995, 16.

14. E-mail correspondence with author, June 20, 2007.

15. E-mail correspondence with author, March 2007.

16. Bill Clark, p. 16.

17. Mike Voorheis, "Hitting: The Swede Science; Pilegard Streaks to Spot in UNCW Record Book," *Morning Star* (Wilmington, North Carolina), March 27, 2001, 4C.

18. Italy did not win a medal at the 1967 European Championships, but they did not participate in that event.

Chapter 9

1. Martin Hoerchner, "A Brief History of Baseball Prehistory" *SABR UK Examiner*, no. 8 (1998).

2. For a discussion of the sport *thèèque*, see David Block, *Baseball Before We Knew It: A Search for the Roots of the Game* (Lincoln: University of Nebraska Press, 2005).

3. Leslie Lieber, "Franççois at the Bat," *Reader's Digest* 49, no. 292 (August 1946).

4. Mark Lamaster, *Spalding's World Tour: The Epic Adventure that Took Baseball Around the Globe — And Made It America's Game* (New York: Public Affairs, 2006), 207.

5. James E. Elfers, *The Tour to End All Tours: The Story of Major League Baseball's 1913–1914 World Tour* (Lincoln: University of Nebraska Press, 2003), 219.

6. Roger C. Panaye, *European Amateur Baseball: 25 Years* (CEBA, 1978).

7. "Baseball in France," *Boston Globe*, August 25, 1901, 27.

8. "Baseball in France," *Los Angeles Times*, May 17, 1908, VIII.

9. "Baseball for France," *Washington Post* on November 5, 1911, 36.

10. "France Has Baseball League," *New York Times*, November 3, 1912, S4.

11. "Baseball in France," *Boston Globe*, March 16, 1914, 7.

12. "Baseball for France, Says A.G. Spalding," *Washington Post*, January 10, 1914, 8.

13. Elfers, 219.

14. "Baseball in France; So M'Graw Predicts," *Washington Post*, September 17, 1916, S2.

15. "French Take Up Baseball," *New York Times*, May 21, 1915, 10.

16. Nearly nine decades later, Andrew Sallee, a former minor leaguer and French national team coach, would somewhat echo Mathewson's concerns. The French "have a soccer mentality and fake injuries and need water poured on them when they get hit by the ball," Sallee said in a 2007 interview. "I heard stories from people before me about teams having wine in the dugouts."

17. Miles Hyman, "Baseball Partners: International Baseball Comes of Age," *Giants Magazine* 3, no. 1 (1988), 101.

18. *L'Histoire du Baseball*, Féédééracion Franççaise de Baseball et Softball, http://www.ffbsc.org/imgs/docu/historique-baseball.pdf. Information on the French game begins on page 12.

19. Associated Press, "American Players Draw Only 20 Spectators in Dublin," *Washington Post*, November 9, 1924, EF3.

20. *L'Histoire du Baseball*, 12.

21. United Press, "Baseball in France," *Washington Post*, February 10, 1929, SM4.

22. Lieber.

23. Ibid.

24. Ibid.

25. "Five Nations Form New European Baseball Federation," *Baseball News: A News Sheet of Baseball* [published by the South Eastern (England) Baseball League], June 6, 1953, 2.

26. Panaye, *European Amateur Baseball: 25 Years*, 12.

27. In 1957, Tunisia would become an independent member of the European federation. With its inclusion, there were even discussions of changing the name of the federation to the Euro-African Baseball Federation. But Tunisia would struggle to meet its financial responsibilities and, in 1962, they were dropped from the organization.

28. The baseball-softball governing federation would also ultimately combine with cricket to further consolidate.

29. "Jeff Zimmerman Chat." *SLAM! Baseball*, April 26, 2000; http://slam.canoe. ca/SlamChats/zimmerman_jeff_042600.html (accessed December 8, 2007).

30. E-mail correspondence with author, July 12, 2007.

Chapter 10

1. "Baseball Ambassador Wins Czech Hearts," *Los Angeles Times*, quoted here from *Washington Post*, October 5, 1969, 164. Quotes from Bill Arce throughout this chapter come from this article.

2. Many sources see this 1920 exhibition as Czech baseball's beginnings (among other sources, "The 2005 European Championship in Baseball Commemorative Postage Stamp," Czech Post, http://archiv.radio.cz/postfila/2005/0443_e.html). But longtime Czech baseball official and player Jan Bagin puts the date a year earlier, with First's introductory classes.

3. Roger C. Panaye, *European Amateur Baseball: 25 Year*, 50.

4. Arce got the general feel of the stadium correct, but his dimensions were slightly off, according to Bagin. The stadium in question was originally built for gymnastics and seated more than 200,000. In addition, the backstop was actually about ten to fifteen feet high.

5. United Press International, July 21, 1990.

6. Stories and quotes from Jones from e-mail correspondence with the author, April 2, 2007 and April 20, 2007.

7. Gaston Panaye, *European Amateur Baseball: 1979–1993*, 79.

8. Jay Berman, "For Love of the Game" *Prague Post*, May 2, 2001.

9. Email correspondence with the author, May 28, 2007.

10. The town of Ostrava, located in the country's northeast near the Polish and Slovak borders, also has a strong baseball presence. The Ostrava Arrows have placed near the top of the Czech Republic's highest league in recent years. Other cities that had teams playing the game at the country's highest level in 2006 were Blansko and Olomouc.

11. The teams in the tournament were Brazil, Guatemala, China, Peru, France, Czechoslovakia and New Zealand. Brazil won the event, going 6–0.

12. Frantisek Bouc, "Big Leagues Scout Czech Baseball," *Prague Post*, January 22, 1997.

13. Glenn Miller, "Not lost in baseball translation," *News-Press* (Fort Myers, Florida), April 9, 2004, 1C.

14. Brandon Swanson, "First Pitch," *Prague Post*, April 19, 2006.

15. Ibid.

16. Joe Connor, *A Fan's Guide to the World Baseball Classic*, Modernerabaseball. com, 2005–2006, 253.

Chapter 11

1. "Croatia: Operation 'Storm'—still no justice ten years on," Amnesty International, http://web.amnesty.org/library/index/engeur640022005 (accessed December 9, 2007).

2. Aldo Vavra, "Baseball Just One Casualty of War in Croatia," *International Baseball Rundown*, September 1992, 3.

3. Peter Bjarkman, *Diamonds Around the Globe: The Encyclopedia of International Baseball* (Westport, CT: Greenwood Press, 2005).

4. It's worth noting that while Panaye dates the founding of the first teams in Croatia to 1973, at least one other source indicates that the first team — Nada in Split — was organized in 1974. See Associated Press, "Hard Way to Learn Hardball: Yugoslavs Determined to Become Respectable Players of American Game," *Boston Globe*, June 18, 1989, 61.

5. J. Brady McCollough, "Home Away From Home-Field Advantage: Weeklong Visit Allows Team to Face Better Opponents before European Championships," *Kansas City Star*, July 28, 2006.

6. Moni Basu, "International Sports: Croats of Summer; Field of Dreams Comes True for Grabrik Ravens," *Atlanta Journal-Constitution*, April 6, 2002, 2D.

7. Bill Clark, "Europe — Now and in 2004," *International Baseball Rundown*, November–December 1995, 6.

8. Thoren also spent extensive time developing baseball in Austria.

9. Ted Thoren, "Baseball Goes on in Croatia — Despite the War," *International Baseball Rundown*, February 3, 1993, 3.

10. Sean Kirst, "For Lover of Baseball, Croatia Keeps Calling," *Post-Standard* (Syracuse, New York), September 23, 1994, D1.

11. Interview via Internet phone with author, March 2007.

12. Japanesebaseball.com, http://www.japanesebaseball.com.

13. Thoren, "Baseball Goes on in Croatia."

14. The CEB Cup is the third of three European Club competitions organized by the Confederation of European Baseball.

Chapter 12

1. "Marlene Campbell behind Austrian Baseball Jump from Six Teams in 1987 to More Than 50 Today," *International Baseball Rundown*, April 1993, 5.

2. "Thoren Returns to Austria," *IBA World Baseball*, winter 1989.

3. "Jack Brenner: The First Bulgarian Baseball Coach in the History of the World," *International Baseball Rundown*, April 17, 1992, 1.

4. Peter C. Bjarkman, *Diamonds Around the Globe: The Encyclopedia of International Baseball* b(Westport, CT: Greenwood Press, 2005), 392.

5. *European Amateur Baseball: 1989–1993*, Confederation Européene de Baseball Amateur (CEBA).

6. Steve Lohr, "Boys of Summer in the Midnight Sun," *New York Times*, July 2, 1988, 4.

7. *European Amateur Baseball: 1979–1993* attributed the founding of the Finnish federation to "fruitful contacts" with their Swedish neighbours" (page 10).

8. The European B-pool Championships is the former name for the qualifying tournament for the top-tier European Baseball Championships. In 1986, Finland placed fourth in a five-team field, beating Switzerland 12–2 in its only victory.

9. Viktor Guseve, "Baseball," *ITAR-TASS*, March 17, 1987.

10. Steve Wulf, "The Russians Are Humming; Now that baseball is an Olympic Sport, the Soviets Are Starting to Fall in Love with the American Pastime," *Sports Illustrated*, July 25, 1988, 38.

11. Basil Tarasko, "Eastern Europe," *International Baseball Rundown*, January/February 1996, 9.

12. Tom Mazarakis, *The History of Baseball in Greece*, Un-official Web Site for Baseball in Greece, 2007, http://www.geocities.com/greek_baseball_federation/history_of_baseball_in_greece2.htm.

13. John Manuel, "Host Greece Sports Unlikely American Roster," *Baseball America*, July 30, 2004.

14. "Greece Hit by Baseball Row," BBC, July 23, 2004, http://news.bbc.co.uk/sport1/hi/olympics_2004/baseball/3920741.stm (accessed December 10, 2007).

15. "One of the Best European Baseball Stadiums Been Closed," Mister Baseball, http://www.mister-baseball.com/one-of-the-best-european-baseball-stadiums-has-been-closed (accessed December 10, 2007).

16. Peter Levine, *A. G. Spalding and the Rise of Baseball: The Promise of American Sport* (New York: Oxford University Press 1985), 18.

17. Mark Lamaster, *Spalding's World Tour: The Epic Adventure That Took Baseball Around The Globe — And Made It America's Game* (New York: Public Affairs, 2006), 234.

18. Gary Bedingfield, *Baseball in World War II Europe* (Charleston, SC: Arcadia Publishing, 1999), 13–14.

19. Roger C. Panaye, *European Amateur Baseball: 25 Years* (CEBA1978), 46.

20. "Recent History of Baseball in Israel," Israel Baseball League, http://www.israelbaseballleague.com/baseballinisrael/recenthistory (accessed December 10, 2007).

21. *Official 2007 Yearbook: The Israel Baseball League*, 6. In 2007, Kurtzer was also the commissioner of the IBL.

22. The 1979–1981 dates come from Marco Stoovelaar, "Europe," *International Baseball Rundown*, March 1995, 12. Stoovelaar writes that baseball "got off the ground to stay in 1988," but the official Web site for the IAB puts the founding date in 1986. See "History of Israel Baseball," Israel Association of Baseball, http://www.iab.org.il/history.htm (accessed December 10, 2007).

23. Ibid.

24. Stoovelaar, "Europe," 12.

25. Bruce Maddy-Weitzman, "Israel Baseball," *Jewish Major Leaguers*, 2006 Update Edition (baseball-card set).

26. "Recent History of Baseball in Israel," Israel Baseball League, http://www.israelbaseballleague.com/baseballinisrael/recenthistory (accessed December 10, 2007).

27. Joel Greenberg, "Here's the Pitch: Baseball in Israel," *Chicago Tribune*, April 20, 2007.

Chapter 13

1. John J. Chernoski (Cerniauskas) and Arvydas Birbalas, "Lietuvos Béėisbolas — A History," *Bridges: Lithuanian American News Journal*, June 2003, 14–18, http://javlb.org/bridges/2003/june2003/june2003_14-18.pdf. Much of the section on Lithuanian baseball is adapted from this article.

2. Nijole Dariute-Mastariene, *Darius ir Girenas*, (Vilnius, 1991), 58. (Quoted in "Lietuvos Béėisbolas — A History," 15).

3. See Fédération Baseball Luxembourg, http://membres.lycos.fr/fbluxembourg (accessed December 10, 2007).

4. Along with Luxembourg and eight club teams, the Great Britain national team also played in the event. Great Britain placed first.

5. *Spalding's 1891 Official Base Ball Guide*, 37. Because I had only a part of this guide and the complete version was not readily available, it is possible that this anecdote actually comes from the 1890 edition (whichever edition, the page number is accurate).

6. Gaston Panaye, *European Amateur Baseball: 1979–1993* (Confederation Europééene de Baseball Amateur), 6.

7. Tim Buckley, "Yankees, Soviets Hit It Off," *St. Petersburg Times*, July 10, 1991, 4 (Citrus Times edition).

8. "History of Club Abator," Clubul Sportiv Abator, http://www.moldbaseball.com/eng/history (accessed December 10, 2007).

9. Marco Stoovelaar, "Europe," *International Baseball Rundown*, April 1993, 4.

10. Norges Softball og Baseball Forbund, http://www.soft-baseball.no/pretenders/stats/index.html.

11. For variations on the story of the first glove for vodka, see Charles T. Powers, "'Give the Old Pilka a Ride, Piotr'; In Poland, Baseball is a Hit with Plenty of Errors," *Los Angeles Times*, August 9, 1987, 1. See also Maciej Mroczek, "Batter Up!" *Warsaw Voice*, September 22, 2002.

12. John P. Tobin, "Palant and Cricket Family Resemblances?" *The World of English*, http://www.woe.edu.pl/modules.php?sid=&mm=4&module=Baseball&mode=show_article&id=15.

13. Although other sources describe this federation as the Polish Baseball Federation, a Polish booklet entitled *Baseball ...... How it Happened*, which was prepared by the Polish Baseball and Softball Federation in 2001, describes the federation as being for *palant* and baseball.

14. Mroczek, "Batter Up!"

15. "Poland Is Admitted to Baseball Group," *New York Times*, January 10, 1960.

16. Powers, "'Give the Old Pilka a Ride, Piotr.'"

17. Baseball is played in the Portuguese speaking country of Brazil, but the level of interest of the sport in that country does not compare to Latin America's Spanish-speaking countries.

18. "Históória do Lisboa Basebol Clube," Lisboa Basebol Clube, http://lbc.planeta-clix.pt/indexhistoria.htm (accessed December 10, 2007).

19. *International Baseball Review*, October 1998. Writer Basil Tarasko discusses the strength of the Venezuelan influence on Portuguese baseball in 1990. He actually says that Venezuelans introduced the game in 1990. As this isn't correct, his other statements should be looked at with a skeptical eye.

20. Other sources credit San Marino's Italian neighbors as the impetus for baseball in San Marino.

21. Associated Press, "Hard Way to Learn Hardball: Yugoslavs Determined to Become Respectable Players of American Game," *Boston Globe*, June 18, 1989, 61.

222. "Baseball Survives in War-torn Country," *Washington Post*, August 15, 1993.

23. "Baseball Club Beograd '96," http://www.beograd96.com/onamae.htm (accessed December 10, 2007).

24. Associated Press, "Hard Way to Learn Hardball."

25. "Vodenlich Family Is Organizing Month-Long Visit of Slovenian 'Team

Zajcki' to United States this Summer," *International Baseball Rundown*, May 1995, 3.

26. E-mail correspondence with author, June 11, 2007.

27. Steve Wulf, "The Russians Are Humming; Now that baseball is an Olympic Sport, the Soviets are Starting to Fall in Love with the American Pastime," *Sports Illustrated*, July 25, 1988, 38

28. Glenn Nelson, "Comrades of Summer — Scoreboard is Just One of the Missing Elements in Soviet-style 'Beizbol,'" *Seattle Times*, July 15, 1990, C1

29. Fred Kaplan, "Moscow's Devils: The Spitting Image of Baseball," *Boston Globe*, August 27, 1992, 1.

Chapter 14

1. According to internal Confederation of European Baseball documents dated July 3, 1969.

2. Following the 1958 Euros, it was decided that "the financial obligations for the participants as well as the organizing country were too much for a yearly championships and it was planned to have the championships every two years," wrote Roger C. Panaye in *European Amateur Baseball: 25 Years*. It should be noted that the Euros were played in back-to-back years in 1964 and 1965.

3. The path to qualification has changed over the years. In the mid-1970s, there were individual qualifying games. Then in the mid-1980s, a European "B-pool" tournament was installed, with the top two clubs earning promotion. This was then substituted with two "B-pool" events (which are now simply called qualifiers), with the winners earning entry to the continent's main group. Following the 2007 Euros, the qualifier process will change again, as the number of teams in the top tier has been contracted from twelve to eight.

4. In a 1969 Federation of European baseball document, officials wrote that Italy protested "against the fact that some players born outside Europe (Dutch Antilles) are included in Holland's list of players."

Bibliography

Books

Archer, Jeff. *Strike Four: Adventures in European Baseball*. Lafayette, CO: White-Boucke Publishing, 1995.

Bedingfield, Gary. *Baseball in World War II Europe*. Charleston, SC: Arcadia Publishing, 1999.

Bidini, David. *Baseballissimo*. Toronto: McClelland & Stewart, 2005.

Bjarkman, Peter C. *Diamonds Around the Globe: The Encyclopedia of International Baseball*. Westport, CT: Greenwood Press, 2005.

Block, David. *Baseball Before We Knew It: A Search for the Root of the Game*. Lincoln: University of Nebraska Press, 2005.

Chetwynd, Josh and Belton, Brian A. *British Baseball and the West Ham Club: History of a 1930 Professional Baseball Team in 1930s East London*. Jefferson, NC: McFarland, 2006.

Connor, Joe. *Fan's Guide to the 2006 World Baseball Classic*, Modernerabaseball.com, 2005–2006.

Crane, Newton. *Baseball: The All-England Series*. London: George Bell & Sons, 1891.

Dariute-Mastariene, Nijole. *Darius ir Girenas*. Vilnius: 1991.

Elfers, James. *The Tour to End All Tours: The Story of Major League Baseball's 1913–1914 World Tour*. Lincoln, NE: University of Nebraska Press, 2003.

Gmelch, George, ed. *Baseball without Boarders: The International Pastime*. Lincoln: University of Nebraska Press, 2006.

Jamail, Milton H. and Dierker, Larry. *Full Count: Inside Cuban Baseball*. Carbondale: Southern Illinois University Press, 2002.

Keith, John. *Dixie Dean: The Inside Story of a Football Icon*. London: Robson Books, 2001.

Klein, Alan M. *Growing the Game: The Globalization of Major League Baseball*. New Haven, CT: Yale University Press, 2006.

Lamaster, Mark. *Spalding's World Tour: The Epic Adventure That Took Baseball Around The Globe — And Made It America's Game*. New York: Public Affairs, 2006.

Litwhiler, Danny. *Glossary of International Baseball Terms*. United States Baseball Federation, 1980.

Levine, Peter. *A.G. Spalding and the Rise of Baseball*. New York: Oxford University Press, 1985.

Miller, Martin with Klages, Andreas. *Base-*

ball: Eine anspruchvolle Sportart auf dem Weg nach oben, Deutscher Baseball & Softball Verband e.V, *http://www.base ball-softball.de/dbv/index.php?id=0000 0860&SXL_Session=783c9bca1c20394a5b d4362dc9ed82cb.*

Panaye, Roger C. *European Amateur Baseball: 25 Years.* Confederation of European Baseball, 1978.

Panaye, Gaston. *European Amateur Baseball: 1979–1993.* Confederation of European Baseball, 1993.

Schiroli, Riccardo; Bugane, Roberto; Caldarelli, Maurizio; and Landi, Marco. *Un Diamante Azzuro: Personaggi e Storie.* Macron Team Uniforms, 2006.

Silverman, Jeff, ed. *The Greatest Baseball Stories Ever Told.* Guilford, CT: Lyons Press, 2001.

Stoovelaar, Marco. *Mr. Cocker Honkbalgids 2000.* M. Stoovelaar, 2000. (Dutch translated by Peter Janssen)

Szymanski, Stefan and Zimbalist, Andrew. *National Pastime: How Americans Play Baseball and the Rest of the World Plays Soccer.* Washington, DC: Brookings Institution Press, 2005.

Wolter, Tim. *POW Baseball in World War II: The National Pastime behind Barbed Wire.* Jefferson, NC: McFarland, 2002.

Articles and theses

Bloyce, Daniel. "John Moores and the 'Professional' Baseball Leagues in 1930s England." *Sport in History* 27, no. 1 (March 2007).

Bloyce, Daniel. "That's Your Way of Playing Rounders, Isn't It? The Response of the English Press to American Baseball Tours to England, 1874–1924." *Sporting Traditions* 22, no. 1 (November 2005).

Carroll, Patrick. "Baseball in Graceland" *The SABR (UK) Examiner,* July 2001.

Cava, Peter. "Baseball in the Olympics." *The National Pastime: A Review of Baseball History* no.12 (1992).

Chernoski (Cerniauskas), John J. and Birbalas, Arvydas. "Lietuvos Béisbolas — A History." *Bridges* no. 5 (June 2003).

Elderkin, Phil. "History of Olympic Baseball." 1984 Olympic Baseball program.

Garrido, Fernando. "Primeros Pasos Del Béisbol Por Barcelona." Secció de Béisbol del Fc Barcelona, http://www.gale on.com/fguillen/fernandogarrido.htm.

Hoerchner, Martin. "A Brief History of Baseball Prehistory." *SABR UK Examiner* no. 8 (1998).

Hyman, Miles. "Baseball Partners: International Baseball Comes of Age." *Giants Magazine* 3, no. 1 (1988).

Jacobson, Louis. "Herman Goldberg: Baseball Olympian and Jewish-American." In *Baseball History 3: An Annual of Original Baseball Research,* edited by Peter Levine. Westport, CT: Meckler, 1990.

Juhase, Kim Steven, and Ruble, Blair A. "Soviet Baseball: History and Prospects." *The National Pastime: A Review of Baseball History* no. 12 (1992).

Mazarakis, Tom. "The History of Baseball in Greece." T. Mazarakis, January 2007; http://www.geocities.com/greek_base ball_federation/history_of_baseball_in_ greece2.htm.

Puff, Richard. "The Amazing Story of Victor Starffin." *The National Pastime: A Review of Baseball History* no. 12 (1992).

Scafella, Igino. *Evoluzione e sviluppo di uno sport d'importazione: Il caso del baseball in Italia.* Presented in the 2000–2001 academic year at the Universita degli Studi di Roma to the faculty of the motor sciences department.

Schrader, Loel. "Former Baseball Olympians." 1984 Olympic Baseball program

Smyth, Ian. *The History of Baseball in the North of England.* Master's thesis, Leeds Polytechnic Faculty of Cultural and Education Studies, 1992.

Stoovelaar, Marco. "Brief History of Baseball in the Netherlands." (This four-page article was given to international baseball sources in the run-up to the 2004 Athens Olympic Games.)

Tobin, John P. "Palant and Cricket Family Resemblances?" *The World of English, http://www.woe.edu.pl/modules.php?sid= &module=Baseball&mode=show _article&id=15.*

Travaglini, M. E. "Olympic Baseball 1936: Was es Das?" *The National Pastime: A Review of Baseball History,* Winter 1985.

Wire services, newspapers, and other periodicals

Ashton-under-Lyne Reporter (UK)
Associated Press
Atlanta Journal-Constitution
Baltimore Sun
Baseball America
The Baseball Magazine
Baseball News: A News Sheet of Baseball, published by the South Eastern Baseball League (UK)
Baseball: Officieel Orgaan Der Belgische Baseball Federatie (Belgium — in Flemish, translated by Peter Janssen)
Birmingham News (Alabama)
Boston Globe
Chicago Record-Herald
Chicago Tribune
Christian Science Monitor
Cleveland Plain Dealer
Daily Mirror (UK)
Daily News and Leader (UK)
Evening Standard (UK)
Hamilton Spectator (Ontario, Canada)
Harper's Weekly
IBAF.news
IBA World Baseball magazine
International Baseball Rundown
International Herald Tribune
ITAR-TASS (Russian Information Agency)
Kansas City Star
Liverpool Echo (UK)
Los Angeles Times
Morning Star (Wilmington, NC)
New York American
New York Times
The News-Press (Fort Myers, FL)
Palm Beach Post
Post-Standard (Syracuse, New York)
Prague Post (Czech Republic)
Reader's Digest
Taipei Times
Time magazine
St. Petersburg Times (Russia)
San Francisco Chronicle
Seattle Times
Sporting News
Sports Illustrated
Stars and Stripes (European edition)
Sun-Sentinel (Fort Lauderdale, FL)
Sunshine Magazine (magazine of the Sun-Sentinel newspaper in Fort Lauderdale, FL)
USA Today
Washington Post
Warsaw Voice (Poland)

Internet sources

Baseball Almanac: www.baseball-almanac.com
Baseball Club Beograd '96: www.beograd96.com/onamae.htm
Baseball Fever: www.baseball-fever.com
Baseball in Wartime (Gary Bedingfield): www.garybed.co.uk
Baseball-reference.com: www.baseball-reference.com
BBC: www.bbc.co.uk
Clubul Sportiv Abator (Kishinev, Moldova): www.moldbaseball.com/eng/history/
Fédération Baseball Luxembourg: http://membres.lycos.fr/fbluxembourg
Fédération Française de Baseball et de Softball: http://www.ffbsc.org
Federazione Italiana Baseball Softball: www.fibs.it
Grand Slam Stats & News (Netherlands): http://home.planet.nl/~stoov/
Israel Association of Baseball: www.iab.org.il
Israel Baseball League: www.israelbaseball-league.com
Japanesebaseball.com: www.japanesebaseball.com
Mister Baseball: Baseball and Softball in Europe: www.mister-baseball.com
SLAM! Sports (Canada): http://slam.canoe.ca
Society for American Baseball Research: www.sabr.org
Norges Softball og Baseball Forbund (Norwegian Softball and Baseball Federation): www.soft-baseball.no/pretenders/stats/index.html
Wikipedia: www.wikipedia.com

Other sources

Baseball.... How it Happened. Polish Baseball and Softball Federation, 2001.
City of Baseball (documentary film). — 2007. Director/producer: Christopher P. Ralph, producer: John Borgonovo.
The Emerald Diamond (documentary film) 2006. Director/writer/producer: John J. Fitzgerald

European Baseball Championships program, 1989.

Jewish Major Leaguers. 2006 update edition. Baseball card set by Dr. Bruce Maddy-Weitzman. (See http://jewishmajorleaguers.org.)

Official 2007 Yearbook: The Israel Baseball League.

Spalding's 1889 Official Base Ball Guide.

Spalding's 1891 Official Base Ball Guide.

Spalding's 1912 Official Base Ball Guide.

Spalding's 1913 Official Base Ball Guide. (John Foster, editor)

Spalding's 1922 Official Base Ball Guide.

Spalding's 1939 Official Base Ball Guide.

Index

Numbers in **bold italics** indicate pages with photographs.